ROMANTIC COMEDIES

EIGHT PLAYS

BY

FERENC MOLNAR

CROWN PUBLISHERS, Inc.
NEW YORK

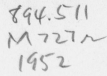

CONTENTS

ACTOR FROM VIENNA

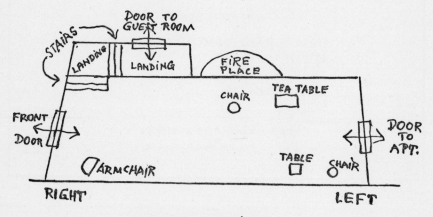

STAIRS

DOOR TO GUEST ROOM

LANDING

LANDING

FIRE PLACE

CHAIR

TEA TABLE

FRONT DOOR

ARMCHAIR

TABLE

CHAIR

DOOR TO APT.

RIGHT

LEFT

SCENE DESIGN
"ACTOR FROM VI'ENNA"

ACTOR FROM VIENNA

ANECDOTE IN ONE ACT

CHARACTERS

BARON PAHLEN-MONTALTO, 60
EDITH, 28
FABRY, 30
DR. BALTIN, 50
BUTLER

PLACE : SOMEWHERE IN EUROPE
TIME : BEFORE WORLD WAR II.

(New acting version of the same author's FELDMARSCHALL as produced at the BURGTHEATER *in Vienna with* OTTO TRESSLER *in the leading role. Produced at the* MAGYAR SZINHAZ *in Budapest with* JENÖ TÖRZS; *on the Italian stages with* MEMO BENASSI; *filmed in Hollywood with* CHARLES BOYER; *produced on television in New York by* BILLY ROSE *with* LEE TRACY.*)*

ACTOR FROM VIENNA

SCENE: *Main hall of a hunting lodge. At the rear wall a few steps and door to the guest room.—Fire place. Armchairs. Doors: front door right; left door to the living quarters. (See floor plan.) Two smoking tables. Ten o'clock at night.*

AT RISE: *As the curtain rises,* EDITH *is alone in the hall, reading by the fire. After a brief pause, enter* BUTLER, *right.*

BUTLER. Mr. Fabry is here.

EDITH *(Getting up)*. Mr. Fabry?

BUTLER. He just got in on the Express Train.

EDITH. Show him in.

(BUTLER *opens the front door right.* FABRY *enters)*

FABRY. Do forgive me for coming so unexpectedly. *(Kisses her hand)*

EDITH. Good evening, Fabry. *(To* BUTLER*)* Wait. *(To* FABRY*)* I trust you haven't dined yet.

FABRY. I'm afraid I did. In the diner.

EDITH. Coffee, then, or tea?

FABRY. Tea, if I may.

EDITH. *(Nods to the Butler. Exit* BUTLER *right)*. This is what I call a pleasant surprise.

FABRY. You aren't annoyed at me, I hope, for bursting in on you so late at night? *(Looks at his watch)* After ten o'clock. In this mountainous wilderness I'm sure you must go to bed early . . . in this lonely hunting lodge . . .

EDITH. No, we're always up until midnight.

FABRY. The others'll be here first thing in the morning. I was planning yesterday to travel with them, but I changed my mind. I couldn't possibly spend a night in a crowded slow train. There's no sleeper, and the windows never shut tight. You know an actor dreads nothing so much as catching cold. In a word . . .

EDITH *(Smiling)*. In a word?

FABRY. In a word, not a word of what I just said is true. I came earlier because I love you, because not an hour passes without my . . .

EDITH *(Interrupting)*. Look out. My husband is right next door here, in his room.

FABRY. I implore you, don't tell him yet that I'm here. Give me these few moments.

EDITH. You upset me. Please sit down. That passionate voice of yours . . . (SHE *breaks off)*

FABRY. Don't be surprised that I'm out of my mind. You've been gone from town for eleven days. In eleven days I haven't seen you. How lovely you are!

EDITH. You're looking pale.

FABRY. I don't sleep. I can't swallow a morsel. I'm in torment. Since that Thursday when you came to my room . . . in the town.

EDITH. For God's sake take care! My husband may come in at any moment.

FABRY. All I thought of on the whole trip was what joy it would be to talk to you about how at last . . . at last . . . you had been with me.

EDITH. Poor Fabry. I stayed with you all of a hundred and twenty seconds. Maybe not quite . . . Less than two minutes.

FABRY. But you sat in my armchair and I held your hand. If it had been a hundred and twenty years the time would have gone just as fast.

EDITH (*Looking around anxiously*). Tell me . . . weren't you supposed to be playing today?

FABRY. How did you know?

EDITH. I look at the repertory in the paper every day. Tonight they're playing Cyrano. That's your part, surely.

FABRY. Way off in the mountains here, you know when I'm playing?

EDITH. I even attend the performance. Look what I was reading. (*Hands him the book*)

FABRY. "Cyrano de Bergerac."

EDITH. The nights you're playing, I sit down by the fire and read. I see you and hear you.

FABRY. Edith!

EDITH. But today you cheated me. You didn't play.

FABRY. I backed out on the pretext I was hoarse.

EDITH. For my sake . . .

FABRY. Spending an evening with you means to me . . .

EDITH (*Interrupting*). You talk as if we two were the only people in this lonely old lodge. The lonely lodge . . . also lodges the Baron.

FABRY. Oh. The Baron.

EDITH. And tomorrow morning there'll be nine noisy guests with us, too. Thirsty hunters, unflagging storytellers.

FABRY. Well, now you can see why I came early.

EDITH. My husband will notice.

FABRY. He doesn't read the repertory.

EDITH. With him one never knows. My husband . . .

FABRY. Is sixty years old.

EDITH. He won the grand prize in the gentlemen riders' steeplechase.

FABRY. These eternally young old men make my flesh creep.

EDITH. His father lived to be a hundred and four. He predicted he'd only make a hundred—too much Austrian blood.

FABRY. And you here with him . . .

EDITH. He gets up at sunrise, he fences, he rides, he hunts. He boasts of descending from that good Italian stock that produces the oldest cardinals.

FABRY. It's outrageous to hear those beautiful young lips praising old age.

EDITH (*Reproaching*). Fabry!

FABRY. The scene it calls up in my imagination tortures me unbearably. You'll be mine, my own wife . . .

EDITH. No.

FABRY. What do you keep praising him for? To be coy? Surely you're past needing that. I go crazy just at the sight of you.

EDITH. Don't torment me.

FABRY. You can't quench the fire that's burning in you.

(EDITH *smiles mysteriously*)

I know why you're smiling. I know the story. You quenched a fire like that once before.

EDITH. Twice. Twice before.

FABRY. This time you won't.

EDITH. It'll be hard. But I will.

FABRY. No, no. You'll come with me. I can't match his millions, but I'm not a poor man, either. And if it's true that you're stage-struck . . .

EDITH. Don't torture me!

FABRY. You're leaving him. You're going to be my wife.

EDITH (*Nervously, looking toward the door, left*). Please, let me call in my husband.

(FABRY *bars her way*)

FABRY. Have you had enough of me so soon?

EDITH. It's not good for me to talk to you so much.

FABRY. It's no use. I'm not giving up.

EDITH. I don't want to listen.

FABRY. Your eyes say the opposite. Edith, I'm going to pursue my object with all the will-power I possess. I'm staying here. No, I shan't go hunting tomorrow. I shall find some excuse to stay with you all day tomorrow. Our fate has got to be decided! Either we never see one another again, or you come with me and marry me.

EDITH (*Frightened*). You aren't going hunting?

FABRY. No.

EDITH. Please, please don't do that. Be careful.

FABRY. I'm all done with being careful!

EDITH. Not so loud, for the love of heaven! My husband . . .

FABRY. I don't care about anything. I'm afraid of no one. (*He goes to her.*)

EDITH (*Pulling away*). You're stark mad!

(*Brief pause.* SHE *rings*)

FABRY. Yes, I'm stark mad.

(*Sits down*)

EDITH. If my husband comes in now, he'll know everything from our faces.

FABRY. Don't forget I'm an actor.

EDITH. Don't *you* forget you're a human being. Go up to your room, and I'll tell him you're changing.

(*Enter* BUTLER, *bringing tea*)
Show Mr. Fabry his room, please.

(BUTLER *goes up the steps*)

FABRY. I'll see you in a minute.

(*Exit, with* BUTLER. EDITH *touches up her hair in the mirror over the mantel. Re-enter* BUTLER)

EDITH. Please tell my husband tea is served.

(*Exit* BUTLER. EDITH *arranges the tea table. Brief pause. Enter* BARON)

BARON (*A powerful, dapper man of sixty. Comes to the tea table*). Three cups?

EDITH. That's right.

BARON. Who's the third for?

EDITH. Why, haven't you seen Fabry yet?

BARON. No. Then Mr. Fabry has arrived already.

EDITH. He's in his room now, changing.

BARON. Interesting. Mr. Fabry here already. He wasn't supposed to arrive till tomorrow, with the other guests.

EDITH. He was afraid of the night trip in the draughty train.

BARON. Then you've talked to him already?

EDITH. Yes. Actors are ridiculously scared of catching cold. (*Sets the tea-cozy over the teapot*)

BARON. He came ahead by the earlier train. Interesting.

EDITH. You're really talking very strangely.

BARON. Who?

EDITH. You.

(*Slight pause*)

BARON. Well, then, my dear child, pay close attention to me. I'm glad you noticed that I'm talking strangely.

EDITH. It certainly wasn't hard to tell.

BARON. What I'm going to say now will be even easier to understand. I shall start with what I think least important.

EDITH. I'd like to point out that Fabry is in his room and may come down at any moment.

BARON. I see you are keeping an eye on the next rooms. Before, you were keeping an eye on this one. *(Indicates his room whence he entered)*

EDITH. What are you getting at?

BARON. As I say, I shall begin with the least important part. This actor is an overwrought person. Young. In love. And your behavior toward him for the past two months . . .

EDITH *(Severely)*. This I will not have.

BARON. I see it better than you can. You don't even realize you're flirting with someone by the time I've become well aware of it.

EDITH. How often have I told you . . .

BARON. Please wait. I was just coming out of the library when I heard loud talk in here. If it hadn't sunk to a whisper, I wouldn't have noticed at all. But there was a sudden silence. There's no mistaking a thing like that.

EDITH. And if . . .

BARON. Then you said to him, "You're stark mad"; and he said, "Yes, I'm stark mad."

EDITH. I said that because . . .

BARON. And then you sensibly sent him to his room. Don't be nervous, dear. Let's talk it over calmly. Sit down, my child.

(EDITH *sits down*)

What's more important is that you visited this actor at his apartment.

EDITH *(Standing up)*. What does this mean? What are you after?

BARON. Don't get excited, my child; you'll have plenty of chance later. Very soon, in fact. Were you at his apartment? Is that true?

EDITH *(Greatly agitated)*. It's true, but if you knew how it happened . . .

BARON. If I didn't know, I shouldn't be so calm. You were back on the street three minutes after you went into the house.

EDITH. You mean you had me watched?

BARON. You can be glad I did. It's the sweep second-hand on my detective's watch that is keeping you safe now.

EDITH. I beg you, stop tormenting me. I can't endure this fake calm any longer. Kill me, or kick me out —but this I can't bear.

BARON *(Calmly)*. I shan't kill you, because without you I couldn't go on living; you know that. Kick you out? So Mr. Fabry can rush after you and lead you proudly to the altar? Really, now! But I shall act, that much is sure.

EDITH. Act as you please, but don't torture me.

BARON. If this man wanted you to be his mistress, I shouldn't need to do anything. I could leave it to you. I could be assured that the gentleman would come a cropper.

EDITH. Yes, and now?

BARON. Now you're in love.

EDITH. And why don't you trust me *now?*

BARON. Because this actor isn't looking for an affair. He's a decent boy. He wants to marry you. That's why I'm stepping in, which I had no need to do before.

EDITH. It isn't necessary now, either.

BARON. My child, you're mistaken. It is necessary. You're a bit chilly at my side, I know, and you warm yourself with that sort of thing. You're decent clear through. And besides, I flatter myself you're afraid of me. You're right to be. This actor chap rehearsed an amateur part with you once, and you fell in love with the actor and his trade together. Love, success, fame . . . and what not . . . You'll be lost to me, if I hesitate now so much as another hour.

EDITH. And what are you going to do?

BARON. We'll get to that, too. A man who is really in love at sixty dies along with his love. I have no time to wait for your repentence and return. My time is short.

EDITH. You're getting too serious. I don't like that.

BARON. Edith, I'm not giving you to that actor. *You* may not know, but *I* know that you want to go with him.

EDITH. You know better than I?

BARON. Much better. *(Pause)* Our forefathers knew what to do in such cases. It was the fashion for the French to cut the heart out of a young fellow like that, and serve it up to one's lovely spouse for dinner. You can read about it in old memoirs from the seventeenth century.

EDITH. How coldly you say it!

BARON. My ancestors in Italy weren't so theatrical. One of the Montaltos fed *his* Fabry something containing a powdered diamond. The diamond . . . pounded to a powder, makes sharp little grains that bore their way slowly through the intestines. But that familiar method departed with the Renaissance, too—I'm sorry to say.

EDITH *(Softly, shocked)*. I've never heard you speak in that tone before.

BARON. My ancestors had a reputation for beating off every robber baron that tried to plunder them. *(Meaningfully)* We defend ourselves, my child.

EDITH *(Alarmed)*. Everything you've been saying indicates some sort of purpose.

BARON. I didn't really need to talk about any of this. But . . . I shall *act,* let me inform you now. You shall feel my strength, my power of life . . . and death.

EDITH. Merciful God . . . what are you going to do?

BARON. I have a feeling you already know that.

EDITH *(Almost hysterically)*. Don't talk like that. For heaven's sake, don't talk like that!

BARON. You know the "Marshal"?

EDITH. Good God!

BARON. You know who the "Marshal" is. "Marshal" is the name of my beautiful slim English hunting rifle, the one I'm taking out tomorrow.

EDITH. You aren't going hunting!

BARON. Who, me?

EDITH. Nor . . . you . . . either!

BARON. You're mistaken. I'll be there. We'll all be there. It will be a fine, old-fashioned, manly, dangerous hunt.

EDITH *(Much agitated)*. I hardly know you. You've lost your poise.

BARON. Something inside me has given way.

EDITH. You're exaggerating the whole matter. I'm not any more interested in this man than in the others I've shown the door to.

BARON. That's a lie.

EDITH. If you wish . . . I'll send him away this very evening, and never see him again.

BARON. Maybe so, but if I don't act at once, *I'll* be done for.

EDITH (*In great agitation*). I'll send him away, I'll show him the door, now, this minute.

BARON. And then follow him.

EDITH. Don't you believe me?

BARON. I envy you, my child, for being able to believe yourself.

EDITH. Have pity on me! Believe me!

BARON. No more, please! (*Pause*) And now I most positively forbid you to say another word about it. (*Pause*)

FABRY (*Enters*). Good evening, Baron.

BARON. How long we take to make ourselves beautiful, my dear matinee *and* evening idol. Good evening. (THEY *shake hands*) So you were terrified of our slow train, eh?

FABRY. It's like a snake—creeps ahead slowly, and is cold all over.

BARON. You've seen my wife already, haven't you?

FABRY. Yes, I've been so fortunate. (*Goes to the tea-table*) Do you mind if I pour myself some tea?

(EDITH *nods, with a forced smile*)

BARON. Is your room all right?

FABRY. It's delightful. Those charming red-flowered curtains and the enormous wide bed.

BARON. It was my bachelor bed.

FABRY. Congratulations.

EDITH (*In a forced conversational tone*). Rum, cream, lemon?

FABRY. Lemon, if I may.—And three lumps.

EDITH (*With a forced smile*). I know.

FABRY. You're looking splendid, Baron. You would, of course, outdoors all day.

BARON. I wish I were. The last few days we've had rain. Dry, clear, sharp cold—that's what I call a good weather. *You*'ve got rather a town complexion.

FABRY. It's the indoor atmosphere.

EDITH. Cafes and clubs, no doubt . . .

FABRY. Oh, very rarely. I'm positively scared of those smoky dives. It goes right to my throat next day. And every time I've experimented with toughening myself, I've had such a cold the very first day that I couldn't play for two weeks. To be quite honest, tomorrow's hunt will be another of those experiments.

(EDITH *looks at* FABRY *nervously*)

BARON. I've been watching the barometer all day. Apparently we'll have fine weather.

FABRY. Where the train turns north, at the big curve after the bridge, the cold suddenly comes and hits you in the face.

BARON. Because the railway—and the highway, too—leaves the sheltered valley at that point.

FABRY. My throat felt it right away. Instantly.

EDITH (*With forced amiability*). I couldn't take the responsibility if your public were deprived of you on our account for even one night.

FABRY. Most kind. But it's really not an affectation, my talking about it so much. I'm a slave of this delicate little instrument. (*Indicates his throat*) Most annoying if it should keep me away from the hunt tomorrow.

BARON. I hope you'll be feeling all right tomorrow morning.

FABRY. I hope to God I shall. But I doubt it. It's behaving most suspiciously. I can always tell beforehand when it's about to have one of its whims.

BARON. Then you won't be along tomorrow?

FABRY. I'm a perfect slave, sir.

BARON (Put out). There, see what happens when a person is afraid of the slow train. He catches cold on the express.

FABRY. Well, it's too late now. Never mind. At any rate I'll wait and see tomorrow.

BARON. I should be sorry if you couldn't come. But . . . if you don't come, you'll simply stay here. (Brief pause. The BARON shrugs) Here by the fire.

EDITH (Laughing nervously). You can play chess with my sister-in-law's grandfather.

FABRY. Please condemn me to anything but that.

BARON (Calmly). I'd been counting on you.

FABRY. Oh, you can manage without me.

BARON. You're upsetting the arrangements a little. (Brief pause) Well, never mind. You can be sorry, if for no other reason, because I was planning to lend you one of my best rifles.

FABRY. Thanks anyway . . .

BARON. And . . . (Gets up) If you will stand me up, wait, at least I'll bring it in and introduce you.

(Exit BARON. EDITH follows him with her eyes, listens to his footsteps, then goes quickly to the door through which the Baron went out)

FABRY. What is it?

EDITH (Softly, agitated). Go away. Get out of here. Tomorrow morning. No. Not tomorrow. Now. Go. This minute.

FABRY. Why? What's happened?

EDITH. The worst. My husband overheard us. Don't ask questions. Go. Go. Please.

FABRY. Really, now . . .

EDITH. For mercy's sake don't say a word; go on, leave at once . . . if you love me . . . this instant.

FABRY. This instant? What's happened?

(EDITH suddenly puts her finger to her lips for silence, goes quickly back from the door to the tea-table, and sits down. FABRY goes and sits down leisurely calm, right. Silence. Enter BARON, carrying two hunting rifles)

BARON. Here they are. My two prima donnas. My "stars." The "Marshal" and the "Colonel." (Lays them on the table downstage left)

FABRY. The "Colonel"? What do you mean? Have they got ranks?

BARON. That's it. See here: this is the "Colonel." That's the one I had assigned to you for tomorrow. (Puts "Marshal" on table)

FABRY (Goes over and takes hold). A splendid piece.

(BOTH are holding the "Colonel")

BARON (Lovingly). "Holland & Holland" made, British, both of them. There'll be none better a hundred years hence.

FABRY. And this is the "Marshal"?

BARON (Puts "Colonel" on table

and picks up "Marshal"). It is. Study him with respect. When I got him he was just a private soldier, like the rest. After each hunt they got promoted according to how they behaved. So this one made colonel, and this one is the marshal.

FABRY. You can't go any higher than that.

BARON. No.

FABRY. Naturally the "Marshal" will go tomorrow with you.

BARON. Naturally. The "Marshal" is not only my best rifle but my best friend. The "Marshal" is as precise as an engineer, as dependable as death.

FABRY. How seriously you do speak of him.

EDITH (*Nervously*). I'm horrified of all firearms. I'm horrified . . . of all . . . firearms.

BARON. Goodness, you're nervous, dear.

EDITH. Please, I can't stand the sight of them.

FABRY. Why? A fine instrument like that is beautiful even to look at.

EDITH. The idea they represent is dreadful.

BARON. To a woman's sensibilities it may be dreadful.

EDITH (*Nervously, almost hysterically, but smiling, in conversational tone*). The only thing they're made for is to cause suffering and death. Please, you make me nervous.

FABRY. How interesting. Madam is seriously annoyed with them.

BARON (*Putting "Marshal" on the table*). She often says I have a sort of diabolical friendship binding me to my rifles.

FABRY (*To* EDITH). That's why you're against these innocent Britons?

EDITH (*Nervously, too loud*). They aren't innocent!

FABRY (*Calmly—he knows by now what is afoot—speaks quietly and plainly*). They are innocent, because they're not responsible for what they do.

BARON. You're affronting my "Marshal." It's not true that he's an instrument. He thinks and acts. Sometimes I'm afraid of the "Marshal" myself—and that's saying a great deal.

FABRY. I respect and honor him; but I guess I'm not hunter enough . . . I'm not afraid of him. (*This is said meaningfully*)

EDITH (*Nervously*). Let's drop it. Let's talk about something else.

BARON. I'm not afraid of men or beasts. There's only one thing I'm afraid of—an inanimate object that suddenly acts as though it had a will of its own.

FABRY. I can't even be afraid of that. (*Meaningly*) And then you have to consider whether a person is much attached to life or not.

BARON. And *you* say that, when your very throat puts you into a panic?

FABRY. My throat, yes. My life, no. I'm an actor. A real, old-fashioned play-actor. To me other people's tears may matter; my own life hardly does. Traveling by train is just as dangerous as looking down the "Marshal's" thirty-caliber barrel.

BARON. It's only twenty-two.

FABRY. So much the better. (*Seats himself downstage right*) Only twenty-two caliber?

BARON (*With "Marshal" in his hands*). That's right. We hunt in the woods here, at short range. Small caliber, great accuracy. Once the bullet hits the heart, what's the difference whether it's a twenty-two or a thirty-thirty? Among other things, it has the advantage that . . .

(During this sentence the BARON, *standing downstage left by the smoking table, has been trying to point out something about the lock. The rifle, happening at the moment to be pointed toward* FABRY *as he sits in the armchair downstage right, goes off.* EDITH *screams)*

(Very long pause. EVERYONE *is rigidly silent)*

FABRY *(Motionless, calmly, softly).* Apparently the "Marshal" isn't so dependable, at that.

BARON *(Staring at the rifle).* I can't understand it . . .

EDITH *(Upset).* Good God . . . I don't even dare ask you . . . Fabry . . . You aren't hurt, are you?

BARON. God has protected you. *(Stands by the table left. Puts "Marshal" on table calmly)*

FABRY. God has protected *us.*

EDITH. Are you all right?

FABRY. Perfectly.

EDITH. But . . . how could it have happened?

(Enter BUTLER*)*

BARON. What do you want?

*(*BUTLER *says nothing)*

BARON *(Excited, very loud).* What do you want? I didn't ring! *(Gives the* BUTLER *a terrible look. The* BUTLER, *as if spellbound, starts to go. As* HE *goes, the* BARON *shouts:)* Even if the house falls down, you've got no business here unless you're called. You'd better go and tell the head gamekeeper I want to give him new instructions for tomorrow. *(*BUTLER *exit. Pause)* We've just escaped a great disaster, Fabry.

FABRY. Please let's not talk about it. Let's not think about what might have happened. I'm no pessimist anyhow . . . and certainly not by hindsight.

BARON. You're quite right.

(Pause)

FABRY. Anyway, it would have been odd to die like that. I never thought of that. And yet it's not so uncommon, comparatively speaking.

BARON. Well, it's the first time in *my* life.

FABRY. It's quite common . . . and the best part of it is, it isn't always an accident. In the cases where it is accidental . . . *(His voice fades)* . . . in the cases where it is accidental . . . in . . . those cases . . .

EDITH *(Frightened).* Fabry . . . Good God!

BARON. What is it?

FABRY. Nothing at all . . . I'm a bit . . . *(Is silent)*

EDITH *(Beside him, very loudly).* Fabry! You must have been hit after all!

BARON *(To* EDITH*).* Please control yourself.

EDITH *(To* FABRY*).* Why don't you say so . . . if the bullet hit you?

FABRY. I must . . . confess . . . Madam . . . don't be alarmed . . . It certainly isn't serious . . . I do begin to feel as if my shoulder . . .

BARON. Your shoulder?

FABRY *(To* EDITH*).* Please don't get excited. I feel something here in my left shoulder. Certainly nothing more than a bare graze. After all, I couldn't talk so easily . . . if it were serious.

EDITH. A doctor must be . . . A doctor must be called at once. *(Rings)*

(BARON *goes upstage, picks up the telephone. Enter* BUTLER)

EDITH (*To* BUTLER). Send the car to the town just as fast as it can get there. Go to the hospital, and bring out the head physician, Dr. Baltin, right away.

(*Exit* BUTLER)

BARON (*On the phone*). Operator? Number 9, the hospital, please. (*Waits*) Thank you. Hospital? This is Baron Pahlen-Montalto. Please call Dr. Baltin to the phone right away. (*Waits.*) All right. I'll hold on.

EDITH. But meanwhile we should . . .

FABRY. No, don't touch it. We learned that in the war—let the doctor be the first to touch a wound. It's nothing serious, certainly.

EDITH. Is it bleeding?

FABRY. I don't think so. Small flesh wounds close right up. The whole thing's a trifle.

BARON (*On the phone*). Dr. Baltin? This is Pahlen-Montalto. Good evening. My car will be there to fetch you in a couple of minutes. There's been an accident. (*Pause*) A gunshot wound. Looks like a . . . small flesh wound. (*Pause*) Thanks very much. (*Hangs up*) He'll be waiting for the car at the gate. (*To* FABRY) Don't you want to lie down? Shall we help you?

FABRY (*Smiling*). Not for anything. I really only agreed to the doctor for Madam's sake.

EDITH. A glass of water, or brandy?

FABRY. Nothing, thanks.

EDITH. I was so horrified when you stopped talking before . . . when you turned pale . . .

FABRY. I'm feeling better already.

I think . . . it was mostly . . . nerves.

BARON (*To* EDITH. *Severely*). Please sit down. Maybe *you'd* like a glass of water or some brandy.

EDITH (*Reaching for a glass*). A drop of water . . . thanks . . . (*Sits down, drinks. Pause*)

FABRY. Well . . . where were we? Oh, yes. It's not so uncommon, comparatively speaking, and the best part of it is, it isn't always an accident. (*Smiling bitterly*) A gun that goes off and discharges a bullet blindly—that's brutal. But a gun that thinks, a gun whose will coincides with the will of . . . (*He breaks off*) . . . That's . . . how shall I say it . . . that's *romantic*. And awful. And beautiful.

EDITH. Strange things . . . you're . . . saying.

BARON. I feel that what you are saying is out of place just now.

FABRY. Once we get to talking about it—a person does think of various possibilities.

BARON. "Possibilities." The term is as out of place as the whole discussion.

FABRY (*Almost rebelliously*). You'll have to forgive my disregarding the rules of conversation somewhat. Though I feel well, so long as we've sent for the doctor I shall claim the prerogatives of a patient.

BARON. Which likewise have their limits.

FABRY. Limits that I shall take the liberty of disregarding.

(*Pause.*)

BARON. You ought to be quiet now.

FABRY. If you're referring to my condition, thank you. But if you mean that the subject I'm discussing is unsuitable, I shall chiefly consider which suits *me*—silence or speech.

BARON. I'll make things easier for you. If you want to discuss the accident with me in that tone, I'm at your service.

EDITH. Please, both of you . . . It's agony to listen to this.

FABRY. True, it isn't altogether amusing, Madam. I confess my well-bred reserve is forsaking me, and my rude peasant forebears are coming to life.

BARON. You still aren't speaking straight out. But I'll help you along. The rude peasant in you says the "Marshal" isn't responsible for what happened. I am.

FABRY. The "Marshal" had nothing to do with any of it.

BARON. Nobody but me?

FABRY. Nobody but you.

(Short pause)

EDITH. Now I won't have this talked about another moment. I won't have it. I won't have it. *(Starts to go out.)*

BARON *(Peremptorily)*. You'll be so kind as to stay here and listen to the rest of what is said.

EDITH. I won't listen to anything. I . . . *(Starts to leave again.)*

BARON *(Peremptorily)*. You'll be so kind as to obey my orders.

(Pause. EDITH sits down)

FABRY. If the bullet didn't hurt up to the last moment, it might still be serious. If it may be serious after all, let's look each other in the eye and talk it out.

BARON. I've already told you I was at your service.

FABRY. The gun may be reasonable, and even the bullet while it's traveling. But once it's landed somewhere in a living body—it may go crazy.

EDITH. But you said it just grazed your shoulder . . .

FABRY. No, it went deeper.

EDITH *(Frightened)*. But then we should . . . then we've got to do something. How can you possibly sit there and talk?

FABRY. Well, assume I can bear pain. And my life . . . has never really seemed my own. It was lent to me. Some time I've got to give it back anyhow.

(He says this with ever fainter voice, like one suffering and manfully hiding his pain)

FABRY *(To the BARON)*. And talking of the matter . . . are you really sure it was an accident?

EDITH *(Screaming)*. It was an accident!

(SHE goes to her husband. Pause. FABRY gives EDITH a long look)

FABRY. Madam has already answered my question.

BARON. If I'd wanted to shoot at you . . .

FABRY. You'd have done it tomorrow on the hunt. But then, I said I wasn't going.

BARON. Then you maintain unequivocally that I intended to fire at you?

FABRY. Let's assume so.

EDITH. You mustn't say that!

BARON. You're my guest. And wounded. What can I say by way of answer? In due time my answer will be forceful.

FABRY. And suppose nobody's left to hear your answer?

EDITH. You can't say it was intentional! You can't say that!

BARON. Don't force me into an argument where I can't speak freely.

FABRY. You're perfectly free. Speak out. Answer. I demand it.

BARON. By what right do you *demand* anything of me?

FABRY. By this right . . . that I may never have another chance . . . to argue the matter with you. I'm inquisitive. I'm interested in people, events, chance, intrigue, motives, crimes . . .

BARON. Please show some consideration for the fact that I'm showing consideration.

FABRY. I'm not saying a word . . . *(To* EDITH) You may rest easy, Madam, I *shan't* say a word. But if that crazy bullet is as crazy as I have reason to think . . . at this moment . . . then my discretion will only last *as long as I'm alive.*

BARON. I didn't ask your discretion.

FABRY. But I shall maintain it. So long as I'm alive, it's a matter among us three . . . it's no concern of anyone else. But . . . if, my dear Baron, I should be so inconsiderate . . . as to die . . . in your house where I was invited to enjoy myself . . . then my silence would be useless. Because then outsiders would mix into the affair. A gentleman usually turns up then who answers to the title of District Attorney. And he's even more inquisitive than I am. He has an easier time asking questions, too, if only because he hasn't got a twenty-two caliber bullet in him while he does it. He finds out everything he wants to know. And, as I say, I'm terribly inquisitive. The thought of my *not* finding out what this gentleman will find out is unendurable. What . . . *(Weakens, falls silent.* EDITH *goes to him)*

EDITH. You've got to lie down. Please, let us help you.

FABRY. No, Madam. Nobody touches me. Only the doctor.

BARON. Now you're openly accusing. And if you really don't claim consideration . . .

FABRY. I don't.

BARON. Then you shall have your answer. Your accusation is groundless, malicious, and contemptible.

FABRY. Now you're lying. (EDITH *screams, runs over again to the* BARON) That was a lie, because the shot has a past history.

BARON. It has no past history. *(Looks at* EDITH.)

FABRY. That's another lie, because it *has* a past history — right where you have your eyes fastened now.

EDITH. Excuse me . . . I've given you no reason to say any such thing. Consider, as a gentleman, what you're saying!

FABRY *(Takes no notice of* EDITH. *To the* BARON). You were jealous.

BARON. Never.

FABRY. Oh, yes, this time you were. I'm proud of that.

BARON. I must destroy your illusions, Mr. Actor.

FABRY. You heard from the next room what I said to your wife.

BARON. I heard nothing.

(FABRY *looks at* EDITH)

EDITH *(Answering the look)*. You didn't say anything . . . that my husband could hold against you.

FABRY. Yes, I did. I tried to persuade you to leave your husband and marry me.

BARON. You couldn't say that to my wife.

EDITH. He didn't, either.

FABRY (To EDITH). You didn't encourage me, but all the same, I said it. (To the BARON) And you heard me.

BARON. You could never have finished saying any such thing to my wife.

EDITH. He didn't say it. He didn't say it.

FABRY. Assuming . . . just assuming . . . that the gentleman I mentioned before . . . the District Attorney . . . were to ask you . . . whether you two had a jealous scene . . . before this accident . . . what would you say?

EDITH (Loud). We had none.

FABRY. Never?

BARON. Never.

FABRY. Please, it's Madam I want to answer.

EDITH. Never. None.

FABRY. Then the Baron did not bring in the "Marshal" as an easy solution to a crisis that . . .

EDITH (Interrupting). No, no, no! How dare you say such a thing? (Keeps looking at her husband) How can you suppose such a thing of my husband?

FABRY. That is to say, you—the only person who knows all about it—you . . . think this . . . was an unfortunate accident . . .

EDITH. Fabry . . . Do calm down a little . . . take a little rest . . . You're so wrought up . . .

FABRY. Answer my question.

BARON (Peremptorily). Answer him!

EDITH (In extreme anguish. Turning to the BARON)). It was an accident! (To FABRY) This is terrible . . . My husband never by so much as a word . . . (Horrified, to FABRY)

Don't look at me like that . . . I'm afraid of you now. (Flees weeping to her HUSBAND, who puts his arm around her)

BARON. Don't cry, my child, and don't be afraid of anything.

EDITH. I'm not afraid . . . when your arm is around me . . .

(BARON kisses her tenderly on the forehead. Brief pause. FABRY surveys the scene with a bitter smile. EDITH slowly slips out of the BARON's arms, and stands for a while beside him, her handkerchief to her eyes; than SHE slowly turns left to go. As SHE gets near the door:)

FABRY. One more moment, please, Madam. (EDITH stops. FABRY gets up) I was supposed to be playing in the theatre this evening. I canceled it to come here. I didn't know then that—I should be playing this evening after all. Well, now I do know, and I say it straight out. I did play this evening . . . and my finest part, too. (Laughs. Pause) How strangely you do look at me. It seems you must suspect what has happened.

BARON. Surely you weren't playacting?

FABRY. Yes, I was. I was playacting, sir, and very well, too, I see. Please don't stare so. It's just as I say. I haven't any bullet in me. The whole thing was just a bit of acting, and if I may say so, not bad acting, either. At any rate it was useful. (Bowing with a smile) My esteemed friends will, I trust, forgive an actor this little exercise in his art.

BARON. You were making fun of me?

FABRY. In point of fact, sir, yes. But not in order to annoy you, or to amuse myself. The play was in earnest. To put it bluntly—I was in love with your wife, and you wanted to put a bullet in me.

BARON. Now that's going too far.

FABRY. You *did* want to. But you didn't hit me. So far the matter is serious. Then came the comedy. I wanted to see what would have happened if the "Marshal" had *not* lost this particular battle. One is always curious about one's own funeral. I have watched it now, esteemed sir and gracious lady. I have learned by it. It was a very sorry funeral. I died as miserably as a dog run over on the highway by the squire's car. The high-born couple does not so much as look back. I had a dreadful death, my dear audience. Really it would make one cry if it weren't so laughable. Please don't be angry. But it was such a tempting idea! Just imagine it for yourselves; it's no everyday opportunity . . . you get killed, and then you see the things that will happen *after* you're dead. No wonder any real actor would be tempted to do something that perhaps isn't permissible. It was not much of a pleasure to see a lady fleeing from the dead man . . . taking refuge in continuing life . . . to see how only the living, the strong, the hard have a friend . . . a *witness* . . . someone to feel *with* them. It was no pleasure seeing it . . . but . . . I'm inquisitive. If you've forgiven me, please deign to be seated . . . *(Points to a seat)* . . . and we'll talk about something else. Well, I must definitely decline to join the hunt, because my throat is really beginning to get painful . . . yes . . . I'm going home by the next train.

BARON *(Brusquely)*. That is enough. I know what you wanted, all right.

BUTLER *(Enters, right)*. Dr. Baltin is here.

(Brief pause)

FABRY. Bring him in. *(To* BARON *and* EDITH*)* If you don't object.

(Exit BUTLER*)*

DR. BALTIN *(Enters with doctor's bag)*. Good evening.

EDITH. Good evening, Doctor. We're grateful to you for being so kind. But we have a pleasant surprise for you.

BARON. Good evening. Have a seat, Doctor.

DR. BALTIN. I beg your pardon . . . ? And the accident?

FABRY. There was no accident, Doctor. It's my fault that you had to come out here this cruel cold night. Permit me to introduce myself: Victor Fabry, the actor.

DR. BALTIN. Quite unnecessary; I've had the great pleasure of seeing you often in the theatre in Vienna.

EDITH. Tea, Doctor? Coffee?

DR. BALTIN. Nothing, thank you very much. But . . . how did this accident . . . happen—or not happen?

FABRY. I'm the culprit. The thing was that while we were looking at that gun there, it suddenly went off. The Baron was holding it when it fired. And after the first fright I couldn't resist the histrionic temptation to play the wounded victim. When they put in the phone call, I had qualms of conscience for a moment, but by then I was in too far to back out. I do hope you'll forgive a crazy actor this rotten joke.

DR. BALTIN. But there's no need for you to apologize at such length.

FABRY. You do forgive me?

DR. BALTIN. With the greatest joy. Now that I know you were the person, I'm ever so much relieved *not* to have been needed.

EDITH. But now you will stay a while . . . surely you'll take a little something.

DR. BALTIN. I can only stop a few minutes. I have a very sick patient in the hospital. I shall have to look in on him tonight.

BARON. Have a cigar?

DR. BALTIN. That I will take. *(Lights up)*

FABRY. You know . . . you must put yourself in my place. I'm sitting there. *(Points downstage right)* We're chatting pleasantly. The Baron is showing off his guns, the "Colonel," the "Marshal" . . .

DR. BALTIN. I know them. The best I ever get is the "Captain."

BARON. There's time yet.

FABRY. And as the Baron is showing them, and praising that wonderful piece to the skies . . . why, it speaks out.

DR. BALTIN. Unheard-of.

FABRY. Yes, really unheard-of. Probably the gun had been lent to somebody who returned it loaded. The Baron is such an experienced huntsman that he could never possibly put a gun back in the rack without unloading it. Well, in short, it goes off. And right in the direction— this direction . . . *(Points)* . . . where I'm sitting. I see their horrified faces . . . and . . . *(Winningly)* Tell me honestly, Doctor, mightn't even a person who was not an actor be tempted to play the wounded victim? Perhaps not so much for the joke of it as to see, to observe how the others would behave, what they would do and say . . . Don't you think so?

DR. BALTIN. Yes, I can quite see. You tell it so well that I'm sorry I wasn't there.

FABRY. You're right to be sorry; it was most amusing.

DR. BALTIN. Amusing?

FABRY. Well, let's say interesting. A socially prominent couple suddenly placed in a situation where they can't help thinking they've killed a man.

DR. BALTIN. Too bad I missed it.

FABRY. Just like a play—the doctor never appears till the end.

DR. BALTIN *(Laughing)*. That's right. *(To the* BARON *and* EDITH) I can imagine that you didn't enjoy it as much as an impressive production. But still . . . seeing a famous star in a part like that . . .

BARON. He did it amazingly well.

EDITH *(Seriously)*. Too well. I'm seriously annoyed with him. I shan't get over it in a long . . . long . . . time.

FABRY. I'm really very sorry for that.

BUTLER *(Enters. The* BARON *looks inquiringly at him)*. The head gamekeeper you sent for is waiting for you, sir. For instructions . . .

BARON. Excuse me a moment. *(Exit, followed by* BUTLER)

DR. BALTIN. And so . . . you played the part of a dying man.

FABRY. I was interested to see what the only witness . . . *(Laughing)* . . . present at the "killing" would say.

(EDITH *laughs uneasily*)

DR. BALTIN. Well, what did she say?

FABRY. Oh, she was splendid. It's a joy to see how a wise, fine wife behaves in a situation like that.

DR. BALTIN (Getting up). The main thing is that there was nothing for me to do. (To EDITH) Forgive me, dear lady, but I'm a little uneasy about my patient.

EDITH. Well, then . . . many thanks for being so helpful.

DR. BALTIN. Please, don't mention it. Goodbye.

EDITH (To avoid being left alone with Fabry). Just a second. Please say goodbye to my husband too; I'll call him right in. (Exit quickly.)

(Brief pause)

FABRY (In an undertone). Just a word, Doctor. Quick, there's no time to lose. Doctor, I want to ask you to treat this as an absolute professional confidence.

DR. BALTIN. Please . . . of course.

FABRY. You . . . didn't miss my performance. You're still seeing it.

DR. BALTIN. How do you mean?

FABRY. Doctor . . . I . . . can scarcely stand . . . I . . . wasn't acting before . . . the performance is now . . . Because you see . . . the bullet is in me . . . the bullet that scoundrel fired at me . . . here, in my shoulder . . .

DR. BALTIN. Why, in that case I must . . . (Makes a motion toward his bag)

FABRY. No, no . . . not here. They must never find out. Please get that straight. I want your word for it.

DR. BALTIN. That's taken for granted. (Steps up to him) In your shoulder?

FABRY. Here. (Stands with back to audience, pushes his shirt out of the way)

DR. BALTIN (Looks at the wound). It's hardly bled at all. But it's a disagreeable spot. Does it hurt?

FABRY. Yes. (Covers up the wound and straightens his coat)

DR. BALTIN. You're coming straight to the hospital with me, in the car. If you can bear it so splendidly as this, it won't be too bad. You were lucky.

FABRY. They both think I was acting before. Now, I guess you know how I was able to act the part of a wounded man so convincingly. Because I wasn't acting at all. I tried right away to hide it, only I suddenly felt rotten. But then . . . when bitterness got the upper hand, I summoned all my strength, . . . and then I began acting again.

DR. BALTIN. Let's go. This is no kind of acting for a doctor.

FABRY. Really, you're very nice. A perfect stranger at last, after all these . . . "friends."

(Enter BUTLER)

FABRY (To BUTLER). Please pack up my things, will you? And take them to the car. I'm leaving with the doctor.

BUTLER. Very good, sir. (Exit up the steps)

DR. BALTIN. It's not proper for me as a doctor to ask, but . . . tell me . . . why should you conceal it now, and suffer doing it?

FABRY (Sweetly, like a child to its father). Well, you see . . . I don't want them crowing over me. He was jealous of me. He fired at me, as if I were a strange animal that had strayed into his garden. I'll take . . . the bullet with me; I'll go . . . but I don't want him to have the satisfaction. Now do you understand?

DR. BALTIN. I understand.

FABRY. I thought that woman . . . Oh, what didn't I think! Then they . . . both . . . showed me . . . that they're right-thinking people.

DR. BALTIN (*Ironically*). Very right-thinking people, I must say.

FABRY. If he'd hit me in the heart, if I'd died, it would have been better. For an actor, an enthusiast, a man madly in love it's a fine way to die. If he *hadn't* hit me, that would have been fine too—to laugh at the old man and be gone, whistling merrily. But as it is . . . trudging off with a bullet in you that hurts . . . these people mustn't know about that. No, Doctor. *I* want to be the one that laughs tonight. For once I don't want the wiseacres to laugh. For once . . . just once I want the poor player to laugh, no matter how . . . it . . . hurts.

DR. BALTIN. It's amazing how you stand it.

FABRY. God has given every creature some means of defence. The bull has horns, the tiger teeth, the rabbit fleet legs, the bird wings . . . the play-actor his play-acting.

(*Enter* EDITH *and the* BARON)

BARON. I hear you're rushing right on, Doctor.

DR. BALTIN. That's right, Baron.

BARON. Well . . . Thank you again.

DR. BALTIN. Good night.

FABRY (*Cheery again*). The doctor is being kind enough to take me to the town. I can catch the express there early in the morning. So I'll make my goodbyes too.

(DR. BALTIN *picks up his bag*)

BARON. Good night.

EDITH. Good night, Doctor.

(*Exit* DR. BALTIN. *The door stands open*)

FABRY. Goodbye, Baron. Goodbye, Madam.

EDITH. Then you're really going too?

FABRY (*Modestly, gently*). For me the hunt is quite over. I had no role as hunter. As game, thank heaven, I got well out of it. What further business have I here? Perhaps I might do as the players did in ancient Rome, turn to the audience at the end of the play, and say *Plaudite:* applause, please! One thing you must grant me. I played my part rather well.

BARON (*Calmly*). You played excellently.

FABRY. And what do *you* say, dear lady?

EDITH (*Softly*). I'm carried away. I'm applauding. (*Makes a few inaudible gestures of applause*)

FABRY (*At the front door*). And I . . . (*Laughs softly*) . . . forgive me, but for my reward, let me laugh heartily over the whole affair. Good night!

(*Exit quickly, softly laughing*)

CURTAIN

PRESIDENT

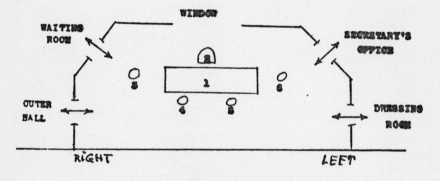

17 DESK
2" SWIVEL CHAIR
3, 4, 5, 6 = STOOLS

SCENE DESIGN
"PRESIDENT"

PRESIDENT

CARICATURE IN ONE ACT

CHARACTERS

NORRISON	DR. FRANK
HARRY	COUNT SAN MARINO-
SYLVIA	SCHATTENBURG
PYNNIGAN	COLLEON
MISS CUNO	KRISTIAN
MISS MARLIN	FELIX
MISS PETROVITCH	TAILOR
MISS SHORTWOOD	HABERDASHER
OSSO	LOUIE
SYRING	CHARLES
WOLF	GEORGE
LOARY	BARBER

PLACE : NORRISON'S PRIVATE OFFICE IN HIS BANK

(New acting version of the same author's EINS, ZWEI, DREI—originally produced at the RAIMUND THEATER *in Vienna and at the* KUENSTLER THEATER *in Berlin with* MAX PALLENBERG *in the leading role. Translated by* SIDNEY HOWARD *and produced under the title* ONE, TWO, THREE *by* GILBERT MILLER *in New York with* ARTHUR BYRON. *Produced at the* VIGSZINHAZ *in Budapest with* SANDOR GOTH; *at the* TEATRO OLIMPIA *in Milan and on the Italian stages with* ANNIBALE BETRONE.)*

NOTE

This play was written for Max Pallenberg, one of the great European comedians of our time. He played its leading role for years in various countries until his untimely, tragic death in 1934 which cut short not only his incomparably successful theatrical career, but prevented the realization of his hope of coming to America in this role.

Pallenberg was not only a highly gifted actor blessed with an irresistible comical genius. When a role demanded it—as this one did—his delivery was a miracle of what his contemporaries liked to call "tempo"—a sharp, penetrating, crystal-clear, amazingly fast *staccato*, like the rapid clatter of a machine-gun.

After these words of introduction it seems almost superfluous to say that a simple reading of this play indicates clearly that *a rapid tempo is necessary and even vital* to its performance. The actor entrusted with the role of NOR-RISON must create what will amount to a record for speed from the moment in which he tells SYLVIA: "Sit there and watch. Attention!" (Page 40), up to the end of the play when NORRISON says, pulling on his gloves: "I think we've cleaned up everything." (Page 77).

This tempo will depend only partly on swift movement and delivery. It requires an inner intensity as well. The actor playing Norrison's role must accomplish everything he does with the almost superhuman celerity of a magician without, however, any lack of poise, presence of mind or precision.

The setting, if its walls are divided into five units (see plan) will also facilitate the swiftness of the action. These units should be so angled that the actors may make every possible saving in the number of steps required to move from any of the entrances to the central desk. Thus, the mechanics of the coming and going of the play's twenty-three characters will be greatly simplified. Curtains should replace doors at all these entrances because the eternal exits and entrances of the twenty-three characters would cause an unbearable opening and closing of doors. It is this coming and going through noiseless curtains that lends to Norrison's "machine" the well-oiled and precise quality which is essential to the play's performance.

PRESIDENT

SCENE: *Norrison's private office in the Norrison Bank. Downstage, in the left wall, an opening the size of a small door, to his private* Dressing Room. *Further upstage, also on the left, another similar opening to the* Secretary's Office. *On the rear wall, a single wide window. On the right wall, opposite the Secretary's Office, is the opening which gives on the* Waiting Room. *Downstage of this, and also in the right wall is the opening to the* Outer Hall. *All these openings have, instead of doors, curtains hanging across the doorways (so-called "portieres"), in order to facilitate the continuous coming and going of the play's twenty-three characters. Behind these curtains, doors are supposed to be, invisible to the audience.*

The center of the room is occupied by Norrison's big desk, an ample, flat piece of furniture, equipped with all manner of telephones and buzzer-buttons and so placed that President Norrison, in his swivel-chair, faces the audience. On the desk a box of big cigars. Four small stools are disposed within close range of the desk.

AT RISE: *At the* RISE OF THE CURTAIN, NORRISON *stands by the Dressing Room door drying his hands on a towel.* GEORGE, *his old servant, a kind of office-attendant, is brushing his coat.* PYNNIGAN, *his old (over 60) secretary stands behind the desk, jots down memoranda in a notebook.*

NORRISON (*Gives quick, sharp orders to* PYNNIGAN *as he finishes with the towel*). You'll put my mail aside for me. Each day in a parcel. Marked with the date. I don't want to be bothered with mail this week.

Further. Look for our friends from London on the thirteenth. Tell them I'll be back to discuss their loan with them the day after. That's the fourteenth. Further. Holstein can handle any trifles that come up while I'm away. Further. I don't want to bother with newspapers either. Turn them all over to the Press Department. Further. Any one who asks for me—no matter who—after this afternoon — four thirty-one — I've gone on a vacation for one week. For winter-sports. During that one week I wash my hands of business. My brain is switched off. (HE *hands the towel to* GEORGE) That's that. (HE *goes to his chair at his desk and sits*)

PYNNIGAN. I'll see to all that, sir.

(GEORGE *takes the brush and towel, going out into the dressing room.* NORRISON *sits lost in thought, staring into the air, tapping his desk absently. A pause, then* PYNNIGAN *continues, humbly, but with less of the employee's formality of manner*) I observe you're drumming on your desk, sir. This is my chance to chat with our great chief.

NORRISON. By all means, my dear Pynnigan. Go on. Talk to me. Can't you forget that you're my secretary? You who've known me all my life? Talk to me . . . just for these few minutes of peace before my train. (HE *glances at his watch*) Two forty-five. At four our dear little Sylvia comes to call for me. Then, at four thirty-one, the train starts to carry Sylvia and me to the snowy mountains, to my family and my holiday! My holiday! I'm already beginning to switch off my brain. Come over here, Pynnigan, old man! I won't listen but talk to me. Help me to relax. Don't be intelligent. That excites me. Be stupid, that soothes my brain.

PYNNIGAN. Your brain is a complex machine, sir. It takes time to switch a brain like yours off.

NORRISON. Pynnigan, you flatter me!

PYNNIGAN. I'm serious!

NORRISON. Don't be!

PYNNIGAN. While you're away, how still and empty this room will be! This room, this shrine of the motive force of all your vast organization!

NORRISON. The metaphor's not bad! Go on!

PYNNIGAN. So . . . you're listening?

NORRISON. To flattery, always. The more, the better. I abhor clumsy flattery. It's depressing. But real good clever flattery works like benzedrine. Cheers a man up. Go on.

PYNNIGAN. Floors above us, floors below us! Hundreds . . . *hundreds* of busy men and women! Wealth! A stupendous furnace, smelting gold out of everything! How beautiful it is!

NORRISON. Do you know when it was really beautiful? When it existed only inside here. (HE *taps his brow*) *Then* it *was* beautiful. Yes, let's forget the bank, though. Let's talk of things we don't have to think about! Chat with me! Empty banter . . . anything . . .

PYNNIGAN. It's funny, sir. Now that I've got the chance to chat with you, I can't think of anything to chat about! What shall I chat about, sir?

NORRISON. Whatever you like! Nonsense! Gossip! Hoary stories. Words, words, words, as Hamlet says. (HE *slaps* PYNNIGAN'S *back*) My dear, old Pynnigan!

PYNNIGAN. That's friendly of you, sir. That's like a horseman, after a hard ride, patting the neck of the horse.

NORRISON. You're too modest, but the metaphor's excellent.

PYNNIGAN. (*Finding a subject*). I *might* ask you how your family is, sir!

NORRISON. Excellent subject! Attaboy, Pynnigan! My family? They must have got up there by this time. In the mountains. They took the morning train. I had to wait for the afternoon train. Sylvia had shopping to do so that she didn't go with them either. She goes with me. At least, I'll have pleasant company. (HE *rises and goes to the window to look out*) A perfect day. Just what my wife needs. She's worn out, poor woman, with all these good works of hers. There's such a thing as too much uplift. Women's leagues. Vocational Homes. Shelters for lost girls. Societies against divorce. Against vice. Against . . . Well, I dunno! They're all of them against!

PYNNIGAN. Your wife fills a magnificent mission, sir. Fighting for morals and purity in this wicked city! She's often spoken of as our highest ethical court! That can't help but be wearing!

NORRISON. Oh, very wearing! Highly ethical, too. You're right. And a bit dull. Just the same, I'm happy to be going to my family. They spoil me. So many women. My wife. My lovely daughters. And Sylvia, our little house guest from

Sweden. She's got to be like our own child to us.

PYNNIGAN. How deeply I admire Miss Sylvia, sir! I'm glad she's coming here this afternoon. She's such a serious young lady.

NORRISON. I'm not sure she doesn't overdo that part. Daughter of one of Sweden's top tycoons — a millionaire's daughter though she is, I always say she's the perfect flower of Puritanism. We'll have to be giving her up soon. Her parents will come and take her home.

PYNNIGAN. It must be six months now that you've had the young heiress with your family. Teaching her our own streamlined production and merchandising methods.

NORRISON. Yes. Last year my daughter Maria spent six months with her people . . . to pick up some good old European culture.

PYNNIGAN. That should have been a profitable visit for Miss Maria!

NORRISON. How good they were to her. Well, we've done what we could to pay back their kindness. And we're proud that those cautious moralists were willing to entrust their only child to us for so long. Now she's leaving us. It's going to hurt, saying goodbye to her. We've grown so fond of her. I must admit though, I've been disturbed about her. She seems so inhibited. Not at all what one would expect from a free democracy like Sweden. She's so terribly reserved for her age.

PYNNIGAN. She scarcely ever returns my greetings.

NORRISON. Ah, these old world people have family pride! Her parents . . . (Brief pause) They're in Canada now. Coming from Lon-don where they saw a famous doctor. The mother has something the matter with her health. (With a sigh, changing the subject) Yes, Pynnigan. Not only one of the wealthiest but one of the most distinguished families!

PYNNIGAN. The old Nordic moneybags with his score of factories should be grateful to you.

NORRISON. I'll see that he's grateful. My wife can have the credit. I'll take the profits. You know how long I've been negotiating with him. Without his co-operation the future looks a bit dark to me, Pynnigan. I've got to have it. (HE sighs) Well, that's enough of that. Now that my wife and I have made ourselves more or less the child's second father and mother, I have hopes of getting somewhere. If only I had a son! I could have made a match of it. That is, if her people would let her marry a son of mine.

PYNNIGAN. *Let* her marry a young *Norrison?* A *Norrison?*

NORRISON. You don't know these rich European snobs with their "historic" names! Bah! Nobody's good enough for them! What they want are great names and great positions. They want a prince, a count, a viscount or a marquess, and a rich one, at that . . . for their only child. (Loud, with pride) When I was a young boy, I sold papers and magazines in our small town! I ran errands for the druggist and for the grocer . . . for a dime, or at the most for fifteen cents, though my parents weren't paupers at all! Yes, Pynnigan! But these people don't understand that. If they knew that part of my biography, they would be horrified! It's ridiculous, isn't it? But . . . what can you do? You have to respect *their* way of life, their century-old prejudices . . . particularly if they have money. And . . . (HE *breaks off*) Anyway, there's no young Norrison, more's the pity. (HE *looks out of the window again.* HE *shrugs*) Still, the sun's out, there's no war-talk in the morning papers, life isn't so bad and everything's all set for my holiday. For my quiet holiday.

PYNNIGAN. It's a real joy to see you so content.

NORRISON. We're hopeful in spite of the hard times. Our organization is efficient. And our personnel . . . I doubt if there's another such "ensemble" on earth!

PYNNIGAN *(Trying to be humorous).* They're like trained seals.

NORRISON. Not exactly. But the metaphor's good, again.

PYNNIGAN. You treat your employees as a father treats his children.

NORRISON. You're wrong! I treat 'em as a machinist treats his machine. With oil. I lubricate the pistons, the wheels and the cogs, and they run smoothly.

PYNNIGAN. Your kindness, sir!

NORRISON. It isn't kindness! It's lubrication. Oil. Oil.

PYNNIGAN *(Getting sentimental).* When I remember how often you used to sit on my lap as a child and pull my nose!

NORRISON. I don't think that that puts me under any obligations, my dear friend. Except . . . maybe . . . some time or other . . . to let you sit on *my* lap, and pull *my* nose. (HE *glances at his watch*) Well, are the skates, skis, bobsleds, bags and trunks all at the station?

PYNNIGAN. I gave orders to have them taken there at one thirty.

NORRISON. Orders aren't enough. Personal supervision, Pynnigan! You should learn from Napoleon as I have. Give orders first. Then supervise their execution. Even with such a personnel as mine.

PYNNIGAN. Yes, sir. (HE *goes into the Waiting Room. Whistling contentedly to himself,* NORRISON *paces the room.* PYNNIGAN *returns)* Excuse me, sir.

NORRISON. Yes? What is it, Pynnigan?

PYNNIGAN. Miss Sylvia, sir.

NORRISON. Sylvia? What about her?

PYNNIGAN. She's here, sir.

NORRISON. So early? Where?

PYNNIGAN. In the waiting room, sir.

NORRISON. Why doesn't she come in? (HE *hurries to the Waiting Room's entrance)* Sylvia! Here already! Come in, child!

(SYLVIA *enters.* PYNNIGAN *goes into the Secretary's Office)*

What's this mean? I didn't look for you till four. Why are you here so early?

SYLVIA. I know I'm 'way ahead of time. And I did have a few more things to buy. I've looked forward so to our trip together. (SHE *sits on one of the stools)*

NORRISON. That's really sweet of you, Sylvia. I'm very touched.

SYLVIA. Yes . . . but . . . I can't go.

NORRISON *(Surprised).* You can't go?

SYLVIA. No.

NORRISON. Why can't you?

SYLVIA. Well, you see, just as I was starting out to do my shopping, this telegram came. (SHE *hands it to him)* Father and Mother aren't coming next week. They're coming today. (*While* NORRISON *reads the telegram*) You know . . . they had to go first to Canada . . . because of that business transaction of father's . . . those important patent-rights. They wanted to spend a few weeks there. But they suddenly changed their mind. So . . . they're coming today. By train. In an hour. So I've got to stay.

NORRISON (*Gives her back the telegram*). But that's splendid! Splendid! So they get here today! I shall be very glad to see them! Even though they will be taking you away. Yes, this really is splendid!

SYLVIA. It isn't quite as splendid as all that.

NORRISON. Why isn't it, my dear?

SYLVIA. Dear Mr. Norrison, I've got something to confess to you.

NORRISON. My God, don't frighten me!

SYLVIA. You mustn't be frightened.

NORRISON. What's happened?

SYLVIA. I thought I'd find time later to bring this up. But this telegram rather changes the situation. I must be frank, quite frank with you, Mr. Norrison.

NORRISON (*Worried*). What's happened?

SYLVIA. Mr. Norrison . . . I love a man.

NORRISON. Oh, God!

SYLVIA. Please. Let's be brief and stick to the point. I've given myself to him.

NORRISON. God in heaven, what are you saying, child!

SYLVIA. Only the bare facts of the case. Those *are* the facts.

NORRISON. Given yourself to him?

SYLVIA. Yes.

NORRISON. Just what do you mean by that?

(SYLVIA *doesn't answer*)

Do you know what you've done if you mean what I think you mean? You've accomplished my moral and economic ruin! You've put me in the position of a man who has a fortune entrusted to him and loses it! What did I do to deserve this of you?

(*No answer*)

Terrible. Terrible. Didn't my wife keep an eye on you?

SYLVIA. You can't keep an eye on us respectable young women. You can keep—you *must* keep—an eye on a girl if she's unethical. Such girls have to be watched but we're not. Even our own mothers can't . . .

NORRISON (*In despair, interrupting her*). Inhibited! Reserved! Puritanical! This is terrible. That's all I can say. It's terrible.

SYLVIA. It's even more terrible than you think.

NORRISON. How much?

SYLVIA. Not very much more. Only a little. Please don't be upset, though. It isn't at all terrible for me. Only for you.

NORRISON. Thank you. Go on.

SYLVIA. And it's terrible only in its social aspect. Morally, no one could say a single word against it. It's not only the normal feminine urge but . . .

NORRISON (*Interrupting; impatiently*). I wish you wouldn't torture me. Don't go into the details, *please! Please!* Go on with your story!

SYLVIA. I am . . .

(SHE *breaks off*)

NORRISON. You are?

SYLVIA. I'm married to him.

NORRISON. You're mad!

SYLVIA. Oh, no. I'm not. I'm respectable. We were married secretly. Just he and I there. I was so frightfully in love, you see.

NORRISON. When did this happen?

SYLVIA. Four months ago.

NORRISON. I feel a little faint. Who is he?

SYLVIA. He's a poor man.

NORRISON *(Into one of his telephones)*. Ice water, please. (HE *puts down the receiver)* Now, my dear child, come here. Come here to me quite calmly, and tell me about him. (SYLVIA *goes to him.* NORRISON *takes her hand and looks at her fingers)* No wedding ring?

SYLVIA *(Casting down her eyes)*. He's a poor man.

NORRISON. Tell me who he is and what he is. (HER *head falls.* SHE *does not answer)* No answer. Then he isn't the Prince of Wales.

SYLVIA. No.

NORRISON. And nothing like.

SYLVIA. Nothing like.

NORRISON. Now we *are* in for it. Is he a government official?

SYLVIA. Lower.

NORRISON. Doorman?

SYLVIA. Lower.

NORRISON. Bus-boy?

SYLVIA. Lower.

NORRISON. Shoe-shine?

SYLVIA. Lower.

NORRISON. Playwright?

SYLVIA. Little higher.

NORRISON. Chauffeur?

SYLVIA. Stop.

(GEORGE *brings a glass of water.* NORRISON *drinks.* GEORGE *goes)*

NORRISON. This is the influence of motion pictures. The handsome,

uniformed, elegant chauffeur of the millionaire eloping with the heiress.

SYLVIA. It's no such thing. I detest elegant men. He's no well-uniformed motion picture chauffeur at all. He doesn't drive a Rolls-Royce.

NORRISON. What is he, then?

SYLVIA. A taxi driver.

NORRISON. A taxi driver! *I'm* going mad! *I'm* going mad! How did this come about?

SYLVIA. He was my instructor. Taught me to drive, when I was preparing for my license. He was the best driver in the garage. He's a fine mechanic and a would-be revolutionary . . . or maybe you'd call him an insurrectionist.

NORRISON. Insurrectionist . . . against whom?

SYLVIA. Against people who have too much money.

NORRISON. Except . . .

SYLVIA. Except me.

NORRISON. I see.

SYLVIA *(Feeling his irony. Reproachfully)*. Only because he loves me.

NORRISON. Of course. Of course.

SYLVIA. But I've cured his subversive ideas. He hasn't resigned from his party yet but he's no anti-capitalist any longer.

NORRISON. I can see that.

SYLVIA. Please don't sneer. You don't know what a pure young man he is. His only fault is to misuse his knife when eating.

NORRISON *(Bitter)*. I understand.

SYLVIA. But he has ambition! He's going places! He's talented!

NORRISON. This marriage he's made amounts to genius!

SYLVIA. Stop sneering! The first

month I loved him without . . . without thinking of our future. But now . . . I've been his wife for three months.

NORRISON. Divorce! Divorce at once!

SYLVIA. I shouldn't dream of it. Neither would he. He's too good and much too pure.

NORRISON. He's pure and I'm sunk. And my poor family! My wife whose Bible is the Social Register! I mustn't think of that! If you knew, though, what you've done to me and my family! We'll have to disappear from this hemisphere! To emigrate! To disintegrate! And you . . . oh, I know your father! You'll be disinherited. And your sick mother! What recklessness!

SYLVIA. Why didn't you look after me better?

NORRISON. Do you think this is any time to be funny?

SYLVIA. Please don't scold me. You'd better help me. I'm very sorry for Mother. I should die if anything happened to her. On the other hand I can't say that *your* financial or domestic catastrophes interest me much.

NORRISON. That's charming of you. Sweet and charming.

SYLVIA. Why *didn't* you look after me better?

NORRISON *(Furiously)*. You're not to ask me that again, do you hear?

SYLVIA. Well, if you can't look after a young girl better than that, you shouldn't have taken her into your house, to broaden her outlook. Suppose you tell me what I'm to do. Father and Mother will be here in about an hour.

NORRISON *(Trying to be calm)*.

Now, my child. In the first place it's absolutely essential that we keep the whole thing a secret.

SYLVIA. That can't be done.

NORRISON. Why?

SYLVIA. I'm going to be a mother.

(Painful pause)

NORRISON *(In a voice stifled by the surprise)*. You're going to . . . to . . . (HE *swallows. Then, pulling himself together, he's again himself)* . . . to be a mother. That's beautiful, absolutely lawful, highly ethical and enormously unpleasant. (HE *rings all the bells, pressing all the buzzer-buttons on his desk.* PYNNIGAN *enters.* NORRISON *speaks in the tone of a commanding general before the battle)* All of you stand by for orders! Not a soul is to leave this building until I say so! General alarm! Complete mobilization, like that of the black Friday on the Stock Exchange!

*(*PYNNIGAN *goes out)*

SYLVIA. There's no point in keeping anything back now. I certainly don't have to spare your feelings. Why should I? What's done is done. When Father wired that he'd be here next week, I wired him right back, "Look forward to seeing you. Break the news to dear mother that I'm married."—I suppose that's what brought this second wire. To expect them today. This afternoon. At four. *(Looks at her wrist-watch)* It's ten to three now.

NORRISON. You haven't overlooked anything, have you?

SYLVIA. I'm naturally thorough.

NORRISON. Thorough. That's fine. Have you thought what your future will be like?

SYLVIA. No, I haven't gone into

that as yet. I did what my heart told me to do. If there's no other way out but suicide . . .

NORRISON. Sylvia! (SHE *wipes a tear from her eye*) Don't cry, child! Courage! Remember this is much harder on me than it is on you!

(PYNNIGAN *enters*)

PYNNIGAN. Everything is in order. Your staff awaits your orders. Every man at his post!

(PYNNIGAN *goes out.*)

NORRISON. Now then. Where is . . . that man?

SYLVIA. Which man?

NORRISON. Yours. The taxi driver.

SYLVIA. He's here. Outside.

NORRISON. Here?

SYLVIA. I brought him with me.

NORRISON. Call him in.

(SYLVIA *goes to the Waiting Room door*)

SYLVIA. Come in.

(HARRY *enters. He is a handsome young man. He wears a poor taxi-driver's worn-out, oil-stained pants and shabby jacket. A muffler protects his ears from the cold. An ugly felt cap is pulled down over his ears. He stands awkwardly near the waiting room door. At first sight he is a deplorable apparition in spite of his good looks*)

NORRISON (*Shocked*). Terrible!

SYLVIA (*To* HARRY). Take off your cap.

(HARRY *removes his cap*)

NORRISON. Still terrible.

SYLVIA. At first sight his exterior isn't much to look at. But that's the result of being poorly dressed. He earns very little and takes nothing from me. I don't ever think of giving him money anyway, because I don't want to humiliate him. (*With a meaningful smile*) I've much better ways of rewarding him. He's my lawful spouse, my husband and the father of my future child. He has a beautiful soul and looks much more dignified without any clothes than dressed in his working-clothes.

NORRISON. That would be an improper statement if you weren't his wedded wife. Even so . . .

SYLVIA (*Interrupting, enthusiastically*). Oh, he's wonderful when it comes to . . .

NORRISON (*Interrupting, indignantly*). Stop!

SYLVIA. Why? (*Finishes the sentence*) . . . when it comes to classical sculptural beauty!

NORRISON (*After having examined Harry for a moment*). What's your name, lucky young man?

HARRY. Harry Foot.

NORRISON. Foot?

HARRY. Yep.

NORRISON. You really mean . . . Foot? Like . . . (HE *holds out his foot*) . . . foot?

HARRY. Yep.

NORRISON (*In despair*). There is absolutely nothing to be done. (*Calmly*) Tell me, Harry Foot, have you ever given a thought to the possibility of a quick divorce?

HARRY. No.

NORRISON. Are you inclined to take the idea into consideration?

HARRY. Nope.

NORRISON. Twenty thousand?

HARRY. No.

NORRISON. Fifty thousand?

HARRY. No.

NORRISON. Harry Foot, every man has his price. How much do you want?

HARRY. Two dollars and fifty cents.

NORRISON. What?

HARRY. Two fifty, just what my taxi meter reads.

SYLVIA. He never takes more than the meter reads.

NORRISON (With utmost calm). A hundred thousand.

HARRY. I wouldn't take a million.

SYLVIA. That's what I call love!

HARRY. I love you. (He embraces her)

SYLVIA. I adore you. Sweet. Dear. Honey. My pet.

(THEY kiss passionately)

NORRISON. Highly expert kissing. It's legitimate and ethical. I hate it. (To HARRY) Hundred and twenty-five thousand.

SYLVIA. You'd do much better not to try to bribe him! That's vile of you.

NORRISON. I never meant to bribe him. I'm only dangling a few large sums of money in front of him. Just to watch closely for any twitching about the eyes or mouth. But I didn't see a twitch.

SYLVIA. He never twitches. (To HARRY) You don't twitch. Do you, darling?

HARRY. I never twitch.

SYLVIA (To NORRISON). You shouldn't try such experiments. You'd much better help us. It's about three now. That train gets in about four.

NORRISON (Agonized). Don't torture me with that time table! You keep holding that train over my head! Sit down, both of you. (He nervously walks the floor) Your mother used to say she wanted you to marry a great man. Now, here he is. (Points at the shabby Harry) This is what you've got yourself. One of nature's noblemen. Only we're going to be blamed for this, my poor wife and I! My poor wife! The highest moral court! I know her. She'll commit suicide. And my poor daughters! (Firmly) Something has to be done, and at once! (He pauses and looks at the pair) There's only one way out of this.

SYLVIA. Is there a way out?

NORRISON. There is. Just one possible way out. If this man could be made over. Into an ideal son-in-law. A son-in-law your family would be pleased with. In an hour, because he'd have to be a finished product before they got here.

SYLVIA (Amazed). Could that be done?

NORRISON. Anything can be done.

SYLVIA. But in an hour . . .

NORRISON. If that's all the time we have!

SYLVIA (Awed). How would you do it?

NORRISON (Mysterioso). I count three. One. Two. Three. Presto! Change! And there you are! . . . But only if your esteemed bridegroom will undertake to obey my orders without flinching.

HARRY. That will depend on how your orders strike me.

SYLVIA (Vigorously, to HARRY). You're not to say another word! You're to think of your wife and child and do as you're told! I'll reward you later in my lawful, legitimate and sweet fashion.

NORRISON (To HARRY). Well?

HARRY (Submitting). As you like. You heard her. (Heroic) There's no sacrifice I won't make for my beloved bride!

NORRISON. You holy martyr, go in that room and wait there till I call you! (HE *points toward the Dressing Room.*)

SYLVIA. Don't vacillate. Go in and wait. Sweet. Dear. Go in. (HARRY *goes into the dressing room*) I don't understand. Do you seriously mean that you can make him over in an hour?

NORRISON. Yes. (HE *rings*)

SYLVIA. Where?

NORRISON. Here in this office.

SYLVIA. How?

(PYNNIGAN *enters*)

NORRISON *(To* SYLVIA). Please don't ask questions. Explanations take just as much time as execution. Sit there and watch! Attention! *(To* PYNNIGAN*)* Is everybody at his post?

PYNNIGAN. Awaiting orders, sir!

(HE *holds his notebook ready to take dictation.* SYLVIA *sits on a stool*)

(From here on all *the characters of the play must enter, speak and go out—obeying and answering Norrison—with utmost rapidity and precision. Beginning here, the role of* NOR-RISON *must be spoken constantly as fast as possible, with an almost unnatural speed and snappiness, in a resolutely go-ahead way, without the slightest sign of weariness)*

NORRISON *(To* PYNNIGAN, *the orders following each other loud, authoritatively, rapidly, without pause or hesitation).* I shall require the immediate presence here of my entire Executive Committee: Mr. Osso, Mr. Syring, Mr. Wolf. Mr. Wolf's telephone number has been changed today. It isn't Turtle 7-3377. It's Val-ley 4-3444. Further. I want the manager of our Supply Department, Count San Marino-Schattenburg. Further. Get me Director Felix here from the automobile factory. Further. Get my attorney Loary here from the Legal Department. Further. Have our press agent Kristian stand by on call. Further. Call Dr. Frank, my family physician, here at once. Further. Phone to that phony diplomat, Armand Colleon, Hotel Queen Elizabeth. Get him here. Further. Ask Louie, the head waiter or captain or maitre d'hotel or what not at the Majestic Hotel, to come here as quickly as possible. Further. See to it that I have an urgent overseas telephone call at 3:30 with Cannes, I spell it: C-A-N-N-E-S, France, Hotel Carlton, General Manager Meyrod, M-E-Y-R-O-D, person to person. Further. All these that I have named are to take taxis, except the hotel manager in France, and they are to tell the drivers to step on it without the slightest regard for red lights, speed laws, or any other traffic regulations. Fines, of course, will be paid by us. Further. I need at once three stenographers and no others than Miss Norman, Miss Marlin and Miss Petrovitch. And send Miss Cuno in here from the office. That's all for now. And see that no one gets in here who hasn't been sent for. To anyone else I'm out of town, on vacation. And now, open all doors and keep them open. I don't want to lose time by all your opening and closing doors when you come in and go out. Hurry, hurry.

PYNNIGAN *(Who has noted all that down, rushes to the four invisible doors, opens them, while speaking excitedly).* Shall I . . . not notify . . .

your wife, sir . . . that . . . you . . .

NORRISON *(Sharply)*. No.

(PYNNIGAN *stands at attention, waiting for orders*)

I shall dine with my wife tonight, in the snowy mountains. And God forbid I should upset her with this! Oh, one thing more. You're not to take time out to think. I shall do all the thinking necessary. My brain's switched on again. You may go. (PYNNIGAN *goes out.* NORRISON *speaks into one of his telephones*) Hello? Get me Stevens, the General Manager of the Hotel Majestic.

(HE *hangs up, while* MISS CUNO — *about 40* — *quickly enters from the office with a notebook, ready to take notes*)

NORRISON. Now, on your toes, Miss Cuno. I want a barber here inside of ten minutes. He will come in by the back door, go to my dressing room and shave the first man who enters the room. Further. That famous English Cutter from the "Old England Tailors." Have him come here immediately. And tell your friend, Miss Shortwood, I shall want her too, in fifteen minutes. Further. you are to find at once and report to me the name of the nearest good store that handles fine ready made suits for men. Further. Phone my jeweler Quarthier. He is to send this very minute a wedding ring with square cut diamonds . . .

SYLVIA *(Interrupting, quick)*. And a star sapphire.

NORRISON *(Continuing, without pause, to* MISS CUNO*) . . .* and a star sapphire, to my office. Price limit $10,000. Further. You will order a handsome bouquet of flowers to be sent here. Orchids. Not for less than $40, and not for more than

$60. Finally. I want a bottle of imported red wine. The name is Chambertin. Year 1937. Not from Rouvillier but from Vamrod. Do you understand? That's the firm name. Vamrod. V for Vanderbilt, A for Astor, M for Morgan, R for Rockefeller, O for Odlum and D for Du Pont. So then, Vamrod: Chambertin 1937. Not chilled but lukewarm. Not standing but lying in a basket on its side so the sediment doesn't get stirred up. Only one glass with it. And in a hurry. *(To* SYLVIA*)* That was Napoleon's favorite wine. He drank that wine before every one of his great battles. (MISS CUNO *starts to go*) Don't go yet, Miss Cuno. There's one thing more. Every ten minutes from now on—it's just three now—you're to come in here no matter who's here with me and tell me the exact time. Every ten minutes. *(Then mechanically* HE *adds)* How is that abscess in your mother's left ear?

MISS CUNO. Much better, thanks. The doctor's opened it.

NORRISON. No temperature?

MISS CUNO. None.

NORRISON. Thank you. Now you can go, Miss Cuno.

(MISS CUNO *goes out quickly*)

SYLVIA. What has her mother's ear got to do with this?

NORRISON. That was oil. I keep my machinery oiled with little thoughtful remarks. (HE *calls to* HARRY) Come in, young man! *(Into the telephone while* HARRY *enters)* Hello? Who's on duty this afternoon at the switchboard? Miss Patrick? You're the pretty blonde girl, aren't you? *(To* SYLVIA, *quick)* Oil. *(Into the telephone)* Now, then, my dear Miss Patrick, on your toes. I shall put through a lot of important calls in the next hour. But I know what a genius you are. *(Puts down the receiver.)*

SYLVIA. Oil again?

NORRISON. Yes. *(To* HARRY*)* How old are you?

HARRY. Twenty-nine.

NORRISON. Are your parents living?

HARRY. I'm an orphan.

NORRISON *(Taking notes)*. My sympathy. What size collar do you wear?

HARRY. Fifteen and a half.

NORRISON. Shoe?

HARRY. Eight.

NORRISON. Hat?

HARRY. Seven and a quarter.

NORRISON. Thank you. That's all. Sit down. *(Into the telephone)* Hello, Miss Patrick? Why haven't I got the Hotel Majestic yet?—Right. —I'm waiting. *(Holds the receiver to his ear)*

SYLVIA. I can't believe it! It's too romantic! It's too much like a fairy tale!

NORRISON. Where would a financier be, these days, without his fairy tales?

SYLVIA. But how do you imagine . . .

NORRISON *(Interrupts her)*. . . . . accomplishing improbable things? I'll tell you, my child. I'm thinking of Napoleon—as children think of him. No really daring scheme is possible except to naive students of Napoleon. His methods are invaluable to me. Even though he did come to a bad end. *(Into the telephone)* Hello, Hotel Majestic? Mr. Stevens? Norrison speaking. How are you?—Thank you, fine. Please hold a suite in my name. Two

bedrooms. Sitting room with each. A private entrance hall. Two baths. Rooms for maid and valet. Charge my account. *(Slams receiver down)*

SYLVIA. Are we going to live at the Majestic?

NORRISON. You're living there already. You hadn't an address. You've got one now. *(To* HARRY*)* Do you grasp that fact?

HARRY. I'd like to know why I should move into an expensive hotel when I've only . . .

NORRISON *(Interrupting)*. You've only to hold your tongue.

SYLVIA *(Peremptorily)*. Yes. Hold your tongue. Stop being difficult. Do as our benefactor tells you.

HARRY. I won't be terrorized! I've got a right to speak!

NORRISON. You've got no right to live!

HARRY. I won't be . . .

NORRISON *(Interrupting)*. Quiet!!! *(Grabs another telephone)* Get Newberry and Co., the travel agency. *(Holds receiver. To* SYLVIA*)* Ah, what a man Napoleon was! How pleased he'd be to see me carrying on. Basically, his thinking was that of a child. How does one conquer the world? By licking the enemies. How does one lick the enemies? By winning all the battles. How does one win the battles? By licking the enemies. It's really very simple. *(Into the telephone)* Newberry Travel Bureau? Norrison speaking. How are you?—Thank you, fine. Please note. For Saturday the eighteenth. Five tickets, airplane and train to Cannes, France. Three with sleepers and two without.

SYLVIA. What's this?

NORRISON. Three *with* sleepers for you two and your secretary. Two *without* sleepers for your maid and valet. The secretary being the brains of the party must sleep lying down. Maid and valet can sleep any way. *(Into the telephone)* All right. I'll let you know the names later. *(Puts down the receiver)* That's that. You leave Saturday.

SYLVIA. For France?

NORRISON. Yes. Cannes.

SYLVIA. Why?

HARRY. That's a point. Why?

NORRISON. I'll tell you later.

SYLVIA. But why not give our names?

HARRY *(Arrogantly)*. That's something I'll . . .

NORRISON *(Interrupting)*. That's something I'll come to when I'm ready. *(Into the telephone)* Get me the Hotel Carlton in Cannes, France.

HARRY. Will you please explain why I should go to Cannes in France with two servants and a secretary when I don't even know where Cannes in France is?

SYLVIA *(Severely)*. You'll find out where it is when you get there and I don't want another word out of you, or you won't be a finished product in an hour!

HARRY. If I'm not allowed to speak, I shall withdraw . . .

NORRISON *(Interrupting)*. . . . into my dressing room, at once, and wait. You can't be seen here looking as you do! *(He sits down and makes notes on a sheet of paper)*

HARRY. I'm not ashamed of my appearance! I'll face the whole world looking as I do! I'll face . . .

SYLVIA *(Interrupting, peremptorily)*. You'll face the whole world when you're properly dressed and not before and you always withdraw

where our benefactor tells you, and quick! Understand? Either you love me or you don't! Understand?

HARRY. You're terrorizing me! *(He embraces her)*

SYLVIA. Yes, I'm terrorizing you! *(They kiss passionately)*

NORRISON *(Writing, He doesn't see that)*. That's right, Sylvia. Use will power on him. *(He looks up. He shouts)* Hey! Hey! I said will power! *Please!* *(Harry hurries into the dressing room. Sylvia sits down as before, bashfully casting down her eyes)* I never heard of such . . . I hate your kissing.

(The stenographers: Miss Marlin, Miss Norman and Miss Petrovitch enter from the Outer Hall. Norrison is writing; He speaks without looking up)

NORRISON. How do you do, Miss Marlin, Miss Norman and Miss Petrovitch. Sit down, Miss Marlin, left of my desk. Miss Norman, right of my desk. Miss Petrovitch, you will wait in the inner office, in reserve. *(Still without looking up)* Miss Marlin is wearing a new dress, Miss Norman's hair is freshly waved and Miss Petrovitch's eyes show signs of weeping.

(He picks up a telephone and speaks without making a pause after the word "weeping,"— while Miss Petrovitch goes hurriedly out into the Secretary's Office and the Other Two take their places)

NORRISON. Connect me at once with Michel and Company, haberdashers. *(He puts down the receiver)* Miss Marlin, take a letter. "To the Committee of the Socialist Party, City. Gentlemen: *(George*

enters with a glass and a bottle of wine in a basket. NORRISON *speaks without making a pause)* Let's see the label. Right. Pour out one glass. *(While* GEORGE *pours out a glass and goes, leaving the bottle on the table)* "Gentlemen": *(The* TELE-PHONE *rings. To* MISS MARLIN) One moment. *(Into the telephone, glancing in his notes, without pause)* Hello, Michel? Norrison speaking. Thank you, and you? Now get this right. Take a pencil. Shoe: eight. Hat: seven and a quarter. Collar: fifteen and a half. Sleeves: thirty-three. I want the following order at my office by taxi in ten minutes, not eleven, ten. Please note. Shoes, hats, gentleman's underwear: white crepe de chine, quality B S. Both shirt and . . . *(Quickly, to* SYLVIA) Pardon me. *(Without pause, very fast, into the phone)* . . . and drawers. Outer shirts. Size: 15½—33. White or white-in-white. Collars low and soft, wrinkle-proof, not to be starched. Assorted socks size eleven in different blue colors: ocean-blue, sky-blue, powder-blue, midnight-blue, navy-blue, indigo-blue and plain honest blue. Also different grays: dove-gray, dust-gray, rainy-day-gray, storm-cloud-gray, hair-gray, and plain honest gray. Six mufflers. One dozen neckties, no crazy variegated surrealistic madhouse-ties, in a word: no ties for playboys and interior decorators but conservative ties for bank-presidents and for luncheon-guests of His Eminence the Cardinal. All of that at my office, I repeat, in ten minutes, not eleven, ten. Goodbye.
*(*HE *slams down the receiver and sips from the wine glass)*
SYLVIA *(Enthusiastically, while* HE *drinks).* All that for my pet!

NORRISON. And what a pet he is! *(Continues at once dictating to* MISS MARLIN) "Gentlemen": *(To* SYLVIA, *quickly making a wry face)* You know, I don't think much of this wine. I don't like it at all. Still, Napoleon always knew what he was doing. — "Gentlemen": *(Dictating)* "I beg herewith to tender you my resignation from the Socialist Party to take effect . . . "

HARRY *(His head appearing from the dressing room).* Is that *my* resignation you're tendering?

NORRISON. Yes, it is. Shut up. Get out. "To take effect as from this date. My reason for this action is that I have to quit your party because I entered the capitalistic employers' camp and . . . "

HARRY *(Only his head visible).* I? A capitalistic employer?

NORRISON. Yes, you. Sylvia, please, do something. The man's annoying me. Go on, Miss Marlin. "I undertake to remain . . . "
(While he dictates, SYLVIA *says to* HARRY, *loudly and severely:)*
SYLVIA. Quiet! You resign! Period!

NORRISON *(Who did not make a pause).* ". . . remain loyal to our unswerving socialistic principles even in my new highly conservative position."—Better make that: "as loyal as possible,"—or better make that: "as loyal as permitted by the overwhelming majority of our stockholders." *(To* HARRY, *who appears in the door of the dressing room and makes frantic gestures)* Don't jump around that way! You've got to be an employer even if you don't employ anybody, my pet. Go back in there and quick!

SYLVIA. Go back inside! Don't

jump around! You've got to be a member of big business! *(As* HARRY *opens his mouth)* Shut up! Think of your wife and child!

HARRY *(In a manly tone).* I have to state that the pair of you are terrorizing me in a manner unheard of outside of totalitarian countries. (HE *disappears, going back into the dressing room)*

NORRISON. Right you are. And you, Miss Marlin, close with: "I remain" and so forth and type it out in a hurry. I like that frock, Miss Marlin. You have taste. Don't answer, please. *(Into a telephone)* Connect me with Mercado's Shoe Shop. *(Slams down the receiver and without pausing speaks to* MISS NORMAN, *while* MISS MARLIN *hurries out in the Outer Hall and at the same time* MISS PETROVITCH *enters from the Secretary's Office to take her place)* Miss Norman, take a letter going to the Board of Governors of my Golf Club. "Gentlemen: It has given me great pleasure to hear from Mr. Morrison of my election to membership in . . .

HARRY *(His head appearing again).* Me? In a golf club?

NORRISON *(To* HARRY, *without looking at him).* Yes! You! *(To* MISS NORMAN, *dictating quickly)* ". . . in that fine exclusive Golf Club of yours. Please accept my warmest thanks." *(To* HARRY, *not looking at him)* Back! Back! Go back! *(He continues to speak while* HARRY *vanishes)* Sign it "Sincerely yours" and type it. Quick! *(*HE *sniffs)* Scented as well as beautifully waved. Bravo, Miss Norman. Don't answer, please. (MISS NORMAN *smiles sweetly and gratefully at him while* SHE *hurries out through the next*

door. Meanwhile NORRISON *takes up the telephone and speaks, without pausing)* Well, what's the matter with Mercado's Shoe Shop? Busy? Keep trying till you get them. *(Slams down the receiver, while* MISS CUNO *enters from the Secretary's Office)*

MISS CUNO. The nearest good shop for ready made suits is in the next block, our street, number sixty-four. Not to be confused with the not so good shop in the same building which calls itself "Best Tailors in this World."

NORRISON. And what's the name of the good one?

MISS CUNO. "Best Tailors in this Building."

NORRISON *(As* MISS CUNO *goes).* Thank you. Miss Petrovitch, take a letter. "Best Tailors in this Building. City. You will please deliver to the bearer of this note, the following articles of clothing: one ready made suit of dark blue virgin wool worsted, double breasted, three pairs of buttons, the upper pair to be left open. Further. One great-coat, heavy enough for winter wear, herringbone pattern, covered button-holes, simple dull facings, comfortable sleeves; dark gray or gray-blue, or blue-gray or blue-in-blue or gray-in-gray. By no means one of those yellowish-tan camelhair things for men-about-cafés. Further. A hat. No dashing Fedora with a showy band. Underline the word 'no.' It shall be a dignified black Homburg. Underline the word 'dignified.' Charge to President Norrison." Type that out at once. *(As* MISS PETROVITCH *starts to go out)* You've been crying, Miss Petrovitch. Your eyes are red. *(As* SHE *stops)*

Why have you been crying? A tiff with boy-friend? Have Kristian and you been quarreling again? *(As* Miss Petrovitch *opens her mouth to answer)* Don't stop to answer. I see everything. Leave that to me. Now, run along! Don't worry, run and type, type, type! Speed, Miss Petrovitch! Speed and tempo, tempo!

(Miss Petrovitch *rushes out)*

HARRY *(Reappearing).* I beg your pardon but there are only big bankers and other millionaires in your Golf Club. *(Rhetorically)* And for that reason alone, I . . .

NORRISON *(Interrupting).* For that reason alone you will be a member.

HARRY. But I can't play golf!

NORRISON. You'll learn.

HARRY. But, please . . .

NORRISON *(Interrupting. Speaks fast).* Don't talk. Sylvia, tell him not to talk and to stop meddling in what doesn't concern him.

SYLVIA *(To* Harry). Will you do as you're told?! You don't see his scheme, darling? He's building you up!

HARRY *(Angrily).* Well, if that doesn't concern me, then I'll be . . .

NORRISON *(Interrupting).* You'll be on your way to Best Tailors in this Building, next block, number sixty-four. You will show them a letter and put on whatever they tell you to put on. Then rush back here.

SYLVIA. In the meanwhile your new shirts will be here!

HARRY *(To* Norrison). Will you tell me what you think you're doing?

NORRISON *(Quickly).* I'm making you into a proper son-in-law, in a ready made suit temporarily. Later you will . . .

HARRY *(Interrupts him. Loud).* Let me tell 'you that my self-respect . . .

NORRISON *(Louder than he).* I have nothing against your self-respect so long as you keep it to yourself!

HARRY. Won't you let me get one word in?

NORRISON. No!

SYLVIA. I must put one in for him. He makes it a rule never to take presents.

HARRY. That rule only applies to women.

NORRISON. It certainly wouldn't prevent his taking a loan from Norrison's Bank. (He *writes)* A loan that will have to be paid back.

(Harry *looks questioningly at* Sylvia)

SYLVIA. Oh, that's all right! That's a legitimate financial transaction. *(To* Harry) Why do you look that way?

HARRY *(Raising his right hand).* I solemnly protest herewith . . .

NORRISON *(Quick).* Herewith your account with Norrison's Bank is opened. *(To the hurriedly entering* Miss Petrovitch) Letter ready about the clothes? (He *takes three letters from her)* Thank you.

SYLVIA *(To* Harry). A bank account *can't* hurt your self-respect! Think of your child.

HARRY. I will. (Norrison *gives him a letter)* What's this?

NORRISON. This is the letter you're to take to "Best Tailors in this Building."

HARRY. Which building?

NORRISON. Miss Cuno will explain it to you.

HARRY. Who is Miss Cuno?

SYLVIA. Don't be so stupid. Ask in the office for Miss Cuno.

NORRISON. . . . at "Best Tailors" you'll undress . . .

HARRY. Undress? Why?

SYLVIA. In order to dress again and hurry back here in a new suit! Dark blue, with three pairs of buttons.

HARRY (Disappointed). Only three?

(The TELEPHONE rings)

NORRISON (Into the telephone). Mercado Shoes? At last! Norrison speaking. Yes, yes, in person.—Thank you, fine. And you? (HE doesn't wait for the answer. Speaks fast) Send me a selection of your custom made hand sewn choice English shoes, both black and brown, good quality, fine leather, quarter linings and innersoles, size eight. To my office, in a hurry. At once, yes. Right away, yes. Wait! Wait! Hard tips, please! The soft ones don't stand up. Thanks. 'Bye. (HE puts the receiver down)

SYLVIA (To the staring HARRY). There! Lovely new shoes, my pet!

HARRY. Hadn't I better go for them, too?

NORRISON. Please don't begin getting ideas of your own. My nerves aren't up to that. I'm the Dictator here and you go where I tell you and hurry back! Time isn't standing still, you know. (HARRY starts to go) Wait. Sign this. (HE shoves a letter toward him)

SYLVIA. Don't stand there that way! Sign it!

HARRY. Whatever the mother of my child tells me to sign, I sign. (HE signs the letter and reaches for another)

NORRISON. No! No! Not that! Only one letter! I said "This." In singular. Not "Those," in plural.

Now he wants to sign everything in sight! For the moment you sign only your socialistic valedictory. What I might call your capitalistic entering in the Golf Club, that will come later. On your way now. Leg it over and see that the clothes fit. (HE sits and writes)

HARRY. Let the tyrant make a clothes horse of me! No sacrifice is too great for my beloved. For my angel. (HE throws his arms around SYLVIA and gives her a big kiss)

NORRISON (Without looking up from his writing). Enough! Stop! No fond farewells. Go along with him if you want to but . . .

SYLVIA. I'll go with my pet to the ends of the earth. (HARRY goes out hurriedly) You don't know how I love him! I mean after so many uninteresting, dull, effeminate escorts to have found a real male . . . a real . . . a real . . . what would you call it?

NORRISON. I know what you mean . . . I'm afraid I know it better than you think. So run along.

(SYLVIA, blushing, runs out after Harry. MISS CUNO enters from the outer office)

MISS CUNO. Ten minutes after three.

NORRISON. Dreadful the way time goes! Here I have only fifty minutes left and we're not even started! (HE hands HER the memorandum he has been writing) This goes down to the cashier. It's a new account. I want a de luxe chequebook for it in a hurry. Something in red leather tooled in gold. One of those we put out for Royalty.

MISS CUNO. One of the kind we gave the King of Egypt?

NORRISON. Are they the best you've got?

MISS CUNO. I'm afraid they are.

NORRISON. Then, they'll have to do. Another thing. Pay close attention, please. I want a good camera. *(Rapidly)* Please note: Eastman, Bell and Howell, Revere, Ciroflex, Keystone, Bausch and Lomb, Wollensak, Rolleifex, Zeiss, Golde, Omega, Leica,—pick one of them; model 1952.

MISS CUNO *(Making notes feverishly. In an undertone)*. Good Lord.

NORRISON. Real competence demands a passion for the tiniest detail. —Further. I want a few dozen General Electric or Westinghouse flashbulbs for snapshots. A pitcher or vase of salt water. A small bottle of aspirin, Bayer, Squibb or St. Joseph. Please don't look at me as if I were an asylum case. I said: Camera, flashbulbs, salt water, aspirin. What is there in that to look so blank about?

MISS CUNO *(Frightened)*. Nothing, sir, nothing. (SHE *hurries out.* PYNNIGAN *enters from the opposite door)*

PYNNIGAN. Here's your attorney Mr. Loary, sir. (HE *goes.* MR. LOARY *enters)*

LOARY. Good morning, sir.

NORRISON *(Talking fast)*. Good morning to you, Loary. I might have known you'd be the first to get here. We've got a life and death business on our hands. Thank God you never ask for explanations. That's your great virtue, Loary. How's your wife? I'm very anxious about her health. How is she? (LOARY *opens his mouth but* NORRISON *continues to speak very fast, not waiting for the answer.)* You'll be good enough to draw up at once some kind of a legal document, the purport of which is that the titled manager of my Supply Department, the old moron Count San Marino-Schattenburg, adopts a son. The son's name is . . . better jot it down . . . Harry Foot.

LOARY *(Baffled)*. Foot?

NORRISON *(Impatiently)*. You never ask for explanations, do you? F, double O, T. Don't stare. That's it. Foot. And see that the courts step on it. (*Ushers* LOARY *toward the secretary's office)* You'd better dictate it right inside here. Use Miss Norman, the one with her hair freshly waved or Miss Marlin, the one with the beautiful new dress. *(To himself, rapidly)* I have to practice so I don't forget which one has the waves and which one the new dress. *(To* LOARY, *without making a pause)* You are looking splendid, my dear Loary! Such fine rosy color! You're rosy, rosy, flushed with health!

LOARY. I happen to be running a high fever, sir. That's why I'm rosy and flushed. (HE *goes into the secretary's office)*

NORRISON *(To himself, rapidly)*. The oil didn't go so well that time. *(To the entering* PYNNIGAN) What now?

PYNNIGAN. The man from Michel the haberdasher, sir.

(The HABERDASHER *enters. His arms are filled with boxes. He is endowed with a superb equipment of whiskers)*

HABERDASHER *(Happily, very loud, triumphantly)*. Good afternoon, sir!!! Good afternoon!!! Here I am and I've brought everything with me!!! (PYNNIGAN *goes out while the* HABERDASHER *speaks)*

NORRISON. Don't shout! Do

you have to make so much noise about it?

HABERDASHER *(Whispering)*. But I'm so delighted, sir, to have you, you!—for a customer at last! *You!* the great President Norrison! My customer! Yippee!!!

NORRISON. Try to control yourself, you fool, and go into this dressing room. Wait for your man there. He'll be with you presently. (HABERDASHER *starts to run*) Stop! Wait! There's a barber in that dressing room with orders to shave the first man he sees. That means extreme danger for your whiskers which I suppose you're proud of. Explain to the barber that you're *not* the man I spoke about. He will try to shave you and I shouldn't want to see your life's work ruined.

(The HABERDASHER *hurries into the dressing room.* PYNNIGAN *enters)*

PYNNIGAN. Mr. Osso, sir.

*(*Osso *enters)*

OSSO. How do you do?

*(*PYNNIGAN *goes out)*

NORRISON. How are you, Osso? Have a cigar. How's your wife? Recuperating? Recuperating?

OSSO. She hasn't been sick for ten years, thank God. But thank you, anyway.

NORRISON *(To himself, quick)*. Oil didn't go well again. *(To* Osso, *without pause)* Sit down, please, till Syring and Wolf get here. When we're all assembled here, we can go into executive session together. I've a very important matter to put before you. How is your dear *healthy* wife? *(Before* Osso *can answer he speaks to* MISS CUNO *who entered)* Yes, Miss Cuno?

MISS CUNO. Here's the cheque-

book, sir. It's the best we've got.

NORRISON. Get after the letters.

MISS CUNO. Yes, sir. Right away, sir. Here's a bottle of aspirin. And here's . . . (SHE *puts the small bottle of aspirin on the desk and points at* GEORGE *who entered meanwhile with a camera and a pitcher)* . . .the camera and the pitcher of salt water.

NORRISON *(Indicating a corner of his desk)*. Put it there.—Where are the flashbulbs? The wedding right?

MISS CUNO. They're coming, sir. (MISS CUNO *hurries out.* GEORGE *puts down the camera and the pitcher and follows her out)*

OSSO. Thank you. She's quite all right.

NORRISON. Who's quite all right?

OSSO. You just asked me twice how my wife is.

NORRISON. Did I? So I did.

OSSO. She's quite all right.

NORRISON. So what? *(Quickly correcting himself)* Er . . . thank God for that.

OSSO. You're very amiable to take such interest.

NORRISON. I do, Osso. Really I do. Always.

OSSO *(Sitting down)*. To be so amiable is a quality of great men, sir.

NORRISON *(Rapidly, impatiently)*. My dear Osso, you're flattering me. I enjoy flattery but sometimes I can't permit myself to listen to it because it takes time. On an average little compliments like these of yours use up, say, a couple of minutes each. With—let's say— thirty compliments a day, there's an hour a day wasted. That's two weeks out of a year. I can use those two weeks for my vacation.

PYNNIGAN (*Who entered during* NORRISON'S *speech*). Mr. Syring, sir.

NORRISON. Let him come in.

SYRING (*Entering*). How are you?

NORRISON (*Rapidly, as* PYNNIGAN *goes out*). How are *you*, my dear Syring? Have a chair. (*As* SYRING *sits on one of the stools in front of the desk*) Have a cigar? How's your wife? How about her insomnia? (HE *doesn't wait for an answer*) Osso would tell you what it is all about, only he doesn't know yet. The main thing is speed, speed. You look splendid, too, Syring. Rosy, rosy. Are you feverish, too?

SYRING. Good God, no. Why should I be feverish?

NORRISON. Your fine color . . .

SYRING. That's the flush of health.—She takes three grains of Sodium Amytal before retiring.

NORRISON. Who?

SYRING. My wife.

NORRISON. Why?

SYRING. Because of her insomnia. You asked . . .

NORRISON (*Interrupting*). Yes, yes. Very good. Sodium is good and Amytal is good. Yes. (*To himself*) What *is* the matter with my oil-duct today?

SYRING. Thank you for your thoughtfulness.

(*The* HABERDASHER *enters precipitately from the dressing room. The* BARBER *follows closely with an open razor*)

HABERDASHER. I can't cope with this brute! He insists on shaving me!

NORRISON. It's a fine feeling that I can always count on my personnel!

HABERDASHER. Well, sir, if you think I'd better let him? For you I'm willing to sacrifice . . . (HE *grabs his beard*)

NORRISON. Oh, no! Never! (*To the* BARBER) This isn't the man I meant. Shave the next one. (*The* BARBER *and the* HABERDASHER *go back into the dressing room*) I take the greatest pride, gentlemen, in the absolute dependability of all my people. (HE *calls into the office*) How's the adoption getting on, Loary?

(LOARY'S *head appears*)

LOARY. We're nearly through.

(HE *withdraws his head*)

NORRISON. No hitch there either. (HE *sips a little of the red wine*) The best machinist's no better than his machine. (*Another sip.* HE *makes a wry face*) I can't see what Napoleon found to like about this wine!

(PYNNIGAN *ushers in* HARRY *and* SYLVIA *and goes.* HARRY *is elegantly dressed except that he has neither shirt nor collar.* HE *is carrying a topcoat over his arm*)

NORRISON. Oh, it is you, my friend! Good! Turn around! (HARRY *obeys*) Excellent! Don't forget, they're your *temporary* clothes, just for a few days. In a few minutes the best tailor in the city will be here to take the measurements for your permanent wardrobe! (HARRY *starts to go*) Hey! Where is your shirt?

HARRY (*Pointing at* SYLVIA). She didn't like it. It was worn and torn. I left it at the tailor's.

SYLVIA (*Answering* NORRISON'S *questioning look*). Yes, I told him to.

You ordered him new ones, didn't you?

NORRISON (*To* HARRY, *pointing to the dressing room*). Now go in there. They're waiting for you in there.

HARRY (*Holding up the topcoat*). Don't you think this coat is a little out of fashion?

NORRISON. Shouldn't say so. Go on. Go on. (*Points at the dressing room entrance.* HARRY *goes*) Sylvia, my dear . . . (*To the* GENTLEMEN) Just a moment, please, gentlemen. (*To* SYLVIA, *in a low voice, speaking fast*) Your pet's elegant enough to be the Duke of Kent, except that his dressing's chronological order is wrong. He has a suit on but no shirt yet. It's *your* fault. Tell him that in the future he *should* put on the shirt *before* the suit. Go in there. The barber's there. So are the underwear, shirt and necktie. See that he gets the underwear underneath the shirt. Dress him, *please*. I'll give you two minutes.

SYLVIA. You *are* a magician!

NORRISON (*Very fast*). I'm not. I look like one but only because people are weak, poor and afraid of being fired. All I'm doing is making use of them sensibly, trying to be as kind as possible.

SYLVIA (*Insisting*). You *are* a Superman! You're a . . .

NORRISON (*Interrupts her, annoyed*). That's sweet of you, Sylvia, but *I* don't need oil or any lubrication whatsoever. (HE *pushes* SYLVIA *hurriedly into the dressing room*) Now, gentlemen . . . (PYNNIGAN *enters*)

PYNNIGAN. Mr. Wolf.

(WOLF *enters.* PYNNIGAN *goes*)

NORRISON. Thank God! Come in, Wolf. Sit down. I won't offer you a cigar because . . . (*Emphati-cally*) . . . *I know you don't smoke!* Now, gentlemen, we must . . .

WOLF (*Interrupting him*). Don't be annoyed with me for not smoking, will you, sir? It's only on account of my faulty digestion. I always feel a terrible pressure here . . . (*Points at his stomach*) . . . after I've been smoking, because, to tell you God's honest truth, exactly ten years ago I and my wife . . .

NORRISON (*Interrupts him, annoyed, impatiently*). Wolf, I give you my word of honor I'm not annoyed. I only observed that you never smoke. But excuse me, now we have to . . .

WOLF (*Interrupting*). But I feel I ought to tell you why . . .

NORRISON (*Very impatiently, nervously*). Don't tell me why, *please*. No! No! Now, gentlemen, we've got our Committee all together. (*The* MEN *all jump up*) Within the next few minutes I look to you to appoint a candidate of mine to the Director Generalship of our United Motor and Automobile Corporation in place of my good friend Felix, the present incumbent. This immediate appointment is vital, not only to the interest of my Bank but of my family as well.

THE THREE MEN. Oh! . . . Oh! . . . Oh! . . .

NORRISON (*Rapidly, but with inner intensity*). Yes, gentlemen. Vital to my family. It's not an exaggeration. Believe me. Thank you for your friendship. It's difficult to restrain my tears. But I will. Thank you. (*In a shaking voice, but as rapidly as before*) A bit of inside information. The man in question is the son-in-law of . . . (*Very impressively*) . . . a very powerful financier whose name I cannot mention for the present. Anyone who knows my business connections all over the world will easily guess. (*The* THREE MEN *murmur*) No murmuring, if you please, gentlemen; and be so good as to step into the conference room. (HE *points to the entrance of the Outer Hall*) Are there any questions?

OSSO. Only one. What happens to poor Felix, the present Director?

NORRISON. I've sent for him. I will accept his resignation. (SYRING *and* OSSO *go out into the outer hall*)

WOLF (*While the others go. Sweetly*). I should like to beg you, sir, not to take my stomach trouble amiss. I'd really enjoy smoking but somehow the acid seems to get the best of me, and I feel deep in my digestive tract something like let's say . . .

NORRISON (*Furiously,* HE *interrupts him and pushes him after the others*). My dear Wolf, let's not discuss our inner lives just now.

(WOLF *is out.* PYNNIGAN *enters*)

PYNNIGAN. Count San Marino-Schattenburg.

(*The* COUNT *enters. A pompous, elderly, poor, shabby, underpaid whatnot—a titled old bum*)

COUNT. Your obedient servant, my dear sir, esteemed friend and revered employer.

NORRISON (*In a hurry*). It's too much, too much, my dear Count. Your greeting has old-world beauty but it's a little long. The matter at hand is urgent. Good afternoon and God bless you, anyway. Now, listen. Last year you were kind enough, my dear Count to *adopt* one of my protégés.

COUNT. I was.

NORRISON (*Talking fast*). I turn to you now, not only as a man

belonging to the highest aristocracy and as my esteemed friend but also as the assistant manager of my Supply Department. I was able to give you—in an extremely down and out moment of your unemployment—a job, a position which I might describe as almost well-paid, but by no means as a permanent one. My dear Count, nothing in this world is eternal. Nothing is perpetual. Here today, gone tomorrow.

COUNT. I know.

NORRISON. So . . . today I turn to you . . . my dear Count San Marino-Schattenburg . . . with a similar request.

COUNT. How similar?

NORRISON. Quite similar. I want still another protégé of mine adopted. And I want him to bear your high-sounding, aristocratic name of San Marino-Schattenburg. My attorney is already dictating a statement of your eagerness to oblige.

COUNT. My eagerness?

NORRISON. You will indicate that by signing the application to the proper lawful authorities and thus gain a second son, a second support for your declining years.

COUNT. It can't be done.

NORRISON. I don't believe that.

COUNT. My friends are still laughing at me for the last one.

NORRISON. Much better they laugh at you than weep for you. As I just said, no job in this world is eternal.

COUNT. Is that a threat?

NORRISON. A gentle warning.

COUNT. And it was only for this that you sent for me?

NORRISON. Only for this.

COUNT (*With a noble gesture of rejection*). Not at any price. (*The following very, very fast, until Miss Cuno enters)*

NORRISON. I see. How much do you want?

COUNT *(Promptly)*. Ten thousand.

NORRISON. Too much. Come again.

COUNT. Ten thousand.

NORRISON. You ought to make it cheaper for a fine, healthy young man!

COUNT *(Stubbornly)*. Ten thousand.

NORRISON. A good son, too, who'll honor his father.

COUNT. Ten thousand. Under the laws of my very small but well-beloved country, he may bear not only my name but my title of Count as well. So . . . ten thousand.

NORRISON. When you're sick he'll look after you!

COUNT. Ten thousand.

NORRISON. He'll wear mourning for three months after you die.

COUNT. Ten thousand.

NORRISON. Suppose he wears it for six months?

COUNT. Ninety-five hundred.

NORRISON. At last. It's still too high, though.

COUNT. You forget, sir, that we have a pretender to the throne of Albania in my family.

NORRISON. Including him, five thousand. Going! Going! . . .

COUNT *(Quickly)*. How soon?

NORRISON. How soon what?

COUNT. How soon can I get the money?

NORRISON. The minute you've signed the legal documents.

COUNT *(Greedily)*. Where are they?

(He begins to search Norrison's desk feverishly)

NORRISON *(Holding him back)*. Hey! Hey! Hey! Wait a minute, for God's sake! Patience! There's no such hurry as all that!

COUNT. You told me yourself it was urgent.

NORRISON. For me. Not for you.

(Miss Cuno enters)

MISS CUNO. Twenty minutes after three.

NORRISON. Terrible! Thank you.

MISS CUNO. And here are the flashbulbs. *(She places a box on the desk)*

NORRISON. Good! *(Miss Cuno goes out. He turns to the Count)* You'll get a handsome bonus in . . . the month of . . . *(He counts the months on his fingers)* . . . July . . . *(The Count look up eagerly)* . . . a grandchild.

COUNT *(Disappointed)*. Thank you.

NORRISON. Don't thank me. Thank your son. I'll keep you in mind for the future, though.

COUNT *(Protesting)*. I won't do any more adopting! No! No! I'd rather starve!

NORRISON. But . . . let's say . . . in case of an emergency . . . it's about a friend of mine . . . how would you like . . . for a substantial sum—that goes without saying—how would you like to marry . . . a pretty girl that her boy friend would like to be rid of?

COUNT. That any time! With pleasure!

(Harry enters from the dressing room, shaved and correctly

dressed. SYLVIA *and the* HABER-
DASHER *follow him)*

SYLVIA. Two minutes. Just.

NORRISON. Splendid! (HE *signs
the* HABERDASHER's *bill)* You present
this at the cashier's window number
five, downstairs. (HE *makes a note)*

HABERDASHER *(In a whisper).*
Thank you so very much, sir, and
forgive me for being noisy when I
came in. It was my happiness, over-
flowing . . .

NORRISON *(Writing calmly).*
Get out of here. Quick.

HABERDASHER *(In a whisper,
starting to go).* May I hope that you
will again . . .

NORRISON *(Writing, interrupts
him calmly).* No. Never again.

HABERDASHER *(Hardly audible).* My compliments. (HE *bows
himself through the door)*

SYLVIA. The barber had almost
nothing to do. My darling's face is
just as smooth as the rest of him.
(SHE *strokes him)*

NORRISON *(To* HARRY, *talking
fast).* Harry, I have the honor to present you to my good old friend the
Count San Marino-Schattenburg, your
father.

HARRY. My what?

NORRISON *(Talking very fast).*
He's just adopted you. You're his
son. You bear his name.

HARRY *(Outraged).* I will *not*
bear his name!

SYLVIA. You will bear everything he tells you to.

HARRY. Am I never to be allowed to say a word?

NORRISON and SYLVIA *(To-
gether).* Never!

SYLVIA. You will bear anything
we put upon you and I shall make it

worth your while in a sweet, ethical
and matrimonial way.

NORRISON *(Hurrying them).*
Father and son, quick, into each
other's arms! (COUNT *embraces*
HARRY) And now, my dear Count,
trot—or rather gallop—into that
office and sign the document. (HE
calls:) The document!

(LOARY *enters from the Secretary's Office)*

LOARY. Just finished, sir.

(The COUNT *hurries into the
office)*

NORRISON *(To* LOARY). How's
your fever?

LOARY. Over a hundred. And
still going up. (HE *sees the aspirin-
bottle on the desk)* Oh! Aspirin!
That'll help! May I take a few? (HE
reaches after the bottle)

NORRISON *(Talking fast).* Sorry,
you cannot. I'll need them later for
other purposes. Go to bed. I don't
think much of medicines. Very few
help. No laughs, please. My theory
is: there are two varieties of sickness. One, the incurable kinds. Doctors try to shorten them. Two, the
kinds which heal by themselves. Doctors try to lengthen them. Going to
bed is good for both. Bed is man's
best friend. Bed, not dog.

LOARY. Thank you.

NORRISON *(Slapping his back).*
Go straight home! Will nothing
teach you to take care of yourself?

LOARY. Not while I still have
work to do for you! (HE *returns to
the office in a hurry)*

NORRISON. There's what I call
a hero! *(Sits down and writes feverishly.* SYLVIA *makes a note)* What
are you writing, child?

SYLVIA. Our new name so I
won't forget it.

HARRY. I beg your pardon, but how's it possible to give up the name I was born with?

NORRISON (Still writing). You will gain nothing by being inquisitive.

SYLVIA (To HARRY). A dictator must never be disturbed. Remember that. Now, let me look at you. (SHE looks at him amorously) Oh, if you knew how . . . how it affects me emotionally to think of you as an elegant gentleman wearing silk underwear! (Ecstatically) I'll be your loving and obedient wife! (Moves toward him with open arms)

NORRISON (Still writing). But not in my office, please!

(SYLVIA steps back)

NORRISON. What's more we've only a few minutes left! We must keep moving! (To HARRY) Your taxi . . . still waiting at the door? (HE rings)

HARRY. Yes. It reads six forty.

NORRISON. How do you know?

HARRY. I suppose so.

(MISS CUNO enters hurriedly. she hands NORRISON a small etui)

MISS CUNO (While NORRISON opens the etui). The wedding ring, sir. $9,990.

NORRISON. O.K. (Putting the ring on SYLVIA'S finger. Rapidly) With this ring he thee weds. (To MISS CUNO, without making a pause) Miss Cuno, there's a taxi waiting at the door. My chauffeur Charles . . .

SYLVIA (To HARRY, admiring the ring). Thank you, darling!

NORRISON (Continues, rapidly) . . . my chauffeur Charles will drive it . . .

HARRY (To SYLVIA, most graciously). Don't mention it, honey.

NORRISON (Continues, rapidly) . . . my chauffeur Charles will drive this taxi immediately to the . . . (Looks questioningly at HARRY)

HARRY (Quick). Metropolitan Taxi Company.

NORRISON . . . Metropolitan Taxi Company's garage, leave the taxi in charge of the garage superintendent . . .

SYLVIA (Interrupting) . . . and give him my love!

NORRISON (Shouting). What?

SYLVIA. He was best man for Harry at our wedding!

NORRISON (Continuing, to MISS CUNO, who made notes) . . . take a receipt and deliver the letter which I will now . . . (HE calls:) Miss Marlin! . . . dictate.

(MISS MARLIN enters right away and sits down quickly to the left end of the desk, while MISS CUNO goes out hurriedly. NORRISON dictates:)

NORRISON. "Metropolitan Taxi Company. City. The undersigned Harry Foot herewith requests his immediate release from duty. His physician has forbidden him to continue his services because of a severe bronchial catarrh. Postscript. My taxi meter reads six forty which sum I will send you by money order tomorrow." That's all. Type.

(MISS MARLIN hurries out)

HARRY. But I have no bronchial catarrh.

(PYNNIGAN enters)

PYNNIGAN. Your family physician, Dr. Frank.

(DR. FRANK enters)

NORRISON (To HARRY, pointing at DR. FRANK). In one moment you will have bronchial catarrh. How are you, Doctor? (PYNNIGAN *goes*) This poor, sick young man . . .

SYLVIA. Oh!

NORRISON . . . needs a doctor's certificate in a hurry. Please examine him. *(To* HARRY*)* Take off your coat. (HARRY *looks at* SYLVIA *hesitatingly*)

SYLVIA *(Peremptorily)*. You take off anything he tells you to.

HARRY. I'll take off everything he tells me to! (HE *takes off his coat and goes to* DR. FRANK)

SYLVIA *(Bashfully)*. May I remain?

NORRISON. He's not to go any further than his coat.

SYLVIA *(To* HARRY*)*. You're not to go any further than your coat.

(SHE *sits, disappointed.* MISS CUNO *enters with a letter*)

MISS CUNO. The letter of resignation, sir.

NORRISON. Thanks. Pay the barber, give him one dollar tip and tell him to go home.

(MISS CUNO *hurries into the dressing room.* MISS NORMAN *enters and sits at the left of the desk*)

Just to save you valuable time, Doctor . . . Miss Norman, take this doctor's certificate, please. "The undersigned, Ulysses W. Frank, M.D., does hereby certify that an exhaustive physical examination has shown Harry Foot to be suffering from . . . *(Very impressively)* . . . a severe bronchial catarrh which . . .

(*Only after hearing that,* DR. FRANK *puts his stethoscope against* HARRY'S *chest,—and during the following dialogue examines him thoroughly*)

HARRY *(As* DR. FRANK *listens to his stethoscope)*. I have to laugh.

NORRISON *(Continuing the dic-*

tation). ". . . bronchial catarrh which renders him incapable of performing any further duties in a taxi-cab."

DR. FRANK. What an exact, correct diagnosis! *(Examines* HARRY*)*

SYLVIA *(To* NORRISON*)*. You said Harry Foot. Shouldn't it be Harry San Marino-Schattenburg?

NORRISON. As a taxi driver he is still Foot.

SYLVIA. You think of everything! You . . .

NORRISON *(Interrupts her)*. Silence. *(To* MISS NORMAN*)* Date it today and type. (HE *leans over* MISS NORMAN'S *head)* What perfume do you use, Miss Norman?

MISS NORMAN. Chafrey. Number eleven.

NORRISON *(Rapidly)*. Try Milomax "My love, my skin." It's eighteen percent cheaper and smells thirty-seven percent more exciting. Go and type.

MISS NORMAN. Thank you so much, sir.

NORRISON. Not at all. Lubrication. A little oil. Quickly now. Go and type. *(As* MISS NORMAN *runs out,* PYNNIGAN *enters)* Well, what's keeping Director Felix?

PYNNIGAN. We've phoned him. He's coming right away.

NORRISON. My friend Felix is very slow to move. He needs to be jolted up. Make him get a move on. Call him again and tell him I'm very angry.

PYNNIGAN. Pardon me, sir, but I'm afraid that will frighten him out of his wits.

NORRISON. That's what I aim to do.

PYNNIGAN. Very good, sir. The English cutter Murgatroyd is here from the firm "Old England Tailors."

NORRISON. Well, trot him in. (PYNNIGAN goes. The TAILOR enters) How do you do, Mr. Murgatroyd? I sent for you because I need a few first class suits made very quickly. The kind of suits you're used to seeing as you stroll on Bond Street.

TAILOR (With broad English accent). With all due respect to you, sir, it is no habit of mine to stroll on Bond Street.

NORRISON. What? You don't stroll on Bond Street?

TAILOR. Never, sir, under any circumstances, sir.

NORRISON. Where do you London tailors stroll in London?

TAILOR. That question, sir, I am not prepared to answer. I have never been to London. My cut and accent may be British but honesty compels me to admit that my nationality is Russian.

NORRISON. "Murgatroyd"?

TAILOR. Formerly Muranoff.

NORRISON. Very good. Now, then, Comrade Mura . . . (Looks at him questioningly)

TAILOR . . . noff.

NORRISON. Noff, will you please . . .

TAILOR (Interrupts him). And no "Comrade." Not Red. White. Call me: "Gospodin." Mister.

NORRISON. That's something else again. Will you please take down my order first, Mister, and take your measurements second, and do both as quickly as possible. Two tweed sport suits, Mister. Two. Dva.

TAILOR (Taking notes; beaming). Dva! Two! Yes! Da!

NORRISON. Two business suits. Two. Dva.

TAILOR. Dva.—Color?

NORRISON. One of good blue. Seenia. Blue.

TAILOR (Beaming). Da, Gospodin Norrison. Seenia. Blue.

NORRISON. The other coconut brown.

SYLVIA. Chocolate brown would be better.

NORRISON. Nyet! Nyet! I said coconut!

SYLVIA (Surrenders). All right. Coconut.

NORRISON (To the TAILOR). And in addition, Gospodin, a dinner jacket and a tail coat. Now take your measurements! (The TAILOR looks at HARRY. DR. FRANK is still examining his chest. NORRISON is impatient)

NORRISON (To the TAILOR). What are you waiting for? The doctor only needs the front. The rear is yours.

TAILOR (To DR. FRANK). Permit me to introduce myself. Murgatroyd.

DR. FRANK. Doctor Frank.

(The TAILOR bows and standing behind HARRY produces his tape-measure and puts the tape-measure around HARRY's chest)

DR. FRANK (With his stethoscope on HARRY's chest). Breathe deeply.

TAILOR (Behind HARRY). One moment, please. Don't breathe. How can you expect your coat to fit if you blow yourself up that way?

DR. FRANK (With deep contempt). Pardon me, but my diagnosis . . .

TAILOR (Interrupting). Pardon me, but his coat . . .

DR. FRANK (To the TAILOR, furiously). You will be good enough to . . .

TAILOR (*Unexpectedly pugnacious, loud*). I insist that I . . .

HARRY. What goes on here? Just don't tear me apart, that's all.

NORRISON. Come now, gentlemen! Please!

DR. FRANK (*Beside himself; to* NORRISON). If you expect me to make my diagnosis, he must inhale.

TAILOR. If you expect the coat to fit, he must *ex*hale!

NORRISON. Quite right. Quiet, please. Make it by turns. Begin with *ex*haling.

DR. FRANK (*To the* TAILOR, *with a bitter smile*). You win. He's all yours. (*To* HARRY, *stepping back*) Exhale.

TAILOR (*As* HE *measures*). Thirty-eight. (HE *jots it down in his notebook*). Now you may *in*hale.

   (DR. FRANK *goes back to* HARRY'S *chest*)

NORRISON. The suits are to be ready in three days, whatever the cost may be, because this gentleman is leaving town on Saturday.

HARRY. For Cannes, France.

NORRISON. Good! (*To* SYLVIA) He's catching on!

   (HE *makes a note. During the following the* TAILOR *goes on measuring and making notes.* MISS NORMAN *enters*)

MISS NORMAN. The Doctor's certificate.

   (SHE *puts it on the desk. Sits, waiting.* MISS CUNO *enters after her and waits*)

NORRISON (*Handing the* DOCTOR *the certificate*). Doctor, sign this, please.

DR. FRANK (*After signing*). May I . . . perhaps . . . read it, too?

NORRISON. It's not necessary at all—but if you wish . . .

DR. FRANK (*After a rapid glance at the paper*). Perfect!

NORRISON. To be frank, I should have preferred pneumonia but I don't suppose you could go quite that far.

DR. FRANK. Out of the question.

NORRISON. You may be right. You're a conscientious doctor. Incidentally . . . if a case of this sort should ever come up again . . . how far would your friendship for me permit you to go?

DR. FRANK (*Severely*). Not over a temperature of a hundred. That is the limit of my friendship.

NORRISON. And of mine. Over a hundred I should most certainly drop you and call in a specialist.

DR. FRANK (*A little hurt*). So long, sir.—How's your wife?

NORRISON. Normal. Ninety-eight six, thank you. (DR. FRANK *is about to leave*). You might look in at my friend, the lawyer Loary. He tells me he's running a temperature of a hundred.

DR. FRANK. A hundred? Now, that makes quite a nice little fever. I will look at him. So long. (HE *goes into the Secretary's Office*)

NORRISON (*To* MISS CUNO). Miss Cuno, will you please see that . . .

MISS CUNO (*Interrupting*) . . . that your chauffeur takes both this medical certificate and the letter of resignation to the taxi garage.

NORRISON. What a pearl you are! Thank you. You may go.

   (MISS CUNO *glances at her wristwatch*)

MISS CUNO. I might as well stay five seconds longer. One. Two. Three. Four. Five. Now it's exactly half past three.

NORRISON. Appalling! Thank you just the same, Miss Cuno. (MISS CUNO *goes out. The same moment* PYNNIGAN *enters from the opposite door.* NORRISON *flies impatiently at him*) Haven't the other gentlemen I sent for come? Neither Director Felix nor Colleon the diplomat?

PYNNIGAN. Both on the way, sir.

NORRISON. God, what delays! Half past three, and . . . (HE *breaks off, going over to the squatting* TAILOR) Aren't you finished yet? Have I nothing but slow-pokes here?

TAILOR. Through in a minute, sir.

NORRISON (*Looks down at the* TAILOR's *head*). I've never before enjoyed a bird's-eye view of you. I see you're getting bald.

TAILOR. I know. I'm doing everything for it, sir. (*Measuring and noting*) Forty-one . . . but nothing seems to help . . . thirty . . .

SYLVIA. Poor, bald-headed tailor man. I'm so sorry for him.

NORRISON (*Rapidly*). Just because *you*'re sorry for him, child, I'll give him a little tip. (*To the* TAILOR) You might try one thing more. Or rather two. (*To* MISS NORMAN) Write down "Omaxolyn pills'" and "Dr. Larsen's ointment." (*To the* TAILOR, *quickly*) The pills have to be swallowed, the ointment has to be rubbed into the scalp. The pills *push* the hair, the ointment *pulls* it. They've given farmers excellent results with sheep. The sheep give twice as much wool after the treatment.

TAILOR. Doesn't it matter that I'm not a sheep?

NORRISON. Why should it? After all, skin is skin, and if wool grows on your head it's a lot better than nothing. (*Suddenly impatient, looking at his watch*) This is disgraceful! Are Felix and Colleon never coming? (*Smelling* MISS NORMAN's *hair*) Scented! Scented and freshly waved. Miss Norman, you must have something on this evening.

MISS NORMAN. I'm going to the Opera.

NORRISON. Ah! With whom?

MISS NORMAN. With my friend Kristian from our Press Department.

NORRISON (*Frowning*). But I thought handsome Kristian was engaged to marry your friend Miss Petrovitch!

MISS NORMAN. He *was* only. They seem to have fallen out.

NORRISON (*Pushes a button, ringing a bell*). They must patch things up. (PYNNIGAN *enters.* NORRISON *continues to* MISS NORMAN) At what time does the Opera start?

MISS NORMAN. At eight.

NORRISON (*To* PYNNIGAN). You will have Mr. Kristian report here to you at seven-thirty and find him something to work him overtime all night. At eight you will take Miss Norman to the Opera in his place. (*To* MISS NORMAN) What is the opera?

MISS NORMAN. A Wagner opera. Lohengrin.

NORRISON (*To* PYNNIGAN). You turn up your nose at Lohengrin.

PYNNIGAN (*In despair, softly*). I've seen Lohengrin thirty-seven times.

NORRISON. So what?

PYNNIGAN. I never liked it.

NORRISON (*Peremptorily*). Tonight you will dislike it the thirty-eighth time. (*Writing on two slips*) I don't blame you. I hate it, too. Herewith I give you a small bonus for your trouble. (HE *hands him one of the slips*. HE *speaks to the* TAILOR, *handing him the other slip*) And here's your hair prescription. Pills and salve. To be swallowed *and* applied. Pills *in*, salve *out*.

TAILOR. Much obliged, sir.

PYNNIGAN. And what are Press Agent Kristian's orders for tonight, sir?

NORRISON. He will spend the whole night, *the whole night* in the office giving dictation to his fiancee, Miss Petrovitch. From seven-thirty until midnight. If necessary, until later! To Miss Petrovitch!

(MISS NORMAN *winces*)

PYNNIGAN. May I ask what he is to dictate?

NORRISON. That speech my wife made last year about the decent love-life of respectable couples who are engaged to marry. You will get a copy from my wife, give it to Kristian, put Kristian and Miss Petrovitch in a private office, hang on the doorknob a sign PLEASE DON'T DISTURB, and disappear. (*To* SYLVIA) Heavy oil.

SYLVIA. Sweet oil. (MISS NORMAN *goes out, deeply hurt*) Poor innocent girl. I'm sorry for her.

(*The* TELEPHONE *rings*. MISS MARLIN *sticks her head through the door*)

MISS MARLIN. Cannes, France, on the wire.

(SYLVIA *steps nearer to* NORRISON, *listening curiously*)

NORRISON (*Into one of his telephones,*—*all the following with utmost rapidity*). Hello, Cannes, France? Hotel Carlton? Directeur Meyrod? Norrison speaking, N-O-double R-I-S-O-N. You remember me? Thank you. How do you do? Fine, thank you. Merci, très bien. How's your wife? (*Without making a pause, to the* TAILOR *who has finished his work, bows, and starts to go*) Da svedanie! Goodbye! (*Into the phone, and no pause until the end of the phone-call*) No, not you. Wait a minute, can't you? (*The* TAILOR *returns. To the* TAILOR) Go away! Go away! (*Into the phone, as the* TAILOR *starts again*) No, not you! Stay where you are. Restez, restez, s'il vous plait! Stay! Remain! (*The* TAILOR *returns*) Not you! Eh, what? Get out! (*Into the phone*) Hold on! Great Scott! (*To the* TAILOR) Out with you! (*The* TAILOR *goes out*) Thank God! The idiot! (*Into the phone*) Not you! No! No! Now, then! Listen, please. Rooms! Chambres! Not for me this time. (*Shouting*) Pas pour moi!!! (*Speaking normally but fast*) For a very distinguished young couple. Jeune gens très distingués. Count and Countess. Quoi! Plait-il? What's that? Children? You ask whether they have children? Just a minute? (HE *counts on his fingers*) . . . May, June, July . . . (*Into the phone*) Well, that depends how long they stay. At the moment, no child. The rooms for the nineteenth, this month. Southern exposure. Windows facing the sea.

(*During this telephone call the* COUNT *entered*. LOARY *and* DR. FRANK *entered the same time, following the Count. The* COUNT *went to* NORRISON. *Now, after the words "facing the sea,"* NORRISON, *who snatched the document from the*

COUNT's *hand, speaks into the phone, without pause)*

NORRISON. I'll give you the name now. *(Shouting)* The name!!! Le nom! Yes! Oui! *(Dictates the name, reading the document)* Count and Countess . . . San Marino . . . hyphen . . . Schattenburg. Yes. "Schatten" and "burg." Read it back, please. — All right. How's the weather there? What? Pluie? Rain? Well, see that you get sunshine. Price no object. It's for me . . . the bill, yes . . . for me, H. W. Norrison, pour moi! Fine! Thank you! Merci! Goodbye! *(Slams down the receiver. —to* LOARY, *who stands with* DR. FRANK *near the Waiting Room door; without making a pause)* Thank you, Loary.

DR. FRANK *(Pointing to* LOARY, *speaking fast).* Fever: one hundred. Diagnosis: flu.

NORRISON *(In a commanding tone).* Loary, to bed! Doctor, thanks! You can go! *(Exhausted, he leans back in his swivel-chair, while* LOARY *and* DR. FRANK *go out through the Waiting Room)*

SYLVIA. Forgive me. Just to make everything clear and orderly. We shall be absolutely without child —or children—until the last week of July. After that, I can promise nothing.

NORRISON. A meticulous young lady. *(To* HARRY*)* Have you a notebook?

HARRY. Yes.

NORRISON. Write this down: San Marino-Schattenburg.

HARRY *(Writing).* What for?

NORRISON. That, my boy, is your high-sounding new name. Be a credit to it. *(With a glance at the* COUNT*)* It could use a little credit.

COUNT. My card. (HE *hands* HARRY *his visiting card)*

NORRISON *(To the* COUNT*).* What's this? Aren't you going to kiss your son?

COUNT *(Reluctantly).* I've already kissed him once.

NORRISON. It takes more than one kiss to be a father.

(COUNT *quickly kisses* HARRY, *then reaches eagerly for* SYLVIA*)*

SYLVIA *(Withdrawing).* Thanks.

COUNT. Thanks? Yes or no?

SYLVIA. Thanks, no.

(MISS CUNO *enters with a bouquet of flowers)*

MISS CUNO. The flowers. And here's the bill for them.

NORRISON *(Rapidly).* The flowers go in the salt water. All the tablets of aspirin go in the salt water with the flowers, to lengthen their lives. Don't stare. Ask any florist. The bill goes with the letters, and the flowers go out in the icebox.

(MISS CUNO *puts the flowers in the pitcher, puts the aspirin tablets in the salt water, puts the bill with the letters and runs out into the Waiting Room with the flowers.*

PYNNIGAN *entered from the outer hall during this operation and said:)*

PYNNIGAN. The gentlemen of the Executive Committee.

(OSSO, SYRING *and* WOLF *enter from the Outer Hall.* PYNNIGAN *goes into the Secretary's Office)*

NORRISON. I'll be with you at once, gentlemen. *(To* HARRY*)* Look here, my friend. Now that you're a San Marino-Schattenburg, you're in a position to sign your letter of acceptance to the exclusive Golf Club.

(HARRY *signs*) Will you be seated, gentlemen? (HE *calls:*) Miss Petrovitch, please! *(To the* THREE GENTLEMEN *who remain standing)* Help yourself to cigars, with the exception of Mr. Wolf who suffers from excessive acidity of the stomach which can cause ulcers, God forbid. (MISS PETROVITCH *enters.* NORRISON *turns to the* COUNT) You run along now, Papa. Go take a walk. We're very busy here. *(The* THREE GENTLEMEN, *still standing, do not touch the cigars. The* COUNT *makes frantic signs that he has not yet been paid off)* What now? I *beg* your pardon! Here's your check. *(Points to the slip on the desk)*

COUNT *(Grabs the check).* Thank you so much. *(Pockets the check)* Yours to command! *(To* HARRY) Bless you, Junior!

HARRY. Goodbye, Dad. *(The* COUNT *goes out quickly through the Outer Hall.)* He makes a very dignified appearance.

NORRISON. For the price. Very. *(To* MISS PETROVITCH) Your lip is quivering, Miss Petrovitch. Have you something to say?

MISS PETROVITCH. Only to thank you for your kindness and understanding. (SHE *dries a tear)*

NORRISON. Don't thank me. You know I don't like thanks. Take this letter to the Golf Club. Write a similar letter to the Auto and Jockey Clubs. Stop crying. All will yet come right. I guarantee it.

(MISS PETROVITCH *goes out)*

SYLVIA. Poor girl! I'm sorry for her too.

NORRISON. That's very sweet of you. (HE *turns to the Committee)* Gentlemen, I present my friend San Marino-Schattenburg. My friends,

Mr. Osso, Mr. Syring, Mr. Wolf. *(General bows)* Now, gentlemen.

OSSO. To make a long story short . . .

NORRISON *(Impatiently).* Even shorter.

OSSO. As short as possible. The candidate is an engineer with a genius for invention. He stipulates that his services are to be rewarded by appointment to an executive position. If he has not as yet invented anything he will oblige us by beginning as soon as possible.

SYLVIA. But he's constantly inventing!

NORRISON. Fine! Let's hear what he's invented. Quick and briefly.

HARRY. I don't know that I can claim to have made inventions. But I've had ideas!

NORRISON. How many?

HARRY. Three.

NORRISON *(Impatiently).* Three? Well, come on. Let's have them, quick, quick.

SYLVIA *(Whispering to* HARRY). Cylinder.

HARRY. Yes. A nineteen-cylinder motor. I say to myself we have six and eight cylinder motors. Why not a nineteen?

NORRISON *(To the men).* And we never thought of it! *(To* HARRY) Stupid. *(To the men)* We buy it. *(To* HARRY) Go on.

SYLVIA *(Whispering).* Headlights.

HARRY. Oh, yes. Another headlight in the rear of the car. For backing.

NORRISON *(To the men).* Magnificent! *(To* HARRY) Stupid. Been done before. *(To the men)* We buy it. *(To* HARRY) Go on.

SYLVIA *(Whispering)*. Bell.

HARRY. That's right. A bell that rings whenever you have a blowout.

NORRISON. It's a little late *after* the blowout but better late than never. *(To HARRY)* Idiotic. *(To the men)* We buy it. *(To HARRY)* Go on.

HARRY. That's all.

NORRISON. It's plenty! (HE *rings and writes out a check)* Mr. Osso, you will have these three ideas worked out with blueprints and all as soon as possible. You will then have these blueprints carefully placed in our secret vault, somewhere near the back and at the bottom so that no one will ever find them. (HE *hands the de luxe cheque-book to* HARRY) Here is your cheque-book, my dear friend. *(To the* THREE MEN) Gentlemen, I thank you for the exemplary speed and keenness with which you have arranged this matter. My compliments to your dear wives. All of you good afternoon. So long, Mr. Osso, Mr. Syring and Mr. Wolf.

WOLF. I hope . . . you're not mad at me . . . because of this . . . stomach trouble of mine.

NORRISON. On the contrary, Mr. Wolf. It was a pleasure. (HE *pushes* WOLF *gently out.* PYNNIGAN *enters)*

PYNNIGAN. Miss Shortwood.

NORRISON. What's keeping Felix? Did you frighten him?

PYNNIGAN. As you directed, sir. I told him you were beside yourself.

NORRISON. Right. What then?

PYNNIGAN. That worked. He's on his way.

NORRISON. Learn from me, Pynnigan, to treat every man according to his character. Let Miss Shortwood come in and send up my chauffeur Charles. (PYNNIGAN *admits* MISS SHORTWOOD, *an ugly girl, and goes)* Miss Shortwood, this is your new chief. From now on you are the secretary of my dear friend San Marino-Schattenburg, Junior, one of the leading executives of our Bank. *(To* SYLVIA) If she's not plain enough, we've got them plainer. *(To* MISS SHORTWOOD) Your first order is to telephone the station and find out if the four o'clock train from Canada is on time.

> (MISS SHORTWOOD *goes out quickly)*

SYLVIA. I'd like to know about the lady's morals.

NORRISON. Can't you see?

SYLVIA. She doesn't look a sensuous type.

NORRISON. I should say not!

SYLVIA. Can you gurantee that?

NORRISON. Without the slightest hesitation.

SYLVIA. That's very comforting. But I'm sorry for her.

> (GEORGE *enters from the dressing room)*

GEORGE. The shoes are here. (HE *goes out)*

NORRISON *(To* HARRY). Go on, son. (HARRY *goes into the dressing room)* Make it fast. *(To* SYLVIA) He's not proceeding properly. It's unusual to have a secretary before having shoes. Dear Sylvia, here's another matrimonial duty for you. Not a sweet one, perhaps, rather a bitter one. Go help him try on his new shoes.

SYLVIA. How many minutes?

NORRISON. One.

> (SYLVIA *runs into the dressing*

room. PYNNIGAN *enters the same moment)*

PYNNIGAN. Mr. Colleon is here.

NORRISON. Well, Mr. Colleon can wait a little.

(MISS CUNO *enters)*

MISS CUNO. Three forty.

NORRISON. Thank you. Terrible!

(MISS CUNO *goes.* MISS SHORTWOOD *enters)*

MISS SHORTWOOD. The four o'clock train will be in on time.

NORRISON. Terrible! Thank you. *(To* PYNNIGAN) Send in my chauffeur Charles. (MISS SHORTWOOD *goes.* PYNNIGAN *admits the uniformed chauffeur* CHARLES. HARRY *enters with* SYLVIA) Let's see, my friend. (HARRY *shows his shoes)* Fine shoes. Are they comfortable?

HARRY. Not very.

NORRISON. Do they hurt?

HARRY. Yes, they do.

NORRISON. I'm delighted! At last you're having a few unpleasant moments, too. *(To* CHARLES) Charles, this is your new master. Miss Sylvia's husband. Count San Marino-Schattenburg. From now on my car belongs to him and you are in his service. You can go. Wait in front of the door. (CHARLES *bows and goes.* NORRISON *turns to* HARRY) Take out your cheque-book.

HARRY. What for?

SYLVIA. Stop asking questions. Do as you're told.

HARRY. Can't I even ask what for?

SYLVIA and NORRISON. No!!

NORRISON. You're buying my car from me. It's a Special Grand Norrison, last year's model. Fully equipped. Low mileage. I'm letting you have it for two thousand. That's a loss of forty percent to me. How about it?

HARRY *(To* SYLVIA). Stupid. *(To* NORRISON) I buy it.

NORRISON. All right. Cash down! Quick!

HARRY. Cash?

SYLVIA. I'll show you how. *(She writes in the cheque-book)* Sign here. (HARRY *signs.* SHE *tears out the cheque and hands it to* NORRISON) So.

NORRISON *(Pocketing the cheque).* That consummates our first business deal very much to my advantage. You have to complete your wardrobe. Let's see your shoes. Marvelous! Tip-top from top to toe. How about a short rehearsal now? (HE *shouts out)* What's your name?

HARRY. Foot.

NORRISON *(Shouting).* Wrong! San Marino-Schattenburg! Take your notebook and go back in there and study! *(As* HARRY *goes)* And don't come out again till you know your name by heart! Whoever heard of such a thing? I buy him an expensive name like that and he doesn't even take the trouble to learn it!

SYLVIA. I'll go in and coach him!

(SHE *follows him out.* PYNNIGAN *enters)*

PYNNIGAN. Director Felix.

(FELIX *enters.* PYNNIGAN *goes)*

NORRISON. It's about time.

FELIX. *(Panting).* How do you do? I came post-haste. What's up? Has anything gone wrong? (HE *sits)* Out of breath! From running!

NORRISON. Good! Fine! Catch your breath. Something most unusual is up!

FELIX. The phone call was frightening. Words like "raging" . . . "Beside himself" . . .

NORRISON. All true. *(A pause. Then, portentously)* You are a man of the world, Mr. Felix.

FELIX. True. Let me say one word, though. We must both be men of the world. So why this scene? Between two men of the world, I admit all.

NORRISON *(Surprised)*. All what?

FELIX. I know why you sent for me. I confess all.

NORRISON. What have you to confess?

FELIX. I see by looking at you that you know all. There's no good lying. I *am* in love with your girl friend, the luscious but highly virginal ballet dancer Begonia.

NORRISON *(Surprised, stuttering)*. Beg . . . Bego . . . Begonia?

FELIX. Yes, sir. The same who had hoped that you'd marry her after divorcing your wife. I am in love with her, I confess. And she *does* love me. With our mutual passion for each other the logical consequences were bound to develop. Including . . .

NORRISON *(Shouting)*. Including *what*?

FELIX. Including marriage sometime in the immediate future. Now, kill me.

NORRISON. Inc . . . including . . . ma . . . marriage? With *my* Begonia?

FELIX. The twenty-seventh of October last year she became *my* Begonia. Isn't it always simpler to be honest?

NORRISON. You're in love . . .

with Begonia? And she . . . with you?

FELIX. We can't help it. *(After a moment's painful pause* HE *recites monotonously the well-known cliche of the newspapers)* The bride-to-be will be given in marriage by her father. She was graduated from the University of . . .

NORRISON *(Interrupting)*. Thank you. I'm not interested. *(Staring at* FELIX. *Loud)* I hadn't the remotest idea of this! I didn't even know you know each other! *I didn't send for you about her at all!*

FELIX *(Horrified)*. Not about her?

NORRISON. Certainly not! And you stand there and name . . . my Begonia . . . with you . . .

FELIX *(Flabbergasted)*. Yes. And it wasn't on her account you sent for me?

NORRISON. No.—And this is how I learn that my Begonia . . . Oh God! *(Into the telephone)* Ice water, please.

FELIX. Make it two.

NORRISON *(Into the telephone)*. Hello. Two.

FELIX. This is terrible. I've been an ass. If you didn't know, though, what made you send for me the way you did?

NORRISON. A matter of business. *(*HE *shouts)* She will marry . . .

FELIX. Me. Yes. *(Quietly)* What *is* the matter of business?

NORRISON *(Suddenly very calmly)*. United Motors. *(Shouting again)* How long has this been going on?

FELIX. *(Quietly)*. Three months. What about United Motors?

NORRISON *(Calmly)*. Just a

business matter. *(Shouting)* And you love her?

FELIX *(Quietly)*. Yes. And she me.

NORRISON. To what extent?

FELIX *(Quietly)*. She's crazy about me. What's that about United Motors?

NORRISON. Just a little business readjustment. I give you my word I'd no idea you knew Begonia?

FELIX. I'm the victim of a bad error in judgment. I'm a bleeding ass. I'm . . . *(Very calmly)* What *is* the readjustment?

NORRISON. The readjustment . . . *(An eloquent pause. Then:)* Well, who cares? Life must go on. (HE *resumes his authoritative manner)* Mr. Felix, in spite of this horrible situation, I'm about to promote you. Will you, without hesitation, resign your present position if, within five minutes, I appoint you General Manager of our gigantic Import-Export Department?

FELIX. Without the slightest hesitation. Yes.

NORRISON. Well, you won't have to wait five minutes. You're General Manager already.

FELIX. I'm overwhelmed.

NORRISON. You're nothing like as overwhelmed as I am! You have ten seconds to write your resignation. (HE *points to the setcretary's room)*

FELIX. One will do.

(GEORGE *enters with two glasses of water.* BOTH MEN *drink.* FELIX *goes out.* GEORGE *leaves)*

NORRISON *(Stands a moment, his hand pressed to his heart)*. Begonia in love. Going to get married. It's a lucky thing I've something else to think of. (HE *crosses to the dressing room)* Sylvia! (SYLVIA *enters)* Dearest Sylvia. Congratulate your husband for me. I haven't time myself. He's just been made president.

SYLVIA *(Crying out happily)*. President! President! *(Triumphantly)* I told you he was going places!

NORRISON. Yes, you did. He's president. Write it down so he can memorize it. Universal United Automobile and Motor Factories Incorporated.

SYLVIA *(Having quickly made notes)*. I'll coach him on that, too. (SHE *runs back to Harry)*

(PYNNIGAN *enters)*

NORRISON *(To himself)*. Quiet, my heart. Life goes on. *(To* PYNNIGAN) Let Mr. Colleon in.

(PYNNIGAN *winks at* COLLEON *who enters.* PYNNIGAN *goes out)*

(COLLEON, *the "phony diplomat" in cutaway and striped trousers, bows deeply from the waist.)*

COLLEON. Good afternoon, Mr. Norrison, or, as we used to say in Old Vienna, under the Emperor, your obedient servant, sir, I kiss your hand.

NORRISON. You don't kiss any part of my anatomy. Please, don't be ceremonious, you old international crook.

COLLEON *(Hurt; reproachfully)*. Crook?

NORRISON. Pardon me. Let's say: "controversial personality."

COLLEON. Isn't it the same?

NORRISON. Approximately. But . . . down to business. This matter is urgent. What have you in stock?

COLLEON. Two honorary consular titles and one of Consul General. Afghanistan, Iraq . . .

NORRISON. No, I don't care for Asia. What have you got in Europe?

COLLEON. I sold the last one we had yesterday. I'm sorry, too. Such a nice southern country with a lovely climate.

NORRISON. Don't break my heart. What else have you got?

COLLEON. There's always the Southern Hemisphere.

NORRISON. I can't use Uruguay or Paraguay! Or any place that ends in "guay." What country is this Consul General post? (COLLEON *looks about guiltily, then whispers in his ear*) That's better. How much?

COLLEON. Twenty thousand.

NORRISON. You're crazy!

COLLEON. My dear sir, as true as I'm standing here, it will cost me eighteen thousand to get it for you. I'll deliver it for twenty thousand, including . . .

NORRISON. Including what?

COLLEON. Escutcheon with coat of arms and flag of that country.

NORRISON. It's too much, just the same. You can certainly let it go for less. My man's a good catch for that country. They'll like him. He's a peace-loving type. He won't get them into war.

COLLEON. I'm sorry but I can't take less, sir. Let him make war.

NORRISON. You must take less!

COLLEON. Monsieur le president, c'est impossible.

NORRISON. May I ask why you're dropping into French?

COLLEON. French has been from time immemorial the language of diplomacy. Si vous voulez . . .

NORRISON (*Interrupts him*).

Enough, old rapscallion. Stop your Viennese French. Write.

COLLEON. Write what?

NORRISON. The honorary Consul General's name. Harry San Marino-Schattenburg.

COLLEON (*Writing*). San Marino . . . Italian extraction?

NORRISON. No. The Bronx.

COLLEON. Still twenty thousand.

NORRISON. How soon can you deliver?

COLLEON. Today. Or . . . if it's urgent, yesterday.

NORRISON. Let me have the papers in an hour and next week the escutcheon with coat of arms to hang over the door. I say next week because he'll only have a door then. He's shopping for a mansion.

COLLEON (*Making notes*). A house?

NORRISON. I said mansion. No house, no shack, no shanty. Mansion.

COLLEON. I see.

NORRISON. The escutcheon has to be a nice bright oval one like that of the British consul. The best quality enamel.

COLLEON. You wouldn't like it painted?

NORRISON. That's like you! Painted ones peel off after the first rain.

COLLEON. Good. Bien. Bon. Comme vous voudrez, cher Monsieur.

NORRISON (*In a hurry*). Thanks. Merci. Fini. Get out. Allez. Marchez. Scram. (*As* COLLEON *is about to speak*) Shut up. Couchez. Out!

(COLLEON *goes out into the Outer Hall. The same moment* FELIX *enters from the Secretary's Office with a letter*)

FELIX. My resignation, sir.

NORRISON. For *this* I thank you. (HE *pockets the letter*)

FELIX. How can I deny you anything you ask now?

NORRISON. I'm glad you feel that way. *(To himself)* This time oil was too expensive, though. *(To FELIX)* I hope you as a gentleman will do the right thing by the lady.

FELIX. Well, I'm doing the very best I know how.

NORRISON. I refer to financial questions. Not— . . . (HE *breaks off*) Now, goodbye to you and my best regards . . . to your *present* wife. How are those five lovely children of yours?

FELIX. All well, thanks. And a sixth on the way.

NORRISON. Congratulations.

FELIX. After the divorce we will divide them. Three remain with my wife, three with me . . .

NORRISON. And with Begonia. Congratulations again. And good afternoon.

FELIX. Good afternoon, sir. I was a bleeding ass.

NORRISON. You may be right. (FELIX *goes out into the Outer Hall.* MISS CUNO *enters the same moment through another door*)

MISS CUNO. Three fifty.

NORRISON *(Lost in thought)*. What's that? Oh, yes. Terrible. (MISS CUNO *goes.* HE *rings*) Begonia hurts more than I thought. (PYNNIGAN *enters*) Press agent Kristian?

PYNNIGAN. He's here in the waiting room.

NORRISON. Tell him to keep on waiting. (PYNNIGAN *goes as* HARRY *and* SYLVIA *enter.* NORRISON *to* HARRY) Congratulations. You've become the honorary Consul General

of a foreign power. Don't look surprised. You're a Consul General.

HARRY. Why?

SYLVIA. Don't you understand? It's very simple. You're a Consul General. A member of the striped-pants set. *(To* NORRISON) I've coached him on our new name and his position. Examine him.

NORRISON *(Rapidly)* What *is* your name?

HARRY *(Fluently, fast)*. San Marino-Schattenburg.

NORRISON. And of what company are you president?

HARRY. Universal United . . . *(Looks at* SYLVIA)

SYLVIA. Auto . . .

HARRY *(Fast)*. . . . mobile and Motor Factories Incorporated.

NORRISON. You do your name quite nicely but you'll have to work harder on the rest. (HARRY *scratches his head*) Don't scratch your head. Don't fret. I'll see you get a typewritten list of everything you've become in the past hour. *(To* SYLVIA) Sylvia, it's time. The train will be here in a few minutes now. Drive to the depot. Welcome your dear parents. Your husband is now a model son-in-law. Even for divorce he's better than he was an hour ago. Hurry, child. (SYLVIA *and* HARRY *embrace and kiss*) And don't stop to be lascivious in my office. That will do, President. Madame Consul General, that will do. In the last few minutes I've become very sensitive about love. I'm beginning to hate it. *(To himself)* Miss B. hurts more than I thought she could. (HE *shrugs*) Who cares? Life goes on. *(To* HARRY *and* SYLVIA) Tempo! Tempo! Countess San Marino-Schattenburg, you will bring your father and mother to the hotel, then telephone me here.

SYLVIA. Isn't Harry going with me to the station?

NORRISON. No. He still needs a few finishing touches.

SYLVIA. All right. Shall I send your car back for Harry?

NORRISON. Never mind. He'll come along in a taxi.

HARRY. Taxi? Not me! Never again for me! No! No!

NORRISON. I beg your pardon for having mentioned a taxi. All right. Send the car back. (HE *rings*)

SYLVIA *(Ecstatically)*. Oh, Mr. Norrison! It's as though he's been born all over again. You've re-born him!

NORRISON. Well, run along. I'm not out of labor yet. (SYLVIA *hurries out into the Outer Hall.* PYNNIGAN *enters from the Secretary's Office*) Where is that ornamental press agent of mine?

PYNNIGAN *(At the Waiting Room door)*. Mr. Kristian!

(KRISTIAN *enters.* PYNNIGAN *goes*)

KRISTIAN. How are you, sir?

NORRISON. Good afternoon. Clotheshorse. Lady-killer. (HE *glares at* KRISTIAN. KRISTIAN's *face falls*) Have you got my orders straight? Overtime all night. With this girl of yours you're trying to get rid of. With Miss Petrovitch.

KRISTIAN. Yes, sir.

NORRISON. You're a philanderer.

KRISTIAN. Quite, sir.

NORRISON. You're a gay Lothario.

KRISTIAN. At your service, sir.

NORRISON. You disgust me. All Lotharios, gay or sad, disgust me.

Ugh! But . . . for the moment I want some striking photographs of President San Marino-Schattenburg . . . (KRISTIAN *bows to* HARRY) . . . for the papers. You'll find a camera and flashbulbs here. (HE *points to the camera and the flashbulbs*)

KRISTIAN. I see, sir. (KRISTIAN *prepares the camera for taking photographs*)

NORRISON. I shall dictate the captions for the photos. (HE *calls*) Miss Petrovitch! (KRISTIAN *starts back in alarm*) Now, don't tremble, my handsome bridegroom. (MISS PETROVITCH *enters, sees* KRISTIAN *and starts, frightened*) Don't wince either, pretty little bride. I don't like affairs of the heart mixed with business. *(Quickly, to himself)* Begonia, Begonia! Who cares? Life goes on. *(To* MISS PETROVITCH *who sits down at the desk)* For the first pose take this: "President San Marino-Schattenburg submits one of his latest inventions to the great H. W. Norrison." *(To* HARRY*)* Come along, young man. *(To appear taller, takes quickly the telephone book and the red Classified Telephone Directory from the desk and stands on top of them.* HE *strikes an attitude, standing before the desk, with* HARRY.*)* Stand there and try to look alive about it. Be talking to me about your inventions. Smile and talk.

HARRY *(With an artificial smile)*. A bell rings whenever you have a blowout.

NORRISON *(With a great big smile)*. Stupid! We buy it! Shoot! *(Flashlight)* Another. Stand out there. (HE *moves* HARRY) Now, as though you were speaking reverently to someone. A little more amiable, please, and just a trifle more devout.

Like this. (HE *demonstrates*) So.
(HARRY *goes through the motions*)
Not bad. Make it a little more
devout. So. Good! Shoot! *(Flash-light)* Take this caption, Miss Pet-rovitch: "President San Marino-Schattenburg in audience with His
Majesty the King of England."

HARRY. Where's the King?

NORRISON. We'll put him in
later. We frequently put him in.
(To MISS PETROVITCH *and* KRIS-TIAN) You may go. (THEY *go
quickly. To* PYNNIGAN, *who enters)*
I'll see Louie the headwaiter, from
the Majestic Hotel.

PYNNIGAN *(At the door of the
Outer Hall).* Will you come in?

(During the following HARRY
*keeps softly murmuring, fre-
quently glancing in his notebook, like a schoolboy learning
his lesson:* "San Marino Schattenburg" . . . "Universal United
Automobile and Motors" . . .
"Consul General" . . . "San
Marino Consul" . . . "General
Motors" . . . etc. LOUIE, *the
maitre d'hotel, enters and bows)*

NORRISON. How are you,
Louie? Please take this down. On
Wednesday evening, the sixteenth . . .

LOUIE *(Repeating the order, murmuring as he writes).* Wednesday
evening. Sixteenth.

NORRISON. President San
Marino-Schattenburg . . .

LOUIE *(With awe, writing).* Oh!
President . . . San Marino . . .

NORRISON *(Rapidly).* Stop talk-ing to yourself. It bothers me. I'll
be brief. The president will entertain
at your hotel in honor of his Scan-dinavian father-in-law. Dinner for
thirty. In the small Green Ballroom.
Six individual tables for five. No

electric light. Just candles. Huge red
candles surrounded with gold laurel
leaves, not real gold, of course,
gilded plastic. Music: small orches-tra of four, five, six or eight, in red
coats; soft sweet northern music, of
course. Please note: music by Linde-gren, Johansen, Nielsen, further-more Grieg's Piano Concerto, Sib-elius' Violin Concerto and so forth.
—Menu: first, that goes without say-ing, Smorgasbord. Then, caviar. No
frogs' legs, *please,* no frogs' legs!
Plenty of Beluga Malossol caviar of
the latest catch. Served in large
blocks of ice. Green turtle soup à
l'Indian. "Maine" lobsters, thirty of
them, one for every guest. Your chef
knows how. Just tell him, à la
Norrison. Further. Choice porter-house steaks, cut from the thick end,
with a large proportion of tenderloin,
one for every guest. Potatoes:
Pommes Soufflées. No "chef's salad."
Please create a new kind of salad
for us. I know what a genius you are
at salads. (LOUIE *bows.* NORRISON
says to himself) Oil. *(To* LOUIE)
Olive oil, of course. Further. Hearts
of artichokes. Green asparagus, tips
only. Dessert: fresh fruit drowned
in old Cognac Napoleon Courvoisier
mixed half and half with Bene-dictine. Then, your specialty:
"Frozen Layer Cake à la Louie," you
know, of course, layers of chocolate
ice cream alternating with layers of
frozen chopped cherries soaked with
Scotch and layers of chopped pine-apples in Danish Aquavit or vodka,
the whole thing covered with a thick
blanket of whipped cream and served
with piping hot vanilla sauce. Coffee.
To finish, of course, plenty of sodium
bicarbonate tablets, large size, ten
grains each. Orchids on the table at

each place. Candles and orchids make a table solemn! White wine: Chateau Yquem, 1920. Red wine: Mouton Rothschild, 1937. Champagne: Lanson Brut Imperial, 1920. *(To himself)* Begonia's brand! Bad girl! It hurts. *(Shrugs)* Who cares? Life goes on. *(To* LOUIE) That's all. Full stop. Goodbye.

LOUIE *(Bowing)*. Many thanks.

NORRISON. These lengthy expressions of gratitude are superfluous. *(As* LOUIE *goes, to* HARRY) Do you understand you're giving a dinner for your father-in-law?

HARRY. I'll be delighted. A fine meal, indeed.

NORRISON. There's one thing I want to emphasize. Merely to ease my mind, you understand. About your knife. Don't eat peas with your knife.

HARRY. You didn't order any peas.

NORRISON. The main thing . . . that is: the fundamental idea is, don't put your knife in your mouth.

HARRY. Don't worry. I'll watch out. I never cut myself.

NORRISON. Anyway . . . I never take unnecessary chances. Let's see now. What have we overlooked? I think I've taken care of everything. There may be a few trifles. Have you a handkerchief?

HARRY. No.

NORRISON *(Handing him his own)*. Take mine. I don't suppose you've anything in your pockets? *(*HE *empties his pockets quickly)* Here are my cigarette case, lighter, watch, fountain pen and some small change. (HARRY *puts the things away in his pockets)*. And here's a little box of Empirin tablets. I always carry it. It's good for headaches.

HARRY. I never have headaches.

NORRISON. You'll have them now. Sure. Put it in your pocket. (HARRY *obeys)* I think that's all.

(MISS CUNO *enters)*

MISS CUNO *(Impressively)*. Four o'clock! *(She goes)*

NORRISON. My friend, the hour is up. I've done what I set out to do. From now on, this office is yours. *(*HE *points to the chair)* I herewith turn my place over to you. I've not only made you, I've set you in motion. Residence. Clothes. Social position. Title. Name. Automobile. Dinner. Travel. Publicity in papers and magazines. The rest is up to you. In the past you've been a good driver. Let's see you slip your new life into gear and step on the gas. My friend . . . *(Indicating his former chair)* . . . the throne is yours! (HARRY *takes his place and bursts into tears)* Now, what's the matter?

HARRY. I don't know. I only feel so . . . so . . .

NORRISON. So, what?

HARRY. I can't help thinking how my old friends will despise me!

NORRISON. That's understood! You have to choose between old friends and career. No man can have both.

HARRY. I'm sorry for that. My conscience is clear though. I've said all along, I'm only a victim of love.

NORRISON. That's very nicely put. Do you like your throne?

HARRY *(Drying his tears)*. It's a little hard.

NORRISON. It's no taxi. Are your feet more comfortable?

HARRY. I can't complain.

NORRISON. Do you miss your brake and clutch?

HARRY. A little. But I'll learn

to use my head instead of my feet.

NORRISON *(Suddenly shouting).* What's your name?

HARRY *(Fluently, very fast).* San Marino-Schattenburg.

NORRISON. Good. And the firm?

HARRY *(Fluently, very fast).* Universal United Automobile and Motor Factories, Incorporated.

NORRISON. Fine! (HE *hands him a sheet of paper on which he has been making notes throughout)* Be so kind as to sign this.

HARRY. What is it?

NORRISON. A mere trifle. The expenses of your transformation. Which you will, of course, pay back to me. (HE *runs them off with utmost rapidity)* Adoption, five thousand. Shoes, linen, suits, five hundred twenty-three fifty. Wedding ring nine thousand nine hundred. Medical examination one hundred. Mother-in-law flowers fifty-five. Telephone to Cannes, France, sixty-five fifty. Airplane and railroad tickets for five, two thousand nine hundred seventy. Barber, three. Tip, one. Consul-generalship, twenty thousand. Miscellaneous, three thousand. Small change from my pocket I just handed you, two sixty-seven. Total: forty-one thousand six hundred twenty, sixty-seven.

HARRY. From which we deduct . . .

NORRISON. From which we deduct six forty, the amount your taxi meter read and which I owe you. The balance stands, forty-one thousand six hundred fourteen, twenty-seven. You have already given me a cheque for your car. The watch, cigarette case, fountain pen and lighter are my wedding presents. And of course, the headache-tablets. (HE *takes from him the signed paper)* I always keep things on a business basis. *(Handing him a one-dollar bill)* Here you are, that's your tip as taxi driver, one dollar; it's four cents more than fifteen percent of six forty. *(To himself, rapidly, without making a pause)* Begonia hurts more than I thought she could.

(The TELEPHONE *rings.* NORRISON *doesn't budge)*

HARRY. The telephone.

NORRISON. That doesn't concern me. I'm not here any more. This is your office. Pick up the receiver and answer for yourself.

HARRY *(Into the telephone).* Hello. How do you do? This is the office of San Marino . . . (HE *looks at* NORRISON)

NORRISON. Schattenburg.

HARRY *(Into the telephone).* Schattenburg. What can I do for you? (HE *listens. Then covers the mouthpiece with his hand)* Somebody wants to know whether he should buy or sell General Motors on the London Exchange.

NORRISON. What's that to me? You're the one to decide.

HARRY. But I don't know what it's all about!

NORRISON. Don't let that trouble you. It's a great advantage! You'd much better know nothing than a little.

HARRY. *(Shrugging his shoulders. Into the telephone).* Buy. But don't overdo it. (HE *puts down the receiver and looks at* NORRISON)

NORRISON. That's excellent. I should have said the very same myself. And at this moment . . . (HE *looks for his watch but cannot find it)* My watch is . . . Oh yes. Just what time is it by my watch?

HARRY *(Looking)*. Eight minutes after four.

NORRISON. Thank you. I was about to say that at this moment your father- and mother-in-law know all. Can you think of anything else you'd like to have?

HARRY. To be frank with you, I'm a bit shy about these fine people of my wife's. What do I talk about at that dinner I'm giving?

NORRISON. Stick to autos. Motors. Talk about gasoline.

HARRY. Is that enough?

NORRISON. You don't have to worry about those fine people. The conversation of a man of the world is simple enough. You might take some notes, though. (HARRY *obeys)* When the U. N. comes up, say: "Better than nothing."—Russia? "A dangerous experiment."—War? "A possibility, as always."—Professor Einstein? I'd go slow on Einstein if I were you. Say you're just reading him.—Hormones? Sexual life? Say you're too young to bother.—Modern music? Say "Stravinsky, yes and no. —Shostakovitch? "No." The rest: no, too.—Psychoanalysis, Dr. Freud? Say: "Complex." And say that you were never in love with your grandmother.

HARRY *(Protesting)*. I never was.

NORRISON. I suppose so. Just the same, keep saying it. And "Complex! Complex!" — About modern love? Easy come . . ." *(With a doleful sigh)* ". . . easy go."—Business conditions? "Not worse than last year, perhaps better." That's always safe.— Domestic politics?

HARRY *(Unexpectedly, loud, with conviction)*. I am . . .

NORRISON *(Interrupts him, peremptorily)*. With the party in power.

HARRY *(Acquiescing without hesitation)*. Yes, sir.

NORRISON. And in election years . . .

HARRY *(Interrupting, loud, with conviction)*. I am . . .

NORRISON *(Interrupts him, peremptorily)*. Sitting on the fence.

HARRY *(Surrenders meekly)*. Yes, sir.

NORRISON. Be sure you get that one. I can't think of any other subjects that are suitable for a distinguished, conservative man of these days.

HARRY *(Feverishly taking notes)*. Much obliged.

(MISS CUNO *enters)*

MISS CUNO. Ten *after* four.

NORRISON. Thank you. *(To* HARRY *as* SHE *goes)* Why don't you do something?

HARRY. What?

NORRISON. Press a button. You're an executive. Executives press buttons.

(HARRY *presses a button.* MISS SHORTWOOD *enters, a pad and pencil in her hand)*

HARRY. Miss Shortwood, I should like to see my photographs before they go to the papers.

MISS SHORTWOOD. Yes, sir. (SHE *makes a note)*

NORRISON *(Seated; looking and listening as a member of the audience in a theatre)*. A particular young man.

HARRY *(A little uncertain, speaking fast, imitating Norrison, and now and then glancing at him timidly, questioningly).* Further. These two letters are to be delivered at once—I said, *at once*—by a messenger. This one to the Golf Club. This to the Automobile Club. Further. You will ask Mr. Norrison to give you a list of my guests for Wednesday, the sixteenth, at the Hotel Majestic. Further. You will have the invitations engraved and mailed.

NORRISON. Bravo!

HARRY *(Rises, holding out the bottle of Chambertin wine).* Further. Take this bottle, copy the label carefully and, from now on, see that I have a case of this wine on tap in this office. That's all. Thank you. You look charming in that frock. Oil. You may go.

(MISS SHORTWOOD *goes, taking the bottle of wine and the two letters with her)*

NORRISON. Immense. I'm delighted. You can shift into second now. And keep moving.

(PYNNIGAN *enters and is about to speak but* SYLVIA *sweeps in, pushing him aside.* PYNNIGAN *goes.* SYLVIA, *wild with joy, throws herself in* NORRISON's *arms)*

SYLVIA. I'm in Heaven!

NORRISON *(Excitedly).* You've seen your mother? Well, well, my dear?

SYLVIA *(Panting).* They're here!

NORRISON. Well? Well?

SYLVIA. They're delighted! I've just left them at the hotel! Both in the tub! In separate tubs, of course! Mother's so happy! They're only staying this afternoon. They've come only to meet my husband. To embrace and kiss him. They have to go back tonight to Canada. Big business

conference. Next week they'll come here. They send their love to you. You mustn't postpone your holiday, they say. Go and join your family, they say. They're so happy! *(To* HARRY) Come, now, my well-dressed elegant executive and diplomat! Come, my pet! Your new father and mother are waiting for you!

HARRY. In the bathtubs?

SYLVIA. Don't be silly. Come on, come on!

(NORRISON *has rung.* GEORGE *enters)*

NORRISON. The president's coat and hat! (GEORGE *goes hurriedly into the dressing room.* NORRISON *says to* GEORGE:) You don't have to hurry any more. Take it easy.

(GEORGE *returns with the things.* NORRISON *helps* HARRY *into the coat.* HARRY *puts on the yellow gloves which he takes from the pocket of the topcoat. Meanwhile* SYLVIA *speaks)*

SYLVIA. Mother's really enchanted. She says: God bless the House of Norrison, she says. She says her ideal for me had always been a young man of genius who had risen quickly in the world.

NORRISON. We're all right on that last!

(HE *carefully puts the muffler around* HARRY's *neck. Meanwhile* SYLVIA *speaks:)*

SYLVIA. He couldn't have risen more quickly. To accomplish that, anybody but you'd have needed at least a whole day. *(Holding out her finger)* Mother's raving about my ring. She says my husband has good taste.

NORRISON *(Busy with the muffler).* He has.

SYLVIA. And that he's a lavish spender.

NORRISON. He is.

SYLVIA *(Looks at* NORRISON *admiringly).* Now you must tell me why you're rushing us off to Europe . . . Cannes . . . France?

NORRISON *(To* GEORGE*).* Bring in the flowers from the icebox. (GEORGE *goes. To* SYLVIA) Don't you think it's better your people shouldn't see too much of your pet just yet? Hadn't you better wait until he's had a bit more training? *(Meanwhile* GEORGE *has entered with the bouquet of orchids.* NORRISON *takes them and hands them to* HARRY) These are for your dear mother-in-law.

SYLVIA. Orchids! How do you know Mother's crazy about orchids?

NORRISON *(Mysteriously).* Little bird . . .

SYLVIA. Magician! Magician! *(Looks suddenly at* NORRISON *wonderingly, opening her eyes in surprise)* May I . . may I ask you something . . . silly?

NORRISON. Shoot.

SYLVIA. It's no stupid superstition. I've seen in the Opera . . . and I've read in immortal books of great writers . . . that . . . *(Timidly)* . . . that now and then . . .some devils appear among us . . . impersonating human beings . . . and . . . and . . . (SHE *breaks off)*

NORRISON. . . . and that I'm one of them? *(Brief pause. Then* HE *says, with a flash of lightning in his eyes:)* Could be.

SYLVIA. Forgive me, but I said this nonsense only because . . .

NORRISON *(Again a mockingly devilish flash in his eyes).* Is it nonsense?

SYLVIA. Don't frighten me. I said it . . . because I still can't believe all this!

NORRISON *(No more a devil).* No more can I. But so long as the world believes . . . Well, good luck to you, Harry. My best wishes go with you in your new life. Just a few questions, quickly.

HARRY. Shoot.

(The following "duet" very rapidly)

NORRISON. What is it you think about the United Nations?

HARRY. Better than nothing.

NORRISON. Italy?

HARRY. We didn't go into that.

NORRISON. My mistake. Russia?

HARRY. A dangerous experiment.

NORRISAN. War?

HARRY. A possibility.

NORRISON. Einstein?

HARRY. I'm too young to bother.

NORRISON. Wrong. That's hormones.

HARRY. My mistake.—I'm just reading Einstein.

NORRISON. Are you? And hormones? Sex?

HARRY. I'm too young to bother.

NORRISON. Modern music?

HARRY. Stravinsky yes and no.

NORRISON. Shostakovitch?

HARRY. No!

NORRISON. Doctor Freud? Psychoanalysis?

HARRY. Complex.

NORRISON. Grandmother?

HARRY. Never.

NORRISON. Modern love?

HARRY. Begonia. *(He corrects himself)* I'm sorry. Easy come, easy go.

NORRISON. How easy!

HARRY. Not so easy!

NORRISON. Business conditions?

HARRY. Better than last year.

NORRISON. Politics?

HARRY. Party in power.

NORRISON. In election years?

HARRY. Fence.

NORRISON (*To* SYLVIA, *triumphantly*). And there you are.

SYLVIA. An accomplished intellectual! You are a magician! (SHE *presses his hand and stares at him*)

NORRISON. What is it? Why are you staring at me that way?

SYLVIA. I was just thinking I could fall in love with you.

NORRISON (*Horrified*). God forbid! That's all I need! Please don't! (*To himself*) What an indemnity for Begonia though! Ah, well! (HE *shrugs*) Who cares? Life goes on. (*To* SYLVIA *and* HARRY) Run along!

SYLVIA. By all means . . . my child's middle name will be "Norrison."

NORRISON. Thank you. Run along!

SYLVIA. So long! (SHE *starts to go. Suddenly* SHE *stops for a moment. Laughing*) When I think how frightened we were an hour ago!

HARRY. I wasn't.

SYLVIA. I knew you weren't, you conceited, impudent seducer of inexperienced young girls! Come on! (SHE *hurries out into the Outer Hall.* HARRY *follows her*)

HARRY (*As he goes*). I say, Norrison! Take care of anything that comes up while I'm gone.

NORRISON. At your service, sir! Slide into high!

HARRY. Toodle-loo! (HE *starts to go*)

NORRISON. Just a minute. One thing more. You've forgotten . . .

HARRY (*In the door*). Yes?

NORRISON. To thank me.

HARRY. What for?

NORRISON. Well, for what I've done!

HARRY (*Quickly, casually*). Oh, right! Thanks! (HE *runs out*)

NORRISON (*After Harry goes out*). You're quite welcome. (*Left alone;* HE *rings*) Wonderful! Open her wide open! A hundred miles an hour! That's what I call tempo! (*To the entering* PYNNIGAN) The general alarm is over. Business as usual!

(MISS CUNO *enters*)

MISS CUNO. Twenty after four.

NORRISON. Miss Cuno, you needn't tell me the time any longer. Everybody can go home. Many thanks for your invaluable assistance. My warmest regards to your mother. And tell her to be sure not to go out in this cold weather. Not until her left ear's entirely healed.

MISS CUNO (*Almost in tears*). You really are the kindest man in the world. (SHE *goes out*)

PYNNIGAN. Your train leaves in eleven minutes, sir.

(GEORGE *enters with Norrison's fur-lined coat and hat*)

NORRISON. Thanks. Thanks.

(GEORGE *goes out. Misses* NORMAN, MARLIN *and* PETROVITCH *enter from the Secretary's Office, dressed for the street, with hats on, bowing to* NORRISON, *cross the stage, starting to go out through the Outer Hall.*)

NORRISON (*As they cross the stage,* HE *puts on his fur coat and hat,* PYNNIGAN *helping him, and speaks to the girls*). Thank you, Miss Marlin.—I hope you enjoy the Opera tonight, Miss Norman.—Miss Petrovitch, will you tell your ornamental but unreliable fiancé Mr. Kristian to report to me here on the morning of the sixteenth at eleven-thirty? Pynnigan, you might make a note of that. (PYNNIGAN *makes a note, as* NORRISON *continues, to* MISS PETROVITCH) Let him know I'm thinking of promoting him. He'll get twenty percent rise in salary and instead of the title Press Agent I'll confer on him the title of Public Relations Director. But raise and title only if he marries you. No marriage, no promotion. Don't thank me. It's nothing but oil. You may go, ladies. Goodbye. (*The* THREE GIRLS *go out into the Outer Hall*) Well, Pynnigan . . . (HE *pulls on his gloves slowly, comfortably*) I think we've cleaned up everything. What a terrible strain this banking business is! One needs a holiday. One has everything packed and ready, then, bang, some trifle comes up and detains one. Because of the stupid prejudices of a snobbish family I might have missed my train. (*As* PYNNIGAN *opens his mouth*) You have something to say, Pynnigan?

PYNNIGAN (*Humble*). I think you can be proud, sir. It must be very wonderful, sir, to be as you are and have *almost* all mankind at your disposal.

NORRISON (*Very simply*). You're quite right, Pynnigan. You're quite right. I can be proud and I am, too. But as regards mankind, my dear Pynnigan . . . after what was just done here . . . I think, mankind—or as you so carefully put it—*almost* all mankind . . . should damn well be ashamed of itself. Well, God bless you, Pynnigan. So long.

(HE *goes out quickly through the Outer Hall*)

CURTAIN

WAXWORKS

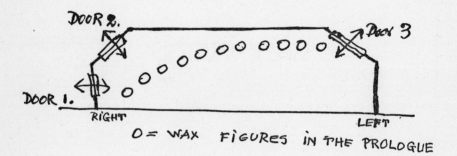

DOOR 2.

DOOR 3

DOOR 1.

RIGHT

LEFT

O = WAX FIGURES IN THE PROLOGUE

SCENE DESIGN
"WAXWORKS"

WAXWORKS

FANTASY-FARCE IN PROLOGUE AND TWO ACTS

CHARACTERS OF THE PROLOGUE

THE MANAGER OF THE WAX MUSEUM

ELEVEN FIGURES.—*(The eleven actors of the play, who, with appropriate makeup and lighting, represent motionless wax figures.)*

A GROUP OF VISITORS.

> PLACE : A ROOM IN A WAX MUSEUM, REPRESENTING A RICH BAROQUE STYLE DRAWING ROOM.
>
> TIME : THE PRESENT.

CHARACTERS OF THE TWO ACTS

PRINCE RUDOLF	GENERAL DUBETZ
KRON-LEITHEN	DR. BLOCK
PRINCESS ANN	BARON ARIBERT
PRINCESS CLEMENTINE	DIEGELMANN
COUNTESS SOPHIE	FRENCH AMBASSADOR
ROBERT THOMAS	LOUISE

TWO LACKEYS (silent parts)

> PLACE : AUSTRO-HUNGARIAN EMBASSY IN ROME. *Act One:* THE SAME DRAWING ROOM AS IN THE PROLOGUE. EVENING. *Act Two:* SAME. A FEW HOURS LATER.
>
> TIME : ABOUT THE TURN OF OUR CENTURY.

(New acting version of the same author's PANOPTIKUM produced at the AKADEMIETHEATER in Vienna with ALMA SEIDLER *in the leading role; at the* KLEINES THEATER *in Frankfort with* BRIGITTE KOENIG, *at the* KAMMERSPIELE *in Cologne (Germany) with* IRMGARD FOERST, *at the* KAMMERSPIELE *in Hamburg with* HILDE KRAHL.—*English text by* ARTHUR RICHMAN.)

DESCRIPTION OF CHARACTERS AND COSTUME PLOT

PRINCE KRON-LEITHEN—50, Ambassador of Austria-Hungary in Rome. He is wearing his diplomatic dress uniform, a gold embroidered frock coat, with a number of orders, etc.

PRINCESS ANN—32-35 years old. The Princess is the Ambassador's wife, and a distant relative to the Emperor. She is dressed in a formal evening frock, following the fashions of the period, with a diadem representing the eleven-pronged ducal crown on her head.

PRINCESS CLEMENTINE—55, mother of Ann. Similar costume.

COUNTESS SOPHIE—40, cousin to Ann. Similar costume, except that she wears a nine-pronged diadem.

ROBERT THOMAS—35, an architect—Tails and white tie.

GENERAL DUBETZ—50, military attaché at the Embassy, in the dress uniform of an Austrian general: Sky-blue coat with gold collar and gold buttons, black trousers with two wide scarlet stripes running down the side. Rows of decorations, etc.

BARON ARIBERT—30, secretary at the Embassy, in the diplomatic dress uniform of his office.

DR. BLOCK—About 50, a famous Viennese lawyer; tails and white tie.

DIEGELMANN—About 50, the Ambassador's butler, a good-looking man, in the gala uniform of the head lackey, gold embroidered colored frock coat, silk knee length trousers, hose, and low cut pumps with a silver buckle.

FRENCH AMBASSADOR—About 60. Diplomatic dress uniform of an Ambassador.

LOUISE—Ann's French maid, dressed in the fashionable maid's uniform of the period, white cap, white lace apron, black dress, black shoes and black stockings.

TO THE DIRECTOR

I.

This play not only satirizes conceited, haughty and hypocritical European aristocrats of its period, but it also is intended to deride those drawing-room plays which fawningly glorified these people as a higher type of human beings—as demigods—throughout half a century.

Therefore this play must be enacted as a discreet *parody* of those old-fashioned elegant drawing-room plays,—in which haughty princes, marquises, counts and their ladies behaved with affectation of superiority and spoke an artificial, elaborately sublime language.

The author's intention is clearly discernible at first reading from the language of the characters and from their ceremonious and ridiculously solemn behavior.

The task of the Director will be made easier if he agrees with the author that the persons of this play are not to be considered human beings, but rather caricatures of human beings. The Director should think of the line from the Prologue in which the Manager says that these people "were wax figures even in their own lifetime."

II.

ANN'S part.

Strange as it may seem, in reading the part of Ann, you are not to believe the words and lines, but to see behind them constantly a woman torn by a guilty sensual passion.

The role is that of *an Olympian goddess, who suffers because she is tormented by shame over falling in love like any mortal woman.* She hides her suffering beneath her cold manner, her silly theories, and her consistent perversion of the truth.

If by sheer acting, inflections and mimicry Ann's impersonator can make the audience aware of the *suffering goddess* behind her absurdly solemn statements, her exaggerated coldness, her ridiculous confessions and occasional outbursts of frankness, then she will be moving as well as comical.

Ann's figure is only comical in the script. On the stage, a hidden suffering should be felt beneath her comedy-lines, without, however, sacrificing any comical effect.

WAXWORKS

PROLOGUE

SCENE: *Room in a wax museum, arranged to represent an aristocratic drawing room of the first decade of our century.*

The room is done in Viennese baroque style. Three doors open off the stage. A few pieces of furniture stand against the walls. A large, gilded sofa, upholstered in red brocade, stands against the rear wall. Matching armchairs and tabourets. A few portraits in gilded frames, among them a big one of Emperor Franz Joseph.

AT RISE: *We see eleven wax figures in a semi-circle across the stage. The room is in semi-darkness, relieved only by the mysterious glitter of gilded frames and furniture. A light falls on the figures. A gramophone outside softly plays Beethoven's Minuet in G.*

Enter by door 3 the MANAGER *followed by a group of* VISITORS. *The latter are dressed in current fashions. Some finger catalogues. The* MANAGER *heads the group, showing off his treasures.*

MANAGER. Ladies and gentlemen, this is Exhibit 9 of our international waxworks. It's the Viennese room and it goes back to the days of Austrian Imperial glory. A lost world, ladies and gentlemen. The people you see before you were famous because of a scandal they were involved in. A mixture of love and diplomacy, that's what you might call it. If you turn to Page 16 of your catalogues, you will find a summary of the scandal. It was a sensation of its day, blazoned in every newspaper of the world. It's forgotten now. It's disappeared from the memory of man, and if it weren't for the story in the catalogue there wouldn't be a single reminder left. As a matter of fact, I'd have thrown this obsolete gang out of my museum long ago if it weren't that they're so typical of their period—such excellent representatives of it—and if there weren't a lot of people today who are interested in this period and this kind of tinselly diplomatic crew which is responsible for a lot of the things that have happened since—and still happen—and which I'd rather not talk about now. *(Points out various figures)* This one is Prince Kron, head of the house, Ambassador, an over-ambitious diplomat whose career was ruined by his wife's peculiar love-affair.—This haughty beauty is his wife, Princess Ann, cold and merciless, a relative of the Emperor.—That one's Princess Clementine, mother of the beautiful Ann.—This lady here is their cousin, Countess Sophie von Witz.—Everyone absolutely lifelike. *(Tapping the heads of the figures)* Made of the best materials. Big as life and twice as natural—not only because the sculptor was clever, but because they were wax figures in their own lifetime. As in all our rooms, the celebrities are shown in their intimate surroundings. *(Continues introductions)* The French Ambassador, one of their enemies.—General Dubetz. He knew more about intrigue than he did about strategy. The one over there is the Ambassador's loyal secretary, Baron Aribert.—This one is Dr. Block, one of the attorneys to the Imperial family. *(Passing*

Thomas, he points to the Butler and Louise) That's their butler. —This is the French maid of the Princess. *(Pointing to Thomas)* I left this figure for the last—purposely. He's Mr. Thomas, a fashionable architect of his day. Ladies, I suggest that you study this gentleman carefully, because he was the hero of the love-affair. He was what is called a romantic. He loved passionately and he was passionately loved. (LADIES *rush about the figure, as* MANAGER *points out the walls of the room to the others)* This is a typical drawing-room in the baroque style. It was in rooms like this that these people lived their exclusive social life, most of the time to the sound of music. They adored music. Sweet strains accompanied their gossip, their scandals, their love-affairs, their politics . . . all to the tunes of the great Viennese composers. That's why I had the phonograph play Beethoven's "Minuet in G" just now. *(Sighs)* Well, I guess they had a better time than we. They lived in the frivolous childhood of our terrible century. But if anybody thinks this a Golden Age, he must be an awful fool! *(Heads for another door)* (1) Now then, ladies and gentlemen, we come to Exhibit 10. (HE *goes out door 1. The group follows him. All go out. Music fades. At the same time lights grow dim, until the stage is left completely dark.)*

CURTAIN

ACT ONE

SCENE: *The same room without the waxworks.*

AT RISE: *The stage is deserted and completely dark as the curtain rises. Slowly the chandelier and the room grow light. A few seconds pass, then door 1 opens and* DR. BLOCK *comes in, carrying a briefcase, followed by the* BUTLER. *During the first few moments the Characters move a little stiffly, reminding the audience that they were wax figures just before.*

BUTLER. Won't you sit down, sir? You're expected. Her Serene Highness commanded me to announce you as soon as you arrived. *(Watches* BLOCK *vigorously shaking his arms and legs)* Is it cold outside, sir?

BLOCK. I feel positively rigid. *(Shakes his legs)* It takes a long time to snap back. It would seem that I've been standing still too long.

BUTLER. It's odd, sir, my legs feel rather stiff, too. *(Shakes his legs)* It would appear that this climate gives me rheumatism.

(Exit door 3. BLOCK *takes papers from his briefcase.—Enter* SOPHIE, *door 2)*

BLOCK. Good evening, Countess Sophie.

SOPHIE. I have told you repeatedly I am not Sophie to you. "Your Grace," if you please. No first name intimacy with lawyers—not even if they happen to be counsellors to the Imperial family. How-ever . . . good evening, Dr. Block. Her Serene Highness will be here shortly. She is dressing at the moment. We're going to a gala performance at the Opera in a little while. There will be a reception here at the Embassy afterward. His Majesty, the King of Italy is to honor us with his presence. *(Sits)* How are you?

BLOCK. Very well, thank you.

SOPHIE. That's too bad.

(Brief silence)

BLOCK. May I sit down?

SOPHIE. I have no right to prevent you.

BLOCK. Thank you very much. *(Sits)* It certainly feels *good* to sit down for a change.

SOPHIE. *You* have that feeling? Strange, but I too find sitting a pleasure today. *(After a short pause)* I am not pleased to see you here.

BLOCK. So I've observed.

SOPHIE. Any time you show up, there's sure to be trouble.

BLOCK. Should we not say, instead, that any time there's trouble, I'm sure to show up? At any rate I have come in response to an urgent summons, not of my own accord. How is the Princess bearing up in the crisis, may I ask?

SOPHIE. Majestically. Cousin Ann is a wonderful woman. Sometimes I feel as if she were a statue—not human at all. A monument to herself.

BLOCK. And her husband, the Ambassador?

SOPHIE. His Highness, the Prince, is a typical diplomat. Like a telescope, he can see things only at a distance. He'll tell you what His Imperial Majesty the Czar of Russia is planning in St. Petersburg. But he doesn't know what his wife's thinking in the room next to his. *(Sighs)* I fear we're facing a difficult situation, Dr. Block.

(PRINCESS ANN comes in by door 3. She is a majestic, royal looking woman, haughty, cold, steadily unsmiling, and rather too solemn in conversation. The goddess-like manner with which she conducts herself verges, actually, on burlesque; but she has more brains than the people of her suite)

(The BUTLER follows ANN with a tea wagon, which he prepares during the following)

ANN *(Cold and unsmiling)*. Good evening, Dr. Block. Welcome to Rome.

BLOCK *(Bowing low)*. Your humble servant, Your Highness.

ANN. I am glad you came so promptly. How are you?

BLOCK. Very well, thank you.

ANN *(Still unsmiling, icily)*. Good. You made an exceptionally quick trip from Vienna to Rome. I think I may say without exaggeration that, as regards reliability, you are a paragon among lawyers. Please be seated.

BLOCK *(Sits)*. Sure feels good.

ANN *(Sitting at the same time; she too leans back, enjoying the comfort of her armchair)*. This *is* nice!

BLOCK. I dashed back to Rome, as you say, Your Highness. I never lose a moment where Your Highness' affairs are concerned.

ANN. Are you attending the gala at the Opera tonight?

BLOCK. Yes, Your Highness. *(Exit BUTLER)*

ANN. I hope you will come to our party afterward. *(BLOCK bows)* Counsellor, this is a great day in my life. His Majesty the King of Italy and Her Majesty the Queen are coming to take tea with us after the Opera. It is the first time I have had the honor of entertaining a King and Queen in my home. I should be excited tonight—if I were at all capable of excitement. But—we haven't much time. We must get to the point of your visit.

BLOCK *(Takes out his papers).* It is always a privilege to serve Your Highness. I am only grieved that my services this time must be directed toward a crisis in your married life.

ANN. Nothing ever grieves a lawyer, Dr. Block, except having nothing to do. As for the crisis in my married life, don't let that grieve you either. I sent for you in order that we might solve it together—smoothly, without scandal, and in accordance with the highest ethical standards, as well as the most exacting demands of our exalted position. The traditions of centuries have raised us above the multitude. We must act accordingly. I would not say as demigods—but nearly so. *(Reaches for the teapot)* Tea?

BLOCK. Might I have a brandy instead?

ANN. No.

(Awkward silence. All three are busy with their tea?)

*(*PRINCESS CLEMENTINE, *Ann's mother, comes in by door 3. She is a forceful woman in her middle fifties, statuesque, as unsmiling as her daughter, but given to sarcasm and sharp words in contrast to Ann's solemnity)*

ANN. Mamma . . . *(All rise)*

CLEMENTINE. Sit down. I don't like to see women stand up when I enter a room. (SOPHIE *and* ANN *sit.* BLOCK *remains standing)*

BLOCK *(Bowing low).* Your very humble servant, Highness.

CLEMENTINE *(Sitting).* Mmmm . . . Aren't these chairs comfortable! —Have you begun your conference?

ANN. Mother . . . Dr. Block was paying his respects.

CLEMENTINE. I heard him.— Have you begun your conference? (BLOCK *sits)*

ANN. Not yet. I didn't want to begin without you. *(To* BLOCK) Mamma has been here for the past three days. She would have gone back to Vienna yesterday, but she insisted on remaining until you came so that she might be present when, in a few minutes, as I intend, I formally announce to my husband, in the presence of my lawyer, that my innermost feminine desires have become fixed on another man. Among ordinary people such delicate confessions are made in private—at the dining table, or sometimes, as I've been told, in bed. Our exalted position, however, demands a conference, and that's why I've asked you three to be present.

BLOCK. The Prince will be distressed by the confession.

CLEMENTINE. That's what I expect to enjoy the most.

BLOCK. Enjoy?

CLEMENTINE. Don't gape at me as if I were a sadist, Dr. Block. You know as well as anybody that I fought against this marriage—tooth and nail —as only a mother can fight. It was in vain. The Emperor's command settled it and my superb daughter had to marry that long-faced simpleton. For ten long years I have been a conquered general, laughed at in my defeat. For ten years I have been waiting for the revenge which will come tonight. It's my turn to laugh now! *And* to enjoy myself. Then, I'm going home to Vienna.

ANN. That isn't how the Emperor's command affected me, Dr. Block. As you will recall, the Ambassador had done the Emperor an important political service in the Balkans shortly before our marriage. The Ambassador wanted me desperately. I didn't want him at all. Other girls might have been unhappy in such a situation, but I was not.

BLOCK. No, Your Highness?

ANN. No. I was happy because I was permitted to make a sacrifice for the Emperor and for Austria.

CLEMENTINE. We've all made sacrifices. I once paid the gambling debt of His Majesty's nephew, in Monte Carlo.

ANN. I'm ready to make any sacrifice for the Emperor. I'd commit a crime for his sake if need be. Even murder, if it helped. (BLOCK *instinctively shrinks back in his chair. Then he clears his throat*)

BLOCK. Where is the Ambassador now?

ANN. The Ambassador? *(She listens and looks up to the ceiling)* My husband is upstairs in his bedroom, dressing to the strains of classical music. The magnificent uniform he wears to galas always stirs him.

BLOCK. No wonder the Ambassador is stirred. It must be a moving thing to know that you represent sixty-five million people.

ANN. He represents no people. He represents the Emperor. That's what moves him. *(Listening again)* He is still in his underwear, that's the reason his phonograph is playing that delicate Mozart. The moment he puts on the gold embroidered frock coat with the orders, the butler has to put on the record with the Imperial Anthem. That's when he experiences his loftiest political flights of fancy.

CLEMENTINE. That's when he ought to be shot.

ANN *(Unmoved)*. Mamma always favors simple solutions.

BLOCK. The Ambassador is a noble spirit. What finer purpose would a man have in life than to work for the return of the monarchy in France with an Austrian Archduchess as Queen? Austria may justly be proud of such a diplomat. How is His Highness' health?

ANN. Excellent as yet. But I fear it won't be, an hour from now.

CLEMENTINE. And I'll be feeling fine.

ANN *(Unmoved)*. Isn't it sad that sometimes the price of our happiness is the misfortune of others? Poor Rudolf. He suspects nothing. What's the news in Vienna?

BLOCK. One good operetta and a very dull melodrama. The cooking is the same as ever and the stock exchange is firm as a rock.

ANN. And how is His Majesty the Emperor?

BLOCK. His Majesty is in splendid form. Past seventy, he looks as fresh and well as the day that portrait was painted. He's been having dinner with his old sweetheart every evening lately. After dinner His Majesty puts on his spectacles and reads aloud to her the detailed monthly report of the Imperial Government's receipts and expenses. The lady accompanies the reading with little giggles and squeals of delight in order to lead the servants who are listening at the door into more interesting paths of conjecture. His Majesty doesn't like it, but the old girl insists. She thinks it's good publicity for them both.

ANN *(Icily)*. I allowed you to finish that abominable recital only because I wished to gain some idea of the abysmal disrespect to which our middle class has fallen. I forbid you ever again to attempt to entertain me with such a story. *(Presses a button)*

BLOCK. Some people think they can't be amusing unless they're tactless. I'm one of them. I beg your pardon.

CLEMENTINE. Not many people are as impertinent as Dr. Block. But I'll forgive him anything tonight.

SOPHIE. I won't. (BUTLER *comes in*)

ANN *(To* BLOCK). Is everything in order for the conference?

BLOCK. Yes, Your Highness.

ANN. In which case, let us begin at once. *(To the Butler)* Diegelmann, we're leaving for the Opera in an hour. No matter who telephones before that, we're out. That applies to visitors also—all except Mr. Robert Thomas, who will be here at 6:30. Announce him the moment he arrives. And see that no one disturbs us.

BUTLER. Very well, Your Highness. *(Exit)*

ANN. All I told my husband was that we were having a conference and that he'd be invited later. He'll learn the rest when he comes. And now . . . you have the floor, Dr. Block.

BLOCK. I shall sum up the situation and my proposals briefly—perhaps a little cruelly.

ANN. I knew I could depend on you, Dr. Block. *(To Sophie)* Why are you fidgeting?

SOPHIE. I want to sit where I don't have to look at Dr. Block.

BLOCK. May I suggest that you stay where you are, Countess, and merely turn your head?

SOPHIE. That's too tiring.

BLOCK. We must pay for our pleasures.

SOPHIE. Evidently.

ANN *(Coldly)*. Proceed, Dr. Block.

BLOCK. Very well. First of all, let us state the facts of the case. *(Takes out his cigarette-case)* May I smoke?

ANN. No.

BLOCK *(Slips back cigarette-case in his pocket)*. Coming back to the facts—Your Highness, as we know, is in love . . .

ANN *(Stiffly)*. Exclude that word from our conference, Dr. Block. I despise it. My condition isn't love, it's an illness.

BLOCK. The symptoms being . . .

ANN. First . . . insomnia. And . . . I am without an appetite. I have palpitations and crying spells. The condition has existed for several months and throughout the time certain base thoughts which society as well as religion forbid to a married woman have focused uninterruptedly on one man. If by chance I don't see the man for any length of time— please make a note of that—if I don't see him for any length of time, I have sharp pains in my stomach because, it appears, suppressed desires, in my case, cause an overproduction of gastric juice. *(Waves Block away)* Don't tell me to take bicarbonate. I've been taking it steadily, but it has no effect where that man is concerned. If it had, you wouldn't be here. Then there are circulatory disturbances too. The first two months I knew him, my pulse went up to 120 every time he came in that door. The last month it's been up to 125, and it's been irregular all along. From the first day of our acquaintance there has seemed to be a mysterious connection between my eyes and my throat. Whenever the man looks at me, the throat dries up so that the tongue sticks to the palate. Moreover not only do my hands and knees tremble but my nostrils quiver, which is most embarassing because everyone can see it. And all my physical sufferings are aggravated by the realization that the man in question is not my husband.

CLEMENTINE. Poor dear. Why don't you send for a doctor?

ANN. If it were my husband who had this effect on me, I would. But since it's not my husband, I've sent for a lawyer.

CLEMENTINE. Good for you!

SOPHIE. I'm so sorry, darling. *(Brushes tears from her eyes)*

ANN *(Coldly, rigidly)*. The disturbances have increased in violence. I can't endure it any longer. But don't cry, Cousin Sophie. This disease is not without a remedy.

CLEMENTINE. It's been known for ages. The treatment is simple, and—if my memory serves—not unpleasant at all.

ANN *(Icily)*. Continue, Dr. Block.

BLOCK. As a lawyer, I have to stick to facts as I see them. Your Highness is in love. And, as you made clear, not with your husband, but . . . *(Glancing at his notes)* with one Mr. Robert Thomas, an architect who has been remodeling your apartment these past three months. I stress three months purposely because, according to expert opinion in my possession, the aforementioned apartment could easily have been remodeled in three weeks. That is to say: Mr. Thomas is more than nine weeks late. And more and more people are coming to the conclusion that the cause of this delay is Mr. Thomas' . . . illness.

ANN. Mr. Thomas is not ill. *He is* in love.

BLOCK. I wouldn't presume to use that word after your previous correction.

ANN. You may use it in speaking of Mr. Thomas. He is a normal man. People differ, Dr. Block. Callous lawyers don't know that, but kind doctors do. As long as I've been able to think at all I've had a horror of everything that might be construed as the romanticizing of sex—an inclination which our Viennese music disgracefully promotes. I hate the inclination and consequently I have a right to call my plight an illness. But Mr. Thomas, who didn't grow up in the chilly atmosphere of Catholic royalty, as I did, but in the sinfully erotic air of Paris and Vienna—Mr. Thomas is not ill. He's in love, poor boy. Continue, Dr. Block.

BLOCK. At any rate—the fact is that as a result of the whole thing, your position has become untenable—

ANN. True.

BLOCK. —and as the loyal counsellor to Your Highness for the past 120 years—which of course includes my ancestors—as your friend, may I say?

(Slight pause)

SOPHIE. I observe that Her Highness did not say yes.

BLOCK. In the sole capacity of Your Highness' lawyer, then; I have been asked to propose a way out of this dilemma.

ANN *(Solemnly)*. A solution

which will preclude gossip and any suggestion of scandal.

CLEMENTINE. We mustn't have a scandal.

BLOCK. Exactly. I therefore propose a divorce. In the shortest possible time.

CLEMENTINE. I'd kiss you, Dr. Block, if you weren't so unattractive.

BLOCK. Divorce is the only solution.

ANN. Cousin Sophie?

SOPHIE. It's not the only one.

ANN. Not? What other is there?

SOPHIE. There is another way to remove your trouble.

ANN. What is it?

SOPHIE. The Almighty forgive those that . . . sin for love.

ANN. I forbid you to apply conclusions regarding the Almighty's habits to me. (To BLOCK) Continue.

BLOCK. Your exalted rank, as well as the position of your husband, permit of no solution but divorce. Your husband is an Ambassador—not in a gay light-hearted city like Paris either, but in Rome where the Vatican and the Royal Family are sensitive about those things. You are related—however distantly—to His Majesty our Emperor. Both you and your husband, up to now, have observed the highest social and moral standards. The Court of Rome and the Church of Rome have hailed your marriage as exemplary. Now, you are a person who cannot pretend, one who is unable to hide her feelings. We can't afford to have Her Majesty the Queen of Italy remark that your throat is dry, that your nostrils are trembling every time you speak to Mr. Thomas at a Court reception. It happens, unfortunately, that these phenomena have not gone entirely unnoticed even in the past. Princes, generals, and cardinals—particularly cardinals—have already remarked them. That's what you might really call the beginning of a . . . (Breaks off)

ANN. I'm afraid you want to use the word "scandal."

BLOCK. You guessed it, Your Highness.

SOPHIE. He growls like a watchdog.

ANN. That's what we pay him for. (To BLOCK) So far I agree with you, Dr. Block. We must learn the lesson which the exploit of the Belgian Princess taught us—the one who recently eloped with a gypsy bandleader and thereby forfeited the respect of the lower classes for the morals of the aristocracy for the next hundred years.

CLEMENTINE. Not to mention the Queen of Saxony and her handsome Italian music master. Horrible!

BLOCK. Quite. Therefore you must not only get a divorce, but you must marry Mr. Robert Thomas at once.

CLEMENTINE. I'm afraid I'll have to kiss the man after all.

BLOCK. It is the only pure solution, complete and free from scandal.

ANN. You agree, Cousin Sophie?

SOPHIE. No. He's wrong.

ANN. So . . . I agree with *you*, Dr. Block. The proposal you advance offers the only ethical remedy for my illness. I must not encourage gossip. The Emperor's watchful eye—to say nothing of my own standards—restrains me. I must be perfect—no matter how it hurts my husband.

BLOCK. The Ambassador will be equal to the occasion. He is a man of lofty spirit.

CLEMENTINE. He's a fool and you're a bootlicker.

BLOCK. He will behave correctly.

CLEMENTINE. He'll behave like a simpleton, but that's exactly what the Emperor expects of a diplomat of his rank.

ANN. His attitude toward Thomas will be perfect. He likes Thomas and appreciates him.

SOPHIE. Why don't you come right out and say that your husband will be proud of his successor?

ANN. This is no time for sarcasm, Cousin Sophie. This is a serious moment.

SOPHIE. It needn't be.

ANN. Don't criticize, Cousin Sophie. You know I never come to a decision without first getting your advice. Because I always do the opposite of what you say.

BLOCK. And what have you decided, Your Highness?

ANN (*Coldly, rigidly*). To divorce my husband, and to marry Mr. Thomas. Without any publicity.

BLOCK. And your orders for me?

ANN. To obtain the Papal dispensation in an amazingly short time. How long will you require?

BLOCK. I have prepared everything. A notary will be here for the necessary signatures at 6:45.

ANN. You're a wizard. In the Middle Ages a man like you would have been . . .

SOPHIE. Burned at the stake.

CLEMENTINE (*To* BLOCK). I'm definitely opposed to your being burned. But on second thought I shan't kiss you. I appoint you and your descendants to be our lawyers for another 120 years.

BLOCK. Your Highness' kindness overwhelms me.

ANN. You haven't answered my question. How long will it be before we're married?

BLOCK. Considering Your Highness' connections and my unusual ability, two weeks should see it through.

(ANN *sighs*)

BLOCK. Is that too long?

ANN (*Casting her eyes down, shamefacedly*). Yes.

CLEMENTINE. Poor child.

ANN. Dear Mamma. (*To* BLOCK) Is there anything else we ought to discuss?

BLOCK. Nothing that I can think of.

ANN (*To* SOPHIE). Do you suppose we ought to call my husband now? What do you say?

SOPHIE. Not yet.

ANN (*Picks up receiver*). Will you ask my husband to come here? (*Puts down receiver*) This is the great moment! Strange, isn't it, Dr. Block—my hands aren't shaking, my lips aren't trembling, and my knees aren't quaking. All I feel is curiosity —as to how my husband will accept the new situation.

BLOCK. The Ambassador is a man of lofty spirit. His love of Beethoven shows that.

CLEMENTINE. He loves Beethoven, but Beethoven loathes him.

BLOCK. How can Your Highness tell *that*?

CLEMENTINE. I can't prove it. But it's impossible that he shouldn't.

(*Enter the* AMBASSADOR, PRINCE KRON)

KRON (*Formally, to* ANN). My secretary informs me that you command my presence here.

BLOCK. (*Bows*). My profound greetings, Your Highness.

KRON. Good evening, Dr. Block. *(Shakes hands)* Is this a conspiracy?

ANN. Yes.

KRON. Not against me, I hope?

ANN. Unfortunately, Rudolf, it is against you.

KRON *(Indifferent)*. Interesting.

ANN. Please sit down.

KRON. Thank you.

(Sits, obviously enjoying the comfort of the chair. Brief silence)

(To ANN*)*

To judge by your mother's beaming countenance, I'm in for an uncomfortable quarter of an hour.

CLEMENTINE. At last an Ambassador whose prediction will come true!

KRON *(To Ann)*. Well?

ANN *(Solemnly)*. Rudolf, I wish to make an announcement in the presence of witnesses.

KRON. Please do.

ANN *(Icily)*. Rudolf, I crave another man's embrace.

(Brief pause)

KRON *(Not at all upset; very politely)*. Who is the man, may I ask?

ANN. Mr. Thomas, our architect.

KRON. Thank you.

ANN. What for?

KRON. The information. Quite interesting and probably reliable.

ANN. Mr. Thomas loves me.

CLEMENTINE *(With obvious enjoyment)*. They adore each other.

KRON. That too is information, but it is neither interesting nor reliable.

ANN. This is no time to quibble, Rudolf. Let me go on with my announcement. Rudolf, we must be divorced.

KRON *(Quietly)*. Yes, Ann.

ANN. You say that very lightly.

KRON. If you tell me we must be divorced, I'm absolutely certain you're right. I wouldn't think of contradicting you. You know all about human problems. I am concerned with the conflicts of nations. With the struggles of continents. Individuals hold no interest for me. My own private life doesn't interest me either. You are a human being. I am a politician.

ANN *(Icily)*. I don't consider myself entirely human.

KRON. But more human than I.

ANN. That will always be a moot question between us, Rudolf. Nevertheless, I am impressed by the immensity of your horizon.

KRON. Very kind of you, Ann. Is there anything else you wish to tell me?

ANN. There is. I think you're entitled to an explanation. You should know how I've always despised the Viennese tendency to glorify carnal instincts in song and poetry.

KRON. Oh, quite—I know best how you feel about that.

ANN. So . . . I shall not offer you any sentimental twaddle, but a medical diagnosis instead. Rudolf, I am seriously ill with an extraordinary, stubborn and constantly increasing desire.

KRON. I'm sorry for you, Ann.

ANN. This isn't romance, but the unexpected rebellion of the flesh against my high conception of life. Forgive me, Rudolf, but this is one time when a pure soul like myself must carry honesty with you to the point of being brutal.

CLEMENTINE. Why not beyond it?

KRON. Mr. Thomas merits our every consideration. He's a good architect.

ANN. And—?

KRON. And a gentleman. He's an ardent patriot, besides, devoted heart and soul to the Emperor.

ANN. I rejoice to hear you say that. I wouldn't have given him a second glance if he weren't.

KRON. But he is.

ANN. He is!

KRON. To such a degree that the Emperor has awarded him the order of Franz Joseph on my recommendation. The confirmation came today, by the morning mail.

ANN. That's wonderful news, Rudolf! It will inspire him not only to love the Emperor even more but to perform brilliant services for the State. I've noticed he has a real gift for politics.

KRON. What a wonderful woman you are—whose chief concern even in love is to serve the Empire.

ANN. My second religion.

KRON *(Very formally)*. I am more than pleased to be the bearer of good news.

ANN. And I thank you, Rudolf. You may speak now, Dr. Block.

BLOCK. Well— The present situation is untenable. Therefore, at Her Highness' command, I am about to take steps toward obtaining a Papal dispensation for divorce.

ANN. It will be easier since we have no children—though many times I authorized Rudolf to take the steps necessary to remedy the lack. *(With a look at her husband)* I have always been dominated by Napoleon's principle—a thing is only done well if one does it alone. But unfortunately the principle cannot be

applied to this. Continue, Dr. Block.

BLOCK. I will try to secure immediately the papers necessary for the wedding.

KRON. What wedding?

ANN. Naturally I intend to marry Mr. Thomas. *(Brief silence)* I seem to sense that you are somewhat touched by this—or am I mistaken?

KRON. Your decision is an honest one, so no objection can be lodged against it. But it wouldn't be natural for a person to hear the announcement—and not bat an eyelash—that his wife would soon be on terms of intimacy with another man.

ANN. As *his* lawful wife. With the consent and blessing of the Church.

KRON. But in the same bed. You have to expect some reaction to that even from an Ambassador.

SOPHIE. An Ambassador is a man too.

KRON. An Ambassador is not a man, Sophie. An Ambassador is a political principle in operation.

BLOCK. What a deep but bitter thought.

KRON. An operating principle, but unfortunately clothed in flesh. When I batted an eyelash a moment ago, it was the reaction of my flesh to a fleeting image—the image of my wife, unclad, in the arms of a patriotic architect.

ANN *(Icily)*. You are suffering, Rudolf.

KRON. How can I suffer since this image means your happiness? I don't suffer. I only react.

ANN. My conscience is clear. I've done everything I could to be cured of this dreadful illness. I even consulted a doctor.

KRON. I didn't know that.

ANN. Now I can tell it. I resorted to a new mode of medical treatment. I went to a psychoanalyst in Vienna. I was examined. Several times. Then I stopped going.

KRON. Why?

ANN *(Majestically)*. Because he offered me the type of treatment that has to be declined with indignation.

SOPHIE. *(Outraged)*. Who was the scoundrel?

CLEMENTINE *(Calmly)*. Don't tell her. She only wants his address.

SOPHIE *(Indignantly, to* BLOCK). Did you hear that?

BLOCK. No.

KRON. I am profoundly touched to think you've gone to such lengths to overcome it.—Is there any more that I should hear?

ANN. I'm finished.

CLEMENTINE. Too bad.

ANN. Why?

CLEMENTINE. I've waited ten years for this scene. And now it's over so soon.

ANN. Not yet, Mamma. *(To* BLOCK, *who signals he wants to speak)* Be brief, Dr. Block. I asked Mr. Thomas to come here at 6:30. (KRON *gets up and starts to go)* Please sit down. I asked him to come here so that he might tell you openly and in my presence that he wants to marry me.

KRON. What a marvelous woman you are! What a feeling for the significance of form! I love you with the greatest respect.

ANN. I'm sure you know that I feel the same about you. The moment may not be opportune, but I can tell you I don't know another woman who loves her husband as much as I do you.—What is it, Dr. Block?

BLOCK. I only wanted to assure His Highness that the divorce will be a masterpiece of dignity and discretion. A divorce far more beautiful than many a marriage . . .

KRON. I feel reassured, Dr. Block. I always knew you were a genius at destruction. *(Glances at his watch)* Six-thirty.

> (ANN *takes a long look at her watch; brief pause —* BUTLER *enters)*

BUTLER. Mr. Thomas.

> *(Enter* THOMAS. BUTLER *exit. Formal bow.* THOMAS *goes to* ANN *and reaches passionately for her hand)*

ANN *(Waves him away with a gesture. Coldly, haughtily)*. Enough. Restrain your ardor, Mr. Thomas. You must have patience. The time will come when I shall not only allow your eruptions of passion but absolutely demand them, for the sake of my recovery. Until then, control yourself. *(To* KRON*)* Rudolf, I hope you appreciate my frankness as much as you used to. So long as you are my husband, I can have no secrets from you. And now . . . Mr. Thomas is here to tell you, man to man, that he loves me and wishes to marry me. *(To* THOMAS) Sit down.

THOMAS *(To* KRON, *explosively)*. Your Highness, after that there is nothing for me to do but . . .

ANN. I said sit down.

THOMAS *(Sits, calmly)*. Your Highness, after that there is nothing for me to do but repeat what Her Highness has said. I love her and I wish to marry her.

> *(Brief silence)*

ANN. I'm convinced, Rudolf, that you'll make a beautiful reply to this beautiful declaration. *(Brief silence, again)* Don't answer right away. Perhaps you'd better think it over for a second or two.

KRON. It isn't necessary. The reply is simple. You've both behaved correctly. It's the only possible solution. Please accept my sincere good wishes. *(To* ANN*)* Are you satisfied with me?

ANN *(Icily).* I adore you, Rudolf.

BLOCK *(Dabs at his eyes).* What display of human grandeur!

CLEMENTINE. I know very few actors who are as good as Dr. Block. But this time he definitely overplayed.

ANN *(To* THOMAS*).* I feel, Mr. Thomas, that . . . Stand up. *(Thomas stands)* I feel that your meeting with my husband can come to an end. A tense situation shouldn't be drawn out a moment longer than is required. (THOMAS *bows.* ANN, *coldly)* I'll see you at the Opera tonight, and afterwards here at our party. We must leave now. A notary is coming to my husband's study at 6:45 to have the papers signed for the divorce and for our marriage. I'll let you know as soon as it's been done. Come along, Mamma, Rudolf, Sophie, Block.

(ALL *start to go)*

THOMAS. Ann . . . if I may address you so . . .

ANN *(Coldly).* Not yet. Not until the papers are signed.

THOMAS. Your Highness . . . You may call it ridiculous sentimentality due to the influence of the years when I lived in Paris, but I cannot refrain from respectfully observing that after the solemn moment we have just passed through, you are saying goodbye very coldly. *(Dabs at his eyes)* It hurts.

ANN *(With the utmost coldness).* When we are together legally for the first time, under the sanction of heavenly and earthly law, in a room somewhere alone—be assured I shall begin to fulfill my wifely duty passionately the very instant the door is locked. But I don't see the necessity of giving you a sample of it, no matter how small, right now in the presence of my husband. *(To the others)* Come along.

(ANN, KRON, SOPHIE *and* BLOCK *line up respectfully at door 3, to make way for* CLEMENTINE)

CLEMENTINE *(To Thomas).* Don't worry. My daughter was magnificent just now and I'm sure she'll be just as magnificent when the door is locked. One of her most beautiful traits is that in doing her duties she doesn't shrink from overdoing them. Come here. For the time being, I'll bid you goodbye in her place.

(THOMAS *steps up to her and bows;* CLEMENTINE *takes his head in both her hands, and raising his face, kisses him. Then, looking at* KRON)

CLEMENTINE. For this moment the suffering of ten years has been worth while!

(Marches out door 3; the others follow)

(At the same time the BUTLER *comes in humbly door 1, with Thomas' hat and gloves, and stands stiffly at the door.* THOMAS *reaches for his hat and gloves as the door shuts behind the others. The* BUTLER, *however, puts down the hat and gloves, and dropping all semblance of servility, speaks in a*

quiet but soldierly and energetic tone)

BUTLER. Just a moment, Captain.

THOMAS *(Snaps to attention)*. Colonel.

BUTLER. Captain, you are in danger. (THOMAS *continues to stand at attention, waiting to hear the rest).* You are in *grave* danger, Captain Bialoskurskov.

THOMAS. Why, Colonel Semionov? *(Bursts into a peal of Russian)*

BUTLER *(Peers around, frightened).* Not another word of Russian! Are you crazy?

THOMAS. I beg your pardon, Colonel. You frightened me.

BUTLER. You may have noticed my boundless regard for the superb lady, who more and more each day is becoming the great love of your life.

THOMAS. I have, and I think of that too daily; with the deepest emotion, Colonel Semionov.

BUTLER. It has made me very happy to follow the development of this love during the past months, even though we haven't spoken of it. But things have come to a head today. The papers are being signed this very moment—permitting your marriage. I should be the happiest of men today, if . . .

THOMAS. If?

BUTLER. If I weren't your superior officer, responsible for you to the Imperial Russian Intelligence Service of His Majesty the Czar. Don't forget that I recommended you for this important post.

THOMAS. I have been deeply grateful to His Majesty the Czar and to you, Colonel.

BUTLER. Captain, I am informed that you are under grave suspicion at home, not only in the offices of the Imperial General Staff but in the intimate circle of His Majesty's the Czar's Court in St. Petersburg.

THOMAS. What is the charge against me?

BUTLER. You did not send anything to our Service from this house. (THOMAS *lowers his head*) I'm sufficiently human to understand the reason. You adore this woman.

THOMAS. The word is too feeble, Colonel.

BUTLER. She is a splendid specimen. An exciting phenomenon. Many of my own most beautiful memories go back to just such haughty, majestic, aristocratic women, rigid and frigid as statues in public, but who in the moments of intimacy bite and claw like tigresses. Do you remember the Countess Natasha Fedorovna Balugtchitchov?

THOMAS. The proud beautiful lady-in-waiting to the Czarina—oh yes.

BUTLER *(In a prolonged passionate sigh, rising almost to a scream).* Oh Natasha, Natasha! *(Suddenly changing his tone)* But let's stick to the subject. The Seventh Bureau of the Imperial General staff of His Majesty's seems to detect a connection between your love for her and the fact that you've sent nothing. I hate to tell you this, but you're suspected of treason.

THOMAS. Treason?

BUTLER. There's an impression in St. Petersburg that the Princess has seduced you, and that to please her you do favors for Austria. *(Nodding toward portrait of Franz Joseph)* For that old man. They're thinking of dropping you.

THOMAS. Colonel, this wonderful creature has raised me with her love to heaven. Betray *her?* Deceive *her?* Never, Colonel!

BUTLER. Who's talking about her? I mean her husband.

THOMAS. I don't care about her husband, but I do care about her feelings. She worships her country and her Emperor. And any feeling of hers is sacred to me.

BUTLER. I personally admire the nobility of your heart. You're a medieval knight. But you have failed in your assignment, Captain. A woman has turned a soldier into a dreamer.

THOMAS. I admit it.

BUTLER. Soldier and man are at grips right now in my heart, brother. How glorious to give up everything for a woman! Ah, I've had such affairs myself! Long, long ago. I too was a young captain once —a fool for romance. I too sacrificed for love. You recall I mentioned Natasha Balugtchitchov?

THOMAS. Yes. The beautiful and haughty lady-in-waiting.

BUTLER. I adored her! How I used to suffer sitting by her fire on winter afternoons! The air was full of romance. Twilight. She would play Chopin. And Tchaikovsky, that sweet poison! I loved her desperately. She wouldn't believe me. She was a cruel girl. She used to torture me. "No," she was forever saying "no" to me. No, no, and no. Then, one day, as I was sobbing collapsed over her piano, she spoke up suddenly. "Tell me, Captain," she asked, "would you give your life for me?" "Without an instant's hesitation," I told her passionately. "What would you do?"—she asked. "I'd draw my revolver and shoot myself any time you gave the word," I said. She

looked at me coldly. "That's not enough," she said. "Is there anything you value above your life?"—"Yes," I said, "my honor." — Her eyes flashed. "Would you give up your honor for me?"—she asked. "Without an instant's hesitation," I answered. "How would you do it?" —she asked. "I'd go straight from here to the Officers' Club and cheat at cards," I said. Natasha was cruel. She looked at me with feverish eyes, burning in those pale cheeks. She said, "I want *that,* the more precious of the two."

THOMAS. What did you do?

BUTLER. I went straight to the Club and cheated. Natasha surrendered to me. She loved me frantically. That's how I won Natasha.— And my fortune.

THOMAS. What a moving, romantic story! A man like you surely ought to understand *me.*

BUTLER. I do understand you. But your fate doesn't depend on me. Your orders came from the General Staff. And the Generals of His Majesty know no mercy.

THOMAS. Then . . .

BUTLER. You must *do* something. If you don't do something to prove yourself—and at once—you'll be tried. And in our profession being accused is the same as being condemned. I hope you realize that. There's only one penalty for treason in our line of work. You know what it is, don't you?

THOMAS. Yes.

BUTLER. So what are you going to do about it?

THOMAS. Run away.

BUTLER. Why, you'll never even get a chance to run. They'll stop you before you start.

THOMAS. Who will?

BUTLER *(Bows his head)*. I am ordered to do so.

(Silence)

THOMAS. And how will you stop me, Colonel?

(Instead of replying, the BUT-LER shows THOMAS *the muzzle of a revolver over the edge of his pocket, then slips the weapon back)*

THOMAS. You mean . . . you'd actually go through with this?

BUTLER. Orders are orders. Our illustrious Czar, Peter the Great, killed his own son for the good of the Empire.

THOMAS. So . . .

BUTLER. You'll have to steal a document. I beg you to, my boy! Any old piece of paper will do as long as it's a document and stolen. I'll build it up in my report. I beg you! Ordinarily there are coded papers in the bedroom safe. I'll make the job easy for you. Here's the key to the safe. *(Offers him a small key.* THOMAS *shudders.)*

BUTLER *(Persuasively)*. He keeps some papers in his desk too—the less important ones. Blood analyses for instance. They're also in code. It's child's play. Here's the key to the drawer.

THOMAS. I couldn't do it.

*(*BUTLER *offers him another key.* THOMAS *shudders and shakes his head)*

BUTLER. Well, since you don't like meddling with locks . . . There's a secret compartment in the desk, lower left. All you have to do is press a certain spot with this button, and it opens. Here it is. *(Shows him the button)* One gentle pressure . . .

and you save your life and happiness. Why are you so stubborn? There's a limit to being romantic!

THOMAS *(In a trembling voice)*. Colonel Semionov, who should understand me better than you? You, whose life has been a succession of great loves! Think of them! Natasha! Natasha! And Vera Grigorovna Balalinkov! And Olga Alexandrovna Krupitkin!

BUTLER *(Sighs)*. It's no use, son, you'll have to go through with it.

THOMAS. Never.

BUTLER. I must save you in spite of yourself, Captain. *(Takes a paper from his pocket)* This is my last offer. Good. Don't steal. But take this coded document. It's a fresh one. I slipped it out of the safe a few minutes ago while you were having your conference. Actually it's a very interesting military document. But I'll let you take the credit. I make you a present of it. All you have to do is hand it over to Agent 423 the minute you leave here, before you go to the Opera. That's all. And remember, it's urgent. Don't take it home with you, for heaven's sake! Hand it right over to 423. See! You didn't steal and you're saved anyhow. And the beautiful cold Princess will be yours. She'll adore you—and bite you. I'm sure she'll bite. I know the kind. Ah, Natasha Fedorovna Balugtchitchov. Oh! Her sharp little white teeth! *(Sighs)* Well — ? *(*THOMAS *sobs brokenly.* BUTLER *hands him the document)* You can thank your lucky stars you have a friend like me. You ought to feel toward me like a son. Love and cherish your marble Princess. I'd like to praise her much more, but I'm afraid you'd be jealous of me.

THOMAS (*Dabbing at his eyes*). Of you, Colonel?

BUTLER. You never can tell. Now go and do what I said. And love her . . . but above all, love your own young life, Captain Bialoskurskov.

(THOMAS *takes the document from the* BUTLER *and slips it into his pocket. He kisses the* BUTLER'S *hand, while the latter dries his tears with his other hand*)

(*Sound of approaching footsteps at door 1.* BUTLER *quickly gathers up Thomas' hat and gloves.* THOMAS *turns away to hide his tears.* LOUISE, *the French maid, comes in by door 1, carrying a huge bouquet of flowers, which she puts into a vase*)

LOUISE. For the Princess, Mr. Diegelmann. Lovely, aren't they? Mr. Thomas sent them. (*Smiles at Thomas and goes out*)

THOMAS (*Surprised*). I did?

BUTLER. Yes. You.

THOMAS (*Examines the card on the flowers*). Thomas . . . (*Surprised*) You ordered them?

BUTLER. At this very moment the Princess is signing your papers of happiness. I thought she might be pleased . . . if . . .

THOMAS (*Seizing his hand*). My friend! My father!

BUTLER (*Repressing his tears with difficulty*). You bad boy. You've awakened the memory of all my loves. You've truly upset me. The fourth movement of Tchaikovsky's Symphonie Pathetique is ringing in my ears. Ah, Tchaikovsky! O sweet, sweet poison! Ah, my melancholy Countesses, my proud Princesses!

They're all grandmothers now. Natasha's little white teeth dropped out long ago, and now she has brand new little white teeth. I wish you luck and happiness, my young friend. May you be as happy as I was at your age!

(*Embraces him. They loudly kiss each other*)

(*Sound of steps outside; both look up at door 3. They separate at once, slipping back into their roles instantly.* BUTLER *stands respectfully, holding Thomas' hat and gloves in his hand.*

THOMAS *stands a few steps away. Enter* ANN, *followed by* CLEMENTINE)

ANN (*Cool, but a little tremblingly*). I knew you wouldn't leave until you heard the happy news from me. It's done, my friend. I signed six different papers—three for the divorce, and three for our marriage. I sent a wire to Vienna, to the Emperor—in which I commended you to His Majesty in the most flattering terms. His Majesty is certain to like you. Mark my words, he will. The vista that has opened before you to-day leads not only to a happy marriage but also to a great political career. (*Hearing this, the* BUTLER, *at the rear, bursts into silent tears*). What lovely flowers! (*Steps up to the vase*) In this solemn moment, too. Only you could be so tender!

THOMAS (*Passionately*). Ah, Ann! I *have* to make a confession to you!

ANN (*Coldly*). Mr. Thomas, I've been your fiancée for the last five minutes. You may leave with that thought.

THOMAS (*Once more approaches* ANN *passionately*). ANN!!!

ANN (*Rigid as a statue, waves him away*). I didn't tell you to come here with that thought; I said, you may leave with it.

THOMAS (*Pressing his hand against the pocket where he has put the document*). Ann, I am the unhappiest fiancé on earth. (BUTLER, *standing discreetly at the rear, starts up at this move*)

ANN. Don't take my rigid behavior too much to heart. It isn't coldness. It's the thing to do.— You're making a dreadful face.

CLEMENTINE. No wonder. Can't you give him one warm word?

ANN. Mr. Thomas . . .

CLEMENTINE. Call him Robert.

ANN (*Evidently considers this a great concession*). I'm looking forward with joy to our marriage . . . Robert. Now, are you still unhappy?

THOMAS. Even unhappier than before.

ANN (*With the greatest astonishment to* CLEMENTINE). What does he expect from me?

CLEMENTINE. Outbursts, darling! Good old-fashioned outbursts!

ANN (*Horror-stricken*). *Before the wedding???*

CURTAIN

ACT TWO

SCENE: *The same room. A few hours after Act One.*

AT RISE: *The* BUTLER *and* TWO LACKEYS *are on the stage.* LACKEYS *each hold a large tray. Sandwiches are piled on one of the trays. The other tray holds drinks.* BUTLER *examines the trays.*

Doors 2 and 3 are wide open.

BUTLER. Sandwiches. Drinks. Very good. (*Points to corner where a number of small tables have been prepared*) We'll serve it all on those tables. Take the trays out to the gallery now. (*Points to door 2.*) Wait out there. Their Highnesses will be back from the Opera in a few minutes and they'll want a bite before the guests arrive. (LOUISE *enters door 1. —Seeing her* BUTLER *says to the* LACKEYS) All right. You may go. (LACKEYS *go out.* BUTLER *closes door 2 after them. To* LOUISE, *anxiously*) Well?

LOUISE. The man just left. He's been cross-examining me right up to this minute. I had to tell him everything I know about Mr. Thomas.

BUTLER. Was he from the police?

LOUISE Yes. The secret police. It's alarming. Why are the secret police interested in Mr. Thomas?

BUTLER. I have no idea.

LOUISE. I guess they're watching him. He must have been in some kind of political trouble. Or sex mixup. And the poor man is sitting at the Opera with Their Highnesses, right now, happy as you please and never suspecting a thing.

BUTLER. Distressing.

LOUISE. Don't be nervous.

BUTLER. Didn't you try to find out what happened from the detective?

LOUISE. Certainly I did. He smiled and told me to say goodbye to

Mr. Thomas because I wouldn't see much of him after this.

BUTLER. Is that what he said?

LOUISE. Those were his words.— Don't be nervous.

BUTLER. Very distressing.

LOUISE. I have a feeling that something terrible must have happened. Don't you think I ought to tell the Princess?

BUTLER. Not for the world.

LOUISE. But *Mr. Thomas* ought to be told.

BUTLER. I'll find a way to let him know. Leave it to me. You hold your tongue whatever you do.

LOUISE. Don't be nervous, Mr. Diegelmann.

BUTLER. If you tell me not to be nervous once more, I'll strangle you on the spot.

LOUISE. But Mr.Diegelmann . . .

BUTLER *(Raises a finger to warn her).* Shh. Go. I hear voices. Their Highnesses must be back from the Opera.

LOUISE *(Listens).* I don't hear anything.

BUTLER. You'd better always trust to my ears.

(Nervously BUTLER *motions to her to go.* LOUISE *goes out door 1.)*

(After a brief pause ANN *and* SOPHIE *enter.* CLEMENTINE, KRON *and* THOMAS *appear on the threshold and remain there talking to each other softly. They have just come from the Opera)*

*(*BUTLER *bows and withdraws to the rear, to await orders. During what follows he tries to signal to* THOMAS, *but he fails to attract his attention)*

ANN. I thought the Opera was quite mediocre. Perotti sang the lover's part too coldly.

SOPHIE. That's something coming from you—the embodiment of coldness yourself.

ANN *(Coldly).* Don't misunderstand me. A moral woman must be cold in love. Burning torrents are the man's part. Iceberg and volcano —that's the way it should be.

SOPHIE. His Majesty the King applauded Perotti. In fact he started the applause.

ANN. That was not enthusiasm, but courtesy. His Majesty is one of the well-bred kings.

SOPHIE. I liked Perotti. It's too bad we had to leave before the third act.

ANN. We must be at home at least half an hour before our guests arrive. What time is it?

THOMAS. Eleven.

*(*CLEMENTINE *leaves the others and walks over to* ANN*)*

ANN *(To* KRON*).* What is the schedule, Rudolf?

*(*SOPHIE *crosses slowly to* KRON *and* THOMAS*)*

KRON *(From the threshold).* The first guests will arrive immediately after eleven-thirty. Their Majesties the King and Queen of Italy a little later. Could we have something to eat?

ANN. Of course. *(To* BUTLER*)* Diegelmann?

BUTLER. Everything is prepared, Your Highness.

ANN. Very well. I'll let you know when we wish you to serve.

*(*CLEMENTINE *and* ANN *are standing at the center of the stage at the moment.* KRON, SOPHIE *and* THOMAS *are still talking at the threshold of door*

3. — BUTLER *makes a last desperate unsuccessful attempt to signal* THOMAS)

ANN *(Seeing this)*. Is there anything you wish?

BUTLER. No, Your Highness. *(Exit despairingly)*

CLEMENTINE. Remember what I told you at the Opera. That poor boy looked so sad sitting with us in the loge. It made my heart ache. You're very cruel to him and it shouldn't go on. Talk to him and act more warmly toward him when you do.

ANN. I will—in Vienna.

CLEMENTINE. Don't put it off. Every man has his vanity and this one's vanity has obviously been hurt. And don't rebuke him every time he tries to speak of love. Your divorce papers are signed, there's nothing you need be afraid of.

ANN *(Sighing)*. All right, Mother. I'll try. But . . . what shall I do with him?

CLEMENTINE. Do I have to tell you that?

ANN. I'm so helpless.

CLEMENTINE. I don't suppose you've ever kissed him?

ANN *(Lowers her eyes)*. Not yet.

CLEMENTINE. Kiss him.—And . . . if you're alone with him don't just talk about the Emperor.

ANN. But if he loves the Emperor so much!

CLEMENTINE. He loves you more. Talk to him about the future. About the children you're going to have. That's the sort of thing that makes a man happy.

ANN. Should I tell him, for instance, about a dream that I had?

CLEMENTINE. Is it flattering to him?

ANN. Very.

CLEMENTINE. Then tell him. *(Seeing* THOMAS *who is coming toward them)* I'll see that no one disturbs you. Courage! Behave like the thing you are, a woman in love.

(THOMAS, *coming from the threshold of door 3, approaches* ANN. KRON *disappears.* CLEMENTINE *starts for door 3, but halfway over she meets* SOPHIE, *who is going toward* ANN. CLEMENTINE *takes* SOPHIE *by the arm and propels her out door 3.* CLEMENTINE *closes door 3 from the outside)* ANN *and* THOMAS *are left alone)*

THOMAS *(In surprise)*. Ann! We're alone.

(Awkward pause)

ANN *(Majestically, but trembling slightly)*. Yes, Robert.

THOMAS. We have a few moments to ourselves.

(Awkward pause)

ANN. Yes, Robert.

(Awkward pause)

Sit down, Robert.

THOMAS *(Coming closer to her)*. I love you, Ann.

ANN. I told you to sit down. *(Both sit. After a short pause* ANN *speaks, trembling, but her head held high)* You've never kissed me.

THOMAS *(Leaps to his feet)*. Ann!

ANN *(Frightened)*. No, Robert. Not yet.

THOMAS. *(Disappointed, sits)*. Well . . . when may I kiss you?

ANN. Not before the wedding.

THOMAS. Not even your hand?

ANN. You may do that.

THOMAS. When?

ANN. At the end of the present conversation.

THOMAS. Thank you.

(Awkward pause)

ANN. This is very awkward. What can I talk about that will make you happy?

THOMAS (Delighted). Anything you wish, Ann.

(Slight pause)

ANN. Tell me . . . As an architect, which do you prefer . . . Ionic columns or Corinthian?

THOMAS. Corinthian.

ANN. I prefer Ionic. But from now on I'll like Corinthian.

THOMAS. Thank you.

(Awkward pause)

ANN. You think I'm cold, don't you?

THOMAS. No. That is . . . I think you're old-fashioned.

ANN. I'm proud of that. A respectable woman can't have any higher ambition than to be old-fashioned.

(Awkward pause)

(Suddenly)

Do you want children?

THOMAS. Lots of them .

ANN. I'm to be their mother, I presume?

THOMAS. Why, certainly.

ANN. That reassures me. There's only one thing I don't want.

THOMAS. What's that?

ANN. Twins.

(Pause)

Not that, I beg of you.

(Pause)

Promise me.

THOMAS. I promise.

(Awkward pause)

ANN. Can you see that I'm trembling?

THOMAS. Yes.

ANN. I tremble more and more, every time you look at me.

THOMAS. Thank you.

(Awkward pause)

ANN. I'm so awkward.

THOMAS. Oh . . .

ANN. This is the first love-scene in my life.

THOMAS. Is it painful?

ANN. Yes and no. It's a strange blending of pain with joy.

THOMAS. How true.

(Awkward pause)

ANN. And now . . . something about your past. When you were a student in Paris . . . did you have a girl friend?

THOMAS. Yes.

ANN (Lays her hand on her heart). That hurts. But I want to know everything.

THOMAS. It's a short story. I was a penniless student. One evening I danced with a girl. I lived with her a year after that.

ANN. In the same apartment?

THOMAS. Yes.

ANN. How many rooms?

THOMAS. One.

ANN. Two beds?

THOMAS. One.

ANN. A whole year?

THOMAS. Yes.

ANN. Now tell me the truth. Swear you'll tell the truth!

THOMAS. I swear.

ANN. Did you have an affair with her?

THOMAS. Yes.

ANN (Sighs with relief). Then she was a prostitute. In that case I can forget about the whole thing. I've already forgotten it.—What was her name?

THOMAS. It doesn't matter.

ANN. What was her name?

THOMAS *(Embarrassed, after a short pause)*. Ann.

ANN. That hurts.

(Awkward pause)

Do you ever dream about me?

THOMAS. Every night.

ANN. What do you dream?

(No answer)

Why do you blush?

*(*THOMAS *lowers his head)*

I've dreamed about you, too.

THOMAS. Thank you.

ANN. Shall I tell you?

THOMAS. Please. Everything you can.

ANN. You were a Knight in armor, clad in steel from head to toe. I approached you longingly. Then, suddenly I discovered—you weren't a Knight at all, you were an iron stove *in the form* of a Knight. Strong fires gleamed in your eyes, in your nostrils, through your parted lips. I continued to approach you. I was myself but I was made of ice. A crystalline transparent statue of ice, and nude. You can imagine how cold I felt. Your warmth attracted me. I stepped close and was eager to kiss you. My husband Rudolf was there and he shouted: "Don't go near him!" —But I wouldn't listen to him and went closer still. Overjoyed, I sank on your bosom . . . and all of a sudden I began to melt. The first thing to melt was my nose. It's a good nose and Rudolf shouted: "Your nose is going! Come back to me, I'll love you without a nose!" And then my hands melted. You took me passionately in your arms and my beautiful breasts melted away. I thought in despair: "If all of me melts away, what will be left for him to embrace?"—But you held me even tighter and I melted away completely.

I began to boil—like water that's poured on a glowing hearth. Then, the next instant, I was steam and I rose high in the air. Up there, in the air, I turned into a little white cloud and a cold wind blew me away.—I woke up. Shivering, I shut my window and took a sedative.—That was all. *(Extends her hand to be kissed.* THOMAS *kisses her hand long and passionately.* ANN *lets him do so. At the same time)* Go now and don't come back until the other guests come, so as not to attract attention.

(After a slight pause)

And now make up your mind to the fact that sooner or later I'll have to withdraw my hand. *(Gently she withdraws her hand)* I'll see you when you return.

THOMAS *(Romantically)*. Au revoir, mon amour.

*(*HE *goes.* ANN *follows him lovingly with her eyes. Then she presses the bell-button—* BUTLER *enters)*

ANN. Sandwiches, Diegelmann! *(She sits at center, majestically, like a queen on her throne.—* BUTLER *motions to the two* LACKEYS *outside door 2. They come in and set up the little tables and bring in the trays with food and drinks. Meanwhile voices can be heard outside)*

KRON'S VOICE. At last we're going to eat.

SOPHIE'S VOICE. I'm awfully hungry. *(*SOPHIE *enters)* Happy, Ann?

ANN *(Majestically)*. More than I can express. *(*KRON *and* BLOCK *enter)* Please, everybody, be seated. *(*LACKEYS *exeunt.* BUTLER *waits on the company, going in and out of the* *room repeatedly. He is unmistakably nervous).* Better have some food now, because it's our last chance to-night. Everybody will be able to eat but us. The sandwiches are master-pieces by our good old cook Emma. Nobody can make sandwiches like her.

KRON. I dislike hearing about servants in such a solemn atmosphere.

ANN. Forgive me if the house-wife sometimes comes out. *(Look-ing about)* Ah, I love these quiet moments just before a big party. Everything glitters, everything is silent, everything is waiting. There is nothing more beautiful than a beautiful room without guests.

(CLEMENTINE *enters.* ALL *rise.* CLEMENTINE *sits.* ALL *sit down again)*

KRON. You're right, it is more beautiful without guests.

(Slight painful pause)

ANN. How did you enjoy the Opera, Mother?

CLEMENTINE. My head was full of your divorce. That gave me a sleepless first act. *(Looking at the sandwiches).* Ah, old Emma's famous sandwiches. *(Takes one)*

ANN. Yes, Mother. *(To Rudolf)* I recommend that one, Rudolf. It's one of Emma's original composi-tions. *(Offers him a sandwich)* Pate de foie gras, caviar, paprika, cheese and garlic, all mixed up.

KRON. Thank you, no garlic to-night. I have to whisper to the King.

BLOCK. I'm not on whispering terms with the King. May I? *(Takes the sandwich)*

SOPHIE. A glass of port?

BLOCK. Your attention is very touching, Countess. *(Taking the glass of wine from her)* Any poison in it?

SOPHIE. I'm afraid not.

KRON *(Solemnly).* Ann, before this small, intimate gathering, I wish to thank you with all my heart for having postponed your departure in order to do the honors as hostess, by my side, on this last day of our married life. I want to thank you for this sacrifice, not only on my own account, but also on behalf of the Austro-Hungarian Empire.

ANN *(Majestically).* I owe it to you to give up these few hours. To you as my husband for the time being, and to you as the representa-tive of His Majesty our Emperor. Further, I owe it to him—the King of Italy—who will lend majesty to our party tonight. *(Raising her head high, she rises and picks up her glass.* ALL *stand)* Gentlemen! (SOPHIE *sits down)* The King! *(Raising her glass, drinks.* CLEMENTINE, KRON *and* BLOCK *follow suit;* BUTLER *at the rear bows low.* ANN, CLEMENTINE, KRON *and* BLOCK *sit)*

KRON *(With a look of exalta-tion).* Yes, my friends. Kings and princes have made this contentious old Europe a happy, peaceful family. The Czar of Russia and the King of England are cousins. The Emperor of Germany is a cousin of both, and a blood relative of the King of Roumania as well. The King of Italy is brother-in-law of a Russian Grand-duchess and son-in-law of the Prince of Montenegro. The King of Spain is a nephew of His Majesty our Emperor. And so on and so on. All together one magnificent, loving, great and happy family. The mar-riages of royalty are a guaranty of everlasting peace! *(Sighs, then sud-denly grows gloomy)* All except that terrible France, which still refuses to enthrone its lawful King!

(A moment of awe-struck silence)

SOPHIE. That was a wonderful speech, I might say an historic one. Too bad there was no music to accompany it.—What piece of music would have been appropriate, Rudolf?

KRON. The wedding march from Lohengrin, of course.

CLEMENTINE. And at the end the Marseillaise. Very softly, of course.

ANN (To the BUTLER). Diegelmann, this little drawing-room is to be our refuge tonight. I don't want any guests in here, as far as it's possible to arrange it. You appear restless.

BUTLER. A trifle nervous, Your Highness. But everything will be in perfect order.

KRON. You can be as sarcastic as you like, Clementine. But my life's aim is to marry an Austrian Archduchess to a pretender to the French throne, a Bourbon. I don't want to die until I've knelt before the throne of Louis XX in Paris.

CLEMENTINE. A wise decision. You're sure to live long at that rate.

ANN (To the BUTLER). The remaining eleven rooms belong to the guests. Keep this one for us, in case we want to rest a while, or have a little chat.

BUTLER. I understand, Your Highness. (Drops the empty silver tray) I beg Your Highness' pardon.

ANN (Coldly, calmly). I notice you've been nervous all evening, Diegelmann. Has anything happened?

BUTLER. No, Your Highness.

Unless it is that I too am deeply shaken by the exceptional significance of this evening.

ANN. This is the first time I've heard that butlers too have nerves.

BUTLER. I'll do my best to get rid of them.

ANN. Meanwhile . . . control yourself. I hope the personnel under you is not as deeply affected.

BUTLER. No, Your Highness. They are nerveless.

ANN (Pointing to the bouquet). In that case take these flowers, give them to my maid Louise and tell her to tend them carefully.

BUTLER. (Takes the bouquet. Stiffly). Yes, Your Highness.

ANN. You look so wooden every time I mention Louise. You don't seem to like being in contact with her.

BUTLER. No, Your Highness.

ANN. You don't like her.

BUTLER. No, Your Highness.

ANN. You hate her.

BUTLER. Yes, Your Highness.

ANN. That doesn't please me. Louise is my personal maid, and you, as head of the staff, will have to like her.

BUTLER. I will try, Your Highness. (Stands stiffly)

KRON. I should deeply appreciate it, Ann, if you would now suppress your excellent Viennese housewifely inclinations of the moment and stop discussing the feelings of servants for one another while I weigh the all-important words by which I mean to present the possibilities of the monarchy to the French Ambassador.

CLEMENTINE. You may go, Diegelmann—on your toes at that.

For heaven's sake, don't disturb the flow of world history.

(BUTLER *goes out with the bouquet. In a few moments he enters again to straighten the room, etc.)*

ANN. Something must have happened in this house. That man just isn't what he used to be. He's hiding something.

KRON *(Deep in thought, to* SOPHIE). We'll have to make sure we marry a healthy Archduchess to a productive member of the Bourbon family. Because we must be assured of having a number of thoroughbred descendants.

CLEMENTINE. Amazing how monarchist politics resembles horse breeding.

KRON *(To* BLOCK). It would be a matter of high political importance to learn which of the Bourbons is most productive. Have you any way of determining that?

BLOCK. Not on the basis of personal experience, Your Highness. But then, there is Your Highness' diplomatic genius! One or two of your subtle questions to the French Ambassador . . .

KRON. I'll try that. *(To* ANN). Leaving tomorrow?

ANN. Yes. With Mother.

KRON. Vienna?

ANN. Vienna. Mamma is having an apartment in her palace done over for Mr. and Mrs. Thomas. She is overwhelmingly happy that I'm leaving you. I'll be staying there by myself for the time being. Thomas is remaining here in Rome until the wedding because, in view of his unbridled passion, I don't want to put too great a strain on my legendary power of resistance.

KRON. A correct procedure. Will Mr. Thomas be here tonight?

ANN. Naturally. An absence is sometimes more conspicuous than a presence.

KRON. Absolutely right.

ANN. He'll be here on time and you can present him with the Emperor's decoration then.

KRON. Which he fully deserves. In my recommendation I gave a detailed account of his patriotism and devotion to His Majesty. One day, when I slipped in here, I found him alone in the center of the room, looking at His Majesty's portrait. I made it a point to watch him. At first he smiled affectionately at the picture, then he was so moved he brushed some tears from his eyes. That was the moment I decided to recommend him for the honors.

(BARON ARIBERT, *secretary of the Embassy, comes in)*

ARIBERT *(A slip of paper in his hand. To* KRON). The chief of police telephoned. *(Seeing the* BUTLER'S *frightened manner)* Is there anything you want?

BUTLER. No, no, thank you.

ARIBERT *(To* KRON). The chief of police informs us that His Majesty will leave his palace at exactly 11:40. (BUTLER *heaves a sigh of relief)* Policemen stationed along the route will telephone the geographic position of the car every three minutes. The time of arrival will be exactly 11:58.

KRON *(Impatiently).* You're an excellent secretary, Baron, but you make me nervous with all this hairsplitting. All I want is to be called in time, since etiquette requires that the Princess and I receive His Majesty at the foot of the stairs, and accompany him up the steps with twenty-four lighted candles.

(ARIBERT *makes a note of something*)

KRON (*Irritably*). What did you just write down?

ARIBERT. Check the candles to see they are firmly placed in their sockets.

KRON. Another morsel that has nothing to do with me. .

ARIBERT. I beg your pardon, but I want to be sure that everything goes smoothly. (*To* ANN, *glancing at his notes*) The orchestra leader has respectfully followed Your Highness' commands, and scrapped his program for the evening.

SOPHIE. Why?

ARIBERT. Her Highness thought the original selections frivolous. Viennese waltzes by Strauss.

SOPHIE. I'll miss them.

ANN (*To* ARIBERT). And now?

ARIBERT (*Reading*). Beethoven, Brahms, Grieg, Tchaikovsky . . .

BUTLER (*At the door, nearly gives himself away*). Ah! Tchaikov— (*Nearly drops his tray, with the dishes*)

ANN (*Coldly*). What's the matter with you today, Diegelmann?

BUTLER. I beg Your Highness' pardon. (*On his way out, softly*) Sweet poison. (*Exit*)

ARIBERT (*Glancing at his notes*). And may I report that one or two of the guests have sent regrets. Minor illnesses. Count . . .

ANN. I don't care about Counts. Any Cardinals among the absentees?

ARIBERT. Cardinal Granelli-Bronchitis.

ANN. He's right to take care of himself. He's ninety-seven.

ARIBERT. It's not he who's ill. It's his mother.

ANN. Thank you, Baron.—You seem tired.

ARIBERT. I've been on my feet since six o'clock this morning. But everything is in perfect order now. I haven't had a bite to eat all day.

CLEMENTINE (*Holding a sandwich in her hand*). I can imagine how hungry you are.

ARIBERT. Yes, I'm frightfully hungry.

CLEMENTINE. Poor Baron.

(*Begins to eat her sandwich with relish.*)

(BUTLER *enters*)

BUTLER. Mr. Thomas telephoned. He wants to know if he may come a little earlier than expected.

ANN. When does he want to come?

BUTLER. Right away.

ANN. I don't understand.—Did he say why?

BUTLER (*Woodenly*). That's all he said.

ANN. Tell him we'll be glad to see him.

BUTLER. Yes, Your Highness.

(BUTLER *whispers to Aribert.* ARIBERT *grasps his head*)

ANN. What is it?

BUTLER (*Nervously*). The detectives have arrived to guard His Majesty.

ANN (*To* BUTLER). Does that make *you* nervous too? It should give you a feeling of security to have detectives in the house.

BUTLER. It doesn't, Your Highness. (*Exit*)

ANN. That man isn't himself today. If he weren't a butler, I'd say there was something tragic about him. *(To* ARIBERT) But *you.*—Why are *you* frightened?

ARIBERT. Because there are forty-five of them.

ANN. There can never be enough detectives where a King is involved.

ARIBERT. We must give them at least ninety sandwiches. And Emma, the cook, is incapacitated. She has an attack of lumbago.

KRON *(Groans).* The servants again.

CLEMENTINE. She should have the lower part of her back well rubbed with alcohol.

(ARIBERT *glances at* KRON)

KRON *(Irritably).* Why do you look at me like that? Do you expect *me* to rub the lower part of the cook's back with alcohol?

ARIBERT. Heaven forbid, Your Highness!

KRON. Then please leave. I don't care about private people's lumbagoes. I'm only interested in the lumbago of Europe.

ARIBERT. A thousand apologies, Your Highness. *(Exit).*

ANN *(Reproachfully).* You're irritable, Rudolf. You offended the poor Baron.

KRON *(Still irritably).* He's an excellent secretary, but I can't rub the cook's behind.

CLEMENTINE *(Calmly).* I don't see why not.

(KRON, *at the end of his patience, stands up threateningly)*

BLOCK. May I speak, Your Highness?

KRON *(Sits down; controls himself).* If you please.

BLOCK. Mr. Thomas will be here soon. We should agree on what instructions to give him.

KRON. Quickly then, because the guests will be here soon, too.

BLOCK. The main thing is: Her Highness and Mr. Thomas are not to see each other alone again until the wedding.

KRON. Quite right. But aren't they likely to feel lonely that way?

(ANN *sighs)*

BLOCK. I can assure Your Highness it won't be long. The waiting period will be cancelled in this case. I already have the special license.

ANN. What for?

BLOCK. Without it you would have to wait a year after the divorce.

ANN. Why?

BLOCK. It is a requirement of our law. If it should happen that the divorced wife has a child by her former husband within a certain time after the divorce . . .

ANN. What a supposition!

BLOCK. Those who made this law know life.

CLEMENTINE. But they don't know . . . *(Glances contemptuously at* KRON)

ANN. Continue, Dr. Block.

BLOCK. And so, the day the decree is granted, Mr. Thomas will take the first train, and you'll be married the day after.

ANN. The same day.

BLOCK *(Makes a note of it).* The same day.—But the train doesn't arrive in Vienna until after eleven at night.

ANN. That doesn't matter. We'll rush right from the station to the Archbishop.

BLOCK. The Archbishop is an old man. He'll be asleep by that time.

ANN. Wake him up.

BLOCK. That's strictly forbidden. Wait till morning.

ANN. No. The Archbishop can't demand that a woman should give herself to a man the night before their wedding.

KRON. But Ann! The Archbishop doesn't demand that of you. He wouldn't suspect that you were capable of such a thing. (*To* BLOCK) Just the same, you'd better wake him up .

BLOCK (*Makes a note of it*). "Wake up . . . Archbishop."—It will be done, Your Highness.

ANN (*To* CLEMENTINE). I hope you realize that I am motivated by powerful ethical factors.

CLEMENTINE. I can't imagine any more powerful.

(BUTLER *enters*)

BUTLER. Mr. Thomas.

(THOMAS *enters.* BUTLER *goes out, giving a secret frightened glance at Thomas.* THOMAS *bows. Formal rigid salutations. Brief byplay.* THOMAS *moves passionately toward Ann; but* ANN *waves him away with a cold gesture*)

ANN. Please sit down. You're the first guest. Thank you for coming so early.

THOMAS. I held it my duty.

KRON. It is a tender thought that you're beginning to consider yourself one of the family.

ANN (*To* KRON). I appreciate this attitude of yours on behalf of Mr. Thomas, Rudolf.

THOMAS (*Wants to say something*). Your Highness . . .

KRON (*Interrupting*). Wait! (*Takes out a box and opens it*) Now if you will all be good enough to rise. (ALL *rise*) Mr. Thomas, His Majesty the Emperor of Austria has — on my recommendation — graciously consented to bestow on you the Commander's cross of the Order of Franz Josef.

(*Takes the order, with its red ribbon, from the box, and holds it against the throat of* THOMAS, *then, holding the two ends of the ribbon, to* BLOCK)

KRON. Dr. Block, will you be good enough to clasp it in back. If I do it, it would look as if I were embracing Mr. Thomas, and that gesture would have some quality of exaggeration, on this particular day.

(BLOCK *fastens the clasp behind Thomas's collar*)

THOMAS. I am deeply grateful, Your Highness . . . I really don't deserve it . . .

KRON. Don't be so modest. (*Smiling*) And don't offend me by saying that a man I've recommended to the Emperor isn't worthy of the honor. (*Shaking hands with* THOMAS) Let me be the first to congratulate you.

ANN. Let me be the second. (*Extends her hand,* THOMAS *kisses it.*)

(SOPHIE, CLEMENTINE *and* BLOCK, *all congratulate him silently, with cordial handclasps.* THOMAS *smiles painfully*)

KRON. Now if you will all be good enough to sit down.

(ALL *sit*)

ANN (*To Thomas*). And now— because our guests will be here in a moment—I want to tell you briefly the plan I've worked out in our family council. I'm leaving for Vienna tomorrow. You're staying here. The decree will be pronounced . . . (*Looks at* BLOCK)

BLOCK. Two weeks from today. *(To* THOMAS*)* Right after that you take the train, arriving in Vienna the following night. Right after that you get married. Right after that the Princess and you . . .

ANN. Stop. That's none of your business.—In a social and ethical sense the schedule is beyond reproach, isn't it, Rudolf?

KRON. The schedule is worthy of us both. I only regret that you'll have to endure the waiting, far from your fiancé. But it is a case of "noblesse oblige." Let that console you in your yearnings. *(Uncomfortable silence)*

SOPHIE *(To* THOMAS*)*. We may interpret your silence, I presume, as meaning that you concur in all the points of this program? *(*THOMAS *is silent. He is embarrassed)*.

KRON. It's unnecessary to ask a gentleman that, Sophie. *(*THOMAS *still says nothing)*.

ANN. Well?

THOMAS *(After some .hesitation)*. I cannot conceal from you that something has happened in the meantime.

ANN. Something . . .

THOMAS. Something that will disturb this perfect solution. That is why I took the liberty of coming before the other guests.

ANN *(Controlling herself)*. What happened?

THOMAS. I've just come from the police.

*(*BUTLER *comes in with a tray of sandwiches for* THOMAS. *Goes toward* THOMAS*)*

ANN. You may leave us, Diegelmann.

*(*BUTLER *turns on his heels without stopping, and goes out,*

tray and all, with a frightened look at THOMAS*)*

ANN. Please continue.

THOMAS. I've just come from the police.

ANN. That's not continuing. That's repeating. *(Short silence)*

KRON. May I ask, Mr. Thomas . . . What you have to tell us . . . is it perhaps confidential?

*(*SOPHIE *and* BLOCK *rise)*

THOMAS. Up to now it's been confidential, but it'll probably be in tomorrow's papers. *(To* SOPHIE *and* BLOCK*)* So you may as well sit down. *(*SOPHIE *and* BLOCK *sit.* THOMAS *speaks to* ANN *and* KRON*)* While I was at the Opera with you this evening, the police searched my apartment. *(Silence.* ALL *freeze)* The reason, presumably, was an anonymous complaint. The men from the secret police dropped in unexpectedly with a search warrant. They found a document in my apartment. They seized it and took it away.

(Brief silence. ANN *sits at her place, rigid as a statue)*

KRON. Is that what'll be in the papers tomorrow?

THOMAS. In all probability. I'm at my wit's end.

KRON. Don't take it so tragically. The police here are overzealous. The Chief of Police is one of our guests tonight. It'll all be straightened out in an hour.

THOMAS. I don't believe it *can* be straightened out.

KRON. Why not?

THOMAS. Because of the polite but definite advice the Chief of the Police himself gave me.

KRON. What was it?

THOMAS. To leave this country's territory as soon as possible.

KRON. You've been expelled?

THOMAS. Yes and no. If I'm to avoid complications, I'll have to go.

KRON. Where?

THOMAS. First of all, across the border.

KRON. And then?

THOMAS. Russia. *(Brief silence.* ALL *sit frozen—five statues of ice)*

KRON. Why Russia?

THOMAS. I'm an officer of His Majesty's the Tsar's Imperial Russian Army.

KRON. That *is* a surprise. You're Russian?

THOMAS. Yes.

KRON. And an officer. I didn't know.

THOMAS. It seems the police did.

KRON. In what branch do you serve? Imperial Guards?

THOMAS. No.

KRON. Cavalry?

THOMAS. No.

KRON. Artillery?

THOMAS. No.

KRON. Infantry?

THOMAS *(After some hesitation)*. You might call it that.

KRON *(Stiffly). I see.*—Colonel?

THOMAS. No.

KRON. Major?

THOMAS. No.

KRON. Captain?

THOMAS. Yes.

KRON. I see.—The name is Thomas?

THOMAS. No.

KRON. What then?

THOMAS. Bialoskurskov.

KRON *(Tries to repeat the name)*. Bia . . . lo . . .

THOMAS. It's hopeless.

KRON. I see. *(Looks at him gloomily.—Silence.)*

THOMAS *(To* ANN). I couldn't leave without bidding you goodbye, Princess. That is why I'm here. A tempest of despair rages in my heart. *(Dreadful silence)*

ANN *(Coldly, as before)*. What's the thing to do now, Dr. Block?

BLOCK. Put a few questions to Mr. . . . Thomas.

ANN *(Solemnly)*. Put them.

BLOCK *(To* THOMAS). What sort of document is it that the police seized in your apartment?

THOMAS. A secret document, in code.

BLOCK. What are its contents?

THOMAS. I don't know. Neither do the police.

BLOCK. Why did they seize it?

THOMAS. They said it could have come to me only in an illegal way.

BLOCK. Why did they say that?

THOMAS. Because it bore the stamp of a foreign Embassy.

BLOCK. What Embassy? (THOMAS *is silent)* Ours?

(THOMAS *nods.* ALL *fall back in their chairs. Brief silence)*

KRON. May I have a large glass of brandy? (SOPHIE *hands him a large glass of brandy. He drinks it in a gulp)*

CLEMENTINE *(Tenderly)*. Wouldn't you like a little soft music to calm you, Rudolf?

(KRON *doesn't answer. He stares stiffly before him)*

BLOCK. Where is the document now?

THOMAS. The police have ascertained that the document is the property of the Austro-Hungarian Embassy. *(With a bow toward* KRON.) As a result of His Highness' brilliant diplomacy, Italy is on the best of terms with the Austrian government. Consequently the Italian Foreign Minister has directed the police to return the document at once to the Austrian military attaché, General Dubetz. The document has been in this very house for the past half hour, here, upstairs, in the office of the military attaché—in his hands, in fact. It's rubber-stamped and bears the two letters: BX.

KRON (*Frozenly*). The letters BX mean that the document is top secret, entrusted to the Ambassador's personal care. "BX"—that's myself. (SOPHIE *reaches for glass of brandy*) Later, Sophie. (*To* THOMAS) If that document is marked BX, it's one of my personal papers.

(THOMAS *lowers his head in silence*)

ANN. Ask him the one and only interesting question, Dr. Block.

BLOCK. How did you gain possession of this document?

THOMAS. I won't answer that.

ANN. Dr. Block, repeat the question.

BLOCK. How did you gain possession of this document?

THOMAS. I repeat I won't answer that. I didn't answer it at police headquarters either.

KRON (*To* THOMAS). You didn't get it from me.—It's horrible to see the Emperor's order around his neck.

SOPHIE. I can't even look at it. (*Goes out crying*)

THOMAS (*To* ANN). Now I have only one thing to say. I am completely at Your Highness' disposal. You may dispose of my life.

ANN (*Icily*). Answer him, Dr. Block.

BLOCK. As Her Highness' legal representative, I flatly refuse this offer in her name. You have ceased to be. You cannot come in any contact whatsoever with Her Highness. Never again.

ANN. Never again. (*Icily*). Not if it breaks my heart. (A QUARTET *outside begins to play Beethoven's Minuet in G softly.* ARIBERT *enters*)

ARIBERT. The first guests are here. Cardinal Maloia. The Greek Minister. The French Ambassador. (ANN *rises*)

BLOCK. Head high, Your Highness.

ANN (*Trembling but controlling herself*). That was unnecessary. We hold our heads high even when we know that they will be chopped off the next second. Like French aristocrats in 1793, approaching the guillotine.—Come, Mother.

(ANN *goes out.* CLEMENTINE, BLOCK *and* ARIBERT *follow.—Brief silence.—*THOMAS *moves toward the exit*)

KRON. Don't go, please. Common sense tells me that any situation can be straightened out.

THOMAS. Not this one, Your Highness. (BUTLER *comes in, looking frightened*)

KRON. What is it?

BUTLER. The house phone. Third floor office calling.

KRON. Who is it?

BUTLER. His Excellency the military attaché wants to speak very urgently to Your Highness.

(*Brief silence*)

KRON (*With a sigh*). My tragedy begins. (*Listens; bitterly*) Minuet, by Beethoven. It would be more fitting if they played a funeral march.

THOMAS. I think so, too, Your Highness.

(KRON *goes out.* BUTLER *and* THOMAS *are left alone.* THOMAS *bows his head in silence. Music fades*)

BUTLER. How did this ever happen, you unspeakable ass?

THOMAS. Just as I told you. They forced their way into my room and found the paper.

BUTLER. The one I gave you?

THOMAS. It's the only one I had.

BUTLER. But I told you not to take it home. I told you to send it off right away, didn't I?

THOMAS. I was weak. I'm in love. *(In a soldierly tone)* Your orders, Colonel?

BUTLER. No orders.

THOMAS. Suggestions?

BUTLER. Take out your revolver, shoot me and then yourself.

THOMAS. If that were an order, I'd obey. But as it's friendly advice, I refuse with disgust. And I also refuse, though without feeling in the matter, the title of ass.—Are you angry with me?

BUTLER. You'll understand my feelings in a moment. A short while ago I told you how I had won Natasha. I wanted you to know me, my son. Now I'll tell you how I lost her. For ten years we lived happily together following the principles taught by our apostolic writer Tolstoy. She was a perfect angel even though she became rather more than pleasantly plump. One day I arrived from Paris before I was expected. I entered Natasha's boudoir unannounced. She was talking to a baby-faced lieutenant, her voice cold and indifferent. Natasha was saying: "I think mathematics is the most abstract of sci-

ences." The lieutenant replied: "I respectfully agree with you." Hearing his answer, I drew my revolver in a rage.

THOMAS *(Wonderingly)*. Why?

BUTLER. Because while he said it, the lieutenant was sitting on Natasha's lap. The next moment they were both on their knees begging for their lives.

THOMAS. And what was your answer to that?

BUTLER. A kiss of forgiveness. With tears in my eyes.

THOMAS *(Moved)*. Natasha must have been thrilled.

BUTLER. I didn't kiss *her*. I kissed the lieutenant. I said to him, brokenly: "I bow before the eternal laws of nature. I love Natasha, but you are young. You have a better right to happiness than I who am growing old. Go in peace and by all means take her with you." They both kissed my hand and left forever. If Tolstoy had been present, I swear he would have caressed his beard with satisfaction.

THOMAS. Why have you told me this?

BUTLER. Because not so long ago I had to cope again with a situation not so very different.

THOMAS *(Frowning)*. You are in love with the Princess.

BUTLER *(Quietly)*. I wouldn't deserve to be called a man if my nostrils didn't quiver when she looks at me.

THOMAS *(Moved)*. And . . . yet . . . you helped me!

BUTLER. Your happiness is more important than mine. Remember Tolstoy and his beard. But it hurts to think that I made this sacrifice in vain. That's why I was excited to the extent of calling you an ass. *(Unexpectedly he bursts into a rapid flow of Russian, accompanied by accusing gestures. Here is what he says:)* Vi menia sdielali niestchastnim i samovo siebia sdielali niestchastnim, Vi sentimentalni durak!

THOMAS *(Interrupts, quickly, as if to excuse himself).* Vi pravi! Ya soshel s'uma iz za etoy . . . *(In a voice instinct with love, accompanied by appropriate gestures)* Ah, Anna moia! Anna! Anna!

BUTLER *(Shouts at him angrily, rapidly)* Brosite razdoriatza! Ya postaraius otsiuda oudrat poka ne pozdno!

*(*THEY *kiss each other unexpectedly and wildly. The* QUARTET *outside softly begins to play the second movement of Tchaikovsky's Symphonie Pathetique)*

THOMAS *(Exultant).* Tchaikovsky!

BUTLER *(Angrily).* To hell with Tchaikovsky! It's all his fault! *(Goes out)*

(Enter FRENCH AMBASSADOR *with* SOPHIE. THOMAS *remains standing beside one of the doors at the rear)*

FRENCH AMBASSADOR. His Highness the Ambassador appears nervous.

SOPHIE. Not at all, Your Excellency. You Frenchmen like to exaggerate. His Highness is an equable man. His only sorrow is that France is still a republic.

FRENCH AMBASSADOR. We are aware of that sorrow. The strings of French monarchist intrigues are pulled in Austria. *(*HE *sees* THOMAS *standing beside the door)* Ah, Mr. Thomas. *(*THEY *shake hands) (Mean-*

ingly, discreetly) If I were as lucky in love as you are, I shouldn't stand there with such a sad face. The news has spread like wildfire. As soon as it's official, I'll congratulate you. Meanwhile I envy you from the bottom of my heart. *(*THOMAS *bows, with a painful smile.* KRON *enters.* FRENCH AMBASSADOR *speaks to* THOMAS)* Let me congratulate you, though, on your new distinction. His Majesty the Emperor assuredly selects the right men on whom to confer his honors. *(Flatteringly, to* KRON) Because he has such excellent advisers.

KRON *(With a painful smile).* Thank you for the compliment, Your Excellency, though I'm sure I don't deserve it.

FRENCH AMBASSADOR *(Ingratiatingly).* Modesty is one of the most pleasing qualities of Austrian diplomats. *(To* SOPHIE, *smiling, though actually addressing his words to* KRON) I could really be fond of them, except that—as I was saying— certain among them show a suspiciously friendly interest in the monarchists. In the pretending Bourbon family.

KRON *(Cautiously diplomatic).* Interest doesn't necessarily mean sympathy, Your Excellency.

FRENCH AMBASSADOR. Believe me, these Bourbons deserve no sympathy. Their women are respectable. But not their men.

KRON *(Wanting to be very cunning).* I've also been told the young pretenders aren't as serious as they might be. They are more engrossed in pretty women than in public affairs.

FRENCH AMBASSADOR. It's common knowledge. *(With pointed sarcasm)* They don't deserve the support of Austria. They run after women all the time.

KRON *(Feigns indignation)*. Awful! And do they ever catch them?

FRENCH AMBASSADOR. I must assume so because one of them—for instance—is now involved in a paternity suit.

KRON. Disgusting. *(Hardly concealing his interest)* Which one is that?

FRENCH AMBASSADOR. Jean-Joseph d'Origny-Bourbon. Still, he's respectable compared with his younger brother. That youth is a bachelor, with two children. Both exactly eighteen months old.

KRON. Twins?

FRENCH AMBASSADOR. No. They have different mothers.

KRON. A monster! *(Delighted)* What's *his* name?

FRENCH AMBASSADOR *(Quickly)*. Philippe-Louis-Adhemar.

KRON. I beg pardon?

FRENCH AMBASSADOR *(Slowly)*. Philippe, Louis, Adhemar.

K R O N *(Smiles mysteriously)*. Thank you. *(Casts a triumphant glance at* SOPHIE*)* ......

FRENCH AMBASSADOR. Believe me, their names aren't worth remembering. *(Takes a drink from the* LACKEY'S *tray at the open door)* Merci bien. *(Goes out;* LACKEY *disappears at the same time)*

SOPHIE *(Overwhelmed)*. Rudolf, I have to bow before this dazzling display of your diplomatic genius, which still functions so brilliantly even after the shock you've suffered. How fortunate that the fate of Europe depends on men like you.

KRON *(Conceitedly)*. It may just be that I have with these few questions set a grandchild of my Emperor, yet to be born, upon the throne of France.

SOPHIE. You're a born diplomatist, Rudolf.

KRON *(Glancing at* THOMAS; *sighs bitterly)* I'm a dead diplomatist, Sophie.

*(*ANN *and* CLEMENTINE *enter)*

ANN *(Sees* THOMAS, *but doesn't deign to notice him)*. Having to receive guests in this state of mind! With smiles! *(Looks at* THOMAS *severely. Then, fixing her eyes upon* THOMAS, *she speaks to* CLEMENTINE*)* Mother, ask him what is he waiting for?

THOMAS *(To* ANN, *humbly)*. I was only waiting to inform Your Highness that I am leaving tonight, but I'll be at my hotel until train time. I'll await your commands there. A tempest of despair is raging in my heart.

ANN *(Icily)*. I've heard that weather-report before. *(*THOMAS, *deflated, lowers his head.* ANN *speaks still fixing her eyes upon* THOMAS*)* Tell him, Mother, that I owe him a debt of gratitude. No medicine could have cured my illness so quickly and so effectively as his foul betrayal. I'll forget him. Tell him to make it easier by leaving at once without saying a word. *(*THOMAS *bows and goes out.* ANN *follows him with her eyes. Then with her hand on her heart)* Mother, do I look like a woman whose heart's been broken?

CLEMENTINE. Not a bit.

ANN. Thank goodness.—My bodily ills have ceased. But I'm experiencing a new and hitherto unknown affliction . . . that has nothing to do with physical things. I think it's what the middle class calls anguish of spirit. Quite excruciating.

CLEMENTINE. The Archbishop will console you in Vienna tomorrow.

ANN. Don't mention the Archbishop. He reminds me of my cancelled pleasures. *(To* KRON*)* Well?

KRON. My tragedy proceeds to its climax. The military attaché just called me. Even over the telephone, his voice was dripping poison. He'll be here in a moment, with the paper. —How could this ever have happened?

ANN. Are you asking me?

BLOCK. It couldn't have happened any way but that Mr. Thomas stole the document. Here, in your apartment. *(To* ANN*)* What does Your Highness say to that?

ANN. The same thing that the peasant said the first time he saw a giraffe.

KRON *(With dignity).* What did the peasant say the first time he saw a giraffe?

ANN. He said, "I don't believe it."

BLOCK. I do. The man is doubtless from the Russian Intelligence Service. He as good as admitted it.

SOPHIE. He begins to get interesting, just when we have to drop him.

KRON. Are you suffering, Ann?

ANN. I hope it doesn't show.

KRON. No. It doesn't. That's why I'm asking you.

ANN. I think I am suffering, Rudolf. And I notice with some surprise that I'm suffering just like any chambermaid. *(Thoughtfully)* That reminds me . . . I was fourteen. One day I saw our young kitchen-maid bathing in the lake. I was startled beyond words when I saw she had breasts just like me, a Princess of royal blood. I cried bitterly all night over that. Next morning I bought gold paint, closed my door and gilded my little breasts. I went around for weeks after that, proud of my golden princessly breasts sparkling under my chemise. Well . . . I've tried to do the same about my sufferings, now. But there is no gilding them. I'm as miserable as any poor servant might be. If this goes on much longer, I'm afraid suffering will make me democratic. Can you imagine, I thought of suicide at first!

KRON *(Reproachfully).* Ann!

ANN. I was hesitating between two kinds of suicide. Physical and moral.

KRON. What do you mean?

ANN. Physical suicide: taking poison. Moral suicide: running away with that scoundrel, right off, this very evening just as I am. Without even changing.

SOPHIE. Without waiting for the King?

ANN. I couldn't look a King in the eye with an adulterous plan in my heart.

SOPHIE. Why not?

ANN. There is only one time we may look a King in the eye with an adulterous plan in our hearts, that is when this plan tends to benefit him personally. *(To* KRON*)* But rest assured. I've dropped the idea of both kinds of suicide. Physical suicide would have been too bitter, the moral kind too sweet. I've found a middle way. A bitter-sweet one.

KRON. And it is?

ANN. I can't remain your wife, but I'll not be his. *(To* BLOCK*)* Go on with the divorce. But call off the wedding.

BLOCK. As Your Highness commands.

KRON. You're behaving like a saint.

(Music fades. ARIBERT appears at the open door and makes impatient gestures)

ANN. Quite correct, Baron. *(Sighing)* We must see to our guests! Coming! *(Exit)*

(CLEMENTINE, SOPHIE *and* ARIBERT *follow her.* BLOCK *and* KRON *are left alone)*

BLOCK. I am afraid the military attaché will use this horrible affair against you.

KRON. He shouted dreadful insults at me over the telephone. You'll hear him in a moment. He's a wicked man and an old enemy of mine.

BLOCK. We must prepare our case quickly, so that I may have the means of counter-attacking him when he attacks.—Where do you keep papers of this sort?

KRON. Since I used to work on them at night, they are sometimes in my private safe, here at home, in my bedroom.

BLOCK. Is there anything else in that safe?

KRON. Jewels.

BLOCK. How many keys are there to the safe?

KRON. Two. One is with me and the other . . . *(Suddenly rigid with fright)* . . . is with my wife. *(Staring numbly)* May I have a large glass of brandy? (BLOCK *hands him brandy.* KRON *drinks it. Muttering softly to himself)* The other key . . . is with my wife . . .

BLOCK. As counsellor to Her Highness' family for the past 120 years, I protest, in my own as well as in the name of my ancestors, against the suspicion that has just arisen in your mind.

KRON *(Pays no attention to him. In a frightened whisper).* The other key . . . is with my wife . . . *(To* BLOCK) Has the safe been forced?

BLOCK. No. It's perfectly all right.

KRON. I used to put every single "BX" document into the safe the minute I got it. Therefore this one must have been in there too. There's no doubt of it. And so, if the safe isn't forced . . . *(He stops)*

BLOCK. I repeat respectfully my protest against any effort on your part to associate the disappearance of this document with your wife's emotional ties to the man in whose possession the document was found.

KRON *(Irritably).* I consider your mind-reading efforts as impertinence. I am only trying to find the solution to this riddle, not thinking of my beloved wife. But it seems that you're the one who dares to think of her in this connection and who is trying to turn my suspicions toward her.

BLOCK *(Angrily).* I reject this insinuation with disgust.

(BUTLER *enters)*

BUTLER *(With tragic look in his face).* His Excellency the Military Attaché.

KRON. My executioner. Don't leave me in this moment of anguish, Dr. Block.

BLOCK. I'll stay with you to the bitter end. Chin up, Your Highness.

KRON *(To the* BUTLER). Show His Excellency in.

(BUTLER *opens the door with a pained look.* GENERAL DUBETZ *enters with a briefcase)*

DUBETZ *(Sullenly).* Good evening.

KRON. Good evening, General.
(ANN *and* ARIBERT *enter the other door.* DUBETZ *bows*)

ANN *(To* ARIBERT). Please, Baron, see to it that no one disturbs us.

ARIBERT. But if the King . . .

DUBETZ *(Angrily)*. Not even he!
(ARIBERT *goes out, frightened.* ANN *motions for all to sit down*)

ANN *(To* BUTLER) What are you waiting for?

BUTLER. Your orders.

ANN. Be sure that no one listens at the door. Above all be sure that *you* don't listen.

BUTLER. I don't deserve this remark from one I love.
(ANN *freezes.* BUTLER *exit*)

KRON *(Maliciously)*. That's the result of fraternizing with servants.

DUBETZ *(Taking papers from his briefcase)*. May I speak?

KRON. You may.

DUBETZ. The facts are as follows: an hour ago the Chief of Police sent me this coded document, which came originally from our Embassy, and which was found by detectives in the riding boots of an architect named Thomas.

BLOCK. Why did they search his boots?

DUBETZ *(With a general's profound contempt for lawyers)*. A lawyer can't ask me questions. This isn't one of your court trials but the report of His Majesty's Military Attaché to His Majesty's Ambassador. (SOPHIE *enters*) The best thing a lawyer can do is to keep his mouth shut.

SOPHIE. That's right.

DUBETZ *(Stands up to greet her)*. Countess!

SOPHIE. General! *(Sits down)*

DUBETZ *(To* ANN). I take the liberty of inquiring respectfully if Your Highness shares my opinion that the presence of the Countess at this conference is not a burning necessity.

ANN *(Coldly, as always)*. Cousin Sophie is present at everything. First, because I need her advice. Secondly, because she wouldn't leave if I told her to.

SOPHIE *(To the General)*. Certainly not.

BLOCK. Which goes to show there are times when the best thing a general can do is to keep his mouth shut.
(DUBETZ *casts a murderous glance at* BLOCK)

KRON. Please continue, General.

DUBETZ. The code department promptly deciphered the document. Here is the original. *(Hands it over to* KRON) And this is the transcription. *(Passes it, too, to* KRON)

KRON *(Glancing at the paper)*. Awful!

DUBETZ. It certainly is awful.

KRON. The carrying capacity of the new railway lines that go to the East.

DUBETZ. In detail!

KRON. The altered plans for frontier mobilization!

DUBETZ. Down to the last detail!

KRON. It is devastating, General. How did this ever get to the man?

DUBETZ. Mr. Thomas comes and goes freely in your house. The document was entrusted to your own person.

KRON. I hope you're not implying that I gave it to him?

DUBETZ. Not for the world. He could get it only from someone who had a key to your safe.

KRON. There are two keys to my safe. One is with me and the other with . . . my wife.

DUBETZ. I wouldn't trust a woman with keys to a safe in which there are secret documents.

BLOCK (*Aggressively*). Do you know what you're saying, man?

KRON (*Energetically*). You wouldn't dare suspect my wife!

DUBETZ. I would. Yes.

BLOCK (*With quiet dignity*). In full realization of what the consequences of such a statement might be I permit myself the release of my justifiable indignation in referring to His Excellency Lieutenant General von Dubetz as a swine.

(ANN *meanwhile sits rigid as a statue*)

KRON (*To* DUBETZ). You are a common slanderer whom I'll meet at pistol point if you dare say a thing like that without proof.

DUBETZ. I have my proof.

KRON. Of what?

DUBETZ. That Her Highness actually handled this document.

KRON. Fingerprints?

DUBETZ. No. Better than that.

KRON. What is this proof?

DUBETZ. That I gave the paper into Her Highness' hands myself. (*Grins*)

KRON. Are you joking, or lying?

DUBETZ. Neither.

(KRON *looks at* ANN, *uncomprehending*)

ANN (*Coldly, as always*). He's neither joking nor lying. He's only tactless.

KRON. How do you mean that?

ANN (*Quietly, coldly, motionless-ly*). Rudolf, I'm going to surprise you with a confession.

KRON. For the first time in my life I have the feeling that I'll be genuinely surprised. Please go on.

(SOPHIE *begins to weep and weeping she pours and drinks a large glass of brandy*)

ANN. Rudolf, the General gave me the paper, and I put it in the safe so a certain person would have an opportunity to steal it.

(SOPHIE *screams, grasps at her heart*)

ANN. Wrong again, Sophie. It wasn't Thomas.

KRON. Who then?

ANN. Diegelmann, the butler. He also has a key to the safe.

KRON. The butler?

ANN. Yes.

KRON. I'm losing my mind!

(ARIBERT *enters*)

ARIBERT. His Majesty the King has just left his palace.

KRON (*Stares at him foolishly*). Why? (*Looks at him fixedly, then wakes up*) Oh yes, thank you!

(ARIBERT *goes out, frightened*)

ANN. I discovered a month ago that the butler was rummaging through our closets and drawers. He had a wax impression made of my safe key. I promptly reported this to the General.

KRON. Why not to me?

ANN. You'd have fired the man, complained to the police, and had him arrested.

KRON. That's right. Wouldn't that be the thing to do?

ANN. No. The butler wasn't after valuables. He isn't a thief, but a spy. And any time we find a spy who goes around looking for secrets in a safe, we ought to be pleased.

We should take advantage of him. He must find things which we have planted there for his benefit. That's the system.

SOPHIE. From whom did you learn that?

ANN. From the General.

SOPHIE. Has he been giving you lessons in counter-espionage?

ANN. Twice a week.

SOPHIE. And this paper?

ANN *(To* KRON*)*. I put it in your safe.

DUBETZ. There isn't a word of truth in what that document says. I wrote it, from beginning to end. A very cunning device. I was proud of it. It would have helped our General Staff enormously to have had it fall into the hands of the Russians. This is the sixth document of the sort I've manufactured.

KRON *(To* ANN*)*. And you took over a role like that?

ANN *(Majestically)*. For Emperor and country.

KRON. Why didn't you tell me all this?

ANN. I promised the General I wouldn't.

KRON *(To* DUBETZ*)*. You had the nerve to forbid my wife to tell me?

DUBETZ. Yes. You'd have spoiled everything.

KRON *(Boiling)*. What do you mean taking this tone with me? You're talking as though I were an idiot?

DUBETZ *(Just as angrily)*. From the military point of view you're an absolute zero. But this friend of yours who couldn't think of a better place to hide the document than in his riding boots . . . ! A crafty spy, I must say!

KRON *(Very angry)*. What's this? Are you reproaching me for not keeping better spies around the house? Really, that's pretty thick!

ANN. Silence, please. *(Both become silent)*. I'm only interested in one question. How Mr. Thomas happened to gain possession of the document. I must know whether or not he was a thief.

DUBETZ. That doesn't interest me at all. The whole case was closed as far as I'm concerned, the moment the police exposed that idiot. *(Angrily again, to* KRON*)* My whole brilliantly conceived plan collapsed in the face of your friend's riding boots! And quite certainly, my career as well! *(As* KRON *holds out the papers toward him)* What's that?

KRON. The document.

DUBETZ. I don't need it any more.

KRON. Shall I lock it in my safe?

DUBETZ. Do you think they'll be stupid enough to steal it a second time? *(Opens door 1, and calls outside)* Please tell the doorman to call my car. *(Closes the door)*

KRON *(Staring gloomily before him)*. I want to see that butler.

SOPHIE *(Opens door 2, calls to the* LACKEY *outside)*. The butler, please.

KRON. To think I didn't notice any of this! I hadn't opened my safe for weeks.

DUBETZ. We opened it every day. So did the butler. I've never seen such a conscientious and reliable thief. It hurts to lose a good customer like that. *(*BUTLER *comes in and stops, with an innocent face)*

KRON. Diegelmann . . .

BUTLER *(Quietly)*. You may as well call me Colonel Semionov.

There's no use being dramatic any more. *(Snapping to attention, introduces himself to Dubetz)* Colonel Vassili Konstantinovitch Semionov, of His Majesty's the Czar's 936th Imperial Infantry Regiment.

DUBETZ *(Ironically)*. Thank you. I knew it long ago.

BUTLER *(Elegantly)*. Nevertheless, as a well-bred man I am bound to observe this formality.

SOPHIE *(Looking at the BUTLER)*. Curious, isn't it? I've never noticed what a good-looking man he is.

BUTLER. Thank you, Countess.

SOPHIE. Hasn't a trace of accent either.

BUTLER. If I had an accent, I'd never have been sent here. But it's all over now. *(To DUBETZ, offering him some keys)* Allow me to present you with my passkeys as a souvenir.

DUBETZ *(Annoyed)*. Thank you, I don't want them.

BUTLER *(Politely to KRON)*. Your Highness sent for me.

KRON. Diegelmann, you're fired. Colonel, you may go.

BUTLER. Right away?

KRON. The sooner the better. Rest assured it is not in the least to our interest to make any complaint against you. No Ambassador would want to make it known his safe had been turned into a mail-box. The whole affair will remain a military secret.

BUTLER. I'm quite aware of that. *(To ANN)* May I be permitted to make a request? *(ANN nods)* Will Your Highness be good enough to fire Louise, the French maid, too?

ANN. Why?

BUTLER. She's my wife.

ANN. Is that why you hate her?

BUTLER. On the contrary, I adore her.

KRON. Was she spying, too?

BUTLER. Yes, Your Highness. For the French Government.

KRON. Amazing. The German Ambassador recommended the girl to us.

BUTLER. We were in service in his household for two years.

DUBETZ. Do you always spy on Ambassadors?

BUTLER. It's my specialty, General.

DUBETZ *(To KRON)*. You have a fine staff, I must say, Ambassador.

(ARIBERT enters)

ARIBERT *(To DUBETZ)*. I'm sorry, General, we can't call your car. We can't find your chauffeur. He's disappeared.

DUBETZ. What do you mean, disappeared?

BUTLER. If I may make so bold as to advise you, don't look for him. It's no use.

KRON. What? He . . . too?

BUTLER. Yes. One of our best.

(DUBETZ looks wildly at the calm BUTLER)

ARIBERT *(To KRON)*. Furthermore it is reported that His Majesty will be here in nine minutes. *(To DUBETZ, explaining)* The royal car is coming along at a moderate pace.

DUBETZ *(Unexpectedly)*. They can drive into the ditch for all I care.

ARIBERT *(Terrified)*. Heavens! *(Totters unsteadily from the room)*

BUTLER. Is there anything else you wish of me?

ANN. Yes. There is. An answer to the question that torments me. Was Thomas a thief, or wasn't he?

BUTLER. Though I have been dismissed as a butler, I would like, as a parting favor, to be permitted once again to announce a guest, and for the last time. *(Opening the door)* Mr. Thomas.

(THOMAS *enters*)

THOMAS *(Introducing himself to Dubetz, with a military air)*. Nikolai Ivanovitch Bialoskurskov, Captain in His Majesty's the Czar's Imperial 1572nd infantry regiment.

ANN. I have a final question to ask you, Mr. . . . Iva . . . Bia . . . Bialo . . .

THOMAS. It's hopeless.

ANN. It would be unbearable for me to think I was the betrothed of a thief. You owe it to me to explain how that paper came into your possession.

THOMAS. I couldn't answer that if I were on the rack, Your Highness.

BUTLER. Thank you, Captain. You have acted in accordance with our rules. But it's all useless now. They know I was the thief. Their darling thief, a love of a thief that they led by the nose. Unfortunately I only learned that tonight, five minutes after I called you an ass. Moral: don't call anybody else an ass until you're sure you aren't one yourself. *(To* ANN*)* I gave that damned paper to the Captain.

ANN. Why did you?

BUTLER. Because it was his duty to steal, but he couldn't bring himself to do it in his sweetheart's house. His feelings caused him to be derelict in his duty. Even though his life was threatened.

ANN. Who threatened him?

BUTLER. I did, by your leave. Under orders. Your Highness can imagine how I felt. But I collapsed with joy when he finally accepted the paper, with tears in his eyes. *(Dabs lightly at his eyes)* I love the Captain like a son. I had to protect his happiness.

ANN. I'm beginning to think that sentiments aren't so ridiculous, after all. Colonel, you really are a sensitive soul, the kind we've been reading about in the novels of His Excellency Count Tolstoy.

BUTLER. That's one of the reasons for my present failure. The other is that I'm not very intelligent. In fact, I must have been very stupid to let one of the stupidest Austrian generals make a fool of me. (DUBETZ *shoots the* BUTLER *a murderous glance)* Sorry, General, this isn't my personal opinion. In the secret instructions of our General Staff about the personnel of your Embassy, you are listed as Number Two in the order of stupidity.

DUBETZ. Who is Number One?

BUTLER. I won't answer that.

KRON. Thank you.

ANN *(To the* BUTLER*)*. Your consolation should be that it wasn't just a General who made a fool of you, but a woman with him.

BUTLER. If it weren't for that, lovely lady, I'd have blown my brains out long ago.

ANN. Thank God you didn't do that. I demand that you keep on living for the sake of those who bear you affection. I hereby permit you to count me among them.

BUTLER. I'm afraid I'm beginning to adore Your Highness already.

ANN. Nobody will prevent you from doing so. Myself, least of all.

THOMAS *(To* ANN*)*. I humbly beg Your Highness' permission to say something.

ANN *(Coldly, as ever)*. You be quiet. I'll do the talking. Will you all be good enough to listen closely to what I say? Please answer my questions.

(The following scene must be enacted without pauses. ANN speaks almost without interruption. The OTHERS respond shortly in answer to a nod from her—as instruments in an orchestra come in at a signal from the conductor—without breaking the continuity of ANN's speech)

KRON. Cross-examination?

ANN. Yes. In short. And quick. Then . . . the verdict.

KRON. Well?

ANN. Defendant.

THOMAS. Present.

ANN. You did not steal.

THOMAS. No.

ANN. You received the document as a gift.

THOMAS. Exactly.

ANN *(To BUTLER)*. The witness?

BUTLER. I swear.

ANN *(To THOMAS)*. You were ready to lose your career, in fact your life, for your fiancé. *(To the BUTLER)* Colonel, as a military expert?

BUTLER. Right.

ANN *(To THOMAS)*. You have done everything in your power to render the Emperor of Austria and his army a great service, but the police tripped you up. *(To DUBETZ)* General, as a military expert?

DUBETZ *(Angrily)*. Unfortunately, that's the case.

ANN *(To KRON)*. Ambassador, as a political expert?

KRON. Correct.

ANN. Just to put my conscience entirely at ease, please tell me I am morally wrong, Sophie.

SOPHIE. You are.

ANN. Thank you. Now then, the verdict. Dr. Block, I command you not to stop my marriage to Mr. Thomas, but to hasten it. *(DUBETZ exit angrily door 1.—ANN speaks to KRON)* Curious. Now that this man has been cleared beyond any doubt, my desire for him has returned—even though it had ceased completely a while ago. Amazing how political annoyances can kill our erotic inclinations.

KRON. I'm glad you understand at last why I have been denied the joys of fatherhood.

ANN *(To THOMAS)*. I have orders for you, too. Take the police commissioner's advice, and make your escape tonight—not to Russia, though, but to Vienna, to my mother's house.

THOMAS *(Overjoyed)*. Ann! Oh joy, oh rapture!

KRON. Vienna? *Before* the wedding-day?

ANN. This will be one of his rewards for having taught me to suffer. It was a new sensation in my life.

SOPHIE *(Amazed)*. I don't recognize Princess Ann!

ANN. Nor do I.

THOMAS. Ann, a tempest of joy is raging in my heart.

ANN *(To KRON)*. These poetic outbursts of his drive me to despair. How fortunate I don't love him for his brains. *(To BUTLER, who bows before leaving)* Goodbye, Colonel. You saved me from a tragedy. And . . . for the first time, Sophie, you are right. He is good-looking. He even has something aristocratic about him. *(To BUTLER)* Are you of noble extraction?

BUTLER. No, Your Highness. But all my life I have loved none but ladies of the highest nobility. They educated and polished me, so to speak.

KRON. If you are telling us this chapter of your autobiography in the position of our former butler, I am compelled to remark that I'm still not interested in your emotions.

ANN. He's not a former butler, Rudolf. I no longer see his lackey's garb upon him.

SOPHIE. For heaven's sake, how do you see him?

ANN. With medals on his breast.

BUTLER (*Enthusiastically*). Your Highness, I cannot restrain the foolhardy observation that if . . . if we had met . . . sooner . . .

ANN. That wouldn't have been good for me. Your Tolstoyan personality would have affected me. Maybe . . . God forbid . . . you would have taught me to smile. Or even to weep.

BUTLER. Or both, Your Highness.

ANN. You'd better go now, Colonel. I shall keep alive the memory of your gallant figure. A handsome stranger who loved me unselfishly.

BUTLER. And how, Your Highness!

ANN (*To* KRON, *raising her head proudly*). Rudolf, in view of the Colonel's invaluable services to my country, would you mind if I went so far as to consider the notion of kissing him on the brow?

KRON (*Looks maliciously at* THOMAS. *To* ANN:) You're addressing this question to the wrong party.

ANN (*To the* BUTLER). Will you come over here, Colonel. Not too close, please.

(BUTLER *steps up to her.* ANN, *cold and stiff as usual, breathes a kiss about one inch from his forehead. Music outside cut abruptly. At the same time* CLEMENTINE *and* ARIBERT *come in door 3.* ARIBERT *freezes in his tracks as he sees* ANN *kiss the* BUTLER)

CLEMENTINE (*Not at all surprised, with calm dignity*). No doubt, my daughter just kissed the butler before her husband and her fiancé. I don't understand why as yet, but I'm willing to swear she did the right thing.

ANN. Thank you, Mother. (*To the* BUTLER) Are you going back to Russia?

BUTLER. Never. I'm opposed to the death penalty in principle but I particularly dislike it if it's pronounced against me.

ANN. But in that case you're left without a livelihood.

BUTLER. There are many Embassies in the world. Anyway . . . (*Bows toward* ANN) Thank you very much for a pleasant evening. (*Exit*)

(ANN *looks at* ARIBERT, *to signify he may speak*)

ARIBERT (*Excitedly*). I want to report that His Majesty's car has turned the corner of our street.

(ALL *rise. Music outside once more begins to play Beethoven's Minuet in G.*—FRENCH AMBASSADOR *walks in door 2, which is wide open*)

ARIBERT. The Ambassador and Her Highness, accompanied by their suite, will receive their Majesties and lead them by candle light. (*Com-*

manding like a general) The lackeys with the candles!

(*Door 1 opens.* TWO LACKEYS *each bearing a silver candlestick with twelve lighted candles, come in.* GENERAL DUBETZ *enters, following them. The door is left open. The* LACKEYS *cross the stage, and go out door 3.*)

KRON *(Deeply moved, solemnly).* Ann, in just a few moments, you'll receive a live King and Queen here in your home.

ANN *(Majestically).* Yes, Rudolf. On a firm moral and legal basis too, and consequently—as always—with head held high. *(Haughtily raises her head very high)*

(LOUISE *and the* BUTLER *appear modestly on the threshold, at door 1, and look in)*

ARIBERT. And now let us start. Please be good enough to line up in the order of your rank.

(The CROWD *whose members had already taken their pre-arranged places, step into position — as they were in the Prologue.* BUTLER *and* LOUISE *imperceptibly slip into their places)*

(When they're all in position, the whole CROWD *becomes rigid, as though they had been changed back into wax figures. The scene slowly goes dim, at the same time that the music becomes softer. For a few moments the whole scene, music, lighting, mood is exactly as at the end of the Prologue, when the wax museum's* MANAGER *and the* VISITORS *had gone out, leaving only the wax figures on the stage)*

(Then gradually, the scene becomes completely dark, and in the total darkness down comes the)

CURTAIN

ARTHUR

ARTHUR

COMEDY IN THREE ACTS

CHARACTERS

FRED CORTIN
EDITH BROOKS
ROBERT GEOFFREY
JULIE
LAWYER
BISHOP
WOMAN

BOY
RIBAUD
HOTEL MANAGER
FLORIST
WAITER
BUTLER
BELLBOY

PLACE : ACT I: TERRACE OF A HOTEL. ACT II: ROOM IN A HOTEL NEAR MONTE CARLO. ACT III: ROOM IN A CHATEAU NEAR MONTE CARLO.

(New acting version of the same author's JEMAND. "Jemand" was produced at the KOMOEDIE in Berlin by MAX REINHARDT, *with* LILI DARVAS *and* ALBERT BASSERMANN *in the leading roles; at the* VOLKSTHEATER *in Vienna with* SYBILLE BINDER *and* LEOPOLD KRAMER; *at the* BELVAROSI SZINHAZ *in Budapest with* ILONA TITKOS *and* SANDOR GOTH; *on the Italian stages with* PAOLA BORBONI *and* RUGGIERO LUPI.—*English text by* P. G. WODEHOUSE.)

ARTHUR

ACT ONE

SCENE: *Summer night. Terrace of a fashionable summer hotel in America, with a few tables and chairs. A door, right, leads to the bar; it is open. Left, door leads to the lobby. In the background, lake, hills and starry sky.*

AT RISE: EDITH, *dressed in evening gown, sits alone listening to the soft piano music from the bar. The music is still in progress when* ROBERT *enters from the lobby.*

EDITH *(Stopping him with a gesture)*. Shhh! (ROBERT *pauses at the door. The piano plays softly on.* BOTH *wait silent and motionless until it is finished. As the song ends,* EDITH *speaks)* All right. You can come now. (ROBERT *goes to her)* I asked the pianist to play that song for me. He left the door to the bar open, so that I could hear.

ROBERT. So you've turned *his* head, too, have you . . . the poor pimply little rat.

EDITH. He is *not* pimply.

ROBERT. Pardon me. He's spotted like a leopard. And he looks at you like a sheep.

EDITH. So do you.

ROBERT. And why not? I love you.

EDITH *(Calling into the bar)*. Thanks so much.

ROBERT. Don't mention it.

EDITH. I was speaking to the pianist. *(Calls)* That was beautiful. *(She closes the door to the bar)*

ROBERT. So now *he's* happy.

EDITH. I hope so.

ROBERT. Quite a change for you, making someone happy. So this is where you've been hiding yourself. Are you alone?

EDITH. Not now . . . unfortunately.

ROBERT. Ouch!

EDITH. Sorry. I didn't mean to hurt your feelings. It slipped out.

ROBERT. Perhaps you would like *me* to slip out?

EDITH. Of course not. Don't be so touchy. Come and sit down.

ROBERT. Thanks. You know, you really are extraordinary. One never knows where one is with you. Take tonight. At dinner you were the life and soul of the party . . . gay, radiant, electric.

EDITH. Thank you.

ROBERT. And now here you are, moping in the moonlight while pimply pianists play you mushy melodies. I can't understand you.

EDITH. You don't have to.

ROBERT. I wish I could. They were discussing you in the bar last night.

EDITH. And what did they say about me in the bar?

ROBERT. They said you were mysterious.

EDITH. Aren't women supposed to be mysterious?

ROBERT. Not so mysterious as you are. There's a limit. Do you realize that nobody here has any idea where you came from?

EDITH. I came from New York. Last week.

ROBERT. But before that. Do you know a man in the hotel named Elsworthy?

EDITH. By sight. Why.

ROBERT. He used to be with our embassies in Eastern Europe for years, and he says that though the way you

131

speak makes him think you were brought up here in America, your appearance and the strange exotic atmosphere you diffuse . . .

EDITH. You talk like an old-fashioned novel.

ROBERT. I have a sister who writes old-fashioned novels. I pick it up from her.

EDITH. Well, go on. The strange, exotic atmosphere I diffuse . . .

ROBERT . . . suggests a Balkan background. Does that flatter you or offend you?

EDITH. Neither. But it offends me that I should be discussed in a bar by a crowd of fuddled topers.

ROBERT. Oh come. Not *fuddled* topers.

EDITH. Fuddled.

ROBERT. Well, all right, if you say so. But you can't include *me*. I'm not fuddled . . . or sozzled . . . or oiled . . . or even blotto. I don't drink to drown my sorrows. When I'm hopelessly in love, I just suffer . . . like a toad beneath the harrow. That's from one of my sister's best sellers.

EDITH. I must get a copy.

ROBERT. No, but seriously. Who *are* you?

EDITH. Ask the tennis pro. He knows me. I played with him in Europe. At hotels in France . . . Switzerland . . .

ROBERT. I *have* asked him. He said he thought you were on the stage. An actress or singer.

EDITH. That wasn't so very clever of him. I always register at hotels under my stage name. I suppose you never heard it in your life?

ROBERT *(Embarrassed).* Well . . .

EDITH. Oh, don't apologize. The countries where that name meant something are a long way away, and it was many, many years ago . . .

ROBERT. "Many, many years ago!" You must have been a baby when you wowed them in Bulgaria.

EDITH. It wasn't Bulgaria.

ROBERT. Are you married? Have you ever been married?

EDITH. It sounds like a radio quiz.

ROBERT. And here's the sixty-four-dollar question. Are you thinking of getting married?

EDITH. Are you so interested?

ROBERT. "Interested" is a feeble word. Didn't you hear me say I loved you?

EDITH. So you did.

ROBERT. They say you can always recognize the *one woman,* when you meet her . . . the one woman you'll never be free from for the rest of your life.

EDITH *(With an ironical smile).* The *femme fatale?*

ROBERT. Exactly. I knew you were my *femme fatale* the instant I saw you. I shall never love anyone but you.

EDITH. I've heard that often.

ROBERT. You don't even like me.

EDITH. I do. I think you're charming.

ROBERT. But . . . ?

EDITH. I was going to say "But I wish you weren't so *mushy.*"

ROBERT *(Outraged). Mushy?*

EDITH. Your own word. Didn't you admit yourself that you looked at me like a sheep? That's not the way to seduce a woman.

ROBERT. Who's trying to seduce you? I'm not one of those wandering hotel-wolves. I'm a respectable British mining engineer.

EDITH. Too respectable. Not

your fault, of course. Just your up-bringing.

ROBERT. Who told you about my upbringing?

EDITH. I know everything. You're a distant relative of royalty. You were brought up by your two sisters.

ROBERT. I lost my parents as a child.—And . . . as to "relative of royalty" . . . Yes. As to "distant"—very distant indeed. But . . . relative just the same.

EDITH. That's one thing that fascinates me. I'm old-fashioned, I confess. I've a great admiration for royalty. And a little . . . for their relatives.

ROBERT. Thank you.

EDITH (*Looking at him with affectionate appraisal*). You . . . *were* brought up by women.

ROBERT. Yes.

EDITH. It has affected your character.

ROBERT. To the extent . . . that . . .

EDITH. It's made you too . . . too correct. Mild. Unenterprising.

ROBERT (*Annoyed*). What do you mean, unenterprising?

EDITH. Oh, just unenterprising. Correct. Mild. Overcautious.

ROBERT. You'd like it better if I sprang at you and bit you in the neck?

EDITH (*Tongue in cheek*). Much better. If you don't mind.

ROBERT. Well, I'm not going to.

EDITH. Of course not. Your sisters wouldn't approve.

ROBERT. I love my sisters! I respect and admire them!

EDITH. Very good.

ROBERT. I . . . Oh, let's change the subject. What made you come out on this deserted terrace?

EDITH. I wanted to get away from that mob of people drinking and talking politics. I wanted to be alone with the lake and the stars and the silent hills.

ROBERT. How poetic! Lake . . . stars . . . hills . . . (*Violently*) I don't believe a damned word of it. You're waiting for a man.

EDITH. How clever of you.

ROBERT. And I know who it is.

EDITH. Cleverer and cleverer.

ROBERT. It's the old man who arrived half an hour ago. I was in the lobby when he got here, and I saw the way he looked at you and the way you looked at him. You were whispering with him.

EDITH. You've been spying on me?

ROBERT. Of course.—The difference in age . . . is appalling.

EDITH (*Coldly*). I think you'd better go.

ROBERT. Oh don't worry. I'm going. I don't suppose you'll have to wait long. He's probably dressing now . . . putting on the perfect dinner jacket, skillfully cut to reduce his stomach to a minimum. (*After a brief pause*) Here he comes. I'll leave you to him.

(ROBERT *stalks out left, as* COR-TIN, *in dinner jacket, enters from the bar right, leaving the bar's door open*)

CORTIN. Been waiting long?

EDITH. Twenty minutes.

CORTIN. I'm sorry. I said ten sharp.

EDITH. I know. But I couldn't wait. I was too excited. So I came and sat.

CORTIN. And thought how much you loved me?

EDITH. All the time. To the accompaniment of soft music. Do sit down, and let me look at you. You're wonderful. So fit, so handsome. Oh dear, how long it seems since we were together.

CORTIN. Eight years.

EDITH. I was twenty then.

CORTIN. Which makes you . . . ?

EDITH. Twenty-four.

CORTIN. Twenty-three. Not a day older.

EDITH. You darling. You always used to say just the right thing.

CORTIN. God! You're beautiful. Enchanting. Let's have a drink.

EDITH. Yes, let's. What would you like?

CORTIN. You know my views. There is only one drink . . . champagne . . . and only one champagne . . . Irroy Brut . . . What music there is in those two words . . . *Irroy Brut.*

EDITH. Captain, please. *(Enter* WAITER *from bar)* A bottle of . . .

CORTIN. Excuse me, darling. *(To* WAITER) A bottle of Irroy Brut, please . . . if possible, 1920. *(Exit* WAITER) I like to do the ordering. Just a whim. Yes, you look beautiful. You still love me?

EDITH. More than ever.

CORTIN. Missed me?

EDITH. More than I can say. You missed *me?*

CORTIN. More than *I* can say.

EDITH. But all these years . . . Why didn't you write?

CORTIN. I'd resigned myself to never seeing you again.

EDITH. Never? Oh, how could you?

CORTIN. I thought it would be best. I heard there was a rich man in love with you, and I felt that I might be an embarrassment. Did he marry you?

EDITH. No.

CORTIN. Is he with you?

EDITH. No. I'm all alone. *(*WAITER *brings champagne)* Well, now that we're together again, we shall have to tell each other all about everything. Just think . . . eight years!

CORTIN. Eight years.

(Exit WAITER)

EDITH. Shall we exchange autobiographies?

CORTIN. Now?

EDITH. Can you wait? *I* can't . . . My dear father! Daddy! Papa! *(She kisses him emotionally. He is a little embarrassed)*

CORTIN. Come, come, my dear. There's nothing to be proud of, having a father like me.

EDITH. My dear, good father!

CORTIN. Would you say "good" was the *mot juste? (He takes her by the shoulders and looks at her)* My God, I've missed you, dear. Ever since I lost your mother, you're the only human being I love.

EDITH. Father!

CORTIN. And so on and so forth. We mustn't get sentimental. You may kiss me once . . . in the center of the forehead . . . and then we'll be calm and cool and practical and start picking up the threads. I last saw you, my child . . .

EDITH. Nineteen forty and . . . wait a moment . . . *(She thinks)*

CORTIN. Just before you divorced your husband.

EDITH. Just before my husband divorced *me.*

CORTIN. Yes, I suppose you are technically accurate there. Damn shame, that was, and all my fault.

EDITH. You mustn't reproach yourself, dear.

CORTIN. What do you mean, I mustn't reproach myself? Of course I must reproach myself. If I hadn't got so stiff in the joints, I'd kick myself. Every time I see myself in the mirror, I point a finger at myself and say to myself "*You* ruined that girl's life, you dirty dog."

EDITH. I don't see why you should say you ruined my life.

CORTIN. Well, I'd like to know who did, if I didn't. There you were, happily married . . .

EDITH. Fairly happily married.

CORTIN. Please! Don't interrupt me when I'm being remorseful. I'm like the priests of Baal, I'm gashing myself with knives and I wish to go on gashing undisturbed. You were *extremely* happily married to a blameless boy from Boston. Old family house *in* Boston. Exclusive, influential friends, all members of the best New England set . . . And then . . . one day . . .

EDITH. It was funny, wasn't it?

CORTIN. *Funny?* What extraordinary adjectives you choose. It was appalling. Your first big lawn party . . . Everybody there . . . everybody . . . Vital to make the thing a success. And what happened? I was playing Bridge in the garden . . . at a rustic table . . . with two Senators and a Governor . . . and I'd just gone three no trumps . . .

EDITH. I wonder if you would have made it.

CORTIN. Unquestionably, I think. I had six hearts to the ace, king, queen . . . However, it was not to be. Just as I gathered in the first trick, two gentlemanly detectives entered through the pergola and gathered *me*

in. Then . . . your papa went with them to the police station.

EDITH. Oh, well, these things will happen.

CORTIN. Tell me, how did the party go after I left?

EDITH. Not too well.

CORTIN. A certain strain?

EDITH. Yes, I would call it that.

CORTIN. I feared as much when I saw your mother-in-law fainting into the fruit salad. And your husband threw you over.

EDITH. Yes . . .

CORTIN. The lily-livered worm.

EDITH. You can't blame him.

CORTIN. Yes. I can.

EDITH. The family hounded him day and night till he agreed to sue for divorce.

CORTIN. He could have defied them.

EDITH. You can't defy the Boston Griffiths.

CORTIN. I suppose it was the publicity they disliked?

EDITH. There was a good deal, you know.

CORTIN. Of course. Yes . . . Your papa was sent to jail as a swindler after a sensational trial in New York. Can you blame them? Who wants a convicted confidence man in the family? A jailbird?

EDITH. People like the Griffiths hate to see their name in the tabloids.

CORTIN. I . . . oh, long, long ago . . . I rather enjoyed seeing mine. Still it takes all sorts to make a world. I suppose your husband could make out some kind of a case for himself . . . though I persist in considering him a worm. Well, back to our autobiography. That about covers nineteen forty . . . and . . .

EDITH. Just nineteen forty . . . *and*.

CORTIN. Nothing else of much interest happened to you?

EDITH. No. I was in Rio.

CORTIN. Dear old Rio!

EDITH. A second-rate singer, a so-called vocalist with a third-rate band in a night club. I called myself Rolly Royce.

CORTIN. Good God . . . And after the war? Still in Rio?

EDITH. Yes, but not in a night club. I had a lovely house of my own . . . and square-cut diamonds in my safe in the bank. There was a millionaire.

CORTIN. I see.

EDITH. And you . . . ?

CORTIN. During the war . . . in the summer months I did some spying for the patriotic French Resistance. They were very pleased with my work and wanted me to go on. But I quit. Cut into my time too much.

EDITH. And after the war?

CORTIN. After the war? Ah, yes . . . I was . . . resting.

EDITH. In a nursing home?

CORTIN. A sort of nursing home.

EDITH. You don't mean . . . ?

CORTIN. Yes.

EDITH *(With sympathy)*. Again?

CORTIN *(Casting down his eyes)*. Again.

EDITH. Oh, you poor darling.— And the next year?

CORTIN. Still the same residence.

EDITH. Two years?

CORTIN. Eighteen months. But it seemed like two years.

EDITH. Where did this happen?

CORTIN. In Sweden. Home of neutrality. But they weren't neutral to *me*.

EDITH. But why?

CORTIN. They didn't like me pretending to be a Dutch promoter trying to raise funds for a non-existent invention. Everything was going fine when a woman in our syndicate made a mistake.

EDITH. Too bad.

CORTIN. She turned sentimental. The old story. Girl meets good-looking old swindler.

EDITH. You?

CORTIN. Who else? Let's skip it. Things came to a bad end.

EDITH. But with your genius and experience!

CORTIN. We're all human. The whole trouble is that in my late profession you spend your time wriggling between the lines of the Law . . . and they keep printing them finer and finer. I bumped into a line.

EDITH. Did you say your *late* profession?

CORTIN. Yes. I've given up the game. If I hadn't, I would never have come into your life again like this. I'd like to read you something. A sort of statement or manifesto which I roughed out in readiness for my first meeting with you. Shall I read it? I want to get it off my chest. *(Takes out a slip of paper from his pocket and reads:)* "That I have not always behaved with scrupulous honesty in the realm of finances towards my fellow man, I admit. That I have ever injured a poor man, I deny. I have pitted my talents against the Law, and from time to time the Law has won our little duel of wits. On such occasions I have invariably paid the full penalty and consequently regard myself as quits with mankind." *(Pocketing the paper)* Forgive this lapse into sentiment. I thought it was something we had better get over.

EDITH. It isn't sentimental. It's true.

CORTIN. Quite true. It is my farewell testament. I have retired and am living on my investments.

EDITH. Have you enough?

CORTIN. Oh, yes. I can afford my daily crust of bread and cup of water . . . or shall we say my caviar and Irroy Brut? But it's a lonely life. No home. Just one damn hotel after another. San Francisco . . . New York . . . Florida . . . London . . . Paris . . . Riviera . . . Rome . . .

EDITH. That's how it is with me. But . . . can you stand doing nothing? After your . . . busy life?

CORTIN. It's hard at times.

EDITH. It must be.

CORTIN. Occasionally when I see a real proposition . . . and God knows you see some beauties nowadays . . . I find the Tempter a little hard to resist. But I've always won . . . so far. Touch wood.

EDITH. You ought to have something to occupy you. There's a Casino here. Why not look in and play a little?

CORTIN. No. Better not risk it. Here in the East too many cops know me by sight. And don't tell me there aren't any around these parts, because I know different. I can smell cops a mile away.

EDITH. But you aren't afraid of them now?

CORTIN. Not afraid, no. But they like me and come running and yoo-hooing after me, offering me drinks. Let's go on. Where were we? Nineteen hundred and . . .

EDITH. No, no more dates. They hurt. Well . . . I lost my friend.

CORTIN. The millionaire?

EDITH. Yes.

CORTIN. He died?

EDITH. Got married.

CORTIN. The same thing. Did he . . . er . . . ?

EDITH. Oh, yes. He was very generous.

CORTIN. You're rich?

EDITH. Quite rich.

CORTIN. Well, that's fine. And where have you been since then?

EDITH. In the Western Hemisphere.

CORTIN. Vague address.

EDITH. Intentionally so.

CORTIN. And what are you planning to do now?

EDITH. Just go on wandering, I suppose.

CORTIN. I don't like that bitter note in your voice. You sound as if you were miserable.

EDITH. I am.

CORTIN. Oh, dear. I wish there was something I could do.

EDITH. There isn't.

CORTIN. I could give you advice, of course . . . but . . .

EDITH. If you don't mind, Papa . . . You have a marvelous imagination but . . . it runs along different lines. Anyway . . . If you did give me advice, what would it be?

CORTIN. To get a man.

EDITH (Musingly). Could be . . .

CORTIN. That was an attractive boy you were with when I came along.

EDITH. Too young.

CORTIN. A passing fault.

EDITH. And naive.

CORTIN. A passing virtue. Not too much brains, I should imagine.

EDITH. No.

CORTIN. Well, who wants brains in a man? They only unsettle him. Look what they've done to *me*. I think this boy sounds promising.

EDITH. At the moment . . . I can't see myself going crazy about him. In spite of his being related to royalty.

CORTIN (*Awed*). Oh. (*Smiling cunningly*) I saw at once that you weren't exactly indifferent to him. That he has some kind of attraction for you.

EDITH. No wonder . . . after all that happened to me . . . to us . . .

CORTIN (*With downcast eyes*). I see, dear.

EDITH (*With a bitter smile*). Royalty! Imagine, Papa! (*Suddenly changing her tone*) But to fall in love with him . . . head over heels . . . ?

CORTIN. Too bad. Such a good family. Such a good-looking fellow.

EDITH. But so . . . *blah*. He was brought up by his sisters, two old maids.

CORTIN. Well, I was brought up by two virgin sisters, and look at me. He probably just wants rousing. For all you know, he may be the devil of a fellow.

EDITH. I don't *want* a devil of a fellow.

CORTIN. What *do* you want?

EDITH. After all these years of humiliation, the one thing I crave for is the respect due a married woman.

CORTIN. Odd. You're rich and independent, and you want to get married. Morbid, I call it.

EDITH. You don't understand. You're not a woman.

CORTIN. That's true. I'm not. So I've been told.

EDITH. Oh, Father, don't make fun of me. I'm deadly serious about this. I want a husband and a home and respectability. It's an obsession.

It's my only hope. I need a name, a good, respectable name.

CORTIN. Good name? But . . . you said he's related to . . .

EDITH. Yes, yes. But so . . . so *blah!* (*Dabbing her eyes*) I'm in a bad nervous state. I'm in no condition to make any weighty decision. I'm tired . . . tired to death of all this scurrying from one hotel to another . . . under a dozen false names . . . It's killing me. It's ridiculous, but I'm afraid of all so-called eligible bachelors . . .

CORTIN. My poor child, I'd no idea you felt like this.

EDITH. I do. And I've taken the first step in the right direction. I'm buying a house.

CORTIN. Really? Where?

EDITH. Just outside a little town on the Mediterranean. Binionville-sur-Mer, it's called. Not far from Monte Carlo.

CORTIN (*Ecstatically*). Monte Carlo!

EDITH. You love Monte Carlo, don't you?

CORTIN. I do, indeed. Beautiful, sunny . . . and artificial! Phony! My spiritual home.

EDITH. It's the sun I value more than the artificiality. Heavens, what I've suffered from the climate in North and South America. Was it very cold in Sweden?

CORTIN. I don't know. I didn't go out much. They didn't let me.

EDITH (*Putting her hand over her mouth*). Oh, I'm sorry.

CORTIN. Quite all right, my dear. Tell me more about this house of yours.

EDITH. My lawyer says if world politics don't get too troubled, it'll be perfectly heavenly living in Binionville.

CORTIN. One of those old Provincial houses?

EDITH. Yes, all gables and spires and all that. Some Baron there is trying to get it, too, but I'll outbid him.

CORTIN. That's the spirit.

EDITH. Just think of me there, Father. A solitary lady living her quiet life far from the world, a refugee from this dreadful age. Benefactress to the whole countryside . . . You know . . . President of the local Red Cross. Intimate friend of the Bishop. Decorating Christmas trees for poor children. Visiting hospitals. Helping poor people with money . . .

CORTIN. You don't want to overdo it. Give 'em advice. Comes cheaper. But I see what you mean. You plan to be Lady Bountiful.

EDITH. Exactly. But there's something missing.

CORTIN. What?

EDITH. Lord Bountiful.

CORTIN. My dear child, they're three for thirty cents. You can't throw a brick in the night clubs of London and Paris without hitting a penniless Prince . . . or even a former King.

EDITH. I don't want penniless Princes and emigré Kings. I'm not going to buy myself a blueblooded gigolo. I want a *man*.

CORTIN. That's what I said just now, and you bit my head off.

EDITH. I'm sick of admitting I'm a divorcee or telling them I'm a widow. It simply means running for my life all the time with a baying pack of fortune-hunters at my heels. The only way to keep them off is to have a husband.

CORTIN (Lost in thought). We'll have a look around.

EDITH (Nervously, whimsically). It's dreadful how timid I've become. You seem to be hinting that you might find me a husband and . . . and . . .

CORTIN. Yes?

EDITH. To tell you the truth . . . the idea terrifies me . . . to live with the horrible fear that some day . . . somehow . . . he would find out.

CORTIN. That you were my daughter?

EDITH. I didn't mean to hurt your feelings.

CORTIN. My dear, you can't hurt *my* feelings. Some of the toughest Judges in both Hemispheres have tried and failed.

EDITH. But that's how it was when I was married to Dwight Griffith. Trembling for fear he would find out . . . and he did.

CORTIN. He did, indeed.

EDITH. I won't go through that again. So, you see, it's hopeless. (With a sigh) And anyway, Papa, to live with somebody . . . whom you aren't in love with! To have to get used to all the thousand habits and faults of a stranger. To hear him coughing in the night. To kiss him . . . and find that he has false teeth. (She shudders) Ugh! I've lost my nerve.

CORTIN. That's all right. I've enough for two.

EDITH. You see . . . the trouble with husbands is that they exist.

CORTIN. How very true. (He stares dismally into space)

EDITH. They exist . . . and find out. (After a moment's pause) I tell you, Papa, I've had such a longing to be the wife of some respectable citizen that once . . . being for a week in London . . . I pretended I was married to a famous American scientist. I registered in the hotel as his wife. I had sampled it for a few days, and . . . I'm sorry to say . . . it tasted marvelous! *(She smiles sadly)*

CORTIN. *(After a pause)*. And all this unhappiness is my fault. *(Waggling his leg experimentally)* I wonder if I *could* kick myself. *(Looking at her lovingly)* To see my only child in such a state . . .

EDITH. Father, please. We mustn't get tragic. I didn't mean to inflict all this on you, but talking it over for the first time after so many years . . .

CORTIN. Exactly. It would have been silly to keep anything back. Well . . . something must be done about this.

EDITH. Nothing can be done. It's no use trying.

CORTIN. That's what they said to Columbus when he told them he was going to discover America. And look how silly he made them feel. Were their faces red! . . . My child, my heart bleeds for you.

EDITH. Oh, I'm all right.

CORTIN. You're *not* all right. You have made me think, my dear, and you have made me examine myself and see myself clearly. And what do I see? An old fraud, an irresponsible, unscrupulous old rascal, at large in this decaying world . . . planning to have a good time for the rest of his life . . . while his child suffers for his sins.

EDITH. Now you're making *my* heart bleed. I wish I'd never brought this up.

CORTIN *(Suddenly firm)*. I'm going to help you.

EDITH. You can't.

CORTIN. Don't tell me I can't do things. It wounds my pride.

EDITH. But how can you help me?

CORTIN. Well . . . I have certain . . . gifts, you know.

EDITH *(Looking at him in alarm)*. Father!

CORTIN. Yes, certain useful gifts. I had intended to retire, but now, for my child's sake, I will go back to work . . . and make things happen.

EDITH. I don't understand.

CORTIN. It's perfectly simple. No need to get frightened. Listen to me. *(Takes a sip)*

EDITH *(Looking at him admiringly)*. Father, your eyes are gleaming.

CORTIN. Why shouldn't they? Good heavens, if a father's eyes can't gleam when he is about to bring joy and contentment to his only child, when the devil *can* they gleam? Bless my soul, I feel like an old firehorse hearing the gong. Once more . . . one more run . . . The last and best. Hasn't the worst jailbird in the world the right to be a loving father?

EDITH. Of course.

CORTIN. Then listen.

EDITH. Yes?

CORTIN *(Briskly, after a short pause)*. Here is the position in a nutshell, as I see it. It was owing to me that you lost your husband. Right?

EDITH *(Looks at him eagerly, curiously)*. Go on.

CORTIN. I'll get you another.

EDITH. What!

CORTIN. I know a husband for you.

EDITH. You do? Who is he?

CORTIN. A big, handsome man. Superb physical specimen. Good family. How does that sound to you?

EDITH. Sounds fine.

CORTIN. Rich. Respected. Not too old and not too young. Say between thirty and fifty.

EDITH. *Fifty?*

CORTIN. You must give me some leeway.

EDITH. Very well.

CORTIN. Can he be . . . let's say . . . a Count?

EDITH. The world has changed, Father. A lot depends on where we live.

CORTIN. You said near Monte Carlo.

EDITH. Yes, there, perhaps, a title might still carry some weight.

CORTIN. That's settled, then. A Count. A gentleman, a scholar, a big-game hunter and a member.

EDITH What of?

CORTIN. Clubs. Scientific societies.

EDITH. Citizen of . . . ?

CORTIN. That remains to be seen. Who cares about citizenship? I have citizen papers of four countries.

EDITH *(Eagerly)*. Go on. Go on.

CORTIN. He's an explorer. Zoologist and anthropologist. At the moment he's on an expedition in Africa with some English scientists. Then he goes to Paris and from there he flies to the jungles of South America.

EDITH. Isn't he ever at home?

CORTIN. Very rarely. That's one of his great advantages as a husband. Another is that he will never, never ask you who your father is.

EDITH. Why not?

CORTIN. Leave that to me.

EDITH. Well, he sounds wonderful. But he won't marry me.

CORTIN. He will, I promise you he will. Whenever you like.

EDITH. Is this a joke?

CORTIN. Of course not. Cross my heart.

EDITH. Then there must be something terribly wrong with him.

CORTIN. On the contrary. He's practically perfect. I see what's on your mind. You think he's a friend of mine, and any friend of mine would naturally be regarded with grave suspicion. But Arthur's different.

EDITH. Is his name Arthur?

CORTIN. Only if you like the name, of course.

EDITH. Why not?

CORTIN. Then . . . it's Arthur. Now listen, my child. You said just now that the trouble with husbands was that they . . . exist.

EDITH. Yes.

CORTIN. Arthur hasn't that drawback.

EDITH *(Starting, as she begins to understand)*. Father, I feel more than ever that I am your daughter because . . . I'm beginning to understand.

CORTIN *(With the excitement of the creative artist)*. You gave me the idea. You're right . . . a husband is an awful thing to have about the house. It's an unforgivable blunder to exist in the world in these horrible times. So I'm finding you a man who doesn't exist.

EDITH. But, Father . . .

CORTIN. Well?

EDITH. It's crazy.

CORTIN. Not at all. It can be arranged. You only need imagination. Listen carefully. All my best work in the old days was done when I was posing as someone else. And why? Because I did it *thoroughly*.

When I was a lord, diplomat, retired admiral, banker, oil tycoon or whatever it might be, I created a full-length figure, with name, mannerisms, accent, complexion and hair-cut . . . every detail perfect. And fools like the police call that imposture.

EDITH. Well, isn't it?

CORTIN. No, my child, it's ART. What had Michel Angelo got that I haven't got? I was an artist . . . an ARTIST . . . Dammit, I was FOUR artists . . . sculptor, painter, playwright and actor, all rolled into one. I made myself a human skin and crawled inside it. It always fitted as if I'd been poured into it. And now I'm going . . . *(Interrupting himself)* You do understand, don't you?

EDITH. I understand.

CORTIN. I'm going to make for you . . . don't be alarmed . . . a similar but of course brand-new, custom-made human skin. But this time I won't be the one to crawl inside.

EDITH. Who will?

CORTIN. Nobody. I'll give you the empty skin as a wedding present. It will be your husband. It will mean a name, protection, position . . . and none of the nuisance of a body to go with it. And no voice to ask you who your father was. I see you understand.

EDITH. A swindle . . . with no swindler.

CORTIN. That's right. Isn't that something?

EDITH. It's heaven.

CORTIN. I thought you'd like it.

EDITH. False papers?

CORTIN. Certainly not. Do you suppose I would allow any phantom I create to shimmer about the place with false papers? Genuine ones are always cheaper and better. But papers aren't important.

EDITH. No?

CORTIN. What matters is relationships . . . personal possessions . . . Those are the things that count. Trust me. Doctors do plastic surgery. I'm going to do plastic psychology. I know exactly what makes an ideal husband. I shall bring to the task all the tried and tested experience of an old specialist in marriage.

EDITH *(Surprised)*. You have . . . practiced that, too?

CORTIN *(Putting his hand over his mouth)*. It slipped out. Never mind. In a word . . . *(He stops for a short moment, meditatively)*

EDITH. In a word?

CORTIN. You buy your husband's house and move in as . . . Well, what do you think? Countess? Baroness? Princess? Any preferences?

EDITH. Let's take the middle road.

CORTIN. Countess?

EDITH. I think so.

CORTIN. All right. Countess. *(A pause)* Well, how do you feel about it? In its broad outlines, does the scheme appeal to you?

EDITH. Tremendously. But . . . suppose . . .

CORTIN. I know. But suppose somebody asks where your husband is. You simply say he's not here just now. Out of town. Out of the Continent. After all, he's an explorer. And rich. Enormously rich.

EDITH. Where did he get his money?

CORTIN. From you. But that's our secret. To the outside world it will be he who has the stuff.

EDITH. And if somebody comes looking for him?

CORTIN. Nobody will. My dear child, who wants a man in person these days? People only want his . . . how shall I say it? . . . his radiations. He pays taxes, so he exists. He has a bank account, so he exists. He writes letters to the editor, so he exists. Who cares about his hundred and sixty pounds of flesh and blood? Apart from the Army, only one person attaches any importance to his body . . . a woman in love with him. And in this case . . . he's not young enough for the Army, and the woman . . .

EDITH . . . doesn't care. (Excited) But . . . but . . . heavens, there are so many questions I want to ask.

CORTIN (Delighted). You like the idea? It appeals to you?

EDITH. Father, you're looking like the cat who swallowed the canary.

CORTIN. You mean like an artist in the fever of creation.

EDITH. Tomorrow . . .

CORTIN. I'll be gone.

EDITH. What! Why?

CORTIN. I couldn't hang around here another minute. I'm all worked up. When I did this sort of thing for money, it never was any real fun. But now . . . to work for love . . . not to make money . . . in fact, to go to some expense . . . that doubles the inspiration of an artist. (Excited) Look at Whistler. Never so inspired as when he painted his mother. Look at Beethoven!

EDITH (Finding this a little extreme). Father, really!

CORTIN. You must excuse me. My brain is on fire.

EDITH. But where are you going?

CORTIN. Who knows? (With a majestic sweep of his hand) Out yonder . . . over the hills . . . into the unknown.

EDITH. Have you a passport?

CORTIN. Three. American, French, Swiss. Let's see. It's July now. Shall I bring Arthur to you in the fall? On a lovely autumn day when the leaves are turning and the air is fragrant with wood smoke? Yes, expect me around the end of September. Heavens, what a fine husband I'm going to bring you! You'll fall in love with him!

EDITH. That's only proper . . . when one's married.

CORTIN. Till then you won't hear from me.

EDITH. No letters?

CORTIN. Not so much as a picture postal card saying "Having wonderful time. Wish you were here." But one day you'll get a telegram, and then you must come wherever I call you.

EDITH. And there my husband will be, waiting for me?

CORTIN. That's right.

EDITH (Laughing). How positive you seem.

CORTIN. I am positive. Keep me informed of your addresses at the American Express in Paris.

EDITH. I will. By the way, what's your name, Father?

CORTIN. Cortin. Fred Cortin. And yours?

EDITH. Edith Brooks. B-R-O-O-K-S.

(BOTH are reaching for their pencils)

CORTIN. C-O-R-T-I-N.

(BOTH make a note of it)

EDITH. Fred Cortin, you've saved my life.

CORTIN. Edith Brooks, I'm glad to hear it. You do love your old papa a little?

EDITH. I worship him. But I

sometimes wonder if you aren't the Devil.

CORTIN. Now, that's a thing I've sometimes wondered myself.

(Enter ROBERT)

EDITH. Come, come, don't be afraid.

ROBERT. I'm afraid I'm intruding . . .

EDITH. Of course not. Mr. Robert Geoffrey . . .

CORTIN. Happy to meet you, Mr. Geoffrey. My name is Cortin. I am this charming lady's lawyer . . . may I say her friend?

EDITH. You may.

CORTIN. Thank you. I have been handling Miss Brooks' affairs since her father died, rest his soul.

ROBERT. I didn't know that your father . . .

CORTIN. She lost him suddenly. Not long ago. Ah, what a man! Forgive me for reminding you of your bereavement. (EDITH bows her head) She loved him very much.

EDITH. Very, very much.

CORTIN. Miss Brooks' father was an exceptional man.

EDITH. Very, very exceptional.

ROBERT (Awkwardly). Ah, well, all flesh is as grass.

CORTIN, Is that your own?

ROBERT. No, my sister's. She often says that sort of thing.

CORTIN. She must be a wonderfully entertaining companion. You ought to put some of her dialogue in a book.

EDITH. Robert's not a writer. He's a mining engineer.

CORTIN (Suddenly radiant). Gold?

ROBERT. No. Salt.

CORTIN (Disappointed). Oh.

(Pause)

ROBERT. You've just arrived, I think?

CORTIN. Yes. And unfortunately I must leave first thing in the morning.

ROBERT. So soon?

CORTIN. I merely came to bring Miss Brooks a message.

EDITH. From my husband.

ROBERT. Your husband?

CORTIN. Charming fellow.

ROBERT. You never told me you had a husband.

CORTIN. She keeps things from you, doesn't she? Too bad, too bad.

ROBERT. Now I see why you were waiting so eagerly for Mr. Cortin's arrival. (To Cortin) She was tremendously excited.

CORTIN. Really?

EDITH. Yes, and now I've seen him I'm even more excited.

ROBERT. I think I can guess what the message was.

EDITH. Yes?

ROBERT. You're getting a divorce.

CORTIN. On the contrary.

ROBERT. What! You don't mean you're being reconciled?

CORTIN. I hope so. And I hope they will both be very, very happy. Well, Mr. Geoffrey, goodbye. I must be going to bed if I'm to be up early in the morning. (To Edith) If I don't see you before I leave, is there any message I can take to your husband?

EDITH. Tell him I send him a million kisses and hope to see him very soon.

CORTIN. I won't forget. Good night.

EDITH. A bon voyage.

CORTIN. Goodbye, Mr. Geoffrey.

ROBERT *(Gloomily)*. Goodbye.
(*Exit* CORTIN)

EDITH *(Looking affectionately after him)*. Nice old gentleman, isn't he?

ROBERT *(Bitterly)*. Charming. Your lawyer, eh?

EDITH. My lawyer. Why?

ROBERT. That look he gave you when he said goodbye was . . . not very legal.

EDITH. He loves me like a father.

ROBERT. *Does* he?

EDITH. He's known me since I was *so* high. I've sat on his knee.

ROBERT *(Exploding)*. To hell with his knee!

EDITH. Well, really! What's the matter?

ROBERT. You know what's the matter. You're getting reconciled to your husband!

EDITH. Yes.

ROBERT. You "hope to see him soon" and send him a million kisses.

EDITH. Yes.

ROBERT. And I suppose you expect me to give three rousing cheers? *(He broods for a moment, then flares up again)* And the way you said it!

EDITH. How did I say it?

ROBERT. So lovingly! So cooingly! So *sensually!*

EDITH. What?

ROBERT. Yes, *sensually!* It's maddening! *(In a burst of jealous fury)* I could murder someone!

EDITH. Who?

ROBERT. You!

EDITH. Splendid!

ROBERT. What!

EDITH. At last you're behaving like a man of flesh and blood.

ROBERT *(Savagely)*. I won't stand for this reconciliation! I'll show you and your husband and Mister by golly Cortin and the whole world! I'll do a job of alienating affection which will go down in history!

EDITH *(Enjoying his outburst of jealousy)*. Really?

ROBERT. It's driving me mad to think I may lose you without ever having so much as kissed you. Up to now I've loved you dumbly, but from now on I'm going to take a different tone.

EDITH. Wonderful. *(Smiling calmly)* How lovely such an . . . active love is. This tornado of jealous fury . . .

ROBERT *(Amazed)*. You *like* this sort of thing?

EDITH. I love it. Why are you gaping at me like that? It's *only* this I like. *(Leans voluptuously back in her chair)* At last a sincere, genuine threat of murder. That sweet old ring of jealousy in a man's voice, how marvelous it sounds. And I owe it all to . . .

ROBERT *(Fiercely and proudly)*. Me.

EDITH. No. To my . . . husband. *(She lights a cigarette)*

(ROBERT, *dejected, leans slowly back in his chair*)

EDITH *(Sentimentally)*. Dear Arthur!

CURTAIN

ACT TWO

SCENE: *Late afternoon in autumn. Sitting-room of a suite in the Hotel du Lion Bleu in the small town, Binionville sur Mer, near Monte Carlo. Left, a window; right, a door to the other rooms of the suite, a door at the rear opens on to the corridor. Center, a low table.*

AT RISE: *The room is empty as the* CURTAIN RISES. *Then* EDITH *enters from the suite and goes to the telephone.*

EDITH. 'Allo . . . Mr. Cortin's suite, please. Four eleven. *(Brief pause)* Father? How are you, dear? . . . Thank you, fine. I've been trying to get you for ever so long . . . Well, I've arrived. I love the suite you engaged for me . . . Yes, I got your wire in Paris the day before yesterday . . . It's a good hotel. Yes. I like it . . . Of course. I'm dying of curiosity. Not a word from you in four months . . . What do you say, *We'll* be right down? You mean you and my husband? So that's why the hotel people have been calling me Countess. A little premature, of course, still . . . Yes, do come at once. I can hardly wait . . . *(Calls)* Julie.

(Enter JULIE, *Edith's maid, from the next room. She is carrying two envelopes)*

EDITH. Julie, my lawyer, Mr. Cortin, will be here in a minute. Don't let anybody in till he's gone. What's that you've got there?

JULIE. A seat for the Regatta, madame. A present from the hotel manager.

EDITH. Very nice of him. When is it?

JULIE. Tomorrow afternoon, madame. It's the great event of the season here. The students' boat race. It's been held every summer for the last hundred years.

EDITH. Really? I mustn't miss it.

JULIE. And this is your sleeper ticket back to Paris on Wednesday.

EDITH. Good. Will you keep it for me. Any news of Mr. Geoffrey?

JULIE. He's here, madame.

EDITH. He must have come on the very next train.

JULIE. Yes, madame.

EDITH. Well, if he wants to see me, he can't till I've finished with Mr. Cortin. That's all, Julie.

JULIE. Excuse me, madame, but could you explain something to me?

EDITH. What's that?

JULIE. Why did the clerk at the desk call you "Countess"? If it's not a liberty.

EDITH. Of course not. It's quite simple. I am a Countess.

JULIE. Goodness! Gracious!

EDITH. Now I'm together with my husband again, I'm using his name. You seem very excited about it.

JULIE. Yes, Countess. You see, Countess, I love you, Countess, because you're an angel of kindness, Countess. But I never dreamed you were a Countess, Countess, as well as an angel.

EDITH. Julie, you're a snob.

JULIE. Yes, Countess . . . *(She utters a cry)* . . . Oo!

EDITH. Now what's the matter?

JULIE. I was just thinking of last night. I was lying awake, and I heard the key turn in your bedroom door.

EDITH. And you thought my husband had arrived?

JULIE. Yes, Countess. And I . . . I was wondering . . . I was picturing

. . . I was imagining . . . Well, I was so excited, I couldn't get to sleep again.

EDITH. Tell me, Julie, where do you come from?

JULIE. Paris.

EDITH. I thought as much. Well, I'm sorry to disappoint you. I was locking my door.

JULIE. I thought you were opening it.

EDITH. No. Some other night, perhaps.

JULIE. Yes, Countess. Shall I unpack?

EDITH. Just enough for a couple of days. Tomorrow morning, we'll have a look at the house I've bought here and see how they're getting on with the redecorating of it.

JULIE *(At the window)*. You can see it from here. It looks like a castle of romance.

EDITH. I don't know that I'd call it a castle, but it's certainly lovely. I'm glad we managed to snatch it from under the nose of Baron . . . What's his name? . . . Baron . . . Amary.

JULIE. I'll bet he's mad.

EDITH. Probably. But we can't help his troubles. *(At the window)* I like the look of this small town, don't you? . .

JULIE. It's beautiful. From my window you can see Monte Carlo . . . the villas, gardens, hotels . . . on the blue beach.

EDITH. Yes, I think we ought to be happy here. (KNOCK *on corridor door)* That's Mr. Cortin. Run away, Julie.

JULIE. Yes, Countess. *(Exit* JULIE *into next room)*

(EDITH *opens the corridor door. Enter* CORTIN. *He is carrying a large, handsome leather suitcase, marked with a monogram and a Count's coronet. In his other hand he carries a bag of golf clubs)*

CORTIN. Good evening, madame.

EDITH. Why so formal?

CORTIN. I thought somebody might be listening. As your friend Mr. Geoffrey's sister would say, walls have ears.

EDITH. No. We're quite alone.

CORTIN. Good. *(He puts suitcase and golf clubs down)* Well, I've just been having a look at your little shack. The plasterers and painters are hard at work. It made me thirsty to watch them.

EDITH. *(At the window)*. You can see it from here. Doesn't it look lovely? Like something right out of the world.

CORTIN. A very shrewd observation.

EDITH. What do you mean?

CORTIN. Well, I have an odd feeling that we . . . you and your husband and I and the house . . . aren't rooted firmly to solid earth but are floating above it . . . somewhere among the pink clouds of a sweet, deceitful dreamland . . . high above the things of this world . . . police, law, jail and so on . . . Just a feeling.

EDITH *(With a sigh)*. I have it, too.

CORTIN. Was that a sigh I heard?

EDITH. A sort of sigh.

CORTIN. Feeling a little low today?

EDITH. Not more than usual.

CORTIN. I'll cheer you up.

EDITH. You always do. I wish there were more people like you in the world, Father.

CORTIN. The Judge at my last trial didn't think so. He said as much. Well, to business, my child. You're probably wondering why we are here, in this hotel. I thought it would be best if you began your new life in the town where you are going to live with your husband. *(Points to the bag of clubs)* His golf clubs.

EDITH. My husband's . . . Arthur's golf clubs?

CORTIN. That's right. He's a great golfer . . . always at his best in a bad lie . . . like me.

(He picks up the suitcase and puts it with exaggerated care on a chair next to the table)

EDITH. And what's inside the suitcase?

CORTIN. He.

EDITH. He? Who?

CORTIN. Your husband. Arthur.

EDITH. What!!

CORTIN. No, he's not a midget. But he's in there.

EDITH. But . . .

CORTIN. You may have read of those fakirs in India who are able to leave their bodies and go where they please.

EDITH *(Frightened)*. My God . . .

CORTIN *(His hand on the suitcase)*. This . . . though similar . . . is a little different. This isn't supernatural. It's a natural swindle. Does that reassure you?

EDITH. Not till you open it.

CORTIN. In a moment. Before we proceed, listen carefully. Don't forget what I told you. If people ask about your husband, tell them he's gone on one of those zoological and anthropological expeditions of his . . . let us say to Brazil. Can you remember that?

EDITH. Of course. Brazil. But

didn't he take his suitcase with him?

CORTIN. Not this one. Only the one containing his dress clothes and his bow and arrows. But let me get on. In here, are his little personal belongings . . . papers and so on. He wouldn't need those in the jungle, so he left them with his wife. Confidentially . . . *(He looks around mysteriously to make sure he is not overheard. Puts his hand on suitcase)* . . . this suitcase contains Arthur. He's in the bag.

EDITH. That's really all there is of him?

CORTIN. That's all there is. There isn't any more. Now, then, let's unpack his Excellency.

EDITH. Excellency?

CORTIN. Former Ambassador.

EDITH. Where?

CORTIN. Oh, all sorts of places. *(He goes to the corridor door and locks it)*

EDITH. What are you doing?

CORTIN. It's all right. Just locking the door. *(Points at the other door)* Nobody'll come in through there?

EDITH. No.

CORTIN. Sure?

EDITH. I gave strict orders. But Father, there's one thing I don't understand. When I registered, the manager told me that my husband's room would be free this evening.

CORTIN. That was dear Arthur's foundations . . . his under-pinnings. I reserved a room for him by telegram. I also sent along a couple of trunks that are supposed to have his suits in them.

EDITH. But . . .

CORTIN. Tomorrow we cancel the room. He will have been unavoidably detained. His trunks will go to the storage room. By that time everyone in town will have heard of him. *(He unlocks the suitcase, then opens it in a gingerly way, takes a briefcase from it and puts the suitcase on the table)* His briefcase.

EDITH. Containing his papers?

CORTIN. Exactly.

EDITH *(Peering into the suitcase).* And in there?

CORTIN. A variety of objects. *(Takes out pajamas)* His pajamas. Not dull English pajamas. Not loud American pajamas. Just the happy mean, as worn by a gentleman of France.

EDITH. He has good taste.

CORTIN. The de Ghuyés are famous for their taste.

EDITH. How did you say? What's his . . . er . . . what's *my* name now?

CORTIN. Countess Ghuyé. He is Arthur Ghuyé. G-H-U-Y-É.

EDITH. Where did you get the name?

CORTIN. Threw all the letters of the alphabet in a hat and drew out five.—I like it.

EDITH. So do I. *(Repeating it)* Ghuyé!—Arthur Ghuyé!—I wish you had given him an easier name to remember. It's hard to pronounce.

CORTIN. That's the idea. People won't be able to pronounce it. That's very helpful to a man who doesn't exist. You, of course, will have to get it down pat.

EDITH *(As* CORTIN *produces a small picture).* What's that?

CORTIN. His picture as a child. Six weeks old.

EDITH. What a darling. And so neatly done up in diapers.

CORTIN. Thank God he *is* done up in diapers. I bought the picture

in rather a hurry, and it may quite easily be a girl.

EDITH. That would take some explaining away.

CORTIN. Yes. But we needn't worry about it. There's never much difference between babies of that age. They all look like Winston Churchill.

(He takes the picture from her and reaches into the suitcase. He takes out a small object, quickly, as if by legerdemain.)

EDITH. And what are those?

CORTIN. His first shoes. Silverplated.

EDITH. Why not goldplated?

CORTIN. His parents were of straitened means. He only became rich through his marriage.

EDITH. Marriage? To whom?

CORTIN. To you. *(Displaying quickly another small object)* What do you think these are?

EDITH. Pearls?

CORTIN Teeth. His first two baby teeth, set as charms.

EDITH. How sweet. Where did you get them?

CORTIN. To tell you the truth, I inherited them from my mother. They're . . . *(With emotion)* . . . my own baby teeth. I hereby bequeath them to your husband. You see the idea? You can't be brandishing a husband's birth certificate all the time, but you *can* throw out an occasional word to your friends—"Look, my dear Arthur's first tiny teeth." As a matter of fact, though, he has an authentic birth certificate. Just in case it should be needed. *(Puts it on the table)* Born in Rio de Janeiro, where his family emigrated many years ago.

EDITH. From what country?

CORTIN. I suggest France. France had several revolutions. Your husband's family fled from the guillotine.

EDITH. When was he born?

CORTIN. Whenever you like.

EDITH (Points to birth certificate). But you said the birth certificate was genuine.

CORTIN. It is. (Tongue in cheek) But some absentminded clerk forgot to put in the date of birth.

EDITH. I see.

CORTIN. The fact that he was born is confirmed under oath by two honorable gentlemen. The oath is false, the document genuine. (He puts away the certificate) Well, that about covers his childhood, I think. Let's get on. (Quickly takes tortoise-shell brush and comb from the suitcase) His hair. (Showing the comb) Tortoise-shell inlaid with a gold monogram.

EDITH. A little ostentatious?

CORTIN. Not at all. He likes nice things. You put these in the bathroom, and when you show visitors over the house you say casually "My husband's marble bathroom. He will leave his things lying about." (Showing a brush) The brush has a few blond hairs in it. I got them from the salesgirl.

EDITH. You think of everything.

CORTIN. I don't miss much. (He shows a small black package) A little personal touch. Once, let's say on a hunting trip, he injured his eye. He has to wear a black patch over it. And here's a bottle of eye-drops. For the bathroom, too.

EDITH. Oh, dear.

CORTIN. Come, come, my child. You can't dish up a palatable man without seasoning him with a few defects. (Quickly putting other articles on the table) This is his face. (Pointing at one object after another speaking with machine-gun rapidity) Shaving cream. Half empty. Shaving brush, some of the bristles missing. Eau de Cologne. Pink talcum. Styptic pencil. Witch hazel. Hair oil. Cold cream. Magnifying mirror.

EDITH. I'm afraid he's vain.

CORTIN. No, no, only careful of his looks. And that's odd, because he hasn't any. (Gives her a book) A book. For his bedside table.

EDITH (Reading the title) "How to Prevent Malaria," by Sir Ronald Ross.

CORTIN. The great problem of every tropical explorer.

EDITH. I see. But tell me . . . a problem that interests me more . . . is he jealous?

CORTIN. It's amazing how well you know him already. Yes, very jealous.

EDITH. Good.

CORTIN. Tell me, my child . . . I don't want to pry into your affairs . . . but am I to infer from that monosyllable that you love the young gentleman with the high moral tone and the high-born relatives . . .

EDITH. Yes. Unfortunately.

CORTIN. Why unfortunately?

EDITH. Because his moral tone is so high. We have . . . what you'd call a platonic friendship. It's beautiful of course, but . . . (Breaks off)

CORTIN. But?

EDITH. Robert has such noble and inflexible principles about love and marriage. I was hoping that my husband would . . .

CORTIN. Rouse him?

EDITH. Yes, rouse him.

CORTIN. Then prepare yourself for good news. In a very short while from now your husband will show himself as jealous as Othello.

EDITH *(Delighted)*. He will? How?

CORTIN. It's all been taken care of. Meanwhile . . . *(He displays colored glittering objects)* His decorations.

EDITH *(Admiringly)*. Oo-ooh!

CORTIN. You may well say "Oo-ooh!" Spanish. Italian. This with the fake diamonds, Turkish. This is French. " Palmes Academiques." You put them in a glass case and say casually "Oh, those? Those are my husband's decorations."

EDITH. They're very sparkling. And . . . seeing that he's a Count, I suppose he has a coat of arms?

CORTIN. Of course. I ordered it from a heraldic expert. It will be stamped in gold and colors on every piece of your dinner china.

EDITH. What's the design?

CORTIN. On a field of blue an old man is standing . . . telling lies. *(Picks up a bundle)* This is his collection of cigarette holders.

EDITH. His what?

CORTIN. Every important man has a hobby. Arthur's is collecting fancy cigarette holders. Give them to the butler to take care of. That will get him used to the idea that there's a master of the house. *(Shows a small box)* Dress shirt studs. Cuff-links. Real pearls. Platinum. *(Shows quickly a top hat)* Here's his head.

EDITH *(Disapproving)*. Oh, I . . .

CORTIN *(Interrupting)*. Only for weddings and funerals. Hang it in the hall. It will create a formal, old-fashioned atmosphere. The aristocratic touch. I put a drop of scented hair tonic in it . . . *(Holds the hat under her nose)* . . . to make it a live

hat. *(With his other hand shows slippers, quickly)* His feet.

EDITH. Aren't they too small?

CORTIN. Not a bit. They've fitted me for years.

EDITH. They're rather shabby.

CORTIN. They should be. Only a newly married bridegroom has new slippers. *(Shows papers)* Documents. To be locked in the safe. They include a diploma stating that he graduated from kindergarten.

EDITH. That doesn't thrill me much.

CORTIN. Nor me. But his character must be complete.

EDITH. What have kindergarten diplomas to do with the completeness of a man's character?

CORTIN *(Pointing to the four small buttons on his coat cuff)*. You might just as well say "What have these four small buttons to do with the completeness of a suit? Nobody knows why they are there, but they have to be. Without them the suit would not be complete. Every profession has its traditions. The tailor's, for instance . . . and mine. *(Showing letters)* These are copies of private letters he has written to prominent people.

EDITH *(Looking at one of them)*. Who's "Dear Glossy"?

CORTIN. The Duke of Gloucester.

EDITH *(Reading from another letter)*. "You know me, Al."

CORTIN. Professor Albert Einstein. And here's one sending his regrets for being unable to attend a royal banquet at Buckingham Palace.

EDITH *(With awe)*. Was he invited by the King?

CORTIN. No. He just sent his regrets. *(Reads)* Dear George . . .

EDITH. Isn't that a little *too . . .?*

CORTIN. Chummy? Not a bit. You've no idea how intimate he is with royalty. *(Reads)* "Dear George. Fear you will have to excuse me for Thursday. Down with grippe. All my best to your good Queen and the girls."

EDITH. I wonder what would have happened if he had really sent that.

CORTIN. He did. Registered, too. *(Shows slips of paper)* Here's the receipt. Show it to the town notables some time. After dinner, perhaps, when they are feeling mellow over coffee and brandy.

EDITH *(Looking into the suitcase)*. What are those magazines?

CORTIN. They contain contributions from his pen. This one, from a sports magazine, is entitled, "New Humane Methods of Lion Hunting." Pompous in spots, but just the sort of thing to get him right with the S.P.C.A. *(Solemnly)* This is his soul.

EDITH. I see.

CORTIN. Can't send the poor fellow out into the world without a soul.

EDITH. Of course not.

CORTIN. And now for his politics. A tricky thing these days, but you've got to have them— He's a fellow traveler.

EDITH. Which side?

CORTIN. On the winning side. Always. Until elections, he sits on the fence. *(Holds up two weeklies)* This one is reactionary, this one left of center. He contributes to both . . . under suitable pen names. We'll wait till the world stops wabbling and then admit one pen name or the other, according to which trend comes into fashion.

EDITH. So he has no political convictions?

CORTIN. Sure he has. Two, as you see. And he upholds them fearlessly. That is what is called "Realism in Politics." Oh, he's quite in the fashion. *(Shows a bundle of letters, holding it cautiously with two fingers)* Here are a few love letters from pretty girls.

EDITH. Why?

CORTIN. That's his heart. A man must have a heart. Love letters have always been convincing evidence of a man's existence. You can show them secretly to your women friends. Remember to blush. They're passionate.

EDITH. Whose . . . ?

CORTIN. Mine. I got them thirty years ago.

EDITH. But . . .

CORTIN. Don't worry. There are no names attached. Just "My sweetest"—"My best beloved"—"My all." Great love knows no names. *(Giving her the bundle)* Be careful how you handle them. They're red hot. They've almost set the suitcase on fire.

(EDITH *takes the bundle from him and immediately drops it on the table like a hot potato)*

CORTIN. Of course, they were written before he knew you.

EDITH. I should hope so. *(Peers curiously into suitcase)* Tell me, have you a photograph of him?

CORTIN. No. But here's a pen-and-ink drawing. *(He hands it to her)*

EDITH. New?

CORTIN. Done in Paris a few weeks ago . . . by Picasso. From my sketches. What you'd call a speaking likeness, is it not?

EDITH. Yes, except that his nose

is more Roman and his chin shows more determination.

CORTIN *(Taking rapid notes)*. Nose. Chin. It shall be attended to.

EDITH. Apart from that, I like the face well enough.

CORTIN *(Replacing the sketch in the suitcase)*. Thank you. *(Quickly showing cards)* Membership cards. Wirehaired fox terrier club. Geographic Society of Paris. P.E.N. Club, London. And so on. Be sure to pay the dues regularly *(Quickly showing a framed picture)* A photograph of Betty Grable. Autographed to you. "To the lovely Countess Ghuye."

EDITH. How does she know me?

CORTIN. She doesn't. Put it on the piano. *(Showing a newspaper)* A Paris paper. See front page. Story about a brawl in a night club, in which your husband knocked out a prize-fighter. Poor fellow had to be rushed to hospital. I gave the paper that story. Got paid for it, too.

EDITH. What's the idea behind that?

CORTIN. It will build him up as a strong man who stands no nonsense. *(Holding up the paper)* These are his muscles.

EDITH. How old did we say he was?

CORTIN. How about . . . forty-five?

EDITH. Good heavens, no. What do I do with him sixty years from now? Tell people he's in his early hundreds?

CORTIN. Thirty-five, then?

EDITH. That's better. *(She reaches into the suitcase, takes out another framed photograph)* Whose picture is this?

CORTIN. You put that on your desk. *(Moved)* His mother.

EDITH *(Moved)*. Oh.

CORTIN. Your mother-in-law. The dowager Countess. With a charming inscription. "To my sweet daughter-in-law" . . . daughter-in-law crossed out and "daughter" substituted. "Mama Ghuyé." A distinguished, stately old lady, is she not?

EDITH. Very.

CORTIN. She used to be our cook . . . when you were a child *(Showing papers—quickly)* Bank statements.

EDITH. He has a bank account?

CORTIN. Several.

EDITH. Why?

CORTIN. Banks write to you. That means mail, and mail means life. When you don't get any more letters, you know you're dead. Of course, all these things are nothing in themselves, but taken together they form a hundred tiny roots that bind a figure to the soil of the real world and let it blossom. For instance . . . these Christmas cards. "Season's greetings, Count and Countess Ghuyé." *(Shows them quickly)* And here . . . *(Shows a sheet of paper)*

EDITH. Another root?

CORTIN. No. My expense account.

EDITH. But, darling, surely you don't need . . .

CORTIN. Must be businesslike. You can say anything you like about me but . . . my bookkeeping has always been flawless. *(Shows another paper)* Here's his will. A few legacies to charity . . . don't worry, quite small . . . everything else to his dear wife. And now we come to something very important, though distasteful.

EDITH. Distasteful?

CORTIN. We must be practical. I've got to protect you against the possibility of my doublecrossing you.

EDITH. What!

CORTIN. Certainly. I'm the only one who knows your secret and I can't have you trusting a fellow like me. You know the sort of so-and-so I am. I'm one of those men my father always warned me against. I refuse to allow me to victimize you. Take this paper, my child. It will protect you against me. It spikes my guns from the word Go.

EDITH (Reading it). "State Hospital for Mental Diseases, Paris." It sounds like . . .

CORTIN. A loony bin. Exactly. Before leaving Paris, I pretended to be crazy and they took me to the State Hospital for Mental Diseases. I wasn't violent, but I bellowed a good deal.

EDITH. Bellowed?

CORTIN. At the top of my voice. I kept bellowing "My daughter's husband, the Count de Ghuyé, doesn't exist! There is no such person as the Count de Ghuyé. I invented him." When they let me go, they gave me a certificate saying I was harmless but unbalanced and that my madness took the form of a fixed delusion that your husband doesn't exist. One tricky move out of me . . . the merest suggestion on my part of a try at blackmail . . . and you foil me by showing that paper.

EDITH. Father, I don't like to be sentimental . . . I know you don't like it . . . but may I kiss you?

CORTIN. Certainly not. This is a business conference. You can't go about kissing people at business conferences. Take care of that certificate. It's unique. A mental strait-jacket . . . Well, then, to sum up. Here we have one complete husband, ready for immediate use. If you don't like him, say so, and the Count de Ghuyé will cease to exist. But if you do, there he is. Well? Do you want him?

EDITH. Of course I want him. Father, I don't care if this is a business conference or not. I'm going to kiss you.

CORTIN. Quite all right now. The conference is over. (She kisses him) That's all settled, then. (A document) Here's your marriage certificate. And here's the ring. (Puts a ring on her finger) With this ring he thee weds. Be happy . . . There. My work is finished. The Count de Ghuyé lives. (He goes to the entrance door and unlocks it) And now . . . (He looks at his watch)

EDITH. What a beautiful watch.

CORTIN. You like it? Swiss. Platinum. A present.

EDITH. Who from?

CORTIN. Your husband. Generous chap.

EDITH. Very.

CORTIN. Give you his shirt if you wanted it. It's nice to think you haven't married a tightwad. (KNOCK on door) Come in.

(Enter BELLBOY)

BELLBOY. A letter for you, Countess.

EDITH. For me? Oh, thank you. (Gives him money)

BELLBOY. Thank you, Countess. (Exit BELLBOY)

EDITH. Now who in the world can this be from?

CORTIN (Looking at it). It's in your husband's handwriting.

EDITH. It looks just like yours.

CORTIN. There is a resemblance.

EDITH (Reads). "It has come to my notice that you have been flirting with a young puppy by the name of Robert Geoffrey . . ."

CORTIN. He has his spies everywhere.

EDITH. "I warn you, madame, respect your husband's honor. Deceive me, and I will murder you and that young whippersnapper without remorse. Love and kisses. Arthur."

CORTIN. He writes a good letter.

EDITH. How thrilling. Oh, how wonderful.

CORTIN. You think this letter will come in handy?

EDITH. Very handy!

CORTIN. There will be others of a similar nature.

(KNOCK *on door*)

EDITH. Oh, dear, I hope that isn't Arthur again. Come in

(Enter WAITER)

WAITER. I beg your pardon, Countess. Would your ladyship be kind enough to receive the manager of the hotel?

EDITH. Certainly. (WAITER *goes out. She looks at* CORTIN) Now what?

CORTIN. It's all right. He wouldn't have been so polite if they were going to throw you out.

(Enter MANAGER)

MANAGER. Good evening, Countess. Good evening, sir.

EDITH. Good evening. Please sit down.

MANAGER. Thank you, Countess, but I only looked in for a moment. We are in great trouble, madame.

EDITH. Really? I'm sorry.— What is the matter?

MANAGER. It is owing to the Count, your husband, madame.

CORTIN. You don't say!

MANAGER. When the Count de Ghuyé wired for rooms, I reserved Suite Number Four for him, the best in the hotel.

CORTIN. Quite right. The best is none too good for the Count de Ghuyé.

MANAGER. Most unfortunately forgetting that Suite Number Four has always been assigned to Monsieur Boutonnier, the Vice-President of the Marseilles Credit Bank.

CORTIN. Never heard of him.

MANAGER. And by the greatest ill luck Monsieur Boutonnier has just arrived. *(In despair)* He insists on his suite. *(Loud noise off.* MANAGER *shivers)* There! That is Monsieur Boutonnier insisting on his suite.

CORTIN. Big man?

MANAGER. No, sir. Very small. A thin man.

(More noise off)

CORTIN. Good lungs.

EDITH. But this is terrible.

CORTIN. Countess, be calm.

(Bellowing off stage. MANAGER *shivers again)*

MANAGER. Listen. What am I to do? He was threatening to kick me.

CORTIN. On the traditional spot?

MANAGER. He specified that. And I bruise so easily. *(He opens the door and remains visible in the corridor outside)* Please, Monsieur Boutonnier . . . I beg you, Monsieur Boutonnier! Not right in front of the Countess' door!

THE VOICE *(Off)*. Don't talk to me about Countesses! I'm interested in the Count! If I find this man in my room, I'll throw him out bodily!

EDITH. Oh, what can we do?

CORTIN. Please. Tact will solve every problem.

(He takes an exceptionally large pair of boxing gloves out of the

suitcase and joins the MAN-
AGER, *also remains in sight.
Speaks loudly)*

I wonder if, now that you are here,
my dear sir, you would be kind
enough to take charge of the Count's
boxing gloves. They need repairing
at the sporting goods shop.

*(He hands over the gloves os-
tentatiously. Comes back. The
door remains open.* CORTIN
*listens. Outside, all is suddenly
quiet.)*

CORTIN *(Softly)*. Well?

MANAGER *(With the gloves in
his hand)*. He's gone.

CORTIN. Then you can give them
back to me.

(He takes the gloves back.
MANAGER *disappears.* CORTIN
*shuts the door and tosses the
gloves into the suitcase like a
juggler concluding a successful
trick)*

You have to be firm with Vice-Presi-
dents.

EDITH. I feel quite faint.

CORTIN. Nonsense. You should
be delighted. Only now has the
Count de Ghuyé really begun to live
. . . because he now has an enemy.
Enemies are the breath of a man's
life.

(Knock on the apartment door)

EDITH. Come in.

(Enter JULIE, *from the apartment)*

EDITH. Yes, Julie?

JULIE. Some mail for the Count,
Countess.

EDITH. Put them on the table.
Hasn't Mr. Geoffrey called?

JULIE. Yes, Countess, twice. And
he's coming again later. And the
desk wants to know, shall he reserve

a ticket for the Regatta for the
Count?

CORTIN. Of course. *(To* EDITH)
He used to row in the Regatta when
he was a student here as a young man.

*(*JULIE *goes out as he says this)*

EDITH. Really?

CORTIN. Well, not really, perhaps. But he must certainly have a
ticket. It all helps to bring him to
life. He now has a wife, a room, a
Regatta ticket and an enemy.

EDITH. Two enemies.

CORTIN. Who's the other?

EDITH. That Baron I told you
about, who wanted the house. Baron
Amary.

CORTIN. Ah, yes. You outbid
him, didn't you?

EDITH. Yes, and he's furious.

CORTIN. He can't be too furious
for me. I hope he froths at the
mouth. This is excellent. Two enemies already, and in a few minutes
there will be a third.

EDITH. A third?

CORTIN. Your admirer, Mr.
Geoffrey.

EDITH. That's true. Robert
won't like Arthur.

CORTIN. He'll hate Arthur's insides. Which is odd, when you come
to think of it, because he hasn't any
insides. Mr. Geoffrey, I gather, is
here?

EDITH. He came after me on the
next train.

(There is a KNOCK *on the door.
A* WAITER *enters with tea things
and busies himself with them,
eavesdropping.* CORTIN *talks for
his benefit)*

CORTIN. Yes, since you are good
enough to ask for my opinion, Countess, I should say that the first thing

we must do is inform the President of the Republic about your husband the Count's ideas concerning the new French Government. And with regard to that very friendly letter from the Queen of England . . . asking you for the address of your dressmaker in Paris . . . (WAITER, *who has started to go out, stops at the door, eavesdropping.* CORTIN *notices what he is doing and winks at* EDITH) That, of course, must be answered *at once.* A nuisance, all this correspondence, but after all, the Queen is an old friend of yours.

EDITH *(Casually).* I think I'll write her.

(She looks suddenly at WAITER, *as if she were surprised to see him still there.* WAITER *slips out.* CORTIN *and* EDITH *smile at each other)*

CORTIN. That ought to settle any doubts about your social position.

EDITH. And, being such a great lady, oughtn't I to start being gracious and charitable? How about a thousand dollar check to the Mayor for the town poor?

CORTIN. It would come better from your husband.

EDITH. I shall send it in his name, of course. I think you said he used to row in the students' race as a young man?

CORTIN. Assiduously. All rowed fast, but none so fast as Arthur.

EDITH. Then how's this? "Now that my wife and I are taking up our residence in your charming town, I am sending the enclosed $1,000 check for the poor. A slight memento of the dear old days when I used to row in the students' race." And so forth. Arthur's clever, isn't he? *(She writes out a check)*

CORTIN. No. He just has a clever wife, whose advice he follows implicitly. *(She gives him the check)* Very touching and human. By the way, while on the subject of checks, you might be writing out another. For fifteen hundred dollars.

EDITH. What!

CORTIN. I'm sorry to say Arthur has been playing the market.

EDITH. Not very successfully, apparently. *(She writes out another check)*

CORTIN. No. He bought for a rise and everything fell, and then he bought for a fall and everything rose.

EDITH. I think he's becoming too alive. Will you please see that he does no more gambling?

CORTIN. Not even an occasional flutter?

EDITH. No, not even an occasional little flutter.

CORTIN. It will be a deprivation to the poor lad . . . Still, just as you say. But these little escapades give him a very vivid personality.

EDITH. He's quite vivid enough without losing fifteen hundred dollars. *(She gives him the check)*

CORTIN. Ah, you can visualize him, can you?

EDITH. Perfectly. Very broad-shouldered. Slim-waisted. Tall. About six foot three?

CORTIN. About.

EDITH. Strong. Tough. Virile.

CORTIN. That's right. An intrepid explorer.

EDITH. Sunburned, weatherbeaten face. Keen, glittering eyes.

CORTIN. Eye, not eyes. One of them has a black patch over it, if you remember.

EDITH. Ugh!

CORTIN. Still, the other glitters

like nobody's business.—He exists!

EDITH. But I'm beginning to wonder *if I do.* I am . . . a little dizzy. Who knows . . . Even I may be just a figment of your imagination.

CORTIN. You're not. Take your father's word for it.

(*Enter* JULIE)

JULIE. Mr. Robert Geoffrey, Countess.

EDITH (*Waking abruptly from her dreams*). Oh! show him in.

(JULIE *goes out.* ROBERT *enters*)

ROBERT. Good evening. (*To* CORTIN, *ironically*) You here again, my dear sir?

CORTIN. I do bob up, don't I? I can see that the fact does not meet with your entire approval.

EDITH (*Reproachfully*). Robert! (*To* CORTIN, *who starts to go out*) Where are you going?

CORTIN. Down to the desk, where men are men. I want to fix up that business of your husband's bedroom. He *must* have it next to yours.

(ROBERT *shudders. Exit* COR-TIN)

EDITH. What's the matter with you?

ROBERT. So your husband is coming?

EDITH. To say goodbye to me before he leaves for Brazil.

ROBERT. That means, I suppose, that you're definitely reconciled. You've started using his name again. And now he's coming here. Grand farewell performance. By day . . . and by night.

EDITH. Please.

ROBERT. And yesterday . . . only yesterday . . . at the station in Paris . . . you told me you were beginning to love me. You don't love him.

EDITH. He loves me.

ROBERT. Is that a bond?

EDITH. He loves me, and he won't give me a divorce. He wants to win me back.

ROBERT. Well, he won't win you back. (*Looks at the table*) What are those?

EDITH. A suitcase of his. His things.

ROBERT. That damned lawyer brought them, I suppose?

EDITH. Must you swear?

ROBERT. Of course I must. What do you expect me to do?

EDITH. The literary circle of your sister would not approve. Nor would your high-born relatives.

ROBERT. Leave His Majesty out of this! And my sister, too.

EDITH. Robert! And I thought she had brought you up so nicely. What are you doing?

(ROBERT *has picked up the pa-jama-trousers.* CORTIN *enters.* ROBERT *does not see him*)

ROBERT. I'm going to have a look at him. See what sort of a man he is. (*Holding up the short, wide trousers*) Ah, short and stout, eh? Fat, pudgy, thickset. Wears a roomy forty-four. And has very short legs.

EDITH (*Snatching the trousers from him*). I won't have you making fun of my husband. (*She throws the trousers to* CORTIN *with a furious look*)

CORTIN (*Whispers to* EDITH *apologetically, as* ROBERT *roars with laughter*). My mistake. The color fascinated me.

ROBERT (*With the brush in his hand*). One light hair. So he's not only stout, but . . . (*Looking at the brush more closely*) . . . a platinum blond. (*Triumphantly*) Peroxide! ! ! (EDITH *snatches the brush from him.*

CORTIN *makes a despairing gesture)*
A little fat chap with bleached hair.
*(He puts on the top hat. It falls
down over his ears)* And with a head
like a pumpkin. *(Picks up the slippers)* Mmmmm. Ladylike little feet.
Patent leather with red velvet lining.
(Picks up the cologne bottle) Perfume! My God, the man's a pansy.

CORTIN. What!

ROBERT. A short, fat, hydrocephalic pansy.

EDITH. He's not!

CORTIN. I'll say he's not. *(Hands
ROBERT the Paris paper)* Read this.
Just the headline.

ROBERT *(Reads)*. "Night Club
Affray. Count Arthur de Ghuyé
knocks out champion boxer with
single punch in brawl."

C O R T I N . "While thousands
cheer." And now the sub head.

ROBERT. "Boxer's condition Critical."

CORTIN. Thank you. *(Takes the
paper)*

EDITH. And now this letter.
*(Hands him letter from the other
side)*

ROBERT *(Reads)*. "It has come
to my notice . . . flirting with a young
puppy of the name of Robert Geoffrey . . ."

EDITH. Go on.

ROBERT. "Deceive me, and I will
murder you and that young whippersnapper without remorse."

EDITH. "Love and kisses. Arthur."

CORTIN. A pansy, eh? *(He takes
two pairs of enormous boxing gloves
from the suitcase, puts them in a row
on the table, points to the four gloves
in succession)* Short . . . Fat . . .
Hydrocephalic . . . Peroxide.

ROBERT. I don't care. Let him
do his worst.

CORTIN. He will, my dear boy.
He will, believe me. *(Exit* CORTIN*)*
*(Several of the articles remain on the
table)*

ROBERT. Thank God *he's* gone.
Now listen to me. I couldn't tell you
in front of that lawyer.

EDITH. That damned lawyer.

ROBERT *(Correcting himself)*.
That damned lawyer. I knew all
about that night club brawl in Paris.
Do you know who was the cause of
it?

EDITH. Who?

ROBERT *(Solemnly)*. A notorious
"demi-mondaine." A prostitute, if
you'll pardon the expression.

EDITH. Good Lord!

ROBERT *(Taking sheet of paper
from his pocket)*. His mistress. His
mistress! She's been his mistress for
the last year. And now she's met this
prizefighter.

EDITH. He has . . . a mistress?

ROBERT. I don't wonder you
clutch your throat.

EDITH. Well, it's always done,
isn't it?

ROBERT. Here is a detailed report from Aristide Passy, the well-
known Parisian private detective.
Read it. It's all there . . . names,
dates, places, everything.

EDITH. How did you get this?

ROBERT. That detective telephoned me one day and asked if I
was interested. I said I was. He then
sent it to me . . . C.O.D.

EDITH. C.O.D.?

ROBERT. Well, I had to pay for
it, of course. The fellow's not in
business for his health. But it was
worth the money . . . because it eased
my conscience. I know now that I'm
not pursuing the wife of a faithful
husband.

EDITH. That must be nice.

ROBERT. It removes my last scruples.

(During these speeches EDITH *has been holding the paper in her hand, suspecting that* CORTIN *is at the bottom of this. She has given a quick look at the door by which he went out.* ROBERT *now starts to walk excitedly to and fro.* EDITH, *unseen by him, looks again at the door by which* CORTIN *left, this time with an affectionate, admiring smile, as if to say "Dear Father, this is your doing."* ROBERT *stops.* EDITH, *quickly changing her expression, clutches at her throat again)*

EDITH. Oh! . . . Oh, how can I bear it? . . . My Arthur. The scoundrel.

ROBERT. That's exactly what he is. So now one need have no qualms about . . . about . . . er . . . well, you know what I mean. I now go right ahead and I don't give a damn what my sister says.

EDITH. How does your sister come into this?

ROBERT *(Rather embarrassed)*. She's been writing me some rather annoying letters . . . about you.

EDITH. Oh? You told her about me?

ROBERT. Er . . . yes.

EDITH. And she doesn't approve of your passion?

ROBERT. Er . . . no. She keeps asking me how long I intend to let you make a fool of me.

EDITH. The old darling!

ROBERT *(Producing letter)*. I have her last one here, if you would care to glance at it.

EDITH. Read me the best bits.

ROBERT *(Scanning letter)*. Well . . . she says . . . *(He finds the passage)* Oh, yes, here it is. She says "With regard to that strumpet . . ."

EDITH *(Screeches)*. What!!

ROBERT. She's a bit old-fashioned.

EDITH. Strumpet, indeed!

ROBERT *(Soothingly)*. You'll find the word in Shakespeare. Othello used to say it to his wife. Quite often.

EDITH. Shakespeare makes me sick. Any dirty word is supposed to become poetry just because he used it.

ROBERT *(He pauses, concerned at her fury, then speaks apologetically)*. I suppose I ought not to have told you. But it would be dishonest to gloss over her simple, Anglo-Saxon expressions. (EDITH *snorts)* It would be deceiving you, and I cannot deceive the woman I love. She writes "She is only playing with you." *(Looks up quickly from letter)* Don't worry. That word does not occur again. "She is using you as a decoy to lure back her runaway husband."

(He reads these last words in a voice trembling with emotion, and EDITH *comes to him feelingly and sincerely)*

EDITH. It isn't true. I'm not playing with you. I love you, Robert. You're a dear . . . dear . . .

ROBERT. My darling. (THEY *kiss, a long and passionate kiss)*

EDITH. And now go.

ROBERT *(Slowly recovering his breath)* Go? After *this.* You can't send me away now. A volcanic first kiss like that . . . should be followed . . . without interruption . . . by . . . earthquakes of love. *(Beside himself)* I . . . I . . . I . . . *(Suddenly matter-of fact)* When can I see you?

EDITH *(Whispering)*. When it's

dark . . . quite dark . . . call for me. Drive me away, away out into the country. We'll have supper out of doors . . . on a quiet terrace . . . under the stars . . .

ROBERT. Of all the fool ideas! Terrace? Stars? What do you want to go out of doors for? We ought to be behind heavy curtains, with all the doors closed.

EDITH. You baby. You must go, dear.

ROBERT. But what do I do . . . until it's quite dark?

EDITH. Write to your sister. You owe her a letter. And thank her from me for using that charming Anglo-Saxon word with which she tried to separate us.

(ROBERT *rushes out.* CORTIN *enters from the suite. He goes straight to the table, picks up the report and folds it*)

CORTIN. You know, this thing is going so marvelously that I almost feel like coming out of my retirement.

EDITH *(Pointing to the "detective's" report).* You concocted that report, of course?

CORTIN. And Passy gave it to the boy. You, very sensibly, entrust it to the care of your lawyer. *(Pockets the report.)*

EDITH. Father, you're incorrigible.

CORTIN. Just what the Judge said that time in Sweden. But, I ask you, who in this world is corrigible at my age? *(Sighs)* Well, goodbye, my child.

EDITH. What do you mean? Are you leaving?

CORTIN. By the night train. My work is done. Your sympathetic husband has started on his way to life. He doesn't need to be nursed along

any more. He has accumulated three enemies already. That's fine for one day.

EDITH *(Embarrassed, apologetically).* I've been so sorry for that sweet boy. What with his scruples and my scruples, we weren't getting anywhere.

CORTIN. But now?

EDITH *(Demurely).* We are. At last I feel free. I'm a married woman. *(Pause. With a mocking smile)* Where is my husband?

CORTIN. I've already put half of him in there. *(Points to the side door, then to the things on the table)* I'll take the other half into your bedroom. That's where he belongs. Except that he has a mistress, he's an ideal husband.

EDITH. I feel sorry for him.

CORTIN. For Arthur?

EDITH. Yes. Tonight he will have to learn how it feels to be a husband whose wife . . . *(She breaks off, lowering her eyes)*

CORTIN. What? You horrify me.

EDITH. . . . a husband whose wife is beginning to be interested in another man. It happens in the best of families.

CORTIN. *Mostly* in the best of families.

EDITH. I'm treating Arthur abominably, I know. And shall I tell you something? I'm afraid of him.

CORTIN. Afraid? What's that? Superstition? Hysterics?

EDITH. Forgive me. I'm nervous. It's silly of me . . . but . . . he's so alive. I wouldn't be a bit surprised if he . . .

CORTIN *(Laughing).* Walked in at the door?

EDITH (*Painfully smiling*). Don't say it, Father.

(*There is a* KNOCK *on the door, a loud ominous* KNOCK. CORTIN *and* EDITH *stare at each other.— Brief, painful pause*)

EDITH. Come in.

(*The door opens slowly. Enter a* MAN *with a bouquet. He looks about as the audience would picture the Count de Ghuyé, after all that has been said about him. He even has a black patch over one eye.* CORTIN *and* EDITH *stare at him*)

THE MAN. I have come . . .

EDITH. Oh!

THE MAN. . . . from the flower shop downstairs. I'm the hotel florist. My name is Philippe Renard.

EDITH (*Relieved, faintly*). Oh! (*After a pause*) I saw your name on the store window, Monsieur Renard.

THE FLORIST. The Count de Ghuyé sent a telegram ordering flowers, with this message for Madame la Comtesse. (HE *gives* EDITH *bouquet and slip of paper.*)

EDITH (*Faintly*). Thank you, Monsieur Renard.

THE FLORIST. Enchanted, madame. (*He goes out*)

EDITH. The relief! I thought I was seeing things.

(*Brief pause*)

CORTIN. You know what that was, of course?

EDITH. What?

CORTIN (*Pointing upward with his finger*). God . . . gently warning us that He objects to our doing what He Himself only succeeded in doing once . . . making a man out of nothing. A man called Adam . . . remember? I've the feeling that He . . . dislikes our trying to repeat his performance.

EDITH (*Faintly*). His eye! . . . He had a patch over it.

CORTIN. Yes, they're very efficient up there. Great attention to detail. (*Points at slip of paper which the florist gave to Edith*) What does the outraged husband say?

EDITH (*Reads*). "With these flowers a thousand kisses to my beloved and faithful wife."

CORTIN. How tactful. Jealous threats in the sealed letter, loving words in the open message.

EDITH. You're right. An ideal husband. (*Tenderly strokes the bouquet*)

CORTIN. And, being ideal, he knows just what to do when his wife is starting out to supper with another man. (*He gathers up the four corners of the tablecloth and throws the whole thing with its contents over his shoulder, like a bundle. Whispering*) He says good night and goes to bed.

(*He tiptoes through the door at the right into Edith's bedroom with the bundle*)

CURTAIN

ACT THREE

SCENE: *Living room in the Chateau, near Monte Carlo. A few ancestral portraits on the walls. Antique furniture. A few African hunting trophies.*

AT RISE: *The time is three months after Act Two, in the afternoon. A tea service on the table indicates that two people have been having tea. A* CATHOLIC BISHOP, *in cassock, with a wide purple girdle, is about to leave. He is saying goodbye to* EDITH *at the door.*

BISHOP *(Folding a check).* On behalf of my poor, I want to thank you, Countess, for this token of your generosity.

EDITH. Don't mention it.

BISHOP. And I beg of you . . . don't take these petty local annoyances too much to heart. The people of this little town of ours are temperamental, sometimes even unruly . . . but fundamentally good and deserving of your many charities. In the long run, you'll like them, I'm sure. And you'll be happy in this beautiful house of yours, you and the Count.

EDITH. I hope so, your Excellency.

BISHOP. I shall see you again quite soon, Countess. Give the Count my very best regards next time you write him. And be sure to tell him how delighted we were with those two speeches he made on the radio.

EDITH *(Embarrassed).* Thank you, your Excellency.

BISHOP. Really, we were delighted . . . myself and a number of my learned friends. The first speech —made, I believe, on his way to Brazil—about foreign politics—was quite a treat. But the second . . . about law enforcement and modern prisons—was positively thrilling. Being one of those old-fashioned humanitarians, I was greatly moved by his sharp criticism of prison conditions in Sweden. He is a man of heart, and a gifted politician.

EDITH *(A little worried).* Do you think it's a good thing, your Excellency, that he is occupying himself with politics?

BISHOP. Oh well . . . political activity is always both good and bad. You make friends . . . and you also make enemies.

EDITH *(Worried).* Yes. It's a pity, isn't it?

BISHOP. To a certain extent, true. But, as I was saying just now, never in all our history was the need so great for a wise far-seeing mentality such as the Count revealed in his broadcasts. Mark my words, Countess, a few speeches like that here in our town, and our people will send him to Parliament.

*(*EDITH *registers uneasiness)*

BISHOP. Yes, yes. Our current representative in the House has been unpopular for a long time. The Count's election . . . next spring . . . in my opinion . . . is practically certain. *(Determined)* I'll see to it.

EDITH *(Worried).* Oh, heavens!

BISHOP. The prospect seems to alarm you.

EDITH. Oh, no . . . but . . . I don't like politics.

BISHOP. Come, come, dear lady. We must be sensible about this. The Count is a brilliant speaker. He is also extremely rich, which in this country is a *decisive* factor in politics.

And, judging by his broadcasts, he is a born diplomat. (EDITH *laughs*) You don't think the Count is a diplomat?

EDITH. Oh, yes. But not a *born* one.

BISHOP *(Tenacious of his idea)*. Anyway, to conclude my burst of enthusiasm, once he is in Parliament, it will be but a step to the Ministry of Foreign Affairs. Yes, yes, I assure you. We have talked it over, some of my influential friends and I, and we all feel that, given the support of myself and my followers, he cannot fail. *(He smiles and speaks energetically)* I don't know if you know the little nickname they have given me in these parts? They call me "Old Stick-to-it."

EDITH. But . . .

BISHOP. I know, I know. The Count for the moment has a bad press. True. But a little patience . . . just a little finesse . . . a couple of good suppers . . . and the critics will change their tone. If they don't . . . we'll have to make them. We will fight them . . . without remorse . . . the Count, my influential friends and I. *(Holding out his hand)* Well, I must not keep you any longer, Countess. Please inform the Count of all this. Mention my esteem and admiration and give him my best wishes.

EDITH. Oh, I will.

BISHOP. And thanks again. *(He raises his hand close to her lips)*

EDITH *(Kissing his ring)*. Goodbye, your Excellency.

> (BISHOP *goes out. The next moment* JULIE *enters by the same door, a newspaper in her hand)*

JULIE. The Bishop's very handsome, isn't he? All the women around here are crazy about him.

EDITH. Except me.

JULIE. Madame seems a little nervous today.

EDITH. And I've enough to make me nervous. *(Sits down again beside the tea table)* Did everybody I asked come?

JULIE. I think so. Four of 'em so far.

EDITH. Where have you put them?

JULIE. In the library. I never saw such a grouchy-looking lot in my life. You should have seen the way they glared at me. Thank goodness Mr. Cortin's here.

EDITH. Are his things unpacked?

JULIE. Yes, madame. He's changing now.

EDITH. Tell him to come down here the moment he's dressed . . . What's this? Another newspaper?

JULIE *(With the paper in her hand)*. The evening one. I hardly dared to bring it to you.

EDITH. Something in it again?

JULIE. Another vile attack.

EDITH. On my husband.

JULIE. As usual. *(Reads:)* "The international playboy and interloper who has shouldered his way into our town on the strength of his money . . ."

EDITH. That's enough. I don't want to hear it.

JULIE. Politics is certainly rough.

EDITH. Our lawyer's here at last. He'll show these people.

JULIE. And about time, too. First we rush around for weeks from hotel to hotel, and then we settle down at last in a quiet house . . . and we haven't had a peaceful day since. It's getting worse, too. Last night, they shot at our dog again . . . twice.

EDITH. Who did?

JULIE. One of Baron Amary's gardeners, so the butler says. He was keeping watch in the garden. And Baron Amary is telling everyone he won't give you a moment's peace till you sell the house to him.

EDITH. A cheerful prospect.

(A loud crash is heard, a window being smashed somewhere in the house. EDITH *takes no notice of it)*

JULIE *(Sighing).* Whenever it gets dark, they always start smashing windows. *(Another crash)* Did you hear that, madame?

EDITH *(Calmly drinking tea).* I hear it every day.

JULIE. Why don't you let me call the police?

EDITH. I won't do anything without consulting my lawyer. Come here, Julie. *(In a confidential undertone)* Anything new about . . . Robert?

JULIE *(Mysteriously).* My sister in Paris has been shadowing him day and night. He's been with those English people again . . . those Jefferses.

EDITH. I know.

JULIE. And Wednesday afternoon, he was alone with the Jeffers girl in a dark corner in a tearoom. Rue Lafayette. And today . . .

EDITH. Yes?

JULIE. He just got here a few hours ago . . . and . . . already he's talked to Paris on the telephone . . . from his hotel . . . for twenty-six minutes.

EDITH. To the Jeffers girl?

JULIE. Of course. *(Mysteriously)* My sister says she's not a bit pretty.

EDITH. Maybe she just doesn't think so. *(Pressing a button)* What on earth has happened to that butler? I've rung for him twice and he doesn't come.

JULIE. He's polishing the Count's cigarette-holders.

EDITH. Well, tell him to stop immediately.

JULIE. Fat lot of good *me* telling him to stop. All he does is sit bleating about how he worships the aristocracy. He says he's a British Conservative—born in the reign of Queen Victoria. He's crazy about the Count.

EDITH. Really?

JULIE. Sits up half the night reading his articles in that hunting magazine. He just can't wait for him to come home.

(Enter BUTLER, *carrying a tray with letters, etc.)*

BUTLER. Mr. Robert Geoffrey is calling, m'lady.

EDITH. Show him in.

BUTLER. Very good, m'lady.

EDITH. And, Hollingsworth, I don't want you spending all your time on my husband. Leave the cigarette-holders alone. We have guests in the house.

BUTLER. Beg pardon, m'lady, but I can't bring myself to leave the master's beautiful things uncared for. *(Putting down the tray)* His Lordship's letters, m'lady.

EDITH. He's not a lord. He's a French Count.

BUTLER. I prefer to think of him as a lord, m'lady.

EDITH. Ask Mr. Geoffrey to come in.

(Exit BUTLER*)*

JULIE. You know, madame, he doesn't like Robert . . . er . . . Mr. Geoffrey. Gives him very ugly looks.

EDITH. Well, if he's devoted to

my husband, I can understand that.

(Enter ROBERT*)*

ROBERT. How do you do?

EDITH. Good afternoon, Robert. Julie . . . tea.

JULIE. Yes, madame. *(With an ingratiating smile at Robert)* I'll make Mr. Geoffrey a lovely fresh cup right away.

ROBERT. Thank you very much, Julie.

(JULIE *exit)*

Nice girl. Say, what's that menagerie doing in the library?

EDITH. I was expecting my lawyer . . . you remember Mr. Cortin . . . so I have asked them here. All sorts of little difficulties have piled up . . . Did you have a good time in Paris?

ROBERT. Edith, I've made an unpleasant discovery. I've found that *you* are spying on *me* now.

EDITH. I?

ROBERT. Yes. And Julie. And her sister. And a cab driver. It's one of those nation-wide hook-ups. (EDITH *wipes her eyes)* Hello! What's the matter?

EDITH. Oh, don't mind me. I'm just nervous.

ROBERT. I don't wonder. I've seen the papers. They certainly seem to have it in for him. Always that way when you go in for politics. By the way, I thought your husband's broadcasts extremely clever.

EDITH *(Embarrassed).* Too clever for a little town like this. They . . . they can't rise to his superior point of view. *(Sighing)* Everybody seems to hate us. And yet my husband has done nothing but good to these people here, and neither have I.

ROBERT. Oh, it's just politics.

EDITH. Well, it hurts one's feelings. And now you're hurting my feelings, too. I can't bear it much longer.

ROBERT. Well, if you want to know, nor can I. If something isn't done, I shall go cuckoo. The way we love each other is humiliating. Climbing in through a window to the woman I feel bound to for life . . . as I had to do at your villa outside Paris . . . it's . . . well, it's humiliating. It can't go on.

EDITH. Oh, Robert, what's the use of pretending? You've been fooling around with that girl for three days, in Paris.

(Enter JULIE *with the tea)*

JULIE. Mr. Cortin will be right down, madame. *(Exit* JULIE*)*

ROBERT. What do you mean, "fooling around"?

EDITH. I mean fooling around.

ROBERT. There's no fooling around about it. She's a serious young lady.

EDITH. Pretty?

ROBERT. Very serious.

EDITH. You mean she's plain.

ROBERT. Strikingly so. *(With an apologetic gesture)* I can't lie to you.

EDITH. You're planning to get married.

ROBERT. Yes.

EDITH. Oh!

ROBERT. Edith . . . I feel that in your heart of hearts you have forgiven your unfaithful husband. So what is there left for me? Nothing . . . except to get married . . . without love. That's the only way I can be free of you. Ours is not one of those trivial passing love affairs and . . . *(In a choked, but manly and determined voice)* . . . in the long run, the only existence I can imagine with any woman is a pure family life. I love you deeply, but as long as you're married to somebody else . . . *(He breaks off with an apologetic gesture)*

EDITH. How very noble of you!

(Enter JULIE)

JULIE. Mr. Cortin.

(CORTIN enters, greets EDITH and ROBERT)

JULIE. Tea, sir?

CORTIN. Not just now, thanks.

(Exit JULIE)

EDITH. How nice to have you here, Mr. Cortin. Did you come straight from Paris?

CORTIN. Started the moment I got your letter. It made me uneasy. All about "difficulties" and "unpleasantness." You seem so nervous. And your eyes . . .

EDITH. Are red. I know. (COR-TIN *throws* ROBERT *a look)* Right, my old friend. He's responsible.

ROBERT. The Countess is amazingly candid today.

EDITH. I have no secrets from my dear old friend.

ROBERT *(Starts to leave)*. Unfortunately, I am not on such delightfully intimate terms with Mr. Cortin. May I look in again this evening?

EDITH. Of course. Have dinner with us.

ROBERT. Thank you. So long.

(He bows and goes out.—There is a brief pause)

CORTIN. So it's a grand passion.

EDITH. Yes. But . . .

CORTIN. But?

EDITH. He's planning to marry some high-born English girl. Probably at the insistence of his royal relatives. *(Abruptly stops talking, then grasps Cortin's hands and ex-*

claims:) Father! Aren't we going to say a word about *that?*

CORTIN. What?

EDITH. Those broadcasts. You promised me a surprise, and I certainly got it . . . when I heard the announcer say, "And now we bring you comments on the political situation abroad by the noted explorer, Count Arthur de Ghuyé." *(Reproachfully, but with unmistakable admiration)* Father, you really *are!*

CORTIN. Pretty good stuff, I thought.

EDITH. So did the Bishop. He was raving about them . . .

(Crash of glass, off)

CORTIN. Hullo! What's that?

EDITH *(Irritated)*. Oh, it's a nightly performance. Just some kindly soul smashing our windows. It happens all the time. They throw rocks wrapped in threatening letters.

CORTIN. How very peculiar. What's been happening?

EDITH. It's Arthur.

CORTIN. Arthur?

EDITH. I didn't mention it in my letter, because . . . you're so proud of Arthur.

CORTIN. I love him like a son. Has he been misbehaving?

EDITH. He's been . . . injudicious.

CORTIN. In what way?

EDITH. Well, for one thing, he sent a thousand dollars to the town poor.

CORTIN. But he did that . . .

EDITH. On my advice. I know. Still, he ought to have remembered that the municipal elections were coming on very soon.

CORTIN. What have the elections to do with it?

EDITH. The leftist press immediately attacked him. Said he had given the money as a bribe . . . to buy a seat on the town council, the first step in a political career. They called him a plutocrat, a wealthy drone. They called *me* a boot-licker of British royalty . . . The Queen's letter . . . about my dressmaker. Remember? A few days later it was in the local newspaper.

CORTIN. The waiter's been gossiping.—And I'd have done better if I'd kept my big mouth shut. *(He looks guilty)*

EDITH. Of course, I denied everything, but it did no good.

(Enter JULIE)

Yes, Julie?

JULIE. Madame, now that Mr. Cortin is here, couldn't we send for the police . . .

EDITH. No . . . Don't go, Julie. Where are the newspapers?

JULIE *(Picking up a stack of newspapers)*. I marked all the nasty things . . . in red pencil.

CORTIN *(Reading)*. "The adventurer from Central Africa and South America who, on the strength of having lured a rich American girl into marriage . . ."

EDITH. That's the organ of the Right.

CORTIN. Are the rightists after his scalp, too?

EDITH. Yes. Their boss is Baron Amary. The man who . . .

CORTIN. Wanted to buy this house?

EDITH. Yes.

CORTIN. Arthur's enemies are certainly working overtime. *(He laughs)* All except Vice-President Boutonnier who bellowed so about his hotel room.

EDITH. Don't laugh. His bank has just called in the mortgage on this house.

CORTIN. We'll pay it.

EDITH. No, we won't. I'm going to sell the house and get out of here.

CORTIN. Where to?

EDITH. I don't know. South Africa. The North Pole. Somewhere far, far away where they've never heard of Count Arthur Ghuyé.

CORTIN *(Reading from newspaper)*. "This singular and perverse blend of Communist and Fascist" . . . *(To* EDITH) The middle of the road paper?

EDITH. Yes.

CORTIN. And all because of that thousand-dollar donation!

EDITH. Now you know why I wrote you that letter. (JULIE *starts to leave)* Wait a minute, Julie. *(To* CORTIN) From the very instant of my arrival in this house, a mob of people started besieging me, demanding to see the Count on what they claimed was urgent business. I put them off. Then, when I knew you were coming, I asked them to come here . . . today. They're waiting outside.

CORTIN. They haven't mentioned the nature of this "urgent business"?

EDITH. Not yet. But I'll bet it's something unpleasant.

CORTIN. Ah, well, they'll tell us.

EDITH. I imagine so. Julie, clear away the tea, and tell Hollingsworth to show these people in, in the order of their arrival.

JULIE. Yes, madame.—Isn't Mr. Cortin having his tea?

CORTIN. Thank you, no. *(Reading, while* JULIE *exit with the tea things)* "Let him chase lions and loose women, but not a seat on our historic town council" . . . Ugh! How provincial. *(Takes another newspaper)* "We want no interlopers in the venerable old mansion" . . . That's Baron Amary again. I recognize his touch.

EDITH. Arthur has only one friend here. The Bishop. And he's worse than all the enemies put together.

CORTIN. Why?

EDITH *(Reproachfully)*. Arthur's broadcasts have infatuated him, and he's resolved to make him a member of Parliament.

CORTIN *(Unpleasantly surprised)*. Oh.

EDITH. The trouble is the Bishop is very influential. And very, very determined.

CORTIN. Most disagreeable. Count Ghuyé will not go on the air again . . . ever.

EDITH. And a lot of good that will do now. You don't know the Bishop.

CORTIN. Tough. Very tough. We aren't getting the breaks.

EDITH. No.

CORTIN. And arising from that, what's the matter with your admirer? Why was he looking like an impending cloudburst?

EDITH. He had just presented me with an ultimatum. My husband or him.

CORTIN. Oh? Well, whatever Arthur's failings, he seems to have succeeded in making that boy fall in love with you.

EDITH. And me with him. I love his youthful naivete . . . his innocence . . . his honesty . . . his fiery passion! I love him more than . . . more than . . .

CORTIN. More than his august relatives?

EDITH. Oh . . . I love them, too. I'm a snob, Papa, I don't deny it. The idea of becoming . . . by marriage . . . even a very, very distant relative of . . . oh, Papa! *(She shudders with pleasure)*

CORTIN. After having been a relative of . . . *(Points to himself)*

EDITH *(Reproachfully)*. Papa, dear!

(Enter BUTLER*)*

Yes?

BUTLER. M'lady, are you prepared to receive the first of the . . . exhibits, m'lady?

EDITH. Yes.

*(*BUTLER *admits* RIBAUD. *Exit* BUTLER*)*

RIBAUD *(Aggressively)*. I'm Jacques Ribaud. Proprietor of Ribaud's Inn, Bar, Grill and Grand International Restaurant, in case you don't know. *(Very loudly)* Have been for forty years.

CORTIN *(Calmly)*. Don't shout. What can we do for you?

RIBAUD *(Loudly)*. I came to see the Count.

CORTIN *(Calmly, patiently)*. I'm not hard of hearing. So much for your information. As to Count Ghuyé, he's in Brazil. I am his lawyer. If something is on your mind, sob it out on *my* shoulder. Why do you want to see the Count?

RIBAUD. I used to know him.

CORTIN. *Really?*

EDITH. You know him personally?

RIBAUD *(Loud)*. Certainly.— Don't you even offer me a seat?

CORTIN. *(Very politely)*. No, Monsieur Ribaud. No.

RIBAUD. Fine people. *(Shrugs)* But . . . down to business. When I read that letter of Count Ghuyé to the Mayor, saying he was giving a thousand dollars to the poor and all about how he'd been a student here and had rowed in the boat race, I remembered him right away. The college boys always come to my place for beer. The Count was a handsome lad. But that's more than fifteen years ago.

CORTIN. You have a good memory.

RIBAUD. I remember every single guest who's come to my Inn in forty years.

CORTIN. How perfectly ghastly for you. But, ceasing for a moment to delve into the past, what do you want?

RIBAUD. The Count owes me money.

CORTIN. Count Arthur Ghuyé?

RIBAUD. That's right.

CORTIN. And how does that come about?

RIBAUD. I'll tell you.

CORTIN. Do. Omitting no detail, however slight.

RIBAUD. It was one night after the boat race. The boys were throwing a party in my restaurant garden. Suddenly there was a terrific storm, thunder and rain and lightning, and the Count left without paying. *(Presents a slip of paper)* Twenty-four francs, ninety.

CORTIN. Interesting. And you're asking for your money *now,* after fifteen years?

RIBAUD. If you give a college boy credit, it always takes a long time to collect.

CORTIN. But my dear Monsieur . . .

RIBAUD. Ribaud.

CORTIN. My dear Monsieur Ribaud, how can you prove it was

Count Ghuyé who left owing you money?

RIBAUD. What? You want proof? From a respected hotel proprietor who has been in the business forty years, here in this town where everybody knows me? You want "proof"?

CORTIN. Yes, if you don't mind.

RIBAUD. It's easy to see you're a stranger here. But, since you insist, it happens I can oblige.

CORTIN. How?

RIBAUD. Simple. Well, look here. There were twenty college boys at that party. And since none of them paid, it follows that the Count didn't pay either. That's logic, that is.

CORTIN. Perfect logic. But how did you arrive at the twenty-four francs ninety?

RIBAUD. That was the largest check. There was no other aristocrat among the students. Naturally a Count would run up the largest bill. These high-born wastrels always do themselves well. (CORTIN *looks at him sarcastically.* RIBAUD *gets angry)* But what's the good of talking? I'll take the thing into court. The Judge knows old Ribaud. Has known me for fifty-three years. He'll see that I get my rights. *(He starts to go)*

CORTIN. Just a minute. You are so impetuous, Monsieur Ribaud. *(Takes out money)* Your subtle reasoning has convinced me. Here you are. *(Gives him money)* Twenty-four francs, ninety. About 1750 at the present value of the franc.

RIBAUD *(Taking the money).* And how about the fifteen years' interest?

CORTIN. Nice work, Monsieur

Ribaud. Interest? At six per cent? *(Calculates)* One hundred and five. Here you are.

RIBAUD. Of course, the big, generous thing would be . . . *(He falls silent)*

CORTIN. Well, what would the big, generous thing be?

RIBAUD. Well, look. Wouldn't the big, generous thing be if the Count was to consider his schoolmates his guests?

CORTIN. The other nineteen?

RIBAUD. Probably would have, too, if it hadn't been for that thunderstorm.

CORTIN. What's it all come to?

RIBAUD. At the present value of the franc . . . Say in round figures 4721.

CORTIN *(Paying)*. Count Arthur Ghuyé hereby invites his nineteen schoolmates to a farewell party. We don't owe you any more?

RIBAUD. I don't think so.

CORTIN. I'm so sorry. If you happen to think of anything when you get home, you *will* let us know, won't you? Come back in the morning. In fact, come back as often as you can. *(He rings)*

RIBAUD. If there's anything due me, I'll come without your smart remarks. I'm a man of integrity, and I never ask for more than my due. *(Savagely)* The hell with it.

(Enter BUTLER)

CORTIN. Next.

RIBAUD. Good night. *(Softly, to himself)* Dirty scum! *(Exit, followed by BUTLER)*

CORTIN. Arthur should never have rowed here as a college boy. *(Crash off. BUTLER re-enters)* What was that noise?

BUTLER. The gentleman inadvertently fell downstairs, sir.

CORTIN. Really? How did that happen?

BUTLER. When about to descend the staircase, the gentleman made an offensive remark about the Count, and I took the liberty of pasting him in the eye, sir.

CORTIN. That's *just* what we needed! Anyway . . . Thank you, Hollingsworth.

BUTLER. Not at all, sir. I desire to give satisfaction.

CORTIN. Whose turn is it now?

BUTLER. There are three persons of various sexes who say they wish to come in together, sir.

CORTIN. Let 'em come, as many as want to. *(Exit BUTLER)* Poor Arthur! They're robbing him of his only real possession . . . his beautiful, enviable lack of reality.

(BUTLER opens the door. THREE PERSONS enter: 1. A pretty WOMAN of about 40, plainly dressed. 2. Her fifteen years old BOY. 3. LAWYER PENDIX)

WOMAN. How do you do? . . . *(To BOY)* Say, How do you do, dear.

BOY. How do you do?

CORTIN. How do you do?

LAWYER *(To WOMAN and BOY, energetically)*. Sit down. Sit down.

CORTIN. I beg your pardon. Is this your house?

LAWYER. No, but if nobody else offers them a seat, I will. My name is Pendix. I'm their lawyer. And, what's more, I'm editor of a local weekly.

CORTIN. Oh, yes. What's it called?

LAWYER *(Emphatically)*. "Scandal of the Mediterranean." *(To the*

WOMAN *and the* BOY, *who are standing about uneasily)* Sit down. Didn't you hear me? (THEY *sit down.* LAWYER *says to the* WOMAN) Don't show so much leg. It's bad for our case. *(Shouting)* And don't look so scared, I'm here.

CORTIN. So I notice.

LAWYER. You can't embarrass me with your supercilious manners.

CORTIN. I wasn't intending to.

LAWYER. And I wouldn't advise you to try. Now then. To begin with, whom have I the pleasure of addressing?

CORTIN. The pleasure is mine. My name is Cortin. I am the legal representative of my friend Count de Ghuyé and his family.

LAWYER. Delighted. This woman is Mademoiselle Marie Bonnard. (WOMAN *starts to get up.* HE *shouts)* Sit down! (WOMAN *sits down)* And the boy is her son, Andre Bonnard *(To* BOY) Get up. Sit down. Andre is fifteen years old. His mother is charwoman at the town hall. She has to practice the utmost self-denial to send her only son to school.

EDITH. I should be happy to contribute a small sum to this worthy cause. If you will see my secretary . . .

LAWYER. I won't see anyone. I will only see you.

CORTIN. But what makes you so aggressive, when you're asking for something? This isn't the way to make friends and influence people.

LAWYER. Pardon me, I'm not *asking.* I'm demanding. This is no matter of charity.

CORTIN. Counselor, you're beginning to get on my nerves.

LAWYER. Just wait. I'll get on them even more. I don't know how closely you were listening when I introduced this lady. In case your mind was wandering, let me present her again. *Mademoiselle* Bonnard—and *her son* Andre Bonnard. From this you will infer—correctly—that Andre was born out of wedlock . . . *(Emphatically)* the illegitimate son of a hardened father who does nothing for the forsaken mother or her child!

CORTIN. The low scoundrel!

LAWYER. So now you see why we are here.

CORTIN. So now . . . I see . . . why you are here?

LAWYER. We intend to confront the father of the child, but if you are his legal representative . . .

CORTIN. Whose legal representative?

LAWYER. The father's. The *noble* father's. Notice how I sneered when I said "noble"?

CORTIN. I got it.

(He gets up and starts to walk quickly to and fro. EDITH *covers her face with both hands to conceal that she is laughing.* LAWYER *makes a speech as if in court)*

LAWYER. Don't cry, madame. Nobody realizes better than I how painful this is for you. But I am a lawyer, an editor, and a publisher, and in all three capacities a fighter for justice. I demand support for this child. I am here to procure my client's just dues . . . amicably . . . in order to avoid involving the already sufficiently unpopular Count in an unsavory trial, which, of course, could hardly be kept out of the press.

CORTIN *(To the* WOMAN). Will you please send your son outside. I have a few questions to ask you.

(BOY *starts to leave)*

EDITH. Just a moment. Come

here, my child. Let me have a look at you.

(ANDRE *goes over to her.* EDITH *looks at him and pats him on the head*)

EDITH. Nice-looking boy.

WOMAN. He looks like his father, don't you think?

EDITH. Very like. That's fine, Andre. You may go.

(Exit BOY)

CORTIN *(To the* WOMAN). You had an affair with the Count?

LAWYER *(Very vehemently).* Yes!

CORTIN. Actually I wasn't asking you.

LAWYER *(To the* WOMAN). Answer him. Is the Count Andre's father?

WOMAN *(Shamefacedly casting down her eyes).* Yes.

CORTIN. What Count?

LAWYER. Count Arthur de Ghuyé, the owner of this mansion, who admits that he spent some summers at college here fifteen or sixteen years ago.

CORTIN. And that's enough reason for you to . . .

LAWYER. Well, it was enough reason for him to seduce this unhappy woman and make her a mother. *(Bombastically)* An unmarried mother!

CORTIN. And you're absolutely certain?

LAWYER. What, that she's the mother?

CORTIN. No, that he's the father.

LAWYER. Well, I ask you. The boat races take place in July, and the boy took place . . . I should say was born in April, nine months later. I can prove that by his birth certificate. But it is not my purpose to present the evidence formally now. I can do that in court. If you are interested, you will be able to read the report of the trial together with a few incisive editorial comments later in my weekly.

CORTIN. "Scandal of the Mediterranean."

LAWYER. Yes, sir. "Scandal of the Mediterranean."—Come, Mademoiselle, we have no further business here.

CORTIN. One moment, Mademoiselle *(To* LAWYER) What on earth are you skipping about for? I haven't said anything yet.

WOMAN *(Speaks up unexpectedly, timidly, but fluently, like a schoolgirl monotonously reciting a carefully memorized lesson—now and then with a glance at the lawyer).* Your Honor, I was a young and inexperienced virgin. It was . . . it was a summer night, about nine-thirty. I was . . . I was lying in bed with my simple but clean nightgown on. There was a knock on the door. "Come in," I said, taking it for granted that it was my father coming to say goodnight. Picture my surprise when Count Arthur de Ghuyé crossed the threshold. He leered at me. His eyes gleamed. His face was suffused. "I want you!" he shouted. *(She stops abruptly)*

LAWYER. Go on.

CORTIN *(Peremptorily).* No! Not here and not now. Let's get down to business. *(To* WOMAN) How much do you want?

WOMAN *(Looking down bashfully).* My lawyer . . . Mr. Pendix has figured it out.

LAWYER *(Laying down a folder).* You'll find it all here. Support, retroactive fifteen years. Regular future payments, or a lump sum in lieu thereof.

CORTIN *(Pointing to an item on the paper)*. And what is this startling sum?

LAWYER. My fee.

CORTIN. Tomorrow morning the Countess' secretary will settle this account. The Count will pay a lump sum.

WOMAN *(To* CORTIN, *sweetly)*. Please accept my most sincere thanks, sir.

LAWYER. Come, come, don't *grovel.* You aren't accepting charity. You're receiving your just due.

CORTIN. Then you're still cross?

LAWYER. Yes! I resent this pampering of aristocratic voluptuaries who seduce unfortunate girls, and then have to be hunted down fifteen years later in unknown continents.

CORTIN *(Calmly)*. I don't think I like your tone.

LAWYER. I don't like it myself. But a father must pay.

CORTIN *(Almost losing his patience—with a flash of a nervous smile)*. You haven't the faintest idea on what thin ice you're doing your figure-skating.

LAWYER *(In an irritating monotone)*. He'll have to pay.

CORTIN *(Regaining his calm—icily)*. I think, my dear colleague, that we have about covered the subject under discussion, have we not?

LAWYER. You mean you want me to go?

CORTIN. As rapidly as you can.

LAWYER *(Indignantly)*. You certainly are . . .

CORTIN *(Interrupting)*. Allergic to you. Good night.

WOMAN *(Timidly)*. Thank you from the bottom of my heart, dear Countess. *(To* CORTIN) And thank you once more, Mr. What's-your-name. Would you like my Andre to come in and kiss you goodbye?

CORTIN. I would not.

LAWYER. Let's go. *(Pushing the* WOMAN *ahead of him to the door)* I wish we'd asked for more.

(The WOMAN *exit)*

LAWYER. Observe that I am taking my leave without salutations.

(Exit LAWYER. CORTIN *rings.* BUTLER *enters immediately)*

BUTLER. Sir?

CORTIN. I just wanted to warn you not to hit these people, no matter what remarks they make.

BUTLER. Not even the elder of the two males?

CORTIN. No, not even him.

BUTLER. Very good sir.

CORTIN. I'm sorry. I know what agony it must be for a man who packs a punch like yours not to be allowed to use it.

BUTLER. Yes, sir.

CORTIN. Still, into each life some rain must fall.

BUTLER. Yes, sir.

CORTIN. Is there anybody else outside?

BUTLER. No, sir.

CORTIN. Thank you, Hollingsworth.

BUTLER. Thank *you*, sir. *(Exit* BUTLER)

(Brief pause)

CORTIN. Well . . . ! I knew I had made your husband a vital and dynamic character. But even so . . . I wouldn't have expected a baby of him. Most disturbing.

EDITH. Not at all.

CORTIN. You are not shocked and horrified?

EDITH. I am not.

CORTIN. What? You defend this woman?

EDITH. Of course. Somebody had to be the father of her child.

CORTIN. Well, there's one thing certain. It wasn't Arthur.

EDITH. What's so certain about it?

CORTIN. Edith, are you delirious?

EDITH. Maybe that isn't his only child. Mightn't he have another?

CORTIN (Beginning to suspect). I don't follow you.

EDITH. Just a question. A legal problem. If for example . . . let's say . . . let's assume . . . that I . . . that I was going to have a baby?

CORTIN. Well?

EDITH. Would it be his?

CORTIN (Suspecting the worst). Darling, you aren't trying to tell me that . . . ? (Breaks off. EDITH casts down her eyes. CORTIN does not know whether to be touched or frantic) Or . . . Or . . .

EDITH (Putting her head coyly against his chest). Father, dear (Looks up into his eyes, smiling blissfully) You see, it's not so impossible.

CORTIN. I . . . I . . . Where's my hat?

EDITH. Your hat?

CORTIN. I want to take it off to Count Arthur Ghuyé. A hell of a fellow!

(Pause)

EDITH. And now . . . do you agree that the situation has become impossible?

CORTIN. It's become so impossible that you might also call it . . .

EDITH. Impossible?

CORTIN. Just the word I was hunting for.

EDITH. Then what's to be done?

CORTIN. Much as it pains me . . . (Gesture of resignation)

EDITH. Robert wants to marry me. I've got to get rid of my husband. And at once, before it's too late.

CORTIN. Sad, but true. Fortunately the procedure is quite simple.

EDITH. Divorce?

CORTIN. No. Never. What will you do with him after the divorce? Keep him hanging around for the rest of our lives? Think of all those club dues and all the other things. Not to mention the determined Bishop. No, it's unthinkable.

EDITH. Then what?

(Short pause)

CORTIN. There's only one way.

EDITH. And that is?

CORTIN. Don't be shocked. We'll have to bump him off.

EDITH. Oh!

CORTIN. There's nothing else for it. We must rub him out.

EDITH. But who will . . . rub him out.

CORTIN. Who else but the man who . . . er . . . rubbed him in? Myself.

EDITH. But how are you going to kill him? With what?

CORTIN (Reaching for his hip pocket). With this. (EDITH screams) Don't be frightened. It's not a gun. It's a far deadlier weapon. (Taking sheets of paper from his pocket) I can reveal to you now, my child, that shortly after your despairing letter arrived, I received these cables from Brazil for you. Be brave, my dear. I'm trying to break it to you gently. (Reads the cables one after another. The first) "Your husband is ill." (The second) "Your husband's condition is critical." (The third)

"Husband is sinking." *(The fourth)* "Husband sunk." *(He hands her the final cablegram and bows his head)*

EDITH *(Reading)*. "Count Arthur Ghuyé . . . Tropical fever . . . Passed away after two days illness. Stop. Have buried him deep in jungle. Stone erected. Authorities informed. Stop. Letter follows." Signed Colonel H. W. Wills, Director of Expedition. *(She bows her head)*

CORTIN. Stop.

EDITH *(Softly)*. Who is Colonel Wills?

CORTIN. I am . . . And here. The letter which follows. *(Gives her letter. Pause)*

EDITH. Father, I feel as sad as if I'd lost somebody.

CORTIN. And you've only lost your husband.

(Short pause)

EDITH. And what do I do now?

CORTIN *(Taking cablegram from her)*. You retire . . . to be alone with your grief. *(Exit EDITH slowly, with bowed head. CORTIN waits till she has gone, then calls through another doorway)* Julie, come here, please, and call Hollingsworth. *(JULIE and BUTLER enter)* My dear Julie. My dear Hollingsworth. *(He almost breaks down)*

JULIE. Are you ill, sir? Shall I fetch the smelling salts?

CORTIN. No, no, 'tis but a passing weakness. Julie . . . Hollingsworth . . . as faithful family retainers you must be informed that your master, your mistress's husband, in short Count Arthur de Ghuyé, has fallen victim to his passion for scientific exploration in the swampy forests of Brazil. This cablegram brought us the sad news. He has fallen ill . . . and died. (JULIE

begins to cry softly. BUTLER *turns away, silently wiping his eyes)* The deep grief of our devoted staff is some small solace to us all. Not much, but something.

JULIE. The . . . the Countess. Does she know?

CORTIN. I hesitated to tell her, but . . . yes, she knows.

JULIE. The poor lamb! Excuse me, sir, but I mustn't leave her alone now. *(She hurries out through the door by which Edith left)*

BUTLER *(Deeply moved)*. I never knew the Count, sir. But anyone who has had the privilege of caring for his beautiful things, as I have, could not but realize how fine a gentleman he was. I learned to love him through his impeccable wardrobe. I read many of his contributions to the press. I listened to his radio comments, too. He was a noble-minded man, my late master. A gentleman from head to foot, sir.

CORTIN. You mean from top hat to shoes. Very true.

BUTLER. May I retire, sir, and weep for him in solitude?

CORTIN. Certainly, certainly. Weep where you like . . . all over the house.

BUTLER. Thank you, sir.

(Exit BUTLER *with bowed head)*

CORTIN. At least one person who loved him. *(Picks up a paper, reads:)* "This neer-do-well who has tried his villainous best to trample the worthy men of our fair city beneath his iron heel . . . An insignificant fellow at best. This Count is a nobody." . . . At long last, a true word. *(Tosses the paper aside)*

(Enter BUTLER*)*

BUTLER *(Still in an emotional voice).* Mr. Robert Geoffrey.

(Exit BUTLER*)*

(Enter ROBERT, *who looks silently at* CORTIN *and solemnly, mournfully shakes his hand)*

ROBERT. I heard . . . from the staff.

CORTIN. I got the cable. *(Takes out handkerchief, wipes away an imaginary tear)* A crushing blow.

ROBERT. We must be brave. The ways of Providence are beyond understanding.

CORTIN. How true. *(Offers him cigarette)* Smoke?

ROBERT. Thank you. Not now. *(Enter* EDITH, *dressed entirely in black)* Edith! *(He takes both her hands)* I want you to know . . . to know . . . I can't find words just now.

EDITH. Thank you, Robert.

(Pause. THEY *stand facing each other, at a loss)*

ROBERT. Edith, I ought to leave you alone now with your thoughts. But may I say this? Your past is dead. Your future . . . at this solemn moment I tell you this without reserve, with full awareness of my commitments under the law . . . your future belongs to me.

EDITH *(Lovingly).* Robert!

*(*THEY *clasp hands warmly)*

EDITH. This evening . . .

ROBERT. No. Tomorrow morning. Till then . . . goodbye.

(He bows formally. CORTIN *bows, also formally. Exit* ROBERT*)*

CORTIN *(Lights a cigarette).* A strange moment, this. I confess I'm moved.

EDITH. So am I.

(Pause)

CORTIN. Where I went wrong was in creating a real man. That's why he had to die. But I couldn't help it. I couldn't have turned out shoddy work. I'm an artist.

EDITH. Arthur was your masterpiece.

CORTIN. I doubt if I shall ever top him. But the trouble was, he was human . . . and so he erred.

EDITH. Wouldn't you say rather that he was too much under our influence?

CORTIN. Well, of course, it's a commonplace . . . the weak man ruled by his wife. Incidentally, he didn't always listen to you. You remember that time he took that toss on the Stock Exchange . . . when he lost that fifteen hundred dollars?

EDITH. Yes.

CORTIN. I expressly told him then that you forbade him to gamble. It was no use. He gambled again.

EDITH. And . . . lost again?

CORTIN. Yes, poor devil. Not much. A measly nine hundred and ninety-five dollars. We'll square accounts tomorrow. Poor dear Arthur only lived about three months, but he didn't waste his time. It's tragic to think he's gone.

EDITH. He was a good husband to me. Apart from being unfaithful, of course.

CORTIN. What do you mean?

EDITH. The loose woman in Paris. You know.

CORTIN. What a perfect example of feminine possessiveness! A woman resents losing even what she never had.

EDITH. I resent it because it lowers my feminine appeal. It shows that my husband was not in love with me but with someone else. I didn't even like those old love letters of his, if you must know.

CORTIN. All we need now is for you to say that he was a sex maniac.

EDITH. Not where his wife was concerned, that's certain. Still, there's one thing. I owe my future happiness to him. So . . . he was the first man who ever made me happy. But not the last, I hope.

CORTIN. All honor to his memory. I knew him. He will forgive us. *(A window is smashed somewhere.* CORTIN *points toward the sound)* And his enemies as well.

(Short pause)

EDITH *(Rather worried)*. I do hope it won't occur to Robert . . . I mean, to ask me that special painful question about . . . *(Breaks off)*

CORTIN. Don't worry. Everything has been arranged. Read tomorrow's papers. They call you "the widow of a martyr to Science." That makes you one of the great ladies of the world. Nobody would dream of asking about your antecedents.

EDITH. Dear, kind Arthur! I owe him even that. *(Gently touches her eyes with handkerchief)* Still . . .

some day the moment will come when I'll confess everything to Robert . . . even if he doesn't ask.

CORTIN. Don't you dread that moment?

EDITH. No.

CORTIN. You love him as much as that?

EDITH. Yes. And I shall tell you why I don't dread it? Because I know now how much he has come to love *me*.

CORTIN. So Arthur has not lived in vain.

EDITH. My God, no.

(Enter BUTLER, *bringing telegrams on a tray.* HE *gives them to* CORTIN *and goes out.)*

CORTIN *(With a sigh)*. The first messages of condolence. *(Opens them, reads in a monotone)* "London, Buckingham Palace. Warmest sympathy. George, Elizabeth and the girls." *(Hands it to* EDITH, *opens another, reads in a monotone)* "Vatican City. On behalf of the Secretary of State of His Holiness . . ." *(Opens a third, reads in monotone)* "Moscow. Profoundly shaken. Joseph." *(*HE *hands it to* EDITH)

CURTAIN

BLUE DANUBE

BLUE DANUBE

A SENTIMENTAL LOVE-STORY IN THREE ACTS

CHARACTERS

PAUL VIRAG
MARIANNE
ELLA
BARNA
BARTENDER
AUTOMOBILE SALESMAN
REAL ESTATE AGENT
WITTNER
WAITER

PLACE : BACKYARD OF THE ROADHOUSE "BLUE DANUBE TAVERN AND BAR" ON THE HIGHWAY TO VIENNA.

(New acting version of the same author's DELILA as translated by SAM JAFFE. *"Delila" was produced at the* PESTI SZINHAZ *in Budapest with* LILI DARVAS *in the leading role; at the* BURGTHEATER *and* AKADEMIE-THEATER *in Vienna with* ALMA SEIDLER; *in Rome and on other Italian stages with* EVA MALTAGLIATI; *filmed in Hollywood with* MARY ASTOR.)*

BLUE DANUBE

ACT ONE

SCENE: *The backyard of the road-house called "Blue Danube Tavern and Bar" on the highway to Vienna. Sunny summer day, before noon.— Two doors lead into the house. To the left a hedge and garden gate opening upon the friendly landscape. To the right trees, shrubs and bushes. In the background glitters the Danube. Two small tables. A few chairs.*

AT RISE: AUTOMOBILE SALESMAN *and* REAL ESTATE AGENT *are sitting at one of the tables, on which two briefcases belonging to each of them are displayed.* MR. VIRAG, *the proprietor of the restaurant, a man of 50, is standing between them. He is a good-looking, dapper, temperamental person.*

VIRAG *(Nervous, excited)*. In the final analysis, what is it all about? What does it come down to? (HE *sits down between them*) You're both trying to sell me a bill of goods. Yes, both of you. And if you want the plain honest truth, I'm fed up and I can't take any more.

AUTO SALESMAN. But my dear Mr. Virag . . .

VIRAG. Don't "dear" me. I can't stand that either. You're both pests. You with your song and dance about buying this house that I've got leased, and you with your sales talk about buying a new car. To what do I owe the honor of your visit, gentlemen? To what do I owe the double honor of both of you at the same time?

REAL ESTATE AGENT. Because . . .

VIRAG. Never mind: I asked and I'll answer. Because you go smelling around . . .

REAL ESTATE AGENT *(Insulted)*. Smelling?

VIRAG. Yes, smelling! How else did you find out that we came into money?

REAL ESTATE AGENT. Certainly not by smelling. It's common gossip. Everybody knows it.

VIRAG. Yes, everybody knows, and everybody keeps adding to it until you'd think we'd inherited a fortune. *(Furious)* Not half, not a quarter, not even an eighth is true! Yes, we came into a little legacy—but we'll settle for the smallest fraction of what they think we have. After all the possible deductions were made and everyone's fee was paid, all I had left were a few measly thousands, that's all. No more. I can prove it to you. The bankbook is there in the safe, with the original deposit untouched. (HE *lashes himself into greater fury*) And for that, for these few measly thousands, I've had to give up my peace of mind. Not a moment's rest any more. People talk about my huge fortune: They envy, despise, berate, exploit, and badger me. I'm forced to listen to all kinds of get-rich-quick schemes. I'm surrounded with swindlers, speculators, and conniving salesmen. *(The* SALESMEN *react)* Forgive me, gentlemen, you are not the first salesmen to pester me: you are the hundred and first. And believe me, I've even been approached by—yes, I've been propositioned by women—yes, women, the shrewd, calculating kind; women who even go so far as to write letters to me. Yes, you can take my word for it. Letters, with their names and addresses. I'm continually plagued, and harassed, and persecuted. But gentlemen, I assure you it won't work. It won't get anyone anywhere. Gentlemen, take my word for it; I'm determined not to buy a thing. I'm just not in the market, see? Not for shoes, a house, an auto, a radio-phonograph, or a woman. We had no need for this money, God knows. We have no children, and this little inn, small as it is, is enough for our needs. We have the reputation of being the best little restaurant of all the roadhouses on the famous Vienna highway. Everybody knows our little but elegant "Blue Danube Tavern and Bar."

SALESMEN. Oh, certainly.

VIRAG. Incidentally . . . I don't know why the tourists call our Danube River . . . (Points at the river) . . . blue. I've always seen it as a muddy milk-coffee. But—if they like it—let them call it "blue" Danube. The customer is always right; so, it's blue for all I care. Yes, gentlemen, we're on the romantic blue river that the foreigners admire, and we have the good fortune to be situated close to the big city. Our customers are well-to-do, and we know how to take care of them, because our former employers were aristocrats. Speaking for ourselves—we're simple people who work hard and manage to earn just enough to keep going. That's all we need and want. We never cared for this unexpected American inheritance from my uncle who died in Cleveland, but since it's here, let it lie buried in the bank. Let it rest in peace. Let it stay locked up for that rainy day, or God knows what, God forbid.

SALESMEN (Enthusiastically). God forbid!

VIRAG. Skip it; save your sympathy. I appreciate it, I can assure you there'll be no occasion for it. It'll lie in the bank. I'm taking no chances. I'm playing safe; it's an old habit of mine. Once more, I appreciate your sympathy, but our few measly pennies aren't worth your trouble.

REAL ESTATE AGENT. Those few measly pennies are still nothing to be sneezed at — even today. "Measly pennies?" No, Mr. Virag. We're in the know. They're not pennies, measly or otherwise. They're dollars, good American dollars, 27,200 of them, at that.

VIRAG. You employ detectives?

REAL ESTATE AGENT (Gaily, whispering). Could be.

VIRAG (Getting angry). That'll do. This winds it up. You must understand, I have other things to do today. (To the AUTO SALESMAN, loud and angry) For your special information, sir, let me inform you that I have no use for an expensive car. I've had enough automobiling to last me a lifetime. Ten years behind the wheel as a chauffeur, and ten more alongside the wheel, glaring out the windshield as a footman.

AUTO SALESMAN. Yes, we know you were Count Esterhazy's chauffeur and then butler.

VIRAG. No, not Count Esterhazy, Prince Esterhazy, who lived in Paris! Prince . . . if you please!

AUTO SALESMAN. Granted — you don't need an auto. But you have a young wife, Mr. Virag. (Showing him a picture in the catalogue) Here's a convertible that'll knock your eye out. A chic little car for the chic little lady . . . for shopping in Vienna.

VIRAG. You're wasting your breath and my time. I don't like your glib talk. My wife is no chic little lady—she's a decent, simple, hardworking woman, and for your special enlightenment, she comes from the same princely household as I did, in Paris. In Paris, understand? In Paris at *Prince* Esterhazy's.

AUTO SALESMAN. Where she was lady-in-waiting.

VIRAG. Don't exaggerate. She was just a good old-fashioned Viennese chambermaid. The first chambermaid of her Grace, the Princess. You know the kind of position that is?

AUTO SALESMAN. Like a court lady.

VIRAG. Pretty nearly. But, well —it's not the title that counts, but the household, and a woman who lives in a household surrounded by art and culture, doesn't think of frivolous things like a chic little car. Not after having lived at a prince's palace, where one learns a simple, modest way of life. Yes, we lived in the best society. *(Bellowing)* And in Paris, you hear? In Paris.

MARIANNE'S VOICE *(From within)*. Ne te fache pas, chéri, ça ne vaut pas la peine.

VIRAG *(Going toward the door)*. Tu as raison, chérie. Pardonne moi.

REAL ESTATE AGENT. Your wife?

VIRAG. Yes, my wife. She's telling me not to excite myself. Is it any wonder I get excited? Who wouldn't? It's been like this all week. I've had to tell dozens of peddlers to get the hell . . .

REAL ESTATE AGENT. Please don't excite yourself. We understand.

VIRAG *(To REAL ESTATE MAN)*.

Then why can't I get it through your heads that I'm not buying anything? I said so in no uncertain terms to your auto-peddling friend. It goes for you, too. I'm not buying this house, understand? Why should I when I have a very good lease! Tell me why? Who sent you here to me?

REAL ESTATE AGENT. Elbogen and Goldfarb.

VIRAG. Well, just tell Elbogen and Goldfarb that I told you to tell them to look around for another buyer. And if they want to know why, say that I'm crazy about the ridiculously low rental and crazy about holding on to my lease, which has twelve more years to run.

REAL ESTATE AGENT. That's just why they want to sell.

VIRAG. Let them sell—but to someone else. I'm not buying.

REAL ESTATE AGENT. How can you pass this up? A house with this enormous acreage! In these surroundings! On the shore of the Danube! And so close to the city! It's the opportunity of a lifetime. The money you've inherited will be more than enough for a down payment. The balance in notes or a mortgage.

VIRAG. I don't want to burden myself with any debts. You want me to go bankrupt? To have to start back from the bottom? To become a servant all over again, without the chance of enjoying the rich life almost within my grasp? *(Excited but sincere)*. Do you know what it means to see your dream of being your own boss come true after twenty years of honest toil? *(Shouting)* I wouldn't exchange this feeling for a row of houses.

(MARIANNE, *his wife, comes out of the house. She looks and carries herself more like a great lady than a former chambermaid who has become a restaurant keeper. The* SALESMEN *rise when* SHE *enters)*

MARIANNE. Why all the noise, my dear? Inside it sounds as though something dreadful were happening.

VIRAG *(Suddenly calm)*. No dear, it's the old complaint: Salesmen, salesmen. *(Introducing them)* Messrs Real Estate and Auto Salesmen—my wife.

(The AGENTS *bow)*

MARIANNE *(To her husband)*. Ne te fache pas, chéri, ça ne vaut pas la peine. Faites les aller, mais doucement.

VIRAG. Tu as raison, chérie. Je te demande pardon de m'avoir rendu si violent. Mais, est-ce-que tu es surprise? *(To the agents)* Now then, gentlemen, much as I like your company, I must make a request and at the same time apologize to you for being abrupt, but please be good enough to leave. It's been nice having you, but I've told you everything. Believe me, there's nothing more. *(Raising his voice)* We're closing for the day. This way, please. *(Pointing to the garden gate)*

AUTO SALESMAN. One final word. Can I interest you in our new streamlined motorcycle?

VIRAG *(Roars)*. NO!

AUTO SALESMAN. One very last word. Positively my last—an offer you can't afford to miss. Our latest gear-shift bicycle.

VIRAG. No. Keep moving and don't stop until you shut the door behind you. Move. No, wait. It just occurred to me you're like flies, yes, like flies swarming on sugar.

AUTO SALESMAN *(With dignity)*. Flies . . . Well, I'll remember

that insult. But on behalf of my fellow traveller and myself, permit me to say, that flies don't always swarm on . . . sugar.

*(*VÌRAG *makes as if to attack them)*

MARIANNE *(Appeasingly)*. Now . . . now . . .

(The SALESMEN *go out through the garden gate)*

VIRAG *(In a nervous loud tone, after they've gone)*. This is what happens when people talk simply to keep their jaws wagging! Yatata ya-tata ya-ta-ta. I hope their faces hurt as much as my head. The whole neighborhood is grinding out rumors. I've inherited a fortune from my uncle in America . . . come into a gold mine . . . fallen heir to a tremendous estate . . . Got . . .

MARIANNE. Ne te fache pas, cela ne vaut pas . . .

VIRAG *(Furious)*. Whenever I get excited you talk French. Why? (HE *sits*)

MARIANNE *(Calm)*. Because I want to remind you that although you were born a poor Hungarian peasant boy, you spent a great part of your life in the glorious city of Paris and in the best of society. Besides, dear, you don't flare up in French so easily. You don't know the language well enough. *(Sighs)* You've never been this way before. It's awful how irritable you are lately.

VIRAG. Can you blame me? You see how they won't let me alone? Is it any wonder?

MARIANNE. Yes, I know. But you mustn't let it bother you so. See what it's doing to you: you don't sleep, you get up much too early, and you drink a little more than is good for you.

VIRAG. If you think I'm going to listen to a sermon . . .

MARIANNE. Don't be so touchy. Take hold of yourself. These flareups aren't good for you. You'll go to pieces if you don't take yourself in hand. Even though you are my big, strong darling lion. Come, be yourself. How about going to Vienna, to the races? You'll enjoy it. The change will do you good.

VIRAG. Stop calling me your darling lion and stop acting like an animal trainer.

MARIANNE. I'm proud of that, sweetheart. Everyone trembles before you. But I need only look at you, they say, and presto, you're a lamb. Lately, though, it doesn't seem to have worked. I look at you—but no lamb; still lion. You don't know your own strength.

VIRAG *(Raging again)*. You, too? Do I have to listen to another sales talk? Do I . . .

MARIANNE *(Interrupting)*. Ne te fache pas, chéri, ne te fache pas.
(SHE strokes his head, continuing the soothing treatment, and gradually he becomes her lamb)

VIRAG. It's true . . . You're right. It's true. There's something in what you say. One loses one's . . .
(His voice dies away. MARIANNE keeps stroking his head. There is a brief pause. VIRAG covers her hand with kisses)

VIRAG. You're an angel . . . to have such patience with me.

MARIANNE. It's love, darling . . . love. I'm no angel. Loving you for ten years has given me all this patience.

VIRAG *(Melting)*. I often wonder what I've done to deserve this . . . great affection. I'm really not worthy of it. I'm not clever . . . I'm not good . . .

MARIANNE. Goodness has nothing to do with it, darling. If goodness had anything to do with it all women would fall in love with the Pope. Why look for reasons? It's love. I love you, that's all. For a peaceful woman like me, a lion like you is the perfect mate. You are my pet lion and I'm devoted to you. Completely given over to you. Your happiness is all I want. Besides being my pet lion, you are my husband and . . . *(Tenderly)* . . . my naughty little boy.

VIRAG. You darling, you lovely little mother. You're so wonderful and I'm cross and contrary, and angry for no reason.

MARIANNE. That's just as it should be, so don't worry. The lion tamer is happy with her pet . . . deliriously happy. Have you any idea how frightfully monotonous a lamb would be?

(ELLA comes out of the house with a large tray of tableware. She is about twenty or twenty-two, exceptionally pretty, gay, piquant, and coquettish. She wears a black dress and a white apron. Her job at the restaurant is a dual one: waitress during the day and cigarette girl at night)

ELLA. Good morning. It's eleven thirty. Shall I set the tables?

MARIANNE. Yes, do . . . please.

ELLA. Just the two . . . as usual?

MARIANNE. As usual . . . just the two. You know we don't bother serving lunch. Our supper trade is sufficient.

(ELLA places the dishes and silverware on the two tables)

VIRAG (*Exploding*). Yes, hang it, we're not after profits—just the chance to serve the right people. It's not money we want, but peace of mind. And now with that damn legacy *that's* all gone. We're supposed to be millionaires—not good simple people any more, like other good simple people. Money! Who wants it?

(MARIANNE *sighs audibly and exit into the house*)

ELLA (*Slowly arranging the table*). It's awful, Mr. Virag, awful. (*Forces a sigh*) I'm only an ordinary cigarette girl and waitress, but I feel for you and Mrs. Virag. You're so nervous, Mr. Virag, that it is really . . . really, Mr. Virag, you are so nervous . . . (*Wiping the plates as* SHE *speaks*)

VIRAG (*Looks around quickly to make sure they are alone, then speaks softly and passionately*). Ella, I haven't slept the whole night.

ELLA. Why, Mr. Virag? Why haven't you slept?

VIRAG. You ask why? You know. You know why, you witch. You just want to hear it again and again. It's you—you I long for, you sorceress. It's you that drives me mad, not the agents and salesmen—just you.

ELLA. Please don't say that. I can't tell you how it hurts. (*With downcast eyes*) I know I should be proud, but it hurts that a fine person like you should have to suffer because of me.

VIRAG. Why let me suffer? Why not help me? You can do it. You alone—only you. Say you'll be mine —you . . . you . . .

ELLA. If only I were free, dear sweet Mr. Virag . . . then both of us would be happy at last. (*With a phony deep sigh*) But I'm engaged. (*Goes to right to set the other table*)

VIRAG (*Passionately*). It can't go on this way any longer. I'm going mad. This uncertainty is driving me mad. I can't stand it. (*Going to her*) What does he say, this . . . fellow you're engaged to—this Mr. Barna— what does he say?

ELLA. Nothing.

VIRAG. Nothing! Did you tell him it was all over between you?

ELLA. No.

VIRAG. But you said yesterday you would. You promised.

ELLA. I tried to tell him. Believe me I tried, but I couldn't.

VIRAG. Which means . . . he's coming here again today.

ELLA. Yes.

VIRAG. Why didn't you tell him? It would have been all over,— finished.

ELLA. I know, I know. But I couldn't. It's not easy. It can't be done just like that, all at once. I'll do it gradually. Remember, we were to be married tomorrow, and I postponed it . . . because of you. That's the fifteenth time I postponed it . . .

VIRAG. And he still wants to marry you?

ELLA. More than ever. He's become my official fiancé.

VIRAG. That settles it. I won't put up with this continual postponing. I'm fed up. We're not playing games any more. Either you make a clean break, a clean break, once and for all, do you hear . . .

ELLA. I hear, but the poor boy . . .

VIRAG. Would you rather I dealt with him? I guarantee I'll do a good job.

ELLA. Heavens, no! Please— don't.

VIRAG. He'll be here soon, this "official fiancé" of yours. Twice daily he roars in on his motorcycle, that panhandler: no job, no trade, not a cent to his name; nothing but a loud motorcycle and a still louder necktie. And he probably bought them both on time. He eats twice a day at my expense, and to cap the climax I have to watch while you get on that machine with him and roar away into the night . . . God knows where.

ELLA. He only roars me home to my mother.

VIRAG (Sarcastically). Your mother. How nice. Well, I don't want to see him here any more. That's final. Final, you hear? He's my pet hate, and I have to watch him gorge himself twice a day here at my expense.

ELLA. You can't keep him out. This is a public restaurant.

VIRAG. Public, but not free. I'd have thrown him out long ago, except for my soft-hearted wife. She stands up for him. (Goes to door, takes a quick glance inside, then speaks softly) It's my wife's fondest wish that he marry you. It's obvious why. She hasn't said anything; not a word . . . she's too clever. But she knows, and I must be calm, keep my head, and not let on. Calm, as I watch you throwing kisses at him between sales, when you make your rounds with the cigarette tray. It's maddening.

ELLA. I can't help it. After all, I'm engaged to him.

VIRAG. Isn't it enough to watch you ride away with him every night? To see you sitting behind him on that damn motorcycle wondering how far into the night you ride . . . heaven knows where.

ELLA (Coquettishly). Jealous.

VIRAG. Jealous? I'm burning up. It must stop. This nincompoop . . .

ELLA. Zoli Barna is a fine, good, decent boy. Don't run him down. He knows you're in love with me.

VIRAG. Well, and what does he say?

ELLA. Nothing. He's in a bad way.

VIRAG. And you? Are you in love with him or me?

ELLA. Don't put me through that again. You know very well who I'm in love with.

VIRAG. But they say you're his sweetheart.

ELLA. My goodness, what people say! People! People! It's a lie. I'm just his fiancée.

VIRAG. That's just what I won't put up with. If, as you say, you love me, then . . . (A shiver runs through ELLA.) What is it? What ails you?

ELLA. I'm thinking of your good-bye kiss . . . yesterday. I just felt it go through me. You hypnotist, you.

VIRAG. You witch. If you love me as you say, then . . .

(The BARTENDER enters. He is in shirt-sleeves and wears the regulation white jacket and apron. A shrewd, sharp-witted man over fifty)

BARTENDER. The truckload of beer is outside.

VIRAG. It can wait.

(The BARTENDER goes back into the house. ELLA sighs deeply again and goes back to wiping the plates.)

VIRAG. It kills me to see you working. You're no menial. You were born to be served, not to serve.

ELLA. Yes, I know. How true. So you see it, too. How well you read people. What a mind!

VIRAG. You, such a tender, delicate creature, doing this kind of work. I can't tell you how I feel when I hear them call after you in the evening: "Hey there—cigarette girl!"

ELLA. You don't know how it wounds me.

VIRAG. You were born for a life of ease and luxury. The right kind of clothes would make you look like the stunning woman you are—the kind I've seen in Paris. All you need is the clothes.

ELLA. True! How true!

VIRAG. In beauty and loveliness . . . you could live your own life, and make one happy who'd shower you with everything money could buy. Oh, I go mad when I think of it . . . you relaxing on a sofa, lying there in silks, laces and satins, and I the happiest of men . . . oh . . . you dear, darling, angel . . .

ELLA. And how I would give myself up to you! Silks, laces, satins . . . oh, just to have someone to be beautiful for! Oh, I would drive you mad! You great lover, you! *(Bending toward him coquettishly)* Tell me . . . will I get my little car?

VIRAG. Of course. A convertible. A chic little car for the chic little woman.

ELLA. And you'll teach me to drive?

VIRAG. Would I?

ELLA. What a delicious dream!

VIRAG. Why a dream? You can make it come true. Just one word . . . a tiny word from you, and you could get away from everyone in a little apartment of your own. We could see each other every day, without anyone knowing. I've never deceived my wife. You are the first and only one . . . or, to be precise, you will have been the first.

ELLA. No, oh no, Mr. Virag. I can't become what you suggest. If I'm not mistaken, you want to make me a respectful prostitute.

VIRAG. Oh, no! No!

ELLA. But I'm not that kind. Respectful or otherwise. My fiancé . . .

VIRAG. *(Interrupting).* I don't want to hear that confounded word again. I'm beginning to believe that deep down in your heart you belong to him . . . to him!

ELLA. No, I don't. I don't belong to him or to you. I've told you a hundred times. I haven't made up my mind. I'm still wavering.

VIRAG. You're what?

ELLA. Wavering. Wavering between the two of you. I can only belong to the one who marries me. And since you can't, I'm afraid I'm bound to belong to him in the end. If not tomorrow, then later, certainly, perhaps. Maybe.

VIRAG. You prefer to starve? To spend the rest of your life on the back seat of a motorcycle?

ELLA. What can I do? He's poor, but he'll marry me. That's what I've been looking forward to. Marriage. In a church.

(VIRAG *is crushed and silent.* MARIANNE *enters and* ELLA *goes back into the house)*

MARIANNE *(Seats herself at a table, spreads out the accounts she has brought along with her and begins checking them).* Twelve and four are sixteen. She always leaves when I come in. Haven't you ever noticed?

VIRAG. No.

MARIANNE *(Continuing her additions)*. Sixteen and five are twenty-one.

(The BARTENDER *enters)*

BARTENDER. I'm sorry to break in again, but the truckload of beer and the brewery men are outside, and they won't wait any longer.

(There is no answer. HE shrugs and goes back into the house)

MARIANNE *(Still working over her accounts)*. For some time now she's been treating me like an enemy.

VIRAG. Aw, go on. You're only imagining it. Why should she?

MARIANNE. I don't know. Ask her. *(With an amiable smile)* Maybe if I cared enough to enquire I'd know, too.

VIRAG. What is this, are you hinting at something?

MARIANNE. Only very mildly.

VIRAG. What can I do if the waitress looks at you one way or another?

(The BARTENDER *enters with a keg of beer which HE places up against the wall)*

BARTENDER. The brewery men are hitting the ceiling. They're leaving.

VIRAG. What brewery men?

BARTENDER. That delivered the beer.

VIRAG. Why didn't you say they were waiting?

BARTENDER. I told you twice.

VIRAG. Don't contradict me. Did you tell them to wait?

BARTENDER. And how!

VIRAG. I'll give them a good piece of my mind. (*HE charges into the house*)

BARTENDER *(To* MARIANNE*)*. Something has got to be done about this. Excuse me for butting in, but sooner or later the lid will fly off, and when it does it'll be too late.

(HE stops to listen to VIRAG *in the house raging at the brewery men)*

MARIANNE. What's the row about?

BARTENDER. Oh, the usual fireworks! He explodes at everybody. This time it's the brewery men.

(THEY listen awhile to the racket)

MARIANNE *(Sighs)*. How excitable he is.

BARTENDER. It's got me. I can't stand by and look on how he's fallen for her. She's the cause of all this excitement. That's why he's all nerves and jumpy. But when *she* talks it's like David with his harp, all sweet and lovely. Excuse the bartender for butting in, but I think it's heading for a big blow-up. He's been after her before. The first time she just played with him—led him on in fun but didn't give a rap about him. She was in love with that poor starved fiancé of hers. Now she's changed, and she's brazen enough to tell the boss she loves him, not Zoli Barna.

MARIANNE. She actually says so?

BARTENDER. All the time. And she keeps stringing the boss along about her boy friend, and that drives him mad.

MARIANNE. Of course the change you speak of came with the inheritance.

BARTENDER. Sure, that's it. Leave it to her. She knows her way around. She's a shrewd dame who means to go places. And the boss falls for her line. You know why he's so easily taken in?

MARIANNE. Why?

BARTENDER. Because he's been loved so much by you. Excuse the bartender for butting in, but that kind—your husband—is always a sucker, excuse me. It wouldn't do her any good to act like that with me, but the chief is a pushover. He keeps telling himself "Why shouldn't she love me?" But take it from me . . . (Whispers) . . . they haven't had an affair.

MARIANNE. No?

BARTENDER. No, of course not. I'll bet my life they haven't.

MARIANNE. Are you trying to comfort me?

BARTENDER. No, just to tell you the truth, because I know how upset you are, and I sympathize with you. It hurts me to see this. Believe me, I know what I am talking about when I say they haven't had an affair.

MARIANNE. Of course they have. You insult my husband by saying they haven't. If he makes up his mind to he can have an affair with any woman any time.

BARTENDER. Maybe, but with this one he hasn't had any. I'll take an oath on it.

MARIANNE (Frightened). What makes you so sure?

BARTENDER. I thought the way you did at first. Was convinced they had one, in fact. (Secretly and with an air of great importance) But I was around yesterday when they took leave of each other about one in the morning.

MARIANNE. Well, what happened?

BARTENDER. It was about one A.M. You like a good little angel had gone to bed a long time before. The boss was up because Count Rudy and his friends were still guzzling champagne. Ella had just put on her coat to go home. Her boy friend was waiting for her outside with the motorcycle. And then the two of them buzzed and whispered and cooed.

MARIANNE. Which two?

BARTENDER. She and the boss. (Mysteriously) Then the boss planted a beaut of a kiss smack in the middle of her mouth. Yes . .. and then I heard . . . "Oh, was that good. My heart stopped."

MARIANNE. Who said that?

BARTENDER. She. The bitch. Ella.

MARIANNE. Oh.

BARTENDER. Wait—you haven't heard the half of it. Listen carefully. The boss took her in his arms again and said: "I'm crazy about you, you sweet darling. Have a heart—see it my way. Don't keep insisting you're pure." Then she said, "I can't, I won't. I want to be pure. I want to be a virgin until my wedding night. My virginity is my only possession." Then he said: "You can't make me believe it. You can't make me believe you're a virgin." Then she said: "But I am, I am. Zoli Barna will be the first." Then the boss said: "Why he? Why not me? Why not me? Why he?" Then she said: "Fate has willed it so." Then the boss said: "Why Zoli Barna, the devil take him?" Why not me?" Yes, madam, those were his very words. Then as soon as she left the boss slapped me on the back. He had a bit of an edge on and he was in high spirits, and he asked me, "Do you think she's really a virgin?" Just like that. Now this very question proves that he doesn't know whether she is a . . . or she isn't . . . you see? (HE *grins tri-umphantly*) You see?

MARIANNE. You heard all that?

BARTENDER. Word for word.

MARIANNE *(Gets up, perturbed)*. That's bad. Very bad.

BARTENDER. Bad? Why?

MARIANNE. It's a catastrophe.

BARTENDER. What! That he hasn't had any affair with her?

MARIANNE. Exactly.

BARTENDER. Why?

MARIANNE. He will marry her.

BARTENDER. How can he? He is married to you.

MARIANNE. It's me, me he'll leave—not her. Don't stand there gaping like that. Yes, he'll marry her. That's just what will happen.

BARTENDER. Ah, no.

MARIANNE. Yes, yes.

BARTENDER. After ten years?

MARIANNE. After ten years. That's when it usually occurs. After ten years. It's the critical point accepted by most people. We're running true to form.

BARTENDER. It may be so for others, but in this case you're way off. It shows you don't know men. Look —a man is like this: If a woman holds back and won't give in, he doesn't waste his time and goes elsewhere. A fellow can't give himself over to coaxing forever. I know from my own experience. It gets to a point where you have to say "Look, I haven't much time. Yes or no."

MARIANNE. My husband is not like that.

BARTENDER. Of course he is.

MARIANNE. Who knows better?

BARTENDER. But . . .

MARIANNE *(Upset)*. Oh, don't talk. *(She blurts out)* That's how he married me, see? (BARTENDER

scratches *his head. There is a slight pause)* The very same way.

BARTENDER. You don't say! Then we'd better do something about it quick. I've got an idea. Threaten suicide.

MARIANNE. Nonsense.

BARTENDER. Don't pooh pooh it. It's damn good. Say . . . how about a very small dose of poison? Just enough to frighten him.

MARIANNE. Don't be silly.

BARTENDER. Then what would you do?

MARIANNE. I don't know yet. I'll think of something. Something will come to me.

BARTENDER. I can tell you now: a big stink.

MARIANNE. Positively not.

BARTENDER. What's to become of me when you leave? I'm an orphan; no father, no mother. And I'm not getting any younger. I'm a man of fifty. You're the only one I have in the world. You're my guardian angel.

MARIANNE. I must go back to checking your accounts. Whenever you begin drooling like that they're usually way off.

BARTENDER. You shouldn't have said that. *(Tenderly)* But I worship you in spite of it . . . my dear, kind, guardian angel.

MARIANNE. Aw, don't be silly. *(A report like the firing of a machine gun, and a motorcycle appears and stops at the hedge. Enter* ZOLI BARNA, *the young fiancé, who comes through the garden gate. He is an attractive, simple, warm kind of person. It's near twelve, and he's coming to lunch, as usual)*

BARNA. Good morning.

MARIANNE. Good morning. Why does your machine make such a racket?

BARTENDER. It's the installment racket. *(Exit into the house)*

BARNA. May I ask what there is for lunch?

MARIANNE. Well, to begin with, a nice slice of rare gossip brought in by the bartender.

BARNA. I've brought some myself. We were to be married tomorrow, as you know. Well, Ella has postponed the wedding again.

MARIANNE. That's no surprise.

BARNA. No, unfortunately. It's no good going on and on this way. I may not show it, but I'm all cut up about it. Something terrible will happen. It's obvious your husband is getting to hate me more by the minute.

MARIANNE. How so?

BARNA. If looks would kill, I'd be a goner. There's murder in his eye. Doesn't say a word to me now— just passes me by. It's not only me. He terrorizes her too—my girl friend.

M A R I A N N E . And your girl friend?

BARNA. Mrs. Virag, you know how madly I love her. Well, she's playing a game now. Yes, it's a money game. A rotten money game. I can't recognize her. She's changed so. Before I was happy—really happy with her. She was flirting with your husband then, too, but it was just in fun —to tease him. It was me she loved, me she wanted to make happy. And she did. She made me deliriously happy. She did—believe me. Spiritually and . . . and . . . otherwise, too, if I may . . .

MARIANNE *(Interrupting)*. No

details, thank you. How is it now?

BARNA. The money has turned her head completely. Nothing has happened between us, but it's the way she talks to me. She keeps picking on me. Reproaches me continually for being poor. Nags me and torments herself at the same time. Then in the middle of everything, she suddenly throws her arms around me and begins to bawl and bewail her sad fate, loving a beggar. But I'm afraid she may still take the leap.

MARIANNE. What leap?

BARNA. Into the arms of your husband.

MARIANNE. But you said she loves you.

BARNA. More than ever. But she'd leave me just the same.

MARIANNE. Leave you?

BARNA. And how. Mine is the tragic fate of any poor young man in any big city today. There are countless tragedies such as mine. It's so commonplace it isn't even interesting. But it's fatal just the same. I'll never survive it. The attachment is such . . . I mean that of the old man . . . forgive me, your husband . . . it's absolutely frightening.

MARIANNE. Why do you allow it?

BARNA. What can I do? When she's with me she sighs and acts superior. Weeping she protests her love for me. She's mine, soul and—excuse me—body and everything. But life calls her—she says. Life!—And she must answer, she says. Evidently from this, matters are still on a level of respectability. It's still in the talking stage. The fact that she confesses so freely . . .

MARIANNE. Through her tears.

BARNA. Yes, through her tears. *(The* BARTENDER *appears.* HE *comes out of the house carrying a case of soda bottles)*

BARTENDER. And through her tears, she tells the boss that she loves only him. Only him. But she can't give you up because you want to marry her.

MARIANNE. Eavesdropping again, eh?

BARTENDER. Always.

*(*HE *disappears into the garden)*

MARIANNE. Well, it's obvious your girl is bent on marriage . . . not with you but with my husband.

BARNA. Isn't it an affair she's after?

MARIANNE. No, Mr. Barna. She's too smart for that. (SHE *gets up)* And the fiancé who permits that . . . forgive me for saying so, I seldom use the word, but I can think of no more appropriate one just now . . . the fiancé, is a jackass. *(Goes over to the other table and sits down)*

BARNA. How do you say jackass in French?

MARIANNE. Ane.

BARNA. If it's the same to you, would you mind using the French word?

MARIANNE *(In despair).* And if it's the same to you, I'd like to break open the safe, take out that damn bankbook, and burn it.

BARNA. Would you really have the courage? So much money . . .

MARIANNE. Yes! Twice, ten times that! And besides . . . I hate it. It's hateful money.

BARNA. What do you mean "hateful money"?

MARIANNE. It's none of your business. Anyway, I hate it. I'd burn it with pleasure! Then your darling would leave him like a shot.

BARNA. Dear Mrs. Virag, you see how desperate I am. Let's do something. This calls for immediate action. I have it. It's the only way out.

MARIANNE. What is the only way out?

BARNA. The grand bounce.

MARIANNE. What?

BARNA. Throw my fiancée out.

MARIANNE. Sure. And have my husband run right out after her! That would be just dandy. At least now I can keep an eye on them.

BARNA. Don't you intend to do something about it?

MARIANNE. Yes, but I intend to give it thought first.

BARNA. I must think about it, too.

MARIANNE. Please don't. Don't go to the trouble. It's one way you can't possibly help. If you were vigorous and aggressive, it might have been different. Unfortunately, you're not.

BARNA. What's wrong with the sensitive type?

MARIANNE. Well, look what happens to them. You have no fighting spirit. No vitality.

BARNA. How do you mean "no vitality"?

MARIANNE. You're the victim type.

BARNA. How do you mean "victim type"?

MARIANNE. A kind of ridiculous martyr.

BARNA. No martyr is ridiculous.

MARIANNE. Except young men whose girls jilt them for a . . . for a . . .

BARNA. . . . for a graybeard.

MARIANNE *(Outraged)*. He's *no* graybeard! *(Proudly)* By God, he isn't!

BARNA *(Cut to the quick)*. And wives whose husbands fall for a sexy pretty kitten . . . are not ridiculous?

MARIANNE. No. They fight.

BARNA. And win?

MARIANNE *(With a mysterious smile)*. Wait and see.

BARNA. I'm afraid I'll just wait. *(Suddenly serious, pleading))* Please bear with me. We share a common suffering. We must stick together. Trust me, I won't let it get me. You are right, I was a jackass. But you've opened my eyes. From now on, I'll fight. Fight like a tiger. If I have to, much as I would regret it, I'll put your husband out of the way.

MARIANNE. How?

BARNA. With a revolver or some deadly poison.

MARIANNE. You scared me for a moment. But since you're talking about weapons that cost money, I feel easier.

BARNA. You, too, mocking my poverty.

(HE *sits down at another table and stares desperately into space.* MARIANNE *gets up, incensed)*

MARIANNE. Ever since the beginning of time when well-to-do old men died, it's always been other people that had the money left to them. What a cross that this time it had to fall on us! But don't lose hope. It hasn't beaten me yet.

BARNA *(Rebelliously)*. Let worst come to worst. I'll speak with him.

MARIANNE. No, don't. Please. Better leave it to me. *(Almost in tears)* Now let's say no more about it. (SHE *tries to restrain her emotions and almost manages, but for a slight*

trembling) What was it you asked when you came in? Oh yes, about today's lunch: Frankfurters, with lentils.

(SHE *goes into the house.* ZOLI BARNA *seats himself at the table to the right.* ELLA *comes in with a plate, exchanges glances with* BARNA, *places knife, fork and spoon before him and is about to leave)*

BARNA. Ella . . . won't you say hello?

ELLA. Hello.

(SHE *goes back into the house and comes right back with a pitcher of water which she places on* BARNA'S *table and is about to leave again)*

BARNA *(Seizing her hand)*. Ella . . . why do you act like this? What's the matter? What have I done?

ELLA. Let me be. *(Tries to withdraw her hand)*

BARNA *(Still holding it fast)*. Can't I hold your hand?

ELLA. Let me alone.

BARNA *(Looking at her hand)*. Say . . . what's this? That screaming red nail polish . . . it's hideous. When did you do that?

ELLA. Early this morning. And if you say another word, I'll have my toes done to match.

(Goes into the house and comes back with a tray and serves BARNA)

BARNA. You're mean to me and you know how devoted I am to you.

ELLA. I'm just as devoted to you. But tell me honestly, on your word as a man, tell me, did you ever buy me a silk scarf, or a rayon one, or even a cotton one, or anything?

BARNA. The minute I lay hands on some money I will.

ELLA. Did you? Answer yes or no.

BARNA. No.

ELLA. That's it. That's just it. And until you become man enough to do so—and not until then—I must ask you to believe me that I'm completely devoted to you . . . but in the meantime let me alone. You must be aware of the fact that I . . .

BARNA. That you . . .

ELLA. That I'm being called.

BARNA. Who's calling you?

ELLA. Life! *Life* is calling me! (SHE *goes into the house. In the house a clock tolls twelve.* BARNA *unfolds his napkin and wipes a tear out of each eye with it, then stuffs the napkin into his collar, emits a heartrending sigh, pours an excessive amount of salt on his lentils and eats.*)

MARIANNE (*From inside the house*). It's twelve. Come, let's eat. (MARIANNE *and* VIRAG *come out of the house and sit at the table left.* SHE *is facing the audience.* VIRAG *is on her left, facing* BARNA)

BARNA (*Getting up halfway to greet* VIRAG). Good morning. (*Sits and continues eating*)

VIRAG (*Sulkily*). Good morning. (*After a pause,* ELLA *enters carrying two plates and two coffee cups on a tray.* SHE *puts the plates and the cups down for the* VIRAGS, *then, moving behind them, with the tray,* SHE *walks over to* BARNA *and remains next to him, at his left, coquettishly smiling. Now all three:* BARNA, VIRAG *and* MARIANNE *are eating. Suddenly,* BARNA *looks up from his plate, gives* ELLA *a lovelorn look, and with his left hand takes hold of hers.* ELLA *encourages him with a coquettish giggle.* VIRAG, *hearing her, raises his head angrily, stops eating and watches silently but furiously* BARNA *and* ELLA *holding hands.* MARIANNE *is taking all this in.* SHE *catches* BARNA'S *eye, whereupon* BARNA *immediately drops* ELLA'S *hand, and frightened, goes back to busy himself with his food. Next moment,* MARIANNE *looks at* VIRAG *and sees him jealously staring at* ELLA *and* BARNA, *whereupon* VIRAG, *frightened, ducks his head down over his plate, exactly as* BARNA *did a moment ago, and shovels the lentils busily in.* MARIANNE *then eyes each of the busy eaters in turn, with a contemptuous smile and after these looks, goes on eating herself. The* THREE *are eating in silence.* ELLA *smilingly observes this, then, still smiling, comes downstage behind* BARNA *and without stopping, passes between the two tables going toward the house, and as* SHE *goes by the* VIRAGS' *table,* SHE *says:*)

ELLA. Hope you enjoy it.

(*And goes into the house*)

CURTAIN

ACT TWO

SCENE: *Set as in ACT ONE. Evening of the same day.*

AT RISE: *All the guests of the restaurant are in the house. From time to time, when the door to the restaurant opens, soft strains of old Viennese PIANO MUSIC (well known Schubert melodies and Strauss waltzes) are heard.* VIRAG *is sitting alone drinking whiskey and soda at one of the tables.* ELLA *comes from the house with her cigarette tray.*

VIRAG. This waiting for you seemed endless.

ELLA. Why so impatient, Mr. Virag? I've been busy. Anyway, I'm here now. (SHE *places her tray on a table.*)

VIRAG. To begin with, come over here. I've got something for you. (*He searches his pocket*)

ELLA. Drinking again?

VIRAG. Yes, drinking again. (*Hands her money*). Put it away.

ELLA (*With the bill in her hand*). What's that?

VIRAG. Don't hold it like that. Put it away before anyone comes.

ELLA (*Pocketing the bill*). Fifty!

VIRAG. This afternoon at the track I placed a little money for you right on the nose. It got you fifty.

ELLA. No!

VIRAG. Honest. Old Count Herbert gave me the tip. His horse came in first.

ELLA. Thanks, darling. It's a fortune. But I beg you, dearest Mr. Virag—be careful about gambling.

VIRAG. Don't worry, they're small bets.

ELLA. Why do you go there at all?

VIRAG (*Sighing*). Because—that is the only place I can get a glimpse of the world I once knew . . . Count Ferdinand . . . Old Herbert . . . Prince Paul . . . His Excellency the British Ambassador . . .

ELLA. But they come here often. They're particularly fond of this high-class place because it is really very, very high-class. It's jammed again tonight. It's going to be a wonderful evening. I must knock on wood. (*Knocks on back of chair*) What a swell crowd.

VIRAG. Many big cars tonight?

ELLA. A Rolls Royce, a twelve-cylinder Packard, two big Cadillacs, five taxis and a motorcycle.

VIRAG (*Getting up*). Damn that motorcycle!

ELLA. Are you starting that again?

VIRAG. I'm not starting that again, baby, I'm finishing it. I told you before lunch that I would put an end to it today. Well, the hour is approaching. That is why I've been drinking . . . if you're interested in knowing the whole truth. Have you got a moment?

ELLA. Yes, a moment. They're having their entrees now. They'll have their cigars and cigarettes later. How many drinks have you had?

VIRAG. I've stopped counting. It's all your fault. You and that boy. This noon, when he took hold of your hand so brazenly, the food stuck in my throat. If my wife hadn't been there, there would have been hell to pay. And after lunch, he simply didn't leave at all. Instead he's been picketing the place. Well, it's not going to go on like this any more. That's over. Finished. There'll be fireworks this evening. Kiss me, you witch.

ELLA *(She looks about.* THEY *kiss)*. Oh, how you kiss . . . You drive me crazy. *(Puts her hand to her heart)*

VIRAG. And you still intend to drive with him tonight . . . to ride away from here? Well, bear in mind you're not riding out of here with him. No, baby, now it's either him or me. You must come to a decision now—immediately. Or else—or else I'll give someone such a beating that he'll remember it for the rest of his life. Understand?

ELLA. Yes.

VIRAG. Is the wretched fellow still here?

ELLA. Yes, darling. Look, I'm beginning to be afraid of him.

VIRAG. Why?

ELLA. There's something suspicious about him today. As though he were going to erupt.

VIRAG. Going to what?

ELLA. Erupt. Like a volcano. He sits in the back at a little table, with his eyes flashing, and every time I pass him, he grabs me.

VIRAG. As long as you're engaged, I can't insult him. Give him the air, and I'll send him flying out on his ear. Unless, of course . . . you love him.

ELLA *(With downcast eyes)*. Mr. Virag knows who I love.

VIRAG. Then make up your mind right now.

ELLA. I can't do it now. Not even if you kill me. I'm on a see-saw.

VIRAG *(Bewildered)*. You're on a what?

ELLA. A see-saw. I've often told you: you are love, he is marriage. The trouble is, he doesn't want to

wait any longer, and I can see why. He senses danger. He's frightened. Oh, he's no fool.

VIRAG. And you? What about you?

ELLA. I'm afraid I'll have to marry him.

VIRAG. What?

ELLA. I know how it must hurt you, but I had to speak out.

VIRAG. You're driving me crazy. What did you say? You're marrying him?

ELLA. I must. I'm miserable one way or the other. But that's not the point. I may look flashy, but I'm a good girl from a good family. Even among physically attractive women there are decent ones. I'm not the butterfly kind. I'm a born wife and mother. And Zoli Barna doesn't want me as a mistress, the way you do. He wants me as his respectable wife. Why should that drive you crazy?

VIRAG. Because I'm absolutely mad about you. I won't let anyone else have you.

ELLA. But I'm not marrying him for love. I'm just playing safe. I'm marrying him because it's the right thing to do. *(With emotion)* Is it my fault if it isn't a love match? If I . . . *(Through her tears)* . . . I am in love with a married man?

(The BARTENDER *enters)*

BARTENDER. They're asking for cigarettes.

*(*ELLA *takes up her tray and goes into the house)*

BARTENDER. Boss!

VIRAG. What do you want?

BARTENDER. Excuse the bartender for butting in. You're going to get into trouble.

VIRAG (Calm). You'll go out on your ear.

BARTENDER. I know, boss. But don't be such a sucker.

VIRAG (Calm). You'll go out on your ear.

BARTENDER. She's playing you for a sucker, boss. Don't let her.

VIRAG (Calm). You'll go out on your ear.

(ELLA comes back)

ELLA (To BARTENDER). You stinker. No one asked for cigarettes.

BARTENDER. It's quite possible. (HE goes into the house)

ELLA. Zoli Barna got hold of my hand again. This time I was afraid he'd break my fingers. There's a mad look in his eye and he keeps one hand in his pocket all the time. I think he has a gun. He keeps insisting that we have to get married tomorrow. I can't stand this any longer. I must marry him and lose you forever.

VIRAG. Even then you will not have lost me. Believe me. What can we do if fate has decided? I'll rent a cozy little apartment where we can meet every day.

ELLA (Indignant). What? How dare you? You want me to deceive my husband? What kind of talk is this? I'll be a model of fidelity as a wife. Ugh—to think that I'd be guilty of such a thing! Anyway, we're going to Vienna right after the ceremony. We'll live there with his parents—No, no, you beautiful dream . . . I've lost you forever. (Pressing close to him) Say goodbye to me. The many passionate kisses you gave me shall stay with me always, as sweet remembrances . . . God, how good they were! (Closing her eyes) Oh, how delightfully you kiss . . . And I am so young and sensual! I'll die

for want of you, I know, but I'll die for you as Mrs. Barna.

VIRAG (Wild). You will not be Mrs. Barna.

ELLA. I must.

VIRAG. You won't.

ELLA. I'll never be Mrs. Loose Woman—never.

VIRAG. Then . . . you'll be something else!

ELLA (Her eyes flashing). Something else?

VIRAG (Gloomily). That's what's been driving me crazy . . . all along.

ELLA (Radiant). What has been driving you crazy all along?

VIRAG. Day and night . . . only that.

ELLA (Jubilant). Oh God . . . What will I be?

VIRAG. Not Mrs. Barna . . . but something else.

ELLA (Happy). What will I be?

VIRAG (Harassed). What will you be? (Embarrassed). You'll be happy.

ELLA. But how? And as what will I be happy?

VIRAG. As—as Ella.

ELLA. As plain Ella?

VIRAG. As . . . Ella.

ELLA. Not as a wife?

VIRAG (Tortured). Perhaps . . . as a wife.

ELLA. As Mrs. Barna?

VIRAG. No! Not that!

ELLA. Then as . . .

VIRAG. As . . .

ELLA (Presses herself lovingly against him). Who will make me happy?

VIRAG. I.

ELLA. What's your name?

VIRAG. Virag.

ELLA. And I'll be happy as . . . as . . .

VIRAG (*Playing dumb*). What?

ELLA. What will my name be when I'm happy?

VIRAG. Your name will be . . . (*Finally giving in*) . . . Mrs. Virag. Now then.

ELLA. I'm fainting.

VIRAG. No. Please don't. Don't do that.

ELLA. Is it really true? Is it possible?

VIRAG. Trust me.

ELLA. What is this? Am I dreaming? Or is this a real promise?

VIRAG. Only . . . let's not forget . . . that my wife also has a say in this. I've been thinking about it all the time. It's kept me awake nights. I don't know how to break it to her. One needs superhuman strength for that.

ELLA. Oh, come . . . she's so gentle.

VIRAG. All the more reason why one needs superhuman strength. I wish she were rough.

ELLA. Think of me when you tell her. It will give you strength.

VIRAG. I'll be open and direct with her. I'll tell her everything, everything. She is so good, . . . and so wise.

ELLA. And she loves you, you darling. You darling, I'll be a faithful wife to you, a passionate and loving little wife! A torrid little wife.

VIRAG. And . . . a rich little wife. Wonderful dresses, fur coats, minks, blue foxes, and a little car. That miserable savings account will take care of all that. I'll spend it all on you. You can even have it in writing this minute.

ELLA. Ugh. In writing! Your word is good enough. You're a gentleman.

VIRAG. How good it makes me feel that you know me. I was brought up with the best people.

ELLA. It's ugly to speak of money now. Ugh! To cheapen love like that. I wish you never had that loathsome money.

VIRAG. Forgive me, sweetheart, but believe me, I can't imagine you except in beautiful clothes. In a gorgeous car, in dazzling surroundings! Believe me, that is the only way I can picture you! And we'll make a trip to Italy. A honeymoon trip to Venice. To the palatial Hotel Danieli.

ELLA (*Enraptured*). Goodness! Gracious!

VIRAG (*Carried away*). And in the evening when you enter the glittering dining room in a cloud of Parisian perfume, in all your splendor, in a low cut gown, imprimé, parfumé . . . plunging neckline . . . all heads will turn in your direction envying me . . . you divine little witch!

(HE *rushes over to take her in his arms. The* BARTENDER *enters from the house*)

BARTENDER. Prince and Princess Lichtenstein have arrived.

VIRAG. Then . . . forgive me, sweetheart . . . I must run. (*On his way out*) I must . . . My one and only love . . . Ah, the Prince! (*Throws her a kiss*) You, my one and only! (*At the door*) The Prince!

BARTENDER. And the Princess!

(VIRAG *dashes into the house*)

BARTENDER (*Quietly to* ELLA). You little hustler!

ELLA. Me?

BARTENDER. Yes, you.

ELLA. Did you listen?

BARTENDER. Of course. You're a hustler, but a very pretty one.

ELLA. Just pretty? That's no compliment. I'm the cover girl type.

BARTENDER. Well, watch yourself, cover girl.

ELLA. What for?

BARTENDER. Because there's going to be an explosion tonight. I'm telling you, kid.

(HE *goes into the house. As* ELLA *nears the door with her tray,* BARNA *appears on the threshold and desperately blocks her way)*

ELLA. Let me in! They're calling for me.

BARNA. No, you'll stay here. I just passed Mr. Virag. He came to greet the Prince with lipstick all over him.

ELLA. What do I care about that?

BARNA. Why not say he got it kissing the bartender?

ELLA. And what if he kissed his wife?

BARNA. His wife is sitting in the bar. You certainly can throw it. Well, I have all the papers with me. The license and everything. We're getting married tomorrow—and you're still playing around with a married man. It's nothing new, you've done it before. But I'm fed up now. We'll go to the Justice of the Peace.

ELLA. What's the rush? Let me be. I've work to do. *(Wants to leave)*

BARNA. I won't let you go.

ELLA. Do you want to marry me here . . . right on the spot?

BARNA *(Fiercely)*. No. But tomorrow noon.

ELLA. Go on. Don't get so excited. Wait. You said there was a possibility of your getting a good job. Then why the rush all of a sudden?

BARNA. Because Mr. Virag wants to take you from me. You can't see anything but that lousy money of his.

ELLA. I love you. You know that.

BARNA. Sure . . . but you tell him that, too. Don't you say it to him when you kiss him?

ELLA. What a dirty mind you have. That's a vulgar insult. I'll never forgive you for it. Never. Yes, I love you, but I know how to control myself. I'm not like you. I'm a smart attractive girl. Am I supposed to waste my best years scrubbing your shirts? No—oh no. It hurts, but I can hold out against it. You might as well know that I've come to a decision. It breaks my heart to say so, but I won't marry you. This is the wind-up. It's final. All over and done with. Goodbye. Now let me out. *(Tries to go into the house)*

BARNA *(Blocking her exit)*. Wait, wait. It's not as easy as all that. (HE *puts his hand to his hip pocket)*

ELLA . Don't be so excited. I know that you have a gun. But I'm not afraid. *(Peremptorily)* Take your hand out of your pocket. (HE *does so)* Now calm down. Stop breathing so hard. Is your heart pounding? So is mine. Make it stop; I will, too. Be still, my heart. And now, goodbye. *(Wants to leave)*

BARNA *(Blocking her)*. Stop. *(Furious)* You spoke those horrible words. You aren't going to marry me.

ELLA. Yes, I spoke those words.

BARNA. You want to be his mistress?

ELLA. Never. What a low thing to say.

BARNA. Then what do you want?

ELLA. My intentions are honorable.

BARNA. Which means that you kept stringing the old man along until he finally made a definite promise to you.

ELLA. Yes.

BARNA. When?

ELLA. Just now. A little while ago.

BARNA. He'll get a divorce and marry you?

ELLA. Exactly.

BARNA. Just now. All of a sudden.

ELLA. And it's all your fault.

BARNA. Mine???

ELLA. You prodded him into it. He was afraid of you.

BARNA. *I* prodded him? It was you—not me.

(ELLA *puts her tray on a table*)

ELLA. You provoked him. It takes a man to provoke another man. You did it out of jealousy. You forced him into it. So out of fear of losing me, he proposed.

BARNA. In other words, I arranged the match.

ELLA. Of course you did. But always remember this. I love you, but I held out against it because this is better for me. I have the right to a good life: to jewels, clothes, fur coats, minks and foxes, a car, and Italy. I know I'll suffer. It serves me right. It's my hard luck that my heart belongs to a poor man. Remember that my heart is yours forever. He is marriage; you are love. (*Throws her arms around him*) I'll always be yours, and when I'm rich I'll take care of you.

BARNA. A gigolo, huh?

ELLA. No. Eternal love.

BARNA. What a nice thing to look forward to.

(*The* BARTENDER *enters*)

BARTENDER. They're calling for you.

ELLA. On your word of honor?

BARTENDER. Cross my heart.

(ELLA *goes off with her tray into the house.* MARIANNE *enters from the other door.* ZOLI BARNA *sinks down at the table and stares bewildered ahead of him*)

BARTENDER (*To* MARIANNE). You're the cleverest woman in the world. You're an angel.

MARIANNE. Why, Max?

BARTENDER. Because you were right.

MARIANNE. How so?

BARTENDER. He'll marry her. He promised to.

MARIANNE. How do you know, Max?

BARTENDER (*Pointing to his ear*). When I tell you something . . .

MARIANNE (*To* BARNA). Did you hear that?

BARNA (*Bitter*). Yes, I've heard the news. He proposed. It's all my fault. Ella says it's my fault. Mrs. Virag . . . that's the sitaution for you and me. For the two of us.

BARTENDER. For the three of us.

BARNA. I knew we were heading for trouble. What will we do now?

MARIANNE. You will do nothing. It's up to me. Before he marries, he must be divorced. And I have something to say about that.

BARNA. But he's determined. He'll stop at nothing.

MARIANNE. In spite of that there's no cause to worry. Go and tell the girl to hand her tray to Elizabeth and come here at once.

(BARNA *goes into the house*)

BARTENDER. For God's sake, don't ever go away from us, little angel.

MARIANNE. For the time being, I'm still here. Now please leave us alone. I want to talk to this "lady." Please go, Max. Besides, it makes no difference whether you're here or in there. You'll listen just the same.

BARTENDER. Righto.

(HE *goes into the house.* MARIANNE *sits down front. There is a very brief pause.* ELLA *enters and remains standing at the door*)

ELLA. I gave my tray over to Elizabeth. Does that mean I'm fired?

MARIANNE. No. It means I want to ask you something.

ELLA (*Comes forward timidly*). Well?

MARIANNE (*Gets up and walks slowly over to her. Speaks quietly but firmly*). You shameless creature. For weeks now you've brazenly see-sawed between my husband and your fiancé. Well, that's got to stop now. It's got to be one or the other. Now tell me which one you love. And don't think you can put anything over on me, because I can read you like a book.

ELLA. What do you want: a lie or the truth?

MARIANNE. The truth.

ELLA. Well, it's fifty-fifty.

MARIANNE. You want to marry one and love the other.

ELLA. You think I want to marry . . . Zoli Barna?

MARIANNE. No. It's my hus-band that you want to marry. You've driven him crazy.

ELLA. Excuse me, it's he who's been driving *me* crazy.

MARIANNE. Well, he didn't succeed. You're not at all crazy—you're marrying him. *He's* the crazy one.

ELLA. What could I do against such a heartbreaker? I'm a weak young girl. I couldn't stand up against passion like his.

MARIANNE. You poor little lamb, you.

ELLA. What could I do? He took me by storm. How could I resist? Dear Mrs. Virag, you know better than anyone how hard it is to resist him.

MARIANNE. Do you love him?

ELLA. He broke off my engagement, wants to be divorced to marry me, promised me a life of ease and luxury, threatens to beat up my fiancé . . . and I shouldn't love him?

MARIANNE. And your fiancé?

ELLA. I love him too.

MARIANNE. Him, too? You don't say. How is it possible?

ELLA (*In tears*). I'm a monster, Mrs. Virag. I love the two of them.

MARIANNE. Nonsense. You're no monster. You're something entirely different.

ELLA. You mean that I am "that" kind?

MARIANNE. That's what I mean, child. Yes. Yes.

ELLA. Why am I that kind? Because I love my fiancé?

MARIANNE. A person is never that kind because she loves somebody, but because she doesn't love somebody.

ELLA (*Irritated*). Who don't I love?

MARIANNE. My husband.

ELLA. But I . . .

MARIANNE. I know, you love both of them. You love your fiancé for himself, and my husband for his money. For the bankbook.

ELLA (Indignant). I don't love him for that. They are two separate things: I love him and he has a bankbook. I would gladly have been his mistress. But what can I do if he wants to marry me no matter what happens? Should I turn down such good fortune? Anyway my conscience is clear. For you, Mrs. Virag, are bright and beautiful. You have no children and your whole life is before you.

MARIANNE. Thanks.

ELLA. That's my whole story. It's a sad one, but what can I do?

(VIRAG enters from the house. HE is embarrassed at seeing them together, and remains standing at the door)

MARIANNE. What can you do? (Catches sight of her husband) For the moment you can go into the house.

(ELLA exit into the house. MARIANNE goes to her husband)

MARIANNE. Well, dearest, have you looked after the Prince Lichtensteins?

VIRAG. Everything is under control.

MARIANNE (Very amiably). Then you'll be able to spare a few moments for me? (Leads him to a table) Sit down.

VIRAG (Sits). What's up, dearest?

MARIANNE (Sits next to him and speaks in a very quiet, matter-of-fact tone). Do you still remember what I once told you in Paris? When you were so jealous because that Jacques Beaumont was so attentive to me?

VIRAG. Yes.

MARIANNE. I told you never to worry about me; that I'd never deceive you; that if ever I fell in love with anyone else, I'd tell you about it and then leave you.

VIRAG. Yes.

MARIANNE. And I told you that I expected that you would do the same for me. And you said: "Naturally—that goes without saying." And we agreed that neither would stand in the other's way. Whoever loved anyone else could leave the other.

VIRAG. Yes.

MARIANNE. So much for the broad outlines. Now to the case in point. Let me ask you: hasn't the situation we mentioned in our agreement come up?

VIRAG. You're absolutely right. There's no doubt that I owe you the utmost candor. Yes, dear, such an occasion has . . . arisen.

MARIANNE. Well then, darling. And isn't there something you want to . . . to say to me?

VIRAG. Of course . . . but it's so difficult.

MARIANNE. You can talk freely. You know that if you have a friend in the world it's me. Speak, darling, and don't be afraid. Besides I know what you're going to say. There's no need of pretty speeches. Be frank. Talk to me not as though I were your wife, but as though I were your mother. Now speak your piece, my little man.

VIRAG (Softly). Marianne . . . I . . . am in love. I love another woman.

MARIANNE. Continue, darling. That much I know! I've watched it develop for a long time. It's an ugly sensual love.

VIRAG. But at my age it's dangerous. It's the only thing that seems to matter. Since I fell in love with you in Paris, dearest, that's ten years ago, I've had eyes for no woman except you . . . and this one. But this one has become an obsession. To be quite frank, I know she's not worth it. I know too that I'm making a fool of myself. But it's a curse, a sensual disease. I feel . . . I must be getting old, or I couldn't have such a longing for such a young girl. It's stronger than I am. I simply can't live without . . . without . . . (HE notices MARIANNE drying her tears) Dearest, I thought you wanted me to talk to you as if you were my mother.

MARIANNE (Drying her tears). Of course, of course. Talk to me as if I were your mother . . . but as for me . . . let me listen to you as your wife.

VIRAG. Dearest, I swear I'll love you always. Only you. Love you forever. Can you understand that?

MARIANNE. Yes, darling. I know it and I believe it.

VIRAG. This girl . . . this is something beyond my control. Like lightning, or an earthquake.

MARIANNE. Yes, it's all clear to me about you and about the girl. The dreadful thing is that . . . (SHE is suddenly silent)

VIRAG. That?

MARIANNE. That . . . the girl really loves you.

VIRAG (Dumbfounded). You . . . say that?

MARIANNE. Yes, I say that.

VIRAG (Delighted). What a noble, magnificent human being you are. Ninety-nine out of a hundred women would say she doesn't love me, and that she's just scheming.

MARIANNE. I can only say what I believe. I had quite a talk with her a while ago. She loves you.

VIRAG. Dearest, you're right.

MARIANNE. Well . . . then . . .

VIRAG (Embarrassed). Well . . . Say it for me, dearest . . . you say it. Make it easier for me.

MARIANNE. You want a divorce. (VIRAG bows his head and is silent.) You want to marry her.

VIRAG (Silent, then in a choked voice). What do you answer to your poor stupid husband? (Almost weeping, he sinks to the table)

MARIANNE (Getting up). Pull yourself together (Stroking his head) It is awful that you had to be taken in this way, poor boy. You must have gone through a great deal. Come, pull yourself together. It would be too bad if someone saw you like this. You, the famous wild lion.

VIRAG (Still in a choked voice, taking hold of her hand). I'll always —always love you, my brave little mother. (Tries hard to pull himself together)

MARIANNE (Quietly). Now dearest, I'll answer you. And the answer will be exactly what you expect. I consent. I won't stand in the way of your happiness. What could I do to stop it? It would be like throwing myself in front of a moving train . . . a much too awful end. I prefer my own kind of sacrifice. You will become a beautiful memory, and I shall continue to love you. I . . . I'm quiet at the moment only because I'm holding on to myself with all my might.

VIRAG. My one and only . . . I knew you'd take it this way. But to be so calm and quiet. It's positively breathtaking. It's . . . It's . . .

MARIANNE. Are you surprised?

VIRAG. No. But . . .

MARIANNE. I have only one concern. Your happiness, my sweetheart.

VIRAG. You heaven-sent angel.

MARIANNE. I'm sure you'll be happy. This girl seems flighty, but she's actually full of soul and feeling. She loves you truly.

VIRAG. Ninety-nine women out of a hundred would have said she loves me only for my money. Such a vulgar viewpoint. Can't they see how a sweet child like her can fall in love with a fiery man, even when he's close to fif . . . (Checked by a look of MARIANNE) . . . er . . . past fifty.

MARIANNE. Of course, you're absolutely right. No one knows it better than I. Any woman would fall for you if you gave her the least encouragement. This poor child is smitten with you just as I was. Do you think if I wasn't convinced of that that I'd consent to a divorce? Would I throw you to a scheming female, just like that? I love you much too much for that. If I ever thought that she loved you only for your money . . .

VIRAG. But . . .

MARIANNE. I know, I know. God grant that you be happy. (SHE touches her eyes with her handkerchief)

(A WAITER enters from the house)

WAITER. Excuse me, madam.

MARIANNE (Drying her tears). What is it, Joseph?

WAITER. Count Bouray has ordered beef-goulash.

MARIANNE. Well?

WAITER. He wants it prepared his special way. But I don't know what his special way is.

MARIANNE (Hardly controlling her tears. In a choked voice). A double portion with very sharp paprika sauce, mixed with Lyonnaise potatoes and a generous helping of onions, and green peppers, some garlic, and a cup of sour cream over it all. And serve it with a side order of sodium bicarbonate on a saucer.

WAITER. Thanks.

(Goes into the house. There is a brief pause. MARIANNE sits table right)

VIRAG. And now—you know I too have learned from refined people —and so I know what my duty is. Let us now talk of material things. (Goes to her)

MARIANNE. No, no.

VIRAG (Sitting next to her). Still, you can't go begging. For ten years you were a faithful, diligent wife. I have a responsibility to you.

MARIANNE. Let's let that go for now.

VIRAG. No, no.

MARIANNE. I rely on you. You were always a gentleman.

VIRAG. Was—and am. Listen, dearest, now . . . this instant, name your terms.

MARIANNE. You insist?

VIRAG. I demand it. Name them at once. I promise to meet them.

MARIANNE. As a matter of fact, it's very simple. I have an idea in that connection. My God, this is embarrassing. But still you did say I couldn't go begging.

VIRAG. No, dearest. Besides, I

want to treat you like a gentleman. You deserve a gentleman.

MARIANNE. My one and only. Well—heavens, what do I need? Just a small allotment will see me through.

VIRAG. How much monthly?

MARIANNE. No, not monthly. That would be continuous worry for you. A burden. It's much better to have a lump sum. An outright settlement.

VIRAG. A lump sum? A settlement? What kind of a settlement?

MARIANNE. The most natural kind. It's obvious, dearest. *(Casually)* Just give me your bank book. *(As* VIRAG *looks at her with wide open eyes, she casts down her eyes)* It's a very modest request.

VIRAG *(Almost speechless).* How? Are these your terms?

MARIANNE. Now dear, you've been insisting that I tell them to you.

VIRAG. The bank . . . book . . . with twenty-seven thousand?

MARIANNE. Yes.

VIRAG *(Gets up).* Must it be just that?

MARIANNE. Yes. You've always hated it.

VIRAG. I did, dear. Yes.

MARIANNE. Well? *(No answer)* You've always told me it's dirty money. You said Uncle Theodore did something wrong in America. He served time, didn't he?

VIRAG. Five or six years. But . . . I haven't the faintest idea what for.

MARIANNE. With all those shrewd lawyers over there if he was sentenced to five years, it was no petty crime—it must have been a beaut. When you accepted the money, you told me that the ancient

Romans used to say that money doesn't stink. But this does, and to high heavens at that. Why do you suddenly cling to it now?

VIRAG. It's disgraceful, but we're living in an age where no one is concerned with the odor of money. *(After a brief but painful pause)* I'll give you an annuity, dearest. I'll have an agreement made with all the details drawn up and notarized.

MARIANNE. But I don't want that, dearest. I only want the bank book.

VIRAG. You want to take that away from me?

MARIANNE. "Take it away?" Why—what kind of talk is that? A month ago it wasn't even here. Just imagine you had wanted a divorce a month ago and I didn't ask you for anything. It comes to the same thing, doesn't it? Or imagine you hadn't had the legacy. Besides, you've always said: "This hateful money is reserved, God forbid, for an emergency or a misfortune." Well, the misfortune has occurred. To me, of course.

VIRAG. And . . . without . . . that . . . you won't consent to be divorced?

MARIANNE. How can you say such a thing? I'm entitled to some sort of a livelihood. A little capital with which to start something, or invest in something so that I won't have to go back to being a . . . chambermaid.

VIRAG. But alimony, a large alimony! *(Sits next to her again)*

MARIANNE *(Amiably, very tenderly).* It would ruin your business, dearest, my only one. I couldn't permit you to burden yourself with an obligation like that, overdoing your generous impulses. No dearest, I can't think of you carrying worries in that handsome head of yours. I can't stand the thought of it. But the bankbook you can give up with a light heart. You wouldn't miss it; it's found money. Dirty money.

VIRAG. And without that you won't have a divorce?

MARIANNE. No, dearest. (Gently, very softly) Never.

(Pause)

VIRAG (Hoarsely). And . . . do you want it after the divorce?

MARIANNE. No, dearest. (Gently, softly) Before the divorce.

VIRAG. It's usually done after the divorce.

MARIANNE. Yes? How interesting. I'll take it before. Your lawyer is a wicked man and might cheat me. Not you, you good dear honest boy, but the lawyer. I want to make sure. You wouldn't want me to go out into the wide world without a penny in my pocket?

(WAITER enters)

WAITER. The British Ambassador has come with a lady.

MARIANNE (Ignoring him). Well? Your answer. Yes or no.

VIRAG. Yes, of course. But . . . (Gets up)

MARIANNE. But?

VIRAG. I want to take a few deep breaths. (Sits down left at a table)

MARIANNE (Gets up). Fine, dear. Take a few deep breaths. (To the WAITER) I am coming, Joseph. (The WAITER goes into the house) Take a few deep breaths, and in the meantime I will sell the Englishman two bottles of champagne, and put a little money in the till. A little here

and a little there, adds up to a great deal in the course of an evening. You won't ever have to starve. Why worry about that measly bankbook that you can buy your freedom with? Be glad you can get it so cheap. Take my advice and act quickly, because the competition is sitting there with his hands in his pockets—one on the gun and the other on his marriage license. (Speaking very softly, almost whispering, downstage, facing the audience) Max, my good old bartender, I don't see you and I don't know where you are, but I know that wherever you are you're eavesdropping. Be an angel and run down into the cellar and fetch two bottles of Irroy Brut champagne quickly. (Cups her hand to her ear, awaiting an answer)

BARTENDER (Unseen, in a clear, resounding voice). Yes, madam!

MARIANNE. I'll be right back, dearest. (Goes quickly into the house)

(Brief pause. VIRAG pours soda into the whiskey and gulps it. ELLA comes in with her tray)

ELLA (Angrily throws a heap of papers on the table). Look here. Zoli Barna jammed these into my hand. All the papers you need to get married, right away. Now he says he won't wait until noon tomorrow. He wants to get married at once. Tonight. He'll wake the Justice of the Peace and pull him out of bed. And in the morning, he'll take me to Vienna. He's stark mad. But thank God it's all over now. I've broken with him. I'm just afraid the poor boy will kill himself. He keeps his hand in his pocket where that gun is. (Coquettishly) I'll calm the poor boy when he drives me home after closing time.

VIRAG (*Gets up. Speaks excitedly*). He won't take you home any more. You've ridden on that piece of junk for the last time. Yes, my child. *I'm* your fiancé now. And your life as a servant is at an end. Hand your tray over to that girl Elizabeth and go home immediately. Immediately, I say. You'll come here tomorrow morning and we'll talk over everything.

ELLA. Did you talk it over with your wife, honey?

VIRAG. Just a few words.

ELLA. Yes—and?

VIRAG. There is . . . hope.

ELLA. Only hope?

VIRAG. No, no. She'll consent.

ELLA. Oh joy, oh joy! But honey, you look so nervous. It must have been painful for you.

VIRAG. No, it wasn't painful. What does it matter? (*Hugs her*) But you'll make me very happy now, won't you?

ELLA (*Promising him everything*). And how!

VIRAG (*With a forced smile to hide unpleasant facts*). Tell me, baby, I have a question. It has only just occurred to me . . . I ask it because . . . but I'd rather not ask . . .

ELLA. But why not?

VIRAG. It was just a joke. A silly idea. I wanted to ask you . . . what you would say If I told you right now that the money was no longer here.

ELLA (*Frightened*). What money?

VIRAG. The hateful inheritance. The twenty-seven thousand.

ELLA. Oh—that. (*Nervous*) Of course you have it.

VIRAG. But suppose it weren't here. Suppose I lost it little by little, betting at the racetrack?

ELLA. You don't joke about a thing like that. Tell me—why did you bring it up? Is it because you believe those wicked people who say the dirty lie that I love you only for your money?

VIRAG. No, no!

ELLA. Then what's all this about? Did you want to try me out?

VIRAG. Why no! It was just . . . just a crazy idea.

ELLA (*Tenderly*). You only torture yourself with things like that because you can't believe that a young girl can go for a man like you. Why —you're just a young girl's ideal . . . a handsome, mature, experienced man! Yes! That's our ideal nowadays. The sensual ideal! Not one of these ghastly modern boys. The devil with your money as long as you love me.

(SHE *embraces him. The* BARTENDER *enters*)

BARTENDER. They're calling for cigarettes.

VIRAG (*Carried away; ignoring the* BARTENDER). You, my one and only . . . you . . . you . . . (*Kisses her impetuously*)

ELLA (*In his arms*). You drive me crazy. You kiss like a fiend.

BARTENDER (*Very loud*). They're calling for cigarettes!!!

VIRAG (*Letting go of* ELLA. *Shouting*). There are no more cigarettes!!! (BARTENDER *goes into the house*) Go, sweetheart. Go right home now. And goodbye till tomorrow.

ELLA. See you tomorrow. (*Exit*)

(MARIANNE *enters from the house*)

VIRAG (*Overjoyed*). I've thought

it over, dearest. I've come to a decision.

MARIANNE. So soon? You didn't have to hurry on my account.

VIRAG. No, but on mine. I'm going to bring you the bankbook. You shall have it at once. (HE *is about to go*)

MARIANNE. Now? At once?

VIRAG. Right now. It belongs to you.

MARIANNE. You are the world's most perfect gentleman.

VIRAG. I was and I am. *(Kisses her hand elegantly and runs into the house drunk with joy)*

MARIANNE. Well, that's settled. So far so good. *(Laughing, then facetiously)* Well, I'll have a drink, too. *(Pours herself a stiff one, but doesn't swallow it, for BARNA enters from the house)*

   (BARNA, without saying a word, reaches for the papers which ELLA has left lying on the table)

MARIANNE. What are they?

BARNA *(Bitterly)*. My papers. A fine mess. Tomorrow is my wedding day, but there won't be a wedding. I won't need these papers. Tomorrow the Justice of the Peace will wait for me and I won't show up. *(Sighs)* Ella's gone home. By bus. She gave me the air, madame. I'm a broken-down shopworn fiancé. Tell me, madame—it's too horrible to believe—did you give your consent to the divorce?

MARIANNE. How do you know that?

BARNA. Do you have to ask? From the bartender. Is it true?

MARIANNE. Yes. I know my husband. It was the only way—to let him go without a fuss—and in friendship. Because he would have gone anyway—but things would have been terrible.

BARNA. This is the end, madame.

MARIANNE. Not at all, my dear man. It's only the beginning.

BARNA. You were my last hope. I knew your husband would triumph over me. He is so powerful. His great strength . . .

MARIANNE. We've taken that away from him, for the present, my dear man. Samson was strong, too, but Delilah found out where his strength lay and she took it away from him.

BARNA. Whom are you talking about?

MARIANNE. Don't you know who Samson and Delilah were?

BARNA. No.

MARIANNE. It doesn't matter. Look them up in the encyclopaedia sometime. And now collect all your papers and go home. And stop looking tragic and pay attention: tomorrow morning, at eight sharp, you must be at my lawyer's office. His name is Herman Wittner. Attorney at law. Look up his address in the telephone book. He'll give you all the information about what you're to do.

BARNA *(Surprised)*. How . . . dear madam . . . what does this mean?

MARIANNE. Do as I tell you. Don't be so inquisitive. Herman Wittner, attorney. At eight in the morning. And be on time. Wittner. At eight.

BARNA. Yes, of course. Attorney. I'll be there. Wittner. At eight. *(Anxiously)* But may I ask what I . . .

MARIANNE. You may not. Now go. Go on now. Furthermore,

I can inform you that you may peacefully dispose of the gun you have in your pocket.

BARNA. How did you know I have a gun in my pocket?

MARIANNE. Do you have to ask? From the bartender. Now go on home. Goodbye.

BARNA *(At the door, excited)*. Now I won't be able to sleep all night. You have something up your sleeve. The way I figure it . . .

MARIANNE *(Threateningly)*. Aren't you going?

BARNA. Oh, of course. (HE *hurries off into the house)*

MARIANNE *(Softly)*. Max.

(The BARTENDER *enters)*

BARTENDER. You called, little angel?

MARIANNE *(Quite gay)*. A bottle of French champagne. My brand. Pommery, Carte blanche 1920. Don't stare like that. Go ahead. Ice it and bring it in. Hurry, now.

*(*VIRAG *enters from the house. The* BARTENDER *goes into the house)*

VIRAG *(With the bank book in his hand)*. Here is the book, my dear love. *(Puts it on the table and opens it up. Reads)*. "Paul Virag or Marianne Virag." And, here is the entry. The original deposit. Untouched, you see.

*(*MARIANNE *examines the book very carefully, but leaves it lying on the table)*

MARIANNE. Sit down here by me.

VIRAG *(Sits next to her)*. My only one . . .

MARIANNE *(Sweetly and with emotion)*. I have ordered champagne. We will say goodbye, now.

VIRAG. Goodbye? Already?

MARIANNE. You don't think that after all that's happened I can stay here in this house . . . where you loved me, and where I . . . *(Overcome with emotion)* . . . loved you and love you . . . so much.

VIRAG. But, dearest!

(The BARTENDER *enters. Brings the champagne, iced in the pail, with two glasses)*

MARIANNE *(To the* BARTENDER, *while he fills the two glasses)*. Old boy, go tell the pianist to play my favorite piece.

BARTENDER. I've already told him.

(Opens the door and points in the direction in which the MUSIC *is coming, then goes into the house. The door remains open. The* PIANO *is heard through the open door and continues to play melodious sentimental Viennese music very softly until the end)*

MARIANNE *(Raising her glass)*. We are saying goodbye, chéri. In the good old sentimental Viennese way . . . Drinking champagne together for the last time . . . just the two of us . . . and . . .*(Breaks into tears)* Now I'm crying. Tomorrow morning I'm going away . . . leaving our Blue Danube . . . forever . . .

VIRAG. But my angel, please don't cry.

MARIANNE *(Through her tears)*. If this house were somewhere in England, near London, on the Thames . . . I would try to keep what they call a "stiff upper lip." But . . . all these years here . . . at the blue river . . . all this music . . . softened me . . . It's ridiculous, isn't it?

VIRAG. No, dear. It's nice and sweet and . . .

MARIANNE *(Holding up her glass, smiling).* A votre bonheur, chéri.

VIRAG. A la votre, chérie.

(THEY *clink glasses and drink)*

MARIANNE. Embrasse moi, chéri.

VIRAG. Chérie. *(Kisses her on the forehead)*

MARIANNE *(Reaching for the bank book).* May I take it?

VIRAG. Of course, dearest, it belongs to you now.

(MARIANNE *kisses the book and tucks it into her blouse)*

VIRAG. Does it make you so very happy?

MARIANNE. Very? More than that.

(Rests her head on his shoulder, and begins to laugh, charmingly, softly, slyly)

VIRAG. What does this mean? A little while ago you wept and now you're laughing.

MARIANNE *(Still leaning on his shoulder).* That's life, dearest. *(Laughs softly while she says:)* Sometimes you cry . . . cry . . . *(Begins to weep softly and says weeping)* . . . sometimes you laugh . . . laugh . . .

(Weeps and laughs by turns on his shoulder, very softly. The PIANO *plays on)*

CURTAIN

ACT THREE

SCENE: *Set as in ACT ONE and ACT TWO. The next morning. Everything is the same except for a number of pieces of baggage: a large trunk, two large handbags, a hat box. The baggage is piled behind a table at which the couple ate their lunch in the first act.*

AT RISE: MARIANNE *enters from the house with a large pasteboard box which* SHE *places on top of the trunk. In the box are a number of packages wrapped in paper, and some smaller boxes. Later* MARIANNE *will busy herself with these small packages.* SHE *will open and arrange them, place them on the table, pack them into the box once more, etc., etc., and the audience will watch her put away her worldly goods as* SHE *keeps moving between the table and the trunk.*

The BARTENDER *enters behind* MARIANNE, *wiping his eyes.* VIRAG *is downstage.*

MARIANNE *(To* BARTENDER*).* Since yesterday everybody in this house has been weeping, except you. Now you're starting.

BARTENDER. Forgive the bartender for bawling. This is terrible to see. Who would have believed that yesterday morning? Why are you in such a hurry to leave us?

MARIANNE. I must go away, Max, I must.

(BARTENDER *goes into the house wiping his eyes)*

VIRAG *(After a short pause).* You don't have to run away. Only yesterday, we were getting along so well, and this morning you seem so eager to get out of here.

MARIANNE. Why should I stay here? Just to torture myself? It's all for the best. I won't be here a moment longer than I have to.

VIRAG *(Much moved).* Yes . . . yes . . . And now that I see you all packed I must confess it breaks my heart. What will happen to me?

MARIANNE. You wanted it this way. I just did what you wanted.

VIRAG. If I were only sure that you understood me, that you believed what I said yesterday, and what I say again now: no matter what happens . . . I will always love only you.

MARIANNE. I know, dearest. I understand you. One can sense it in you. I see what you're going through. It was the same way with Count Ferdinand when he divorced his wife, exactly the same.

VIRAG (Sighs). I know. I know that some day I will regret this bitterly. But what can I do . . . ? I am lost, dearest . . . I can only explain it as something I can't help—an earthquake, a fire, a hurricane.

MARIANNE. You don't have to explain it, dearest. Every woman knows about these accidents that happen to older men. (A slight reaction from VIRAG at this thrust) I've been unlucky, that's all. My husband is full-blooded. My husband fell. Don't waste time trying to explain. We women understand about that. I'm fortunate in having enough strength and understanding not to fight against it. Against a . . . hurricane.

VIRAG. If I could only be sure that there was some hope . . . that you might . . . not right now, but in good time . . . that you might adjust yourself, and find peace of mind.

MARIANNE. I've already adjusted to it.

VIRAG. I mean . . . that you . . . might find happiness.

MARIANNE. That's impossible. (Without the least trace of sentimentality) You know that there can be no happiness for me without you.

You shouldn't even speak such nonsense.

(Pause. MARIANNE pretends to busy herself)

VIRAG. And . . . with what will you occupy yourself?

MARIANNE (Offhand, while SHE is working with the packages). First of all, I shall try to marry.

VIRAG. You don't say! Why marry?

MARIANNE. As a matter of principle. A respectable woman needs a husband.

VIRAG. Who's the lucky man?

MARIANNE. Don't get excited. I shall make a very careful selection. I must get myself another lion.

VIRAG. And you haven't found one yet?

MARIANNE. No. But I know I will.

VIRAG. Amazing. How lightly you can talk of it.

MARIANNE. Tell me, dearest, what good would it do me to cry and carry on?

VIRAG. Come to think of it, it's true. You have every right to live your life. I see that, and I envy you your calm and self-possession. Fortunately, you have no nerves.

MARIANNE. I'm a poor hard working woman and I can't afford the luxury of nerves.

(Pause. — MARIANNE arranges her things again)

VIRAG. And . . . and what will you do with the money?

MARIANNE. I will invest it.

VIRAG. Invest it? Where? For heaven's sake don't speculate.

MARIANNE. Why not?

VIRAG. Anything but that.

MARIANNE. Why are you worrying? It isn't your money now.

VIRAG. I know it isn't . . . but I still think of it affectionately . . . from a distance.

MARIANNE. Have confidence in me. I have a very good investment in mind.

VIRAG. There are no good investments nowadays.

MARIANNE. You will see. There are.

(ELLA *comes out of the house in a black dress and white apron as in* ACT ONE *and* TWO)

ELLA *(To* VIRAG). Good morning. I am a little late because I didn't come with . . . (SHE *breaks off)* I came by bus.

(Sees MARIANNE. *Turns and is about to go back into the house)*

MARIANNE. Where are you running to? (ELLA *stops)* Come here. Aren't you even going to say goodbye to me? Do come here. (ELLA *walks over to her timidly)* Don't be afraid. I won't bite your nose off. We're not angry at each other. There'd be no sense to that. I'm not angry at you. Why should I be? Because you want to make my husband happy?

ELLA *(Moved)*. Dear . . . dear . . . Mrs. Virag.

MARIANNE. Let us be friendly again. It's very important to me to stay friendly with my husband from whom I'm quietly being divorced. The better class of people behave this way. *(To* VIRAG) You remember how Count Ferdinand was the best of friends with his wife after the divorce. *(To* ELLA) Write to me now and then. Write to me whatever news there is about the business.

VIRAG *(Almost dissolving)*. You angel on earth.

(ELLA *bursts into tears)*

MARIANNE. What's the matter?

So you're joining the crying chorus, too. What have *you* to cry about?

ELLA. I can't tell you how very much I feel for you, Mrs. Virag. I'm not as bad as you think. *(With frankness)* My heart actually aches to think of you.

MARIANNE. It shouldn't. As you once said, I'm bright and beautiful, and my whole life lies before me. (ELLA *sobs)* Don't cry, you little silly, you. Why are you sorry for me? You can see for yourself I'm not sad.

ELLA. Yes, but I know you know how to suppress your feelings.

MARIANNE. There's nothing to suppress, my child. Don't carry on like that. Now brace up. Let me comfort you. Take my word I'm not to be pitied. My husband has made things easier for me. What a gentleman. There isn't another like him. I have no fear of the future; he took care of that. He gave me . . . as a parting gift . . . to see me through . . . *(Playing for time.)* . . . his . . . bank account. The twenty-seven thousand. The whole of it.

(ELLA *stops crying, looks at* MARIANNE, *perplexed.—Pause.* —MARIANNE *fills the pause with her merry humming as* SHE *arranges her little packages.* ELLA *stares into space, dumbfounded.* VIRAG, *in anguish, gets up and walks up and down.)*

ELLA *(Without restraint)*. So that's why . . . he told me yesterday the money wasn't there!

MARIANNE. Did he? It was very nice of him. *(Hums)* Well — and what did you say to him?

ELLA. I . . . thought he was joking . . . that he wanted to test me. *(Pause)*

MARIANNE. Well, I see you are comforted a bit. You're not sorry for me now.

ELLA. No . . . not so very.

(Brief pause. ELLA stares stupidly into space. VIRAG sits and watches ELLA intently)

MARIANNE (Playing with her packages). You don't have to worry about that any more. It shouldn't affect you.

ELLA (Nervously). No, it's not me, it's him it affects.

VIRAG (Embarrassed). It doesn't affect me. (Distressed) A month ago it wasn't even here. It was found money.

(ELLA starts to weep again)

MARIANNE. Now what are you crying about?

ELLA. I'm afraid of something. Awfully afraid.

MARIANNE. About what?

ELLA. I'm not at all happy.

MARIANNE. Why? My husband loves you, doesn't he?

ELLA. That's true. But after all this he won't.

MARIANNE. After all this?

ELLA. Yes. He won't want to have me like this.

MARIANNE. Like this? How?

ELLA. Without the money he won't want me.

MARIANNE (Puzzled). What?

ELLA (Getting more and more excited). He pictured me in beautiful dresses . . . in a fur coat . . . at the wheel of a roadster . . . a chic little lady in luxury. But this way he won't want me, I know. He positively won't want me as a housewife, a drudge. I'm not the type for that.

VIRAG (Stalling). But listen, child . . .

ELLA (Irritated). No, no. This isn't what you imagined.

MARIANNE. And you? How did you imagine it?

ELLA. That has nothing to do with it. It isn't how I pictured it, but how he pictured me.

VIRAG. But dear child . . .

ELLA (Excited). Don't you talk. You definitely said you could only picture me that way . . . traveling to Italy with you . . . in a swell hotel . . . in Venice. And when I'd enter the luxurious dining room . . . beautifully dressed . . . how everyone would turn and look at me. (To MARIANNE, becoming more agitated) That's how he pictured it. A gorgeous woman in expensive silks . . . with plunging neckline . . . jewels! Now he's stuck with a poor waitress . . . a common drudge. His hopes are disappointed . . . (Through her tears) Poor, poor Mr. Virag.

MARIANNE. In a word—now you're sorry for him.

ELLA. Yes. His illusions are gone.

MARIANNE. How touching. What a sensitive soul you are.

ELLA. Poor Mr. Virag expected Parisian perfume from me, not kitchen smells. Not onions.

MARIANNE. He expected Parisian perfume from you? Maybe it was you who expected Parisian perfume from him.

ELLA (Impudent). What does it matter who expected what? Since you're the one who has it now.

MARIANNE. Oh—so that's what you're sorry for.

ELLA. Of course! (With sincere feeling). And I'm very sorry too that I can't support the poor boy who suffered so much on my account. Our marriage was scheduled for this noon.

I can imagine what anguish he must be going through now . . . and I had hoped that this decision of mine would enable me to make it up to him for his misfortune.

MARIANNE. Suffering relieved by money.

ELLA. Why not? Wasn't Madame's suffering relieved by money?

MARIANNE. What makes you think it's been relieved?

(ELLA *weeps*)

VIRAG *(With much embarrassment, to* ELLA, *after a brief pause).* Look . . . I can't talk about it now in front of my wife, but believe me, my child . . .

ELLA *(In a rage, weeping and screaming).* I believe nothing! Don't talk to me! Go away! *(Sobbing loudly)* My dream is ruined!

MARIANNE. Anyhow, that at least is spoken from the heart.

(VIRAG *walks to within a few steps of the women. Stands there and then boxes both his own ears.* HE *then sits down at a table with his back toward the two women. Pause.* MARIANNE *humming loudly, begins packing again, this time with ostentatious merriment. From the garden enter* ZOLI BARNA *and* WITTNER, *the attorney.* THEY *exchange greetings with the others.* BARNA *seems overjoyed)*

M A R I A N N E *(To* BARNA). What's happened? We didn't hear all the explosions that usually announce your arrival. Didn't you come on your motorcycle?

BARNA. No, ma'am. Mr. Wittner brought me over in his car. *(To* VIRAG *as* HE *bows)* Mr. Virag. *(Goes over to* ELLA*)* Hello there, Ella— what is it? You've been crying.

ELLA. It's no business of yours.

BARNA. What's the matter? Has anything happened?

ELLA. It's no business of yours. *(Turns away from him)*

WITTNER *(Briefcase in hand, introducing himself to* VIRAG). Attorney Herman Wittner, attorney for Madame.

VIRAG. Virag.

WITTNER *(Bowing to* ELLA). Wittner.

VIRAG *(To* MARIANNE). What does this mean? A lawyer? Already?

MARIANNE. I called him up last night. We've got to get this over with. The sooner the better. I don't want to keep putting things off. *(To* WITTNER). Are the papers ready?

WITTNER. Everything, as Madame requested in last night's telephone conversation. (HE *is about to take out the legal documents)*

MARIANNE. Never mind, not now. Did you speak to that man as I asked you to?

WITTNER. Yes. It's eleven now. He's expecting us at twelve.

MARIANNE. Good. Please be seated. *(Looks smilingly at* BARNA*)*

BARNA *(Overjoyed, almost stuttering).* Dear Mrs. Virag . . . I really don't know . . . I can't find words . . . to thank you . . .

MARIANNE. Oh, it isn't worth talking about.

BARNA. No, no . . . this . . . this . . . a thing like this has never happened before.

MARIANNE. Don't exaggerate, child.

BARNA. Such generosity.

MARIANNE. I've only done my duty to my fellow man.

BARNA . . . but . . .

VIRAG. What are you talking

about? I can't follow a word of this conversation.

MARIANNE. I've tried to make up for his . . . that is, to make good his loss. He came to his good fortune through my failure, you might say . . . Yesterday, the poor boy said I was his last hope, and since he was deceived in that, I owed him this.

VIRAG. What did you owe him?

MARIANNE. A little material help. Ella also said only a while ago she wanted to help him.

BARNA. But so much money, Mrs. Virag! So much money!

ELLA (Pricking up her ears). How much?

BARNA. I don't trust myself to say it—it's that much.

MARIANNE. Oh, come—Rockefeller has more.

BARNA. Not much more.

ELLA (Nervous). What did you get?

BARNA. May I tell her?

MARIANNE. Certainly.

(BARNA—his hand to his heart —is unable to speak)

ELLA. Well, speak up! What did you get?

BARNA. Wait . . . it cannot be said so easily. Ask again.

ELLA (Screaming). What did you get?

BARNA. Twenty . . . twenty-seven . . . thous . . . and.

VIRAG (Shouts). It's not true!

MARIANNE. It is true!

VIRAG. You gave him all of it?

MARIANNE. Yes.

VIRAG. You're joking!

MARIANNE. No, I swear it's true.

VIRAG (In despair). Then it's not legal. (Shouting to ATTORNEY

WITTNER) It isn't valid . . . no, no . . . it . . . it isn't legal ! ! !

MARIANNE (Calmly). Mr. Wittner?

WITTNER (With the documents). It is absolutely legal and bona-fide . . . here is the deed of gift . . . drawn up and executed according to law and properly signed . . . the model of a legal document. I . . . personally, as an attorney . . .

VIRAG (Unable to control himself). It isn't an attorney we need, but a doctor! A psychiatrist! You are crazy! (Sinks into a chair)

MARIANNE. Maybe I'm not as crazy as you think. (To WITTNER) Mr. Wittner . . . would you like a drink?

WITTNER. Well . . . since you ask, I'd like a glass of beer.

MARIANNE (To BARNA). And you?

BARNA. Dear Mrs. Virag . . . Is there any aspirin in the house?

MARIANNE. Of course.

BARNA. Then I'd like a couple. I've got a terrible headache from this . . . this excitement.

MARIANNE (Calling very softly out front). Max, a glass of beer and a glass of water. (Takes a box of aspirin out of the large box) Here's your aspirin. Does it hurt much?

BARNA. Well, as befits the amount. (Takes the aspirin from her)

(The BARTENDER enters with a glass of beer and a glass of water. He puts the glasses down and starts bawling)

MARIANNE. Max! . . . Max! . . . What's this? Crying again?

BARTENDER. I see a lawyer . . . why shouldn't I cry?

MARIANNE. What of it?

BARTENDER. What will become of me, dear madame? *(Goes out)*

WITTNER *(Raising glass, to* MARIANNE). Here's to you. *(Drinks)*

*(*ZOLI BARNA *swallows the aspirin.* VIRAG *and* ELLA *stand petrified through all this.* ELLA *watches every move of* ZOLI BARNA. VIRAG *remains staring at his wife.)*

VIRAG *(Coming to).* This is madness. *(Yelling)* What have you done? What have you done?

MARIANNE *(Calmly).* Ne te fache pas, chéri.

VIRAG. It is madness! I'll have you examined by a doctor! I'll start a court action to stop this!

MARIANNE *(Quietly).* Mr. Wittner?

WITTNER. It is too late for that. The bank book no longer exists. I withdrew the deposit in cash for Mr. Barna—according to instructions.

*(*ELLA *quietly, slowly, and smiling sweetly, makes her way over to* BARNA *and stands close to him)*

WITTNER. Twenty-seven thousand. A trifle, of course, has been deducted.

MARIANNE. How's that?

WITTNER. Madame, we are living in a highly civilized country. Something must always be deducted from everything.—The money is in my keeping. *(*HE *slaps his pocket, showing where it is. To* VIRAG) Do you wish to see it? *(Takes a wad of bills out of his pocket, while* ELLA *cranes her neck to look.* HE *gives her a special view)*

ELLA. Good heavens.

*(*SHE *claps her hands, sits down, and then puts her hand to her heart)*

BARNA *(Tenderly).* Aren't you feeling well, dearest? *(Hands her his glass of water)*

ELLA. Thank you . . . It's over . . . you dear . . . thank you for being so nice to me. *(Takes a sip)* Only you know how to be so nice, so considerate, my sweet, my one and only. *(Looks at him lovingly)*

WITTNER *(To* MARIANNE). Want to see? *(Holds the bills out to her)*

MARIANNE *(Turning up her nose).* It stinks.

WITTNER *(Smelling the bills).* Not at all. They smell sweet as flowers.

MARIANNE. To a lawyer's nose, yes.

VIRAG *(To* MARIANNE, *hoarsely).* Between us . . . us two . . . I want to call your attention to the fact that there was nothing in writing about the bank book . . . I . . . I . . .

WITTNER *(Smiling).* Between the two of you, there was no need of anything in writing. There is no need of a written agreement between married people. This is a gift from husband to wife. Absolutely bona fide. Legal.

VIRAG *(Despairing).* Then I'll try a psychiatrist—for her.

MARIANNE *(Quietly, to* ELLA). Well, my child, get dressed.

ELLA. Why? Am I fired?

MARIANNE. Take off your apron. Get your hat. You have things to do.

ELLA. Where?

MARIANNE. In the city.

ELLA. In the city? What have I . . . to do . . . in the city?

MARIANNE. Well . . . take a guess.

ELLA *(Bewildered).* I haven't the slightest notion.

MARIANNE. Then I'll tell you. You're going to the city to get married. (SHE *looks at* VIRAG)

ELLA. I?

MARIANNE. Yes, you. You're going to be married.

ELLA. To whom?

MARIANNE. To the man you love. (ELLA *looks at both men uncertainly.* MARIANNE *points to* BARNA) This one here. I believe the marriage was scheduled for today, wasn't it?

BARNA. Yes, for this noon.

M A R I A N N E *(To* ELLA) As you've undoubtedly heard, a certain person is expecting you at twelve. The person in question is the Justice of the Peace. *(Stealing a glance at* VIRAG. *Pause.* ELLA *looks at everybody in turn, perplexed)* Come, let's go. On your way. Mr. Wittner will take you there in his car. Step lively. Come on. To the wedding.

ELLA *(Pointing to* BARNA *timidly).* With him?

MARIANNE. Don't be so startled, my child. It isn't so surprising. It's happened before that somebody's married her own fiancé. Come, let's go. Off with the apron.

ELLA *(Timidly).* Right now?

MARIANNE. Yes, yes.

ELLA. But . . . please . . . let me think it over for a minute.

MARIANNE. Why?

ELLA. Because I called it off between us yesterday . . . I told him yesterday that I . . .

MARIANNE. Don't you love him any more?

ELLA. I love him . . . but . . . but . . . *(Looking at* VIRAG)

MARIANNE. Don't look at him, child. He agrees. Don't you feel it? I do. And just imagine that the money . . . is his wedding gift to you. *(Glances smilingly at* VIRAG) He wants to make you happy, the way he promised you. He is the greatest gentleman in the world.

ELLA. Yes . . . but my word . . . my promise . . .

MARIANNE. Do you want to throw away such a stroke of fortune? This is no time for hesitation. You . . . if you don't go at once and marry him, I will.

BARTENDER *(Whose head appears through the door).* No, no, little angel—no! *(Disappears)*

MARIANNE. Well? Will it be yes or no?

ELLA. But . . . *(Takes a step toward* WITTNER)

WITTNER. I must let you know why the money is on my person and not in Mr. Barna's hands. You see, Mr. Barna will only get the money after the ceremony. Immediately after. Mrs. Virag's instructions. If ceremony's at twelve, then cash at twelve-thirty.

(ELLA *exchanges looks with* VIRAG *and* MARIANNE, *then begins slowly to untie her apron strings)*

VIRAG *(At this* HE *gets up and starts to go into the house, but remains standing in front of the door and begins yelling agonizedly).* Twenty-seven . . . thous . . . *(Suddenly stops, controls himself, and says to his wife softly and quietly as he bows elegantly)* Pardonnez moi, chérie. *(Exit into the house)*

(ELLA, *very frightened, takes up her apron and puts it on again. Looks at* MARIANNE *perplexed).*

MARIANNE *(To* BARNA). Have you got the tickets?

ELLA. For Vienna?

BARNA. No, not for Vienna. *(Shows them to her)* For Venice, Italy. Honeymoon. Hotel Danieli. Round trip. A real honeymoon. Seven days in Venice.

(ELLA *finally throws her apron down)*

MARIANNE. Well, at last.

ELLA. My God . . . what shall we say to poor Mr. Virag.

MARIANNE. Are you sorry for him?

ELLA. Very sorry. You won't believe me, Mrs. Virag, how sorry I am for him.

MARIANNE. Really, you are goodness itself. Heart of gold. Well, you must go now. I will fix it for you with him.

BARNA *(In an unexpected superior tone, commanding* ELLA). Let's go, let's go. And no show of sentimentality.

ELLA. What? You dare to talk to me like that? You ought to be the first one to keep your mouth shut.

BARNA. Why should I?

ELLA. Because I'm mad at you.

BARNA. Why?

ELLA. Because you turned me down.

BARNA *(Puzzled)*. I?

ELLA. Yes, you. It was your faint-heartedness that let me get away. Why weren't you man enough?

BARNA. I wasn't a man?

MARIANNE *(To* ELLA). Let him be, my child. Believe me, it's hard to be a man without money. He'll be a man now. You'll see. Well—go on. *(Noticing a reaction from* ELLA*)* What's the matter with you?

ELLA. Dear Mrs. Virag . . . Just one more request.

MARIANNE. Well?

ELLA. Be so good as to bless us.

MARIANNE. Gladly. *(Then, with a little movement of her hand)* My blessings.

WITTNER *(Who is now standing with the young couple)* Am I also included in the blessing, madame?

MARIANNE. It's all right with me.

WITTNER. Many thanks. So sweet of you.

(ELLA *kisses* MARIANNE'S *hand.* BARNA *kisses her other hand)*

BARNA. And now once again from the bottom of my heart . . .

MARIANNE *(Interrupting him)*. No speeches, please. Go now. It is eleven-thirty.

BARNA. And give Mr. Virag my warmest regards, my . . . my . . .

MARIANNE. Yes, yes. I'll take care of that. *(Pushes them out)*

(BARNA, ELLA *and* WITTNER *leave by the garden.* MARIANNE *picks* ELLA'S *apron off the ground, hums, as* SHE *shakes it and folds it carefully and places it on the table. Humming more loudly and joyfully,* SHE *begins packing and arranging her things in the paper box. Now* SHE *hums the wedding march. There is a brief pause.* VIRAG *enters from the house staggering, looks around, sees that the others have left, sits down a little to one side, depressed, with his back to his wife. Then* HE *commences to speak softly, like a broken man, without looking at* MARIANNE*)*

VIRAG. Tell me, my child, whereabouts is this . . . this quiet sanitorium that you recently made mention of . . is it somewhere near the city?

MARIANNE. That is no place

for you, my dear. It is a sanitorium for morbid . . . *juvenile* delinquents.

(Brief pause)

VIRAG *(Looks at her now)*. What are you doing?

MARIANNE. I'm packing.

VIRAG. What for?

MARIANNE. I keep my word. I'm going.

VIRAG *(Stares ahead of him)*. What have you done to me?

MARIANNE. To you? Nothing.

VIRAG *(Insisting)*. But why . . . did you give it away . . . why did you give it to that . . .

MARIANNE. I do what I please with my money. I told you I knew of a good investment. I invested. *(Puts the cover on the box, takes a hat from the table)* Well, dear, farewell. . . . .

VIRAG. What's the meaning of this?

MARIANNE. I'm leaving.

VIRAG. Well. You don't have to hurry so. Stay a while. Just make one thing clear to me, or else I'll go crazy. Why did you take the money away from me?

MARIANNE. Because I knew, dearest, that the girl had no use for you without your bank book. You've just seen this for yourself.

VIRAG. All right, but why didn't you keep it?

MARIANNE. That would only have been half the job. I had to play safe. Forgive me, but it was a matter of my own life. I had to make a good match of Zoli Barna, exactly as good as you were yesterday. So that the sunflower would turn in his direction.

VIRAG *(Lost in thought, and playing with ELLA's apron)*. Sunflower . . . A calculating little minx

. . . a pretty scheming little minx. *(Throws the apron down)* And you could bring yourself to say that she loved me!

MARIANNE. If I hadn't convinced you, you would never have trusted your bank book away from you. At that it was hard enough getting it away from you. Tell me, my friend, I suppose you miss all that money dreadfully now?

VIRAG. No. Really not. Ill-gotten gain never thrives. Do you miss it?

MARIANNE. I must say I do miss it *terribly*. You have no idea how I miss it. But it had to be so. Nothing happens for nothing in this world. Everything has its price. That was the price tag the Almighty put on my happiness. Expensive, but worth it.

VIRAG. I'm not sorry about that damn money. Believe me, I don't care. But one thing makes me boil. That is that you made that little chiseler happy, too.

MARIANNE. When my own happiness is at stake, I'm cruel enough not even to mind making someone else happy.

VIRAG *(Looking at her fixedly)*. And now, after all this, I really don't know whether I should beat you or adore you.

MARIANNE. Make it a little of each.

VIRAG. Why?

MARIANNE. Because I've deserved both.

VIRAG *(Looks at her enraptured, then speaks sincerely)*. I will always . . . always love you.

MARIANNE *(Stroking his hair)*. Believe me, that's the smartest thing you could do.

VIRAG *(Lost in thought, with a bitter ironic smile).* Earthquake, fire, hurricane.

MARIANNE *(Stands next to the seated* VIRAG *and strokes his hair. Then, in the tone of one telling a fairy story).* Earthquakes pass, fires die down, hurricanes subside.

*(*BARTENDER *noiselessly appears in the rear. Stands silently, with a happy grin on his face.* MARIANNE *turns around and sees him)*

MARIANNE. What do you want?

BARTENDER. I'm not crying any more. I'm laughing now.

VIRAG. Max, my boy.

BARTENDER *(Steps forward, military fashion).* At your service, chief.

VIRAG. Max, do be a good fellow and take the bags into the house.

BARTENDER *(Happy).* And how! *(Throws* MARIANNE *a kiss)* Little Angel, I'm so happy. Forgive the bartender for being happy. *(Picks up the two suitcases, feels that they're empty. Shakes them and is startled)* What is this? They're empty. *(Opens the lid of the large trunk)* The trunk, too. You . . . You never packed at all.

MARIANNE *(Very quietly).* Why should I have packed? Just to unpack again?

*(*VIRAG, *sitting, looks up at her.* MARIANNE *smiles down at him)*

BARTENDER *(With baggage in each hand).* There isn't another woman like her. Forgive the bartender for being in love. *(Goes toward the house)*

CURTAIN

THE GOOD FAIRY

THE GOOD FAIRY

COMEDY IN THREE ACTS AND EPILOGUE

CHARACTERS

LU, 25	*Silent Parts:*
SPORUM, 48	HEAD WAITER
KONRAD, 45	CLERK
METZ, 48	MAN FROM PICTURE
WAITER, 32	SHOP
KAROLINE, 28	TWO WORKMEN
MANAGER	

PLACE : ACT ONE AND EPILOGUE: A SMALL PRIVATE DINING-
ROOM IN A FIRST-CLASS HOTEL-RESTAURANT. ACT
TWO AND ACT THREE: A LAWYER'S OFFICE.

(Acting version of the play; translated by JANE HINTON. *Produced in New
York by* GILBERT MILLER *with* HELEN HAYES *in the leading role; in Berlin
by* MAX REINHARDT *with* GRETE MOSHEIM; *in Vienna by* MAX REINHARDT
with PAULA WESSELY; *in Budapest at the* VIGSZINHAZ *with* FRANCISKA
GAAL; *in Paris at the* THEATRE DES CAPUCINES *with* NICOLE RICHE;
on the Italian stages with MARTA ABBA; *in Hollywood's first film version
with* MARGARET SULLAVAN; *in the second film version with* DEANNA
DURBIN; *made into a musical comedy by* PRESTON STURGES, *produced in
New York at the* WINTER GARDEN *under the title* MAKE A WISH *with*
NANETTE FABRAY.)*

THE GOOD FAIRY

ACT ONE

SCENE: *A private dining room in a smart hotel.*

TIME: *Evening.*

AT RISE: *A table is set for three persons. At rise of curtain the* HEAD WAITER *is bustling about in silence. Another* WAITER *enters with bottle of champagne in bucket. He uncorks champagne.* HEAD WAITER *at serving table. Suddenly* KONRAD *rushes into room. He gives coat to* WAITER. *He calls* HEAD WAITER *to him and proceeds to hurl orders at him wildly.*

KONRAD (*To* WAITER). Quick, waiter—quick! Go to the side entrance immediately. There you will find a car with curtains drawn. In the car is a lady. Show her up here discreetly . . . without attracting any attention! Don't speak a word to her! Don't even say "good evening" and the moment she arrives serve supper at once.

(WAITER *takes* KONRAD's *hat and exit.* HEAD WAITER *listens attentively and then exit. There is a few moments' pause, during which* KONRAD *fusses about and picks up champagne bottle and looks at label, puts bottle on table.* LU *enters. She is in evening dress. She seems very excited.* KONRAD *relieves her of her wrap. Both* LU *and* KONRAD *are obviously trying to put on the "grand manner.")*

LU (*Smiles and presses hand to her heart*). Oh, how my heart is beating!

KONRAD. But, Madame! What are you afraid of? Why this exces-sive caution? This game of hide and seek? This coming in separately instead of together?

LU. I must be so careful! . . . My husband! . . . Oh, my husband! If anyone sees me, I'm lost!

KONRAD. But I made the car stop in the side street. At the side entrance which leads directly to this room!

LU. You don't know my husband! He's terrifying! If I'm seen here alone, I can always say that I'm calling on a friend, who lives in this hotel. But, if I'm seen with a man . . . and just the two of us . . . then, Heaven protect me!

KONRAD (*As the* WAITER *enters to serve hors d'oeuvres*). Ah! Caviar a la Konrad. My own creation!

(WAITER *exit*)

LU. Please . . . where is your friend? You said that your friend would be here, too! That was understood. It was absolutely understood that there would be three of us! You haven't lured me here under false pretenses, have you?

KONRAD. Oh, no. For Heaven's sake, calm yourself. You see there are three places. I was unable to reach his Excellency the Minister in time. He had already arranged to attend a political dinner.

LU. Oh.

KONRAD. But the dinner is being held in this hotel. In the ballroom on the first floor. And His Excellency has promised to divide his evening. He will join us later on. This caution . . . is fantastic. Are you afraid of me?

LU. I . . . I . . . don't like to be alone . . . with a man . . . in a private room! I am not a tart! *(Sits left of table)*

KONRAD *(Laughing)*. But all this excitement is nerve-wracking . . . every time we meet! *(Sits right of table)*

LU. Now, now! "Every time?" This is only the third time we've met. The first time, at the Tea Room, where you and your friend His Excellency the Minister introduced yourselves . . . doesn't count! *(Coquettishly)* Even then, you must have noticed from the way I looked at you . . . that . . . although His Excellency is a very fine looking man . . . I liked you best!

KONRAD *(Encouraged)*. Oh, sweet little Lu! *(He pours wine)*

LU. We have only met twice so far! Just count! This is the third time.

KONRAD. And what fine times they were! The first, at five o'clock in the afternoon, in a crowded tearoom. The second also in the afternoon at a "thé dansant"! Always with a thousand people present!

LU. You'll get used to it, my dear! What do you expect? You've hardly known me a week!

KONRAD. Known you? That's an exaggeration. I only know that you are a lady, the wife of a lawyer, that much you have told me. Nothing else. You envelop yourself in mystery. I have told you everything about myself. You know that I was born here, and worked thirty years in South America. You haven't even told me your name.

LU. My name is Lu.

KONRAD. That's very little.

LU. Then . . . Louise.

KONRAD. That's a bit more, but still not enough.

LU. Isn't it more beautiful this way?

KONRAD. No.

LU. So romantic . . .

KONRAD. Why do you torture me with romance? Romance has been out of date for a long time. We live in a different age! Progress is the motto of our time. But . . . how shall I put it . . . there doesn't seem to be any noticeable progress between us!

LU. Sir! This crude expression of impatience . . .

KONRAD. What do you intend to do with me? You can see that I love you, that I'm crazy about you! You're in my thoughts day and night. You interfere with my work . . . with my business. Why are you here with me, if you don't love me?

LU. Patience, patience!

KONRAD. That's what you always say! How much longer . . .

LU. I want to know you better. I'm not that kind of person. How often must I repeat that? I'm married. I have my scruples. For me, this is a most unusual experience! A . . . tremendous experience! Not just a brief cynical adventure!

KONRAD. Oh, charming, charming! (HE *makes a move towards her*)

LU. Now, now! Control yourself, President! Be a nice man and let's talk quietly. How much longer are you staying in Europe?

KONRAD. Oh, a long time. Perhaps a whole year. Until I have organized our branches all over Central Europe. That takes time.

LU. And then, you will return to . . . *(Sighs)* To your wife!

KONRAD. Yes. Why do you

look at me so reproachfully? You have your husband. . . .

LU. Oh, my dear! Life is so horrible! Why does one always find the right man too late?

KONRAD (*Rising and leaning over her*). Lu! Lu! Lu! You drive me crazy when you talk like that! (HE *makes another move towards her*)

LU (*Pointing to a chair*). Please don't go crazy, President, it's so bad for you.

(KONRAD *sits again*)

KONRAD. Look here. I know that you can't fall in love with someone . . . on the spur of the moment. But I'm so nervous, because I feel that you are on the verge of a decision. My happiness is a matter of days . . . or perhaps only hours.

LU. Patience! We respectable women go at things more slowly. You rich gentlemen are used to the tempo of fast women. You are spoiled, President!

KONRAD. Oh, please don't say that! Especially, since you know that my love for you is based on respect. I love you because you are a lady, because this love is fraught with danger for both of us, because you are making a sacrifice!

LU. Let's be frank! And because an open affair would damage your business reputation here and get you in trouble with your family.

KONRAD (*Laughing*). Very clever! Very clever!

LU. Oh yes! A society woman has her great advantages. We are discreet: we remain unseen, voila! All that—is worth a little patience!

KONRAD. Yes, yes, of course. You talk so sensibly. It's a pleasure to listen to you. Please forgive my . . . gross importunities. They are really due to the fact that I've been denied feminine society for a very long time. On the ship . . . not a single flirtation. And on my other journeys since then . . . not a single one! And now, I am suddenly thrown into your presence, for a whole week . . . your nearness, your perfume, your haunting voice . . . have all bewitched me, and yet . . .

LU. You're too ardent, sir! Oh, much too ardent! Still, I like that! However, all you have said just now only concerns . . . shall I say . . . the physical?

KONRAD. What worries me, too —you won't accept anything from me! I'd be so happy, if you would occasionally permit me to offer you a few trinkets. . . .

LU. Sir!

KONRAD. Yesterday, for instance, that beautiful ruby necklace in the shop window. . . .

LU. President, these remarks are very distasteful!

KONRAD. Well, it's something that you accept a few flowers!

LU. Flowers, yes! But preferably only wild flowers!

KONRAD. Oh!

LU. There must not be the slightest relation between my eventual surrender . . . (KONRAD *starts*) . . . and your financial status!

KONRAD. What delicacy!

LU. That's lucky, too, isn't it? Let's be frank about this, too! We are not expensive. That's another point in favor of us respectable women! (*Gesture from* KONRAD) Oh, I know, I know you're generous, sir! . . . Aren't you a lord?

KONRAD. No. I am the President of a large corporation.

LU. Oh, that's better than being a lord, isn't it?

KONRAD. In our country . . .

LU. And . . . in ours!

KONRAD. I am a business man, Madame, and proud of it! I'm a business man.

LU. I just dote on business men. I always bring them luck!

KONRAD. That, too? Oh, you angel. *(Starts to take her hand, stops as* WAITER *enters with chicken and salad, crosses to serving table)* Ah, here we are. Cold chicken and salad. And as far as luck is concerned, Madame, we'll soon see, for at this very moment, I'm waiting to hear the outcome of a very important business deal. I'm phoning later on to find out the result.

LU. Really? Now, you've made me curious to see if I'll bring *you* luck!

> (LU *exchanges glance with* WAITER)

KONRAD *(To the* WAITER*)*. Bring me the telephone book.

> (WAITER *exit)*

LU *(Looking over her shoulder at the door. Frightened)*. Good Heavens!

KONRAD. What is the matter?

LU. That waiter knows me! . . . Oh, how awful! . . . It's just occurred to me! . . . I've dined here once or twice with my husband! . . . And now, that impudent waiter dares to smile at me! . . . Oh, I was a fool to come here! What *will* he think of me?

KONRAD. Why should that matter to you?

LU. I . . . I . . . don't like to be alone . . . with a man . . . in a private room! I'm not a tart! *(Nervously)* What's happened to your friend? . . . And if I ever dine here again with my husband . . . that wretched waiter will be sure to grin at me!

KONRAD. A waiter wouldn't do that!

LU. Oh, I'm so nervous! . . . Oh, how nervous I am! *(Nervously)* Please, give me a cigarette.

KONRAD. With pleasure. *(Takes out cigarette case and leaves it on table)* Extra special! *(He lights her cigarette)* Made especially for me in England.

LU. Especially for you?

KONRAD. Especially for me.

LU. What an extravagance! *(Puffing cigarette)* Your friend, the Minister, His Excellency, is a fine looking man. And he seems to be a gentleman, too.

KONRAD. He is a perfect gentleman, Madame.

LU. He inspires confidence. His appearance is very distinguished. His manners are charming. But I can't wait for him very much longer. I lied to my husband. I told him I was going to the theatre with my girl friend . . . (KONRAD *starts)* Oh my friend can be trusted. She goes to the theatre alone and then afterwards, over the telephone, she tells me about the play, so that I can talk to my husband about it . . . Oh, yes. A single woman doesn't need to complicate her life with lies. But we married women are slaves to them. *(Nervously)* My position here is intolerable . . . Oh that waiter . . . Go and fetch the Minister. *(Irritably)* At once.

> (WAITER *enters with telephone directory.* KONRAD *rises and takes it.* WAITER *is about to exit when* KONRAD *calls him)*

KONRAD. Wait a minute, please. *(Takes the directory)* You must get me the number.

LU *(Nervously)*. Please, don't bother about business now! My honor is at stake! Go and fetch him here! *(Takes the directory away from him)*

KONRAD *(Laughing)*. Well done, little tyrant! Dictator! Dictatress!

LU. I hope you don't mind, President! Au revoir!

KONRAD *(In the doorway)*. Madame. I highly appreciate the psychological import of your remark and I am happy to conform thereto!

(KONRAD exit. Brief pause. The WAITER walks to LU's table, fills a glass with champagne, sits on table and drinks it calmly. He and LU then begin a hurried, whispered duologue)

WAITER. Why all the elegant talk?

LU. I'm not talking. I'm making conversation. Please don't give me away! I told him I was a lady . . . a society lady!

WAITER. And why are you so cautious? Why are you playing hide and seek?

LU. That's why! So that he'll believe I'm a lady! I told him I was the wife of a lawyer!

WAITER. Why did you say that?

LU. So that he'll respect me! . . . Say! What does "psychological import" mean?

WAITER. The way you think about something.

LU. And what does "conform" mean?

WAITER. To do as you're told!

LU. Thanks.

WAITER. The dress?

LU. Borrowed. *(Weeps)*

WAITER. Why are you crying?

LU. Please, don't give me away!

WAITER. Oh! What do you think I am? *(Pause)* I haven't seen you for a long time.

LU. I don't come here for tea any more. Do I owe you much?

WAITER. That's unimportant.

LU. You are a gentleman.

WAITER. *(Finishing his champagne)*. Always.

LU. You'll get your money . . . *(Pause)* Do you still love me?

WAITER *(Crossing to serving table)*. Still. How long have you known him?

LU. A week.

WAITER. Do you love him?

LU. No. I don't love him, but he . . . shall we say . . . he pleases me. Or shall we say . . . he doesn't please me.

WAITER. Well then—

LU. Only he's too important . . . Rich and in love. But there's been nothing between us, so far . . . We have only danced . . .

WAITER. The waltz?

LU. Yes.

WAITER. Well, that's a beginning . . .

LU. Don't make fun of me. I don't love him. But he loves and respects me . . . like a married lady! That's what his love is based on! Respect. That's why he treats me so nicely! You see, again tonight, he has brought me to a fashionable place! If he knew that I'm only a movie usherette . . . A sort of glow worm . . . with my flashlight blinking in the dark . . . all dressed in lemon yellow coat and glaring red skirt . . . What did you just tell me? What does "psychological import" mean?

WAITER. The way you think about something.

LU. And what was that other one? . . . Oh, yes . . . "conform!"

WAITER. To do as you're told.

LU. Thanks.

WAITER. Why do you ask?

LU. I like to learn.

WAITER *(Crossing to center table)*. You watch out that some day he doesn't wander into your movie theatre.

LU. Oh, I left the movie theatre a week ago. For his sake. He respects me so!

WAITER. How do you know that he respects you?

LU. He doesn't give me money! But don't worry . . . I wouldn't take it anyway . . . I won't sell myself.

WAITER. Then—what do you live on?

LU. Oh, I eat a lot of popcorn. And then, I've saved a little . . . enough for two weeks. And I have debts, too! Nice, big ones!

WAITER. Debts! Who would give you credit? *(Sits at table)*

LU. Everybody! Everybody likes me! *(Sadly)* That's why I have so many debts! *(She drinks)* Board bills, dressmakers, shoemakers, hairdressers, manicures, sleeping-pills, permanent waves, reducing tablets, dentists, cigarettes, Eau de Cologne, powder, rouge, mascara, magazines, dog license . . . all on credit! There's only one person to whom I pay cash . . .

WAITER. Who?

LU. The beggar. *(Drinks)* That's because I expect that some day he'll have to support me. So far, I've never been able to sell myself. *(With great determination)* But now . . . I'm going to gather all my strength and try it. I'm so unhappy.

WAITER. You're tight.

LU. Yes, a teeny-weeny bit. Why do you look at me like that?

WAITER. I'm not looking at you *like that.*

LU. I really am to be pitied, am I not?

WAITER. You are.

LU. I'm not in the story.

WAITER. What story?

LU. Life! I'm always the next installment.

WAITER. You're what?

LU. The next installment. And when the next installment arrives . . . I'm the one after that! I'm a peninsula.

WAITER. A peninsula?

LU. Yes! Like a peninsula, I reach out from the old life into the new . . . but never succeed in breaking away.

WAITER. That's clever.

LU. I don't know what I am. What do you think? Am I a tart?

WAITER. No.

LU. I don't think so, either. Am I a working girl? (WAITER *tries to speak)* No . . . and yet, that would be my ideal! But, I can't work.

WAITER. Too bad.

LU. I can't work. Maybe I am a tart, after all?

WAITER. I've already told you . . . No!

LU. I'm unable to sell myself for money. And yet, that would be my ideal! But I just can't!

WAITER. Well then, what are you doing here with this . . .

LU. I've already told you. I want to have one last try. He's very rich.

And I can't go on like this any longer. But it's so hard. I keep putting it off like a visit to the dentist's. It's dreadful! . . . I'd rather starve than have anything to do with a man I don't love . . . I don't matter that much . . . On the other hand, you know . . . for the sake of my poor, sick, little mother . . . I could even walk the streets! But I haven't got one! . . . Or, if I had a child . . . Then I could rip the heart out of a rich man's body! But, I have no one! *(Drying her tears)* What's the use of talking? I can't . . . for money! *(Weeping)* I can't . . . with a man I don't love!

WAITER. What are you crying about? That's a very beautiful sentiment.

LU. Nowadays? . . . It's a disease!

WAITER. What?

LU. I've already seen a doctor about it!

WAITER. And what did he say?

LU. A change of air . . . and lots of vitamins! *(Weeps bitterly)*

WAITER. Don't cry.

(Pause)

LU. Do you know what I'd like to be?

WAITER. What?

LU. An idiot. They say idiots are happy.

WAITER. Do you think you're so wise?

LU. No. But I'm not an idiot, either! Fifty-fifty. And that's the worst of all! But . . . God loves me.

WAITER. That's a lot!

LU. Because I'm good. Am I not?

WAITER. Oh, yes.

LU. I do good whenever I can. Do you know what I am?

WAITER. What?

LU. A fairy! *(She drinks)*

WAITER. Don't drink so much. It makes you conceited.

LU. Don't say that. If I hadn't that illusion I'd have eaten a pound of sleeping-pills long ago! Besides I've brought you luck, too!

WAITER. When?

LU. Tonight. There's going to be a huge bill tonight. That's lucky for you, isn't it? *(Getting her handbag and starting to repair her make-up)*

WAITER. Yes. That's lucky for me.

LU. So, I'm a useful member of society after all! Am I not?

WAITER. Oh, you are!

LU. Only . . . I'm a "member-in-bad-standing," I suppose you'd say?

WAITER. I'm afraid so.

LU. I have no one. Have I?

WAITER. If you say so. And if you don't count me.

*(*LU *pulls something out of the corner of the armchair. She shows it to the* WAITER)*

LU. What is this?

WAITER. Good Lord! Baron Aribell's gold cigarette case! We've been hunting for it all week. I've even been to the police about it! Where was it?

LU. Right here. It had slipped down in the corner.

WAITER. You darling! You can't imagine how happy you've made me! They even suspected me!

LU. Now, you see? I found it without even looking for it!

WAITER. You really *are* a fairy!

LU. Oh, I am. *(Puts some of* KONRAD's *cigarettes into the Baron's case)*

WAITER. What are you doing?

LU. Performing a little miracle. What is the name of the baron who lost this?

WAITER. Baron Aribell.

LU. Well, let Baron Aribell have a little extra special happiness. A few extra special cigarettes. A little present from the fairy.

WAITER. A present? But, you're stealing them, my dear child! You're stealing them from someone else!

LU. When one can do good, one shouldn't hesitate at a little sin!

(Gives him the case. They laugh. WAITER *kisses her hair.* KONRAD *enters. He doesn't see the kiss, but notices that they are smiling)*

WAITER *(Going to serving table).* Would Madame care for some French pastry?

LU *(Very aristocratic).* Thank you, waiter . . . no!

WAITER. Very well, Madame.

KONRAD. The Minister will be here shortly. Your command has been duly executed, Madame!

LU. *(With exaggerated refinement).* I'm very grateful, President. Pray forgive me, for having troubled you. You see, these fears and precautions are the disadvantage of us society women. But what can we do? We must . . . conform . . to the psychological imports . . . of our husband's wishes. Ahh!

(She sighs triumphantly at her elegant speech. WAITER *smiles)*

KONRAD. Will you permit me to make my telephone call now? *(He goes to the sofa and picks up the phone directory)*

LU. I was just going to ask you to . . .

KONRAD. *(Looks for the number in telephone directory. Speaks to* WAITER). Will you get me 181-92. And if no one answers there, try 949-49.

*(*WAITER *writes down the number and exit)*

KONRAD. That waiter really did smile at you . . . rather meaningly. And . . . as a matter of fact . . . you didn't look at him any too severely. *(Moving to her.)* Quite good looking . . . for a waiter!

LU. What does this mean, President? Are you jealous of a waiter?

KONRAD. Of every man, Madame! And particularly of this one! I don't know why . . . but I'm particularly jealous of this one!

LU. But, sir! He belongs to a totally different social class!

KONRAD. Never mind. Anything can happen in this troubled age!

LU. How ardent you are! . . . And what wild imagination! But how interesting!

KONRAD *(A step to her).* Oh Lu . . . Lu . . . Lu . . . I'm going crazy. You're so divine! *(He tries to embrace her)*

LU. No! . . . No! *(Pushes him into a chair. Moves away from him)* Sit down like a nice man, and have something to eat. You've hardly eaten anything.

KONRAD. That's what love does to me.

*(*LU *serves from serving table; then sits back of table.)*

LU. A little cold chicken. This cold supper is very wholesome, my dear President. It contains heaps of calories and vitamins, but still it isn't fattening. Do you like calories?

KONRAD. I adore them!

LU. So do I. Have you ever seen a calorie?

KONRAD. No.

LU. Neither have I.

(They eat)

KONRAD. I'm happy the supper pleases you! *(Pours champagne)*

LU. Pleases me! . . . That's putting it mildly! You know how to appreciate the good things of life! My dear President. You're an epi-epi-cur-ist!

KONRAD. Oh Lu! . . . what thrilling words!

(He moves his chair nearer and tries to embrace her)

LU *(She reaches out and pushes him slowly)*. No . . . no! Be quiet, sir! Let's eat! *(She eats)*

KONRAD. Didn't you tell me that you were on a reducing diet?

LU. Yes. But there is one rule for every reducing diet.

KONRAD. What is it?

LU. It starts tomorrow! *(She eats)*

KONRAD. Oh, Lu . . . *(Tries to embrace her again)*

LU. Now stop that, please! Don't be so grabby. *(Points to a chair)* It's high time His Excellency arrived.

KONRAD. I warn you . . . His Excellency is a little . . . er . . . drunk.

LU. Oh that's all right! I like them like that!

KONRAD. Let us drink too.

LU. With pleasure, President.

(They drink)

KONRAD *(Moving his chair nearer the table)*. And now, darling, tell me about yourself. What is your name? Where do you live? How do you live? You are so shy! . . . so mysterious! Where do you spend your evenings? Do you go to the movies often?

LU. There was a time when I went every night. But not now.

KONRAD. I hope you don't mind my asking you these questions. But you are not just a fleeting adventure to me, you know.

LU. What do you love about me?

KONRAD. Everything . . . your charm . . . your enchantingly aristocratic manner which, if I may say so, is in such striking contrast to your . . . your bubbling personality.

LU. Does my personality really bubble?

KONRAD. Like champagne, dear lady! It intoxicates me . . . I must know who you are . . . and I should also like to ask you most respectfully about your financial status.

LU. Fair.

KONRAD. Have you a car?

LU. No.

KONRAD. Furs?

LU. No.

KONRAD. Jewels?

LU. No! . . . These questions are very distasteful. One can easily see you're not a lord. I'm not a tart. What would my husband say if he saw me wearing costly presents?

KONRAD. Your husband's a lawyer?

LU. Oh . . . yes!

KONRAD. As I've already told you, I am now engaged in organizing here branches of my firm. I am greatly in need of a good lawyer, so that if . . .

LU. President, that's a plain financial proposition!

KONRAD *(In a business-like manner)*. But look here . . . forgive my saying this, but I hate successful lawyers. Once they are rich and famous they don't care a hang for anything! What we want is a good, hard-working lawyer! Really, you'd be doing me a favor if you'd help me find one.

LU. Do you mean it?

KONRAD. I'd be very grateful to you . . . oh, they're only *small* cases but quite a lot of them. I won't go into details; it would only bore you. It is sufficient to say that it means a very large but assured income.

LU. And it all depends on you?

KONRAD. Entirely! I can make someone rich with the stroke of my pen!

LU. It sounds like a fairy tale!

KONRAD. It's real, nevertheless. And it wouldn't be a present either . . . he'd have to work for it!

LU. And it wouldn't be your money.

KONRAD. You are right! It would be the firm's money. *(Coaxingly)* Why should I let it go to others . . . strangers? Wouldn't that mean everything for you: a car, jewels, furs?

LU. Oh, my husband would shower me with presents. He's so generous!

KONRAD. But won't you tell me now, who is your husband?

LU. When you have earned my confidence I will tell you everything.

(The WAITER enters)

WAITER. I've got your number at last, sir. The first number didn't answer, but 949-49 is now on the wire.

(Goes to fetch the grapes on the little table and offers them to LU.)

KONRAD *(Rises, crosses to the door)*. You'll excuse me, Madame, won't you?

LU. Certainly! I'm dying to hear if I brought you luck or not! . . . What's this? Oh, grapes! And so out of season too! You will spoil me, President.

KONRAD. That's my one ambition! *(Exit)*

LU *(Rises. Looks after him and goes excitedly to the door, then back to the* WAITER). A name, a name of a lawyer, quickly.

WAITER. What for?

LU. He wants to know my husband's name! Give me a name!

WAITER. Invent one.

LU. Oh no! I must have a real one! We've got a chance to make someone happy!

WAITER. How's that?

LU. He wants to make my husband rich!

WAITER. But you haven't got a husband, have you?

LU. That's why I'm asking you for a name, idiot! Quickly! He's just crazy to make my husband rich! Quickly! Name me a lawyer! I tell you we've got a chance to make someone very happy!

WAITER. What a crazy idea! Anybody could see that you've been drinking.

LU. Well it's a good thing I have been drinking. Now that I've decided to surrender at least someone is going to profit by it. Sweetheart, who's *your* lawyer?

WAITER. He doesn't deserve it!

LU. I don't know any lawyers at all, thank goodness! But quickly!— Let's take one from the telephone book! *(She crosses to the sofa, he follows her; she grabs the book from the sofa)* We will open it anywhere and the first lawyer on the page will be the lucky one! *(Opens the book. They bend over it, searching and whispering "s-s-s")* I've got him! Here he is! Sporum, Max, attorney at law, Telephone 911-19.

WAITER. Don't know him.

LU. Neither do I! (WAITER *jots down the name and number*) But I'll make him rich—I will!

WAITER. What if he is rich already?

LU. Then he won't get anything. But I'm sure he's poor. Don't worry . . . I only make mistakes when I think. When I do something blindly I always hit the mark! I bet that he's the poorest lawyer in the whole city! I'm either a good fairy or I'm not.

WAITER. What if he's married?

LU. Then he'll never know how it all happened. His good fortune will have just dropped from heaven!

WAITER. And if . . .

LU. Don't ask so many questions. I haven't any use for logic. *(Hides the note in her dress)* There we are: I'm so excited, I'm so happy! *(She goes to the window)* Oh! Isn't it lovely! It's midnight now and somewhere a poor man lies asleep in his bed and doesn't even dream that at this very moment he is rich. Don't you see? That's how a good fairy works!

(Through the open window we see the midnight illumination of the big city with its rows of lighted windows)

WAITER. You ought to get a commission.

LU. Oh! A good fairy and a commission!

WAITER. That happens very often.

LU. No! I'm performing miracles, not taking profits!

WAITER. Well, I hope it turns out all right. *(Then as* KONRAD *enters radiantly, the* WAITER *goes to the serving table)* French pastry, Madame?

LU. Thank you, waiter, no!

WAITER. Very well, Madame. *(He replaces the plate)*

LU *(To* KONRAD, *giving him her hands)*. Well, I can see by your face . . . It was good news!

KONRAD *(Happily)*. Oh, and what good news, dear lady! My men have won all along the line! Or to put it more plainly, we had hoped to conclude a deal involving a million and it has turned out to be a million and a half!

LU. Oh, President, I'm so glad!

KONRAD. You're a mascot, Lu! Let's drink to it! (WAITER *starts to pour the champagne)* Never mind, my friend, you may go. I'll attend to that! *(Exit* WAITER *looking back at* LU*)* Remarkable, the way that waiter always manages to be *in* when I'm *out*!

LU. Sir!

KONRAD. I hate that waiter! But don't let's bother about him now. *(They both drink)* Where were we? Oh yes! You were at last going to tell me who is your husband? What is his name?

LU. You will make him rich?

KONRAD. I will . . . at once!

LU. Promise?

KONRAD. I promise!

LU. Oh, the great moment has come! Shall I or shall I not?

KONRAD. Please, I beg you to!

LU. Max Sporum. S-P-O-R-U-M.

KONRAD. At last! *(He jots down the name)* His address? He's in the phone book, isn't he?

LU. He most certainly is!

KONRAD. Well, you will have no reason to complain of me, little girl . . . tomorrow you will hear from me . . . I'm a man of my word . . . and by this time tomorrow the contract will have been signed!

LU. Only, for heaven's sake, go about it cleverly! You mustn't say you know me!

KONRAD. That goes without saying, my dear. I'm a gentleman.

LU. You say that a little too often, President! But no matter . . . oh dear, if only Max doesn't suspect . . . I'm sure he'd strangle me!

KONRAD. Nonsense, Madame! Nonsense! I'll say he was recommended to me by the Embassy!

LU. And not a word about knowing me!

KONRAD. But my dear lady, I'm a gentleman! I mean to say, I give you my word of honor! Won't that suffice?

LU. Oh, yes! That'll suffice. Thank you, President, I'm so happy that I can make Max happy!

KONRAD *(Taking her hands)*. And I am so happy that I can make *you* happy! *(Kisses her hand)*

LU *(Delighted)*. Oh, aren't we having a lovely chat?

KONRAD *(Overjoyed, puts his arm around her)*. At last you are beginning to enjoy yourself! Now the Minister need not come at all, eh?

LU *(Coquettishly)*. You're right. Now that I have had a little to drink, I have more courage! You are so good to me, you dear man!

(They move towards each other. The WAITER *enters)*

WAITER *(Announces)*. His Excellency, Minister Metz!

*(*KONRAD *and* LU *rise. The* MINISTER *reels in drunkenly, in evening dress. He bows deeply.* WAITER *exit)*

LU *(To* METZ*)*. Sir, you have kept a lady waiting!

METZ. A thousand pardons, Madame. *(Kisses her hand)*

LU. Sit down, and eat and drink and make conversation.

METZ *(Sways, as he sits down)*. Thank you!

LU. On the chair, Your Excellency . . . not next to it!

METZ. Thanks for that most practical bit of advice.

LU. I understand that you are drunk, Excellency?

METZ. That is a fact, Madame.

LU. Well, I'm surprised at you . . . a Cabinet Minister!

METZ. We are only human.

LU. Oh, absolutely! Do you mind telling me where you minister?

METZ. At the Ministry, of course!

LU. You don't say! And what do you do there?

METZ *(Jokingly)*. I am the Minister of Futilities. *(Laughs)* I'm the man who decides who is to have a Medal of Merit and who is not.

LU. And all that depends on you?

METZ. It does. And what's more, it's very delicate work. I am said to be the most tactful cabinet minister in existence!

LU. You must be a very powerful man. But I'll bet that you're a severe one, too.

METZ. I should say I am! But those who are nice to me . . . you charming lady . . . those who are nice to me can have anything that they want. *(He tries to embrace her)*

LU. Sir! This is indeed a painful surprise! Are you trying to paw me?

METZ. That *has* been done!

KONRAD. Steady, Harry Metz, steady!

METZ. What? You're not jealous, Bob Konrad, are you?

LU. Of course he is! He's terribly jealous! And you mustn't forget that you are a very handsome man.

KONRAD. But, Madame . . .

METZ. Am I intruding?

LU. No, no! We were just having a chat.

METZ. What about, may I ask?

LU. We were talking about my husband.

METZ. Oh, that interests me too. Who wouldn't be interested in the lucky man who owned such a jewel? Ah, what eyes, what hands, what legs, what neckline . . .

LU *(Interrupting)*. Your Excellency! What lewd language!

KONRAD. My dear friend, I must really ask you to adopt another tone in speaking to this lady. It happens that she *is* a lady. She is the wife of a distinguished lawyer!

METZ. Oh!

LU. Of course I am! What did you think I was?

METZ *(Laughing loudly)*. Shan't tell you!

LU. Well, if you are the most tactful of ministers, I can just imagine what the others are like!

METZ. And what sort of man is your most fortunate husband? What does he look like?

LU *(Crisply)*. Handsome . . .

METZ. Young or old?

LU. Older than I and younger than you.

METZ. Tall or short?

LU. Taller than a thimble and shorter than a skyscraper. *(Laughing)*

METZ. What's the color of his hair? Dark or fair?

LU. Well, let's see. How can I describe it. Well, it's . . . attractive.

METZ *(With a drunken laugh)*. That's a new color . . . attractive— ha, ha. And tell me, does Mr. Attractive know Mr. Konrad as yet?

LU. No.

METZ. But he is a very good person for a lawyer to know! Can Mr. Attractive boast of many acquaintances as worthwhile as Mr. Konrad? *(He laughs)*

LU. Please, Mr. President, protect me! The Minister is being tactless!

KONRAD *(His arm around her)*. Excellency, I humbly beg your pardon. Madame is so sensitive, you must be careful how you speak to her, or she will wilt like a flower.

LU. He is rude enough to wilt an oak.

KONRAD. Really, Madame, this is very painful to me! I am very sorry, very sorry.

METZ. Tell me, is this the way Mr. Attractive makes all his worthwhile acquaintances?

LU. This is outrageous! Stop it, please! President, protect me!

KONRAD. Your Excellency!

METZ *(Stammering)*. Mr. Attractive . . . Mr. Thimble . . . Mr. Skyscraper . . .

LU *(Very angry, a little drunk)*. I won't have you make fun of my husband! It's insulting! You ought to be ashamed of yourself!

KONRAD *(Hopping to and fro in consternation)*. Please, Madame! Excellency . . . Madame . . . Excellency . . .

(WAITER *enters and whispers to* LU)

WAITER. Don't get excited, Lu.

LU *(Rising; screaming)*. I demand that my husband be respected! I demand it!

KONRAD. But Madame—before the waiter . . .

LU. Before the waiter or behind the waiter, it's all the same to me! I go crazy when anybody insults my husband!

METZ. But Madame. I . . . I . . . I . . .

(Rising to bow, but falls back in chair. He is unable to continue for laughing)

LU *(Angrily. Going to the sofa and getting her things).* Go home and sleep it off! *(To the* WAITER*)* Waiter, get me a taxi! *(To* KONRAD*)* President, get your bill! I am not going to stay here and listen to my husband being slandered!

METZ. But my dear Madame, I am really sorry. I regret extremely . . .

LU *(Turns to* METZ*).* Oh, go to the devil!

KONRAD *(To the* WAITER*).* Let me have my bill, please.

LU *(Calls after the* WAITER*).* And a taxi! *(*WAITER *exit. LU flares up again)* I am not going to have my husband slandered! *(Thumping her fist on the table)* I am not going to have it! *(Hurls a glass against the door)* I am not going to . . .

KONRAD. But dear lady, there will be a scandal!

LU. I don't care! I won't have my poor dear husband treated like that! At this very moment he is sitting at home . . . at his desk . . . working his fingers to the bone for me, and you . . . here . . . *(Sobs wildly)* . . . dare to insult him . . . and make fun of him . . .

METZ *(Rises).* Well, there's nothing for me to do but leave! That *may* clear the air. *(Walks to the door)* I bid you good night. And please don't forget to invite me to your next jolly little party! *(Goes out, offended)*

(Brief pause)

LU. Can you imagine that? Now *he's* been insulted!

KONRAD. And my Medal of Merit is off for at least another year!

LU. I could have boxed his ears for him!

KONRAD. Coming from you even that must be sweet.

LU. I'd advise you not to try it, President!

*(*WAITER *enters)*

WAITER. Your bill, sir. *(To* LU*)* The taxi will be here in a moment, Madame.

KONRAD *(Looking at the bill).* Waiter, this bill is outrageous!

WAITER. Outrageous? What do you mean, sir?

KONRAD. I don't usually say anything, but this is much too much. 120 for caviar!

LU. Mr. President, that isn't done.

KONRAD. Oh, I beg your pardon. *(He pays angrily with notes. The* WAITER *exit with the money)*

LU *(Nervously).* And now you must go first . . . We must leave . . . separately . . . as we came.

KONRAD. But what's the use of all this . . . this . . .

LU. Please don't make me nervous. Do as I tell you! I must be so careful! Can't you ever understand that? Poor Maxie is so jealous!

(At the mention of the name "Maxie" she again breaks out in tears.)

KONRAD. And when will I see you again, darling?

LU. Tomorrow.

KONRAD. At what time?

LU. At ten o'clock . . . like tonight. . . . Call for me at the Tea Room, but don't come in. Send your chauffeur.

KONRAD. Thank you . . . thank you. And then may I hope that to-morrow—please, answer me!

LU. Oh, darling.

(She falls into his arms. There is a long passionate kiss)

KONRAD. The first kiss! Oh, Lu . . . Lu . . . I'm going mad! I'm going mad!

LU *(Pushing him away)*. No, don't go mad. . . . Just go! . . . Go quickly! . . . that's best.

(WAITER enters)

WAITER. The taxi is here, Madame. *(Offers KONRAD his change on the tray)* Your change, sir.

KONRAD. So! I get something back after all? I'm surprised!

LU *(To KONRAD, as he reaches for it)*. Leave it, President. *(To the WAITER, very grandly)* That's for you, waiter.

WAITER. Thank you, Madame. *(Goes to the table and busies himself)*

LU. And now . . . once again, President. Adieu!

KONRAD *(Kisses her hand)*. Permit me to apologize for the Minister's behavior.

(KONRAD exit)

WAITER. The Minister is rather common.

LU. *Very* common! *(Smiles)* But he has made me happy!

WAITER. But you were crying!

LU. With happiness! It was so good to defend someone, to belong to someone . . . I cried so beautifully . . . I'm so grateful to the Minister for having insulted poor Max.

WAITER. If Max knew about this he would probably give you a good beating.

LU. I don't care! I need Max . . . Oh, I've got such a big heart and no one to put in it! *(Moving to him)* I'm so lonely . . . so lonely . . .

WAITER. You can have me, Lu. *(A step nearer to her)*

LU. What, again? Don't be silly! I can't . . . now!

WAITER. Have you arranged to meet him tomorrow?

LU. Yes.

WAITER. Then you finally decided . . .

LU. Well . . . half and half . . . you never can tell . . . though I do think I'll succeed this time . . . for now I'll be helping my little Maxie. Why do you look at me like that?

WAITER. I am *not* looking at you *like that*.

LU. Does it hurt you to think about it?

WAITER. Can't deny it.

LU *(Nearer to him)*. Oh dear, you are a good friend.

WAITER. A better friend than you think.

LU. The very best!

WAITER. I'd like to marry you, Lu.

LU. But not *now*, you foolish boy, not now!

WAITER *(Arm around LU's shoulder)*. I've been offered a nice little place in the suburbs . . . One could almost call it a first-rate restaurant . . . there you could have a clean, respectable, quiet life . . . a little house . . . a bit of a garden . . . and babies . . .

LU *(Looking up at him)*. How many babies?

WAITER. One every year.

LU. Oh, that's always been my ideal! But unfortunately this isn't the time for it. Please, please, don't try to ruin my career! *(The* WAITER *kisses her hand and laughs softly)* Why do you kiss my hand?

WAITER. Because I'm so grateful to you for having made me rich. *(Shows her the bill)* And because you found the gold cigarette case.

LU. I'm so glad I did!

WAITER *(Whispers)*. May I take you home?

LU. No. . . . What are you thinking of?

*(*WAITER *hangs his head)*

LU. Don't despair . . . Wait and have patience . . . Your time will come . . . Don't worry . . . I shan't let you suffer . . . I shan't let anybody suffer . . . Give me my wrap.

(The WAITER *goes to the sofa, takes the wrap and comes to her)* The Minister will make Max a judge. I'll speak to him about it. (WAITER *helps her into her wrap)* Oh, Maxie is gently sleeping somewhere in the distance. Somewhere in this big city . . . in the night . . . and doesn't know that tomorrow he'll be rich . . . rich and envied . . . Oh . . . I'm too happy for words. I shan't be able to sleep all night. Kiss my hand again. *(She holds out her hand)*

WAITER. Again?

LU. Yes! I don't know why . . . I feel like it tonight. . . . That's right. *(She walks to the door, smiling)* And now . . . *(The door opens slowly)* Adieu!

(She slips through the door. the door closes slowly)

CURTAIN

ACT TWO

SCENE: MAX SPORUM'S *office. It is a shabby office. On the left two doors leading to his living quarters. At the right main entrance.*

TIME: *The next day.*

AT RISE: SPORUM *is seated at a small table, with his back toward the audience. He is finishing his mid-day meal, eating salami and drinking beer.* MISS KAROLINE *serves him and stands beside him while he eats.* SPORUM *is forty-eight years old, very pompous. He is not what you'd call a handsome man.* KAROLINE *is his secretary and chief-clerk in one. She is a pretty, energetic person, deeply attached to* SPORUM.

SPORUM. I'm not even looking at you, Miss Karoline, and yet I know what you're thinking.

KAROLINE. Well, what am I thinking, Mr. Sporum?

SPORUM. You're thinking what you always think at lunchtime, that a lawyer ought to be ashamed of himself if at the age of forty-eight he can't afford anything better than a small beer and cheap salami.

KAROLINE. Money doesn't bring happiness, Mr. Sporum.

SPORUM. That's true enough. Money never brought me happiness. But then, it never tried to. Still, I believe it could if it ever tried. *(Stands up and walks to the desk which faces the audience. Lights a cigar)* May I have a cup of coffee, Miss Karoline?

KAROLINE. We haven't any coffee, Mr. Sporum.

SPORUM. What about a very *small* cup of tea?

KAROLINE. We haven't any tea or coffee. *(The* DOORBELL *rings)*

SPORUM. The doorbell is ringing, Miss Karoline. It's probably another creditor. All I wish is that the first of the month would never come. Go and see who it is.

KAROLINE. I'm sure it isn't a client. *(She exit)*

SPORUM *(To himself)*. No tea— no coffee. What a success!

KAROLINE *(Returns, holding a slip of paper)*. Telephone bill! Final notice—Max Sporum, attorney at law, is hereby requested, etc., etc. If we don't pay twenty-three fifty the phone will be cut off!

SPORUM. Well, we won't pay! The telephone company is crazy! Where would I get twenty-three fifty? Let them cut it off! Throw him out! *(He sits down)*

KAROLINE. I *have* thrown him out. *(Adoringly)* You are nervous today, Mr. Sporum.

SPORUM. Oh, please don't fuss over me.

KAROLINE. I'm not fussing over you. I'm merely stating a fact.

SPORUM. Then stop stating facts to the effect that I'm nervous. That's a medical diagnosis and you are a law clerk and not a physician!

KAROLINE. Very well, Mr. Sporum.

SPORUM. Oh, all right. Have it your way. I *am* nervous. This first of the month is terrible! All the bills come today. I won't pay a single one, but nevertheless it's terrible! Why do you look at me so significantly? I know I haven't even paid you! But rest assured, you're the only one who will be paid.

KAROLINE. I am greatly honored, Mr. Sporum. *(She exit with the tray)*

SPORUM *(While she is moving about)*. Don't be sarcastic, Miss Karoline. Things are going very badly with me. (KAROLINE *re-enters*) I'm afraid you have made a foolish choice. I doubt if there is another lawyer in the whole city who is doing as poorly as I am. I'm so worried that I'm unable to sleep. I read the Bible all night long. It's the only thing that still affords me a little comfort. Those in search of justice have no use for me because I uphold the standard of ethics. What was that phone call a few minutes ago? Who wanted me? Let me see the slip. *(Reads)* Mr. Robert S. Konrad, President of the Argentine Meat Packing Co., Ltd. What does he want?

KAROLINE. His secretary phoned to ask when Mr. Konrad might see you on business. I told him at any time.

SPORUM. And that is right, my child.—I am upholding the standard of ethics, so I have to starve. Shady cases, I refuse to handle, and the honest ones do not pay. Friends I have none. Politics, I hate. So here I am, nearly fifty years of age, with all my knowledge and integrity, eking out an existence by scribbling articles for law journals. My practice is nil. How is it going to end? Only one thing is certain . . . it is not going to end by my abandoning the strict standards of ethics. *(Shouting)* It is not going to end that way, Miss Karoline!

KAROLINE. Don't shout at me as though I wanted you to abandon your precious ethics. I don't! I admire you just because you're willing to endure this poverty!

SPORUM. I'd prefer you to despise me for my wealth! *(Picks up some papers on desk)* A fine list of cases I have here . . . Ammo vs. Bergman—the fee won't pay for a pair of shoes. . . . Legros vs. Julius—at the most that'll pay for a new pair of trousers and short ones at that! My biggest case—Adam vs. Coloman . . . I worked on it for two full nights. Yet I'll bet it won't pay for next month's rent. *(Throws the documents aside)* Now look at this desk again. And over there! Everywhere . . . disorder!

KAROLINE *(Arranging papers)*. But you always throw things around! Now if you had a wife . . .

SPORUM. Yes, that's all I need, isn't it? . . . a family! Well, I'm thankful I haven't got one! There'd be more of us to starve. As it is, I'm the only one to suffer because of my misfortunes, my integrity, my . . . handicaps. *(Looks at the slip again)* President Konrad—I'm positive that someone is playing a practical joke on me.

KAROLINE. Yes, Mr. Sporum, I thought so too at first, but I called the secretary at his hotel. He said it was about an important legal matter and so I made an appointment for the gentleman to call here at about this time.

SPORUM. Now?

KAROLINE. Yes, Mr. Sporum. He said he'd be here within an hour.

SPORUM. A big business man . . . coming to my shabby office on an important legal matter! Impossible! Those things don't happen, Miss Karoline! *(The* DOORBELL *rings. He starts)* I'll go into the other room, Miss Karoline. You'd better see him first, if it is he.

> *(Rushes off stage.* KAROLINE *hurries out and returns a moment later with* LU)

LU *(Entering)*. Good morning. *(Looks at* KAROLINE*)* I wish I were like you. . . . Exactly like you. *(Sigh)* But I can't be. . . . I can't.

KAROLINE. Excuse me, Madame . . . I don't quite understand.

LU. Don't worry. . . . I'm not crazy. That remark was just a sigh with words. I'm looking for Mr. Max Sporum.

KAROLINE. May I ask your business, Madame?

LU. It's a personal matter. Are you his secretary?

KAROLINE. Yes. Who shall I say is calling?

LU. Mrs. . . . *(She doesn't finish the word)* Oh, please tell me quickly. . . . Is Mr. Sporum married?

KAROLINE. No.

LU *(Relieved)*. Oh, thank Heaven!

KAROLINE. Why? . . . You haven't any designs on the old man, have you?

LU *(Alarmed)*. Oh, is he old?

KAROLINE. Yes.

LU. I hope he's not *very* old.

KAROLINE. Well—he's much nearer fifty than forty. *(She exit)*

LU *(Looks at the desk)*. He *is* poor! I'm sure of that! (SPORUM *enters. He looks pompous and forbidding.* LU *is awed)* Mr. Sporum?

SPORUM. Yes. Pray be seated, Madame. (LU *sits)* What can I do for you?

LU. I want some legal advice.

SPORUM. You said it was a *personal* matter.

LU. It is . . . to me.

SPORUM. Might I ask your name?

LU. I'll tell you later. Won't you let me explain my business first?

SPORUM. If you wish, Madame. (LU *gives* SPORUM *a furtive look. She is awed again*)

LU. I'm an unemployed glow-worm.

SPORUM. You're a what?

LU. I show people to their seats in the movies. I glow with my little flashlight in the dark.

SPORUM. I see. A well-known insect. Please go on.

LU. Well, on my day off I went to a tea room and met a very wealthy married man. He took a fancy to me, but you see, he just hates immoral women.

SPORUM. What of it?

LU. But Mr. Sporum, it's very important in this case. He hates loose women! He knows that they're hard to get rid of, and besides an open affair would damage his reputation. He's right, of course, he has the proper "psychological import" and realizes that the best thing for him is a married woman!

SPORUM. Continue. So far you haven't told me anything.

LU. Well, we danced together, and during a waltz I told him a lie, I said I was married to a lawyer. You know, I can always lie more convincingly during a waltz.

SPORUM. Go on, please! And I ask you to come to the point! Why have you come to see me?

LU. Because I'm frightened! What will happen to me when he finds out that it was a lie? Is it a case of fraud—a crime? What shall I do? (*Weeping*) I'm prepared to pay well for your legal advice. (*Still weeping,* *but coquettishly*) I'll be grateful to you in every way.

SPORUM. Where is the Bible? (*Searches and finds a big Bible*)

LU (*Rises, awed*). Is there advice for that sort of thing in the Bible?

SPORUM. No, but my glasses are in it! (*Takes glasses out, puts them on. Looks at her through them*) You're a very pretty girl!

LU. Oh yes, I know that. That's why the men run after me.

SPORUM. Oh, do they run after you?

LU. They all want to teach me the facts of life.

SPORUM. And you?

LU. Well, I am very poor, so I have decided to lead an immoral life.

SPORUM (*Caressing her*). Poor, pretty, frivolous child.

LU (*Sinks into his arms*). Oh, thank you! Thank you! Thank you! (*Sniffs*) I smell perfume. What is it?

SPORUM. Lily-of-the-valley. But let us get to the point. I have only one question to ask you. Did you accept money or jewels from him under your assumed name?

LU. Under what name?

SPORUM. The name of the lawyer's wife.

LU. Oh, no . . . I never accepted a single penny under any name. All I had was a few teas, a cold supper; flowers. . . .

SPORUM. They don't count. You'd have had them in any case. Well, then . . . (*As though reciting a lesson*) Your thoughtless procedure whereby you did cunningly and artfully mislead someone into an erroneous belief, but from which you did not derive any unlawful gain, does not fall within the legal interpretation of fraud according to the provisions of Section 379 of the Penal Code. As you gave no name you are innocent of the charge of impersonation according to Section 143 of the Penal Code. Thus, my child, from the legal point of view, you are not guilty of anything. I'm in a position to completely reassure you on that point.

(He *pats her. He has been caressing her throughout the speech and now makes a bolder gesture*)

LU *(With a sigh)*. Oh, I envy the woman whose fate lies in the hand of a strong man!

SPORUM. Pardon me, but my hand slipped.

LU *(Pointing to her dress)*. It's this slippery material.

SPORUM. Well, don't worry, my child. Be happy that you are young and pretty. You still have all your life before you.

LU. You are so kind-hearted, Mr. Sporum. You give me courage.

SPORUM. Not at all. I am only doing my duty.

LU *(Sits down)*. Oh, I've just remembered! . . . I forgot to mention something when I told you my story. It's a mere detail but I'm sure it has no importance, legally.

SPORUM. What was it?

LU. Well—this man insisted so much that I finally had to tell him my husband's name.

SPORUM. How do you mean?

LU. The telephone directory happened to be lying on the table, so I opened it at random . . . and chose the name of a lawyer.

SPORUM. Excellent! *(Laughs, greatly amused)* Just on the chance.

LU. Yes.

SPORUM *(Laughing loudly)*. Excellent! And who was it?

LU. You.

SPORUM. What?

LU. You.

SPORUM. Me!

LU. Yes. I gave him your name . . . I told him you were my husband.

SPORUM. That I—am your husband?

LU. Yes. That's right . . . Your name was the first on the page—in the top left-hand corner.

SPORUM. In the top left-hand corner!

LU. A while ago you asked me my name. I will tell you now. *(Rises and makes him a bow)* Mrs. Max Sporum! *(Sits down again)*

SPORUM *(Angrily)*. I'll have you jailed for that!

LU. But didn't you just say . . . ?

SPORUM. This is different! . . . You gave a false name, and you are therefore guilty of impersonation . . . but not according to Section 143 of the Penal Code, because you did not assume a false name in order to deceive a public official. Instead, you cunningly and artfully deceived a wealthy individual, and therefore your offense is far more serious! It comes under Section 379 of the Penal Code. And this cold supper at an expensive hotel cost a great deal of money. It represents something of value received by you. It constitutes an unlawful gain which you obtained by means of a false name. It is fraud, according to the provisions of Section 379 of the Penal Code! The penalty is twelve months in prison or five years in the house of correction. You will go to jail, Madame! You'll serve time for this!

(LU *weeps softly.* SPORUM *demands furiously*)

SPORUM. Why did you do it? Were you drunk?

LU. A little.

SPORUM. What made you marry into the telephone book? Why didn't you invent a name?

LU. I wanted to make someone rich.

SPORUM. What is that you say?

LU. He is looking for a lawyer.

SPORUM. *Who's* looking for a lawyer?

LU. My friend. He can make you rich with the stroke of his pen.

SPORUM. How?

LU. It's enough to tell you that it means a very large but assured income, and he is willing to give it all to us. By the stroke of his pen he can make some lawyer rich and happy. So why should we miss such a golden opportunity? Why let it vanish in the air like cigarette smoke? *(She sobs)*

SPORUM *(Suspecting evil).* Good Heavens! What's this man's name?

LU. Konrad.

SPORUM *(Pulls out the slip and reads).* Robert S. Konrad, President. Is that the man?

LU. Yes . . . yes.

SPORUM. And this gentleman wishes to assist your husband as a reward for your . . . your . . .

LU. Yes . . . yes . . . At last you understand.

SPORUM. And this gentleman will call on me this morning because you . . . you . . .

LU. That's it, Mr. Sporum. My, but it takes you a long time to get things.

SPORUM. It's unbelievable! How utterly vicious and how fiendishly clever!

LU. Don't look at me so murderously, you awful man! Why, I thought you'd be pleased!

SPORUM *(Indignantly).* Do you think everyone is as corrupt as you are? There are still some people who have moral scruples.

LU. Oh, excuse me, I didn't know that.

SPORUM. How horrible! How perfectly horrible! A monster with a pretty face.

LU. All right, then . . . If that's the way you feel about it, I'll confess everything and call it all off!

SPORUM *(Furious).* Don't do that!

LU *(Happily).* Then you accept?

SPORUM. Certainly not!

LU *(Sadly).* You don't accept?

SPORUM. No . . . that is to say . . . Wait a minute. *(Excitedly)* It isn't as simple as that. You just wait a minute please! What's the hurry? You just wait a minute, will you? You've placed me in a very awkward position.

LU. Why? If I were really Mrs. Sporum then you'd have a right to say that, but I'm not.

SPORUM. If you were my wife, nothing like this could happen. Wait! I must try to think clearly. Well, let's consider the facts. How horrible. That man will be here almost immediately! He's already made the appointment!

LU. There, you see, everything I've said is true.

SPORUM. What a dreadful blow! It is all so sudden, too. Just a minute, please . . . I'm so upset . . . My thoughts have scattered to the four winds . . . Oh, it's horrible. *(Shouts, facing her)* What do you want of me?

LU. I'm not asking you to take part in any deep-dyed plot. All I want you to do is to accept. It will give me strength, if someone else's fate depends on it. It will help me to make a decision.

SPORUM *(Blustering)*. Let me see . . . if you haven't as yet . . .

LU. No. But it's been arranged for tonight.

SPORUM. How horrible. It's been arranged! What shall I do?

LU. Why ask me, darling?

SPORUM. What? You call *me* darling!

LU. Why not?

SPORUM *(Blustering)*. Let me see . . . if you haven't as yet . . .

LU. And I haven't. . . .

SPORUM. And it's been arranged for?

LU. Tonight.

SPORUM. Horrible! *(Flaring up)* If you had only held your tongue about how I was to get this contract. I uphold the standard of ethics, so how can I possibly accept? *(Despairingly)* Oh, why did you come here? Why! Why!

LU. Well, when I do a good deed, I hope to get a little something in return . . .

SPORUM *(Suspiciously)*. Ah-h!

LU. Say, a little gratitude, or a little love from somebody.

SPORUM. If you'd only come to me afterwards!

LU. I thought of that, too, but if you'd happened to let slip that you weren't married, the whole thing would have fallen through. I have to be businesslike, even though I am a good fairy.

SPORUM. Oh, never mind about your good fairies! You're not a fairy —you're a little goose.

LU. Really? Oh, you make me so happy, darling. That's my ideal.

SPORUM. Why didn't you say you are my daughter?

LU. Oh, go on! Who does anything for a father? And besides, how was I to know that you were old enough to be my father? But it's a good thing you *are* such a fiftyish old fool, because it seems more likely that I *would* be unfaithful to you . . . right and left.

SPORUM. Right and left?

LU. Yes.

SPORUM. Thanks, awfully. And how did you know that I was poor?

LU. I never make mistakes because I never think. Please, dear Max, don't send me to prison. Don't you see I could have undone everything with a single word? Yet I have come down to earth with a lovely miracle, and I want these dull people on earth to believe in the miracle. Think it over calmly. Let me make you happy. You really deserve it, you dear old idiot, you.

SPORUM *(Exasperated)*. I object to the tone in which . . .

LU. Don't you worry about my tone, darling. A little rudeness will do you good, now that you are weakening.

SPORUM. Witch! . . . goose! . . . witch! . . . you're a perfect cross between a witch and a goose!

LU. Oh, it's a good sign when you begin calling me names. Look here, you must be sensible. Konrad will be here any minute. Afterwards I'm going away forever and you'll be happy . . . Oh, don't be angry . . .

Let's have a little talk. Or shall I go?

SPORUM. Courtesy forbids me to ask you . . . to leave. And, anyway, I know that you wish to stay here till your millionaire arrives so that he will find you with me.

LU. That's right. We might as well be honest about it . . . Although it wasn't so hard to guess, was it, Judge?

SPORUM. I'm not a judge!

LU. No, but you will be, and then you'll laugh.

SPORUM. I won't laugh.

LU. I promise you, you'll be a judge.

SPORUM. I positively will not laugh.

LU *(After a long pause)*. Isn't this too bad? But it's just like me. Now that I should talk I can't think of anything to talk about!

SPORUM. That's the time to keep quiet.

LU. All right. *(Resigns herself. Silence. Looks about her)*

SPORUM. What are you looking for?

LU. The dog.

SPORUM. What dog?

LU. There's a sign outside that says "Beware of the dog."

SPORUM. There is no dog here!

LU. Then what's the sign for?

SPORUM *(Embarrassed)*. Bill collectors.

LU. Oh! What's that over there on the wall?

SPORUM. A map.

LU. What's *that* for?

SPORUM. I have to hang *something* on the wall. *(Pause)* Old masters are too expensive this year.

LU *(After a pause. With a sigh)*.

What's that great big green country over there?

SPORUM. Russia!

LU. What's that little red spot in the corner?

SPORUM. That, my child, is Europe.

LU. Thanks.

SPORUM. That's all right.

LU. I've learned something.

SPORUM. I'm very glad.

(Pause)

LU. I've got a heart but no one in it.

SPORUM *(Bitterly)*. Except me!

LU. Except you, darling.

SPORUM. I'm a fine figure of a man!

LU. Yes . . . for your age . . . May I ask an indiscreet question?

SPORUM. Please do!

LU. I know you're not married, but there's some woman in your life, isn't there?

SPORUM *(Nervously)*. Oh . . . I say . . . really . . .

LU. Then there isn't a woman? *(BELL rings. KAROLINE enters from left, crosses room and exit right. LU looks at KAROLINE and back to SPORUM, meaningly)*

LU. Oh, I see . . . Max, you must make this woman happy!

SPORUM. What?

LU. That girl ought to have a baby by you.

SPORUM. What!

LU. Give her a beautiful baby! It's your duty!

SPORUM. My what?

LU. Your duty! Good gracious, are you deaf? I have to tell you everything twice.

SPORUM. I'm *not* deaf! But you

are so brazen that I always think I haven't heard you correctly.

LU. Don't snap, you funny old bear! *(Smile)* You foundling!

SPORUM. Foundling? That's a libel on my parents. Penal Code, Section 402. I was not a foundling!

LU. To me you are a foundling, darling, because I found you in the telephone book! Don't be angry. That's nothing to be ashamed of. Moses was a foundling, too, and he became . . . general manager!

SPORUM. Tch . . . how perfectly awful!

LU *(Imitating him impishly)*. Perfectly awful!

SPORUM *(As though to himself)*. I'll end by killing her, this tactless glowworm. You're a triple cross between a witch, an idiot and a glowworm.

LU. Thanks.

(KAROLINE *enters; stops in the doorway*)

SPORUM. Who was that?

KAROLINE. A collector . . . for the installment on the books . . . Shakespeare's works.

SPORUM. Have you thrown him out?

KAROLINE. Yes. *(She goes out. Little pause)*

LU. Oh . . . "Midsummer Night's Dream" is so beautiful . . . Titania . . . that *should* have been my name . . . or Puck, perhaps. *(Pause)* I'm much better with music. Without music I can't really be a good fairy.

SPORUM. How are you fairies doing nowadays?

LU. We are dying out!

(Pause)

SPORUM *(To himself)*. Strange! I'm sitting here with her and I don't kill her! I don't know what's the matter with me! *(Looking at* LU*)* Well? What now?

LU. I don't know anything else to talk about. Aren't any more collectors coming?

SPORUM. Oh, certainly!

(The BELL *rings.* SPORUM *nods his head to indicate there's another.—*KAROLINE *enters)*

KAROLINE. A collector from the laundry.

SPORUM. Did you throw him out?

KAROLINE. Yes. (KAROLINE *exit*)

LU. Laundry! I love laundry! *(Pause.* SPORUM *stares)* But then, I need nice undies. *(Pause)* With me they are always on display. Oh, don't misunderstand me, please! *(In tears)* It is one of my greatest sorrows. The first thing they all do is undress me. The painter, the photographer, the tailor, the theatrical manager, the film director, and the doctor. Once I was even undressed by a dentist!

SPORUM. Surely not by force!

LU. Oh no! He just asked me to.

SPORUM. Whereupon you immediately undressed yourself?

LU. Why, of course! You see, I always say to myself . . . you know, I *have* a nice little figure . . . so I always say to myself, "Let the poor boys see it. It makes them happy." . . . Would *you* like to see it? *(Half rising. Lifts her dress coquettishly)*

SPORUM *(In great consternation)*. No, thank you! No . . . no!

LU. That's my one passion—doing good, no matter how it has to be done.

SPORUM. You ought to go on the stage!

LU. Oh, no. I don't want to do

too much good! (DOOR BELL *rings energetically*) Oooh, that's the President!

SPORUM. So you recognize his ring.

LU. No, that's the first time I've heard it. But I know it's the President.

(KAROLINE *enters excitedly*)

KAROLINE. President Konrad is here!

SPORUM *(Presses his hand to his heart)*. Good God!

LU *(Quickly to* KAROLINE*)*. Let him come in, Miss.

SPORUM *(Nervously)*. Wait, Miss Karoline. *(Buries his head in his hands, in a panic of indecision)*

KAROLINE. I can't keep him waiting. Shall I let him come in or not?

LU *(To* SPORUM *in a whisper)*. Let him in. You'll see. He'll act as though he didn't know me. He's going to lie like anything. He is a *real* gentleman! (SPORUM *nods affirmatively to* KAROLINE. *Grips the table.* KAROLINE *exit happily.* LU *speaks to* SPORUM) What's the matter with you?

SPORUM. I'm going to faint in a minute. I'm not used to all this excitement.

(KAROLINE *shows* KONRAD *in and exit*)

KONRAD. My name is Robert S. Konrad.

SPORUM *(Rising and crossing to* KONRAD*)*. I am Max Sporum.

KONRAD. Won't you introduce me to the charming lady?

SPORUM *(Stammering)*. As a matter of fact she is . . . is . . .

LU *(Interrupts)*. Why, Max! Aren't you going to introduce the President?

(Almose fainting with excitement, MAX *points to* KONRAD *and then to* LU*)*

KONRAD *(Steps forward and kisses her hand)*. President Konrad.

LU. I am pleased to meet you, President. Won't you sit down? May I get you a cup of coffee or perhaps you'd prefer tea?

KONRAD. Thank you, Madame. Neither. Well, may I come to the point at once?

SPORUM *(Uneasily)*. As far as I'm concerned, I'd like to say . . .

LU *(Interrupting)*. But, Max . . . *(To* KONRAD*)* Please go on, Mr. President.

KONRAD. Well, my dear Mr. Sporum. I wish to appoint you as the legal representative for Central Europe of my firm, the Argentine Meat Packing and Export Co., Ltd.

LU. Bravo! This month is starting off beautifully! But, Maxie, didn't I predict this morning . . . just when you kissed me? (SPORUM *darts her an angry look*)

KONRAD. We can leave the details for another time. To be brief, we have an immense number of contracts and countless small law-suits, all simple work but a lot of it. Your income would be very considerable.

LU. How lovely! That's what we've always dreamed of . . . when you kissed me . . . *(Another angry look from* SPORUM*)*

KONRAD. Later on, when we are accustomed to working together, there will be larger cases. But for the present I have come here only to learn whether or not you accept.

SPORUM. And, may I ask, sir, why you come to me?

KONRAD *(Blows kiss to* LU, *secretly)*. The Embassy recommended you. Mmm . . . there seems to be a strong odor of lily-of-the-valley here.

SPORUM. That's me, sir. Won't you go on?

KONRAD. Very well. All the particulars which will be of interest to you are contained in a document which I will send you. So that for now that's all I've got to say.

SPORUM. Are you *sure* that I was recommended by your Embassy?

KONRAD. What do you mean by that, Mr. Sporum?

LU. But Maxie, the President is not a fool!

(SPORUM *looks at* LU)

KONRAD. I've become quite a stranger here. That's why I turned to them for advice. You see, we've got law suits, contracts, et cetera. But above all, tax cases, which are especially important to a foreign firm.

LU. Oh, very important!

SPORUM. I am pleased to hear you say that. Just a few months ago I wrote an article for the "Judicial Review" on Legal Rights of Foreign Firms in Tax Cases. Perhaps the article might interest you. Would you care to read it?

KONRAD. Certainly.

SPORUM. I think I've still got a copy left. Excuse me a moment.

(Exit left, with a terrible look at LU. KONRAD *blows kiss to* LU)

LU *(To* KONRAD, *in mock anger).* What did you mean by all those signs?

KONRAD *(Going to her).* They were kisses, my angel!

LU. How dare you, here in my own home, in front of my husband! Are you crazy?

KONRAD. Yes . . . you've driven me crazy! Well, aren't you pleased with me now?

LU. Aside from the kisses, very much pleased.

KONRAD. Then tonight . . . I see you . . . at ten?

LU. Yes. I have decided.

KONRAD. One more thing, Lu.

LU. Yes?

KONRAD. These talks with your husband . . . when he kissed you . . . I go mad when I think that that ugly man . . .

LU *(Turning away).* No details please! Let's not talk about it.

KONRAD. But you must promise me . . . you must swear . . . that you will never again . . . permit him to kiss you . . .

LU. You ask me to be cruel. But I promise. Oh how Max will suffer . . . ! With his temperament and his sense of justice. *(Coquettishly)* You tyrant!

(SPORUM *comes back, papers in hand)*

SPORUM. Here's the article, sir.

KONRAD. Thank you. I will read it later. *(Absent-mindedly crumples papers in pocket)* Well, Mr. Sporum. What about your answer?

LU. I'll leave you two alone now. *(To* SPORUM) And Maxie, I hope you won't go to your club today as you did yesterday without saying goodbye to your little wife. *(She starts for the next room)*

SPORUM. Where are you going?

LU. I'm going to lay out your dinner jacket and dress shirt. *(To* KONRAD) I spoil him so. *(o* SPORUM) You big baby! *(Exit into his apartment)*

KONRAD. What a charming woman! Well, what is your answer?

SPORUM *(Stammering)*. My answer? You want my answer?

KONRAD. You seem to hesitate.

SPORUM. Oh no. It's only my nerves. Yes . . . my shirt and dinner jacket . . . Yes, my nerves are none too good. I don't know whether it will pay me for the sake of fifty or sixty little cases a year.

KONRAD. Fifty or sixty . . . ha ha . . . ! According to our estimate there will be about nine hundred. If conditions don't improve there will be a thousand or more. We can't help running into these nasty little suits, because our business entails so many monthly accounts. And so many people don't pay their monthly instalments. People throw out . . . collectors.

SPORUM *(Weakly)*. I know. It's awful!

(BELL *rings*. SPORUM *jumps*)

KONRAD. I beg your pardon . . . is something the matter?

SPORUM. No, no. It's nothing.

KONRAD. In our budget you will find estimates according to which you will earn forty thousand from contracts and about a hundred thousand from law suits. That makes a total of a hundred and forty thousand yearly, without counting the larger cases.

SPORUM. A hundred and forty thousand a year?

KONRAD. At least.

(SPORUM *grasps his chair, sways and faints*. KONRAD *rings the bell frantically*. KAROLINE *rushes in*)

KAROLINE. What's the matter?

KONRAD. Mr. Sporum has fainted!

SPORUM *(Gasping)*. Forgive me . . . I haven't been feeling well for days. It's the sultry weather.

(KAROLINE *exit*)

KONRAD. Well, Mr. Sporum. Will you accept? I'm in a hurry!

SPORUM. Couldn't I have a little time to think it over?

KONRAD. Ten seconds, Mr. Sporum. *(Looks at his watch. Counting)* One . . . two . . . three . . . six . . . nine . . . ten . . .

LU *(Enters with a shirt)*. Excuse me, President . . . *(To* SPORUM*)* Will this one do, darling?

SPORUM *(Softly, very furiously)*. Now she brings my underwear to the office.

LU *(To* KONRAD*)*. He is so particular about his linen.

KONRAD. What a model housewife you are! Well, what's your answer, Mr. Sporum? Is it yes?

LU *(Persuadingly)*. Of course it's yes.

SPORUM *(Stammering)*. Yes.

KONRAD *(Energetically)*. Did you say yes?

SPORUM *(Surrendering)*. I *said yes!*

LU *(Happily)*. At last, darling . . . at last . . .

SPORUM *(To her under his breath)*. Get out! (LU *exit. To* KONRAD) And when do I start work, sir?

KONRAD. At once.

SPORUM. Is it so urgent?

KONRAD *(Wickedly)*. You have no idea how urgent it is to me, Mr. Sporum!

SPORUM *(Looking at door where* LU *left)*. I see, Mr. President.

KONRAD. You will have to get used to modern methods. *(Indicating furniture)* New office equipment, everything up to date.

SPORUM *(Reeling)*. Certainly ... certainly. *(He is very nervous. He wants to see what* LU *is doing, but hesitates as he reaches the door)*

KONRAD. Later on you will require a more imposing office . . . a larger staff . . . a finer apartment ... a car . . . Furs and jewels for your wife. (SPORUM *looks at him, dazed)*

SPORUM. Yes. But you don't know me. To you I'm merely a pig in a poke.

KONRAD. Sir! Let me tell you this ... when the Ambassador recommends someone to me there is no pig about it—either in a poke or—otherwise. I can't allow you to insinuate that.

SPORUM *(Frightened)*. I beg your pardon, sir. I didn't mean to insult His Excellency the Ambassador.

KONRAD. I should hope not . . . When will the contract be ready?

SPORUM. I will send it to you early tomorrow morning.

KONRAD. No, no —not early! I'll be sleeping late tomorrow. I'm going out on a spree tonight . . . to a night club.

SPORUM. With the Ambassador?

KONRAD. Yes . . . What? Oh no.

SPORUM. Something slim and pretty . . . eh?

KONRAD. Well, you know . . . each to his own taste.

SPORUM. And if I am not too inquisitive, is this—ah—slim—an old affair?

KONRAD. Oh, no. First time tonight. Tonight for the first time!

SPORUM. Bravo! Have a good time in the night club, President.

KONRAD. Thank you, Mr. Sporum. *(They shake hands. Walks to the door, then turns significantly)*

Please remember me to your wife. She is so much in love with you. Ah yes, there are still a few happy marriages!

(Exit. SPORUM *remains alone for a moment. He is deliriously happy.* LU *enters)*

LU. Well darling, are you happy? As happy as I?

SPORUM. I am dazzled . . . bewildered as though in a dream. A hundred and forty thousand! A fairy treasure!

LU. Oh! How beautiful to see someone happy! *(In ecstasy)* I will get you still more business. Much, much more!

SPORUM *(Alarmed)*. Oh, no! I can't have that! I don't want you to. *(Suddenly clutches his head as though worried)* Now, how do matters stand? What are the facts? Oh how my head is swimming! Let's go over the facts. You recommended me. You were entitled to do that . . . *legally*. You are utterly mad and immoral but that's not my fault . . . *legally*. The one who is recommended is not responsible for the recommender's state of mind . . . *legally*. It is the recommender who is responsible that the person recommended is of sound mind and unimpeachable character. And I am both of those . . . *legally*. Thieves and burglars recommend lawyers to each other. Does that reflect upon the lawyers? *(With emphasis)* Certainly not!

LU. All right. Now, kiss me. *(She comes close to him)*

SPORUM. No!

LU. Not passionately, darling. I don't care a fig for that. I want you to kiss me out of gratitude.

SPORUM. I'm not going to kiss

you. I'm like you . . . if I don't like a person . . . I can't. I'm not a lady of the evening.

LU. No. You certainly don't look like one.

SPORUM. Thank God for that . . .And another thing . . . This is an important point. You must be careful. Nothing must happen between you and him until my contract has been signed.

LU. Are you afraid he won't sign afterwards?

SPORUM. No. But if he signs before . . . then at least I shall not be . . . how shall I say it? . . . a third person profiting from feminine immorality.

LU. Legally.

SPORUM (Repeats mechanically). Legally. This is very important to me because of my conscience.

LU. Then we haven't a minute to lose. I'll call Karoline. (Starts to door. SPORUM interrupts)

SPORUM. But . . .

LU. You must dictate the agreement to her at once.

SPORUM. Is it as urgent as that? What time are you going to meet him?

LU. At ten tonight! (Shouting) Karoline! Come in!

SPORUM. And . . .

(KAROLINE enters)

LU. Karoline, my child, come and sit down. (KAROLINE looks surprised) Yes, yes . . . I'm talking to you. Get a pencil and sit down. Mr. Sporum is going to dictate an agreement. (KAROLINE sits down) You've had a great piece of luck, Karoline.

KAROLINE. Good heavens!

SPORUM. Yes. (With trembling voice) A great piece of luck, Miss Karoline. This office must be reorganized at once for big business.

KAROLINE. Big business!

SPORUM. Yes. Big business!

KAROLINE. But Mr. Sporum, you're quite beside yourself!

SPORUM (Wiping away tears of joy). It's joy, Miss Karoline. Joy.

LU (With a wink). Maxie, darling, please start your dictation.

SPORUM (To KAROLINE). Yes. You will type it immediately, and then take it to President Konrad at his hotel, and tell him that I asked him not to sign tomorrow afternoon but this very evening. And . . . (With a significant look at LU) before ten . . . without fail. (In despair) Before ten!!!

LU. Maxie.

SPORUM. Eh? (Going towards her)

LU (In a low voice). I'll say goodbye now. I'm going. I have nothing more to do here. Please don't think I'm to be envied. There is only great unhappiness in store for me. Think of me at ten . . . think of me . . . intensely! (SPORUM sinks his head)

SPORUM. I thank you and I'm deeply moved.

LU. And please pity me very much.

SPORUM. At ten.

LU (With tears in her voice). Yes, dear.

SPORUM (Looks at his watch). Let's adjust our watches. (LU looks at her watch)

LU. I have four thirty. (SPORUM adjusts his watch)

SPORUM. Thank you. (Stands beside her, very much moved)

LU. And now . . . goodbye. You need not worry. You'll never see me again. (On the verge of tears) I only wanted to be your good fairy. And now, you see, I must vanish. *(Dries her tears)*

SPORUM. No tears, please. Let's be strong in this moment. *(To KARO-LINE)* Now take this. *(He dictates, his voice choking with emotion)* Contract . . . between . . . Robert S. Konrad . . . party of the first part, and . . . *(He cannot repress his tears)* Max . . . Sporum . . . attorney-at-law . . . *(Cries silently)* . . . party of the second part . . .

(He turns his back to the audience, crying. KAROLINE also begins to cry. During this speech LU goes slowly to the door)

LU *(Deeply moved. She cries. Then in a whisper to SPORUM).* Maxie, don't forget the baby.

(The door opens slowly. She slips through the door. The door closes slowly)

CURTAIN

ACT THREE

SCENE: SPORUM's *office.*

TIME: *The next afternoon.*

AT RISE: *Large and small parcels are lying all about the office. On the right, three different typing machines are placed upon three chairs.* KARO-LINE *stands by picture at back, with man from picture shop.*

KAROLINE *(To PICTURE MAN).* That's fine, just wait outside. *(To SPORUM)* Mr. Sporum, the picture's here—come and have a look at it. *(She goes to the door and back to picture.* MAN *goes out)*

(SPORUM bursts in like a hurri- cane. He is smoking a large cigar. He has a handful of papers. He doesn't even look at KAROLINE, but throws himself immediately into his chair. He is followed by a CLERK, *who stands at attention in front of his desk.* SPORUM *feverishly ar- ranges his papers and parcels, as he speaks)*

SPORUM. What's the matter, Miss Karoline? What's happened? *(Mak- ing notes)*

KAROLINE. The picture!

SPORUM *(Without looking up).* Has it arrived? *(Puts packages in order)*

KAROLINE. Yes. A few minutes ago. Won't you have a look at it?

SPORUM. That was quick work, Miss Karoline!

KAROLINE. I know it was al- ways your dearest wish to have a pic- ture—so I made the arrangements as quickly as possible. Not only that— but we can have it on credit!

SPORUM. But this is a bit too quick—this change, from one day to another! We only got the contract last night! Here it is hardly past noon and we've already got the pic- ture! God doesn't like such haste, Miss Karoline!

KAROLINE. Didn't you say that it was necessary for us to hurry with the furnishings?

SPORUM. Yes, but not so much— not so much!

KAROLINE *(With enthusiasm).* That's the modern influence. Our client's energy is contagious!

SPORUM *(To the* CLERK*).* Well there's nothing further to discuss, my friend. We are agreed in everything. You enter my service today, and together with Miss Karoline, you will attend to the vastly increased volume of my business. If you can't cope with it—we will engage a third clerk next week!

KAROLINE *(Joyously)*. And a fourth!

SPORUM. Quiet, please. *(To* CLERK*)* You start immediately. *(Noisy hammering outside)* What's all that noise?

KAROLINE. They're fixing the telephone extension.

SPORUM. Already?

KAROLINE. Yes. I gave them a rush order yesterday afternoon. *(Calls to workmen)* You must be more quiet, please.

(The hammering stops)

SPORUM *(Points to one of the packages)*. What's this?

KAROLINE. Letter heads. A new design. I had it done in two languages. Spanish and English. Our new client is an American. South and North. And these are business cards.

SPORUM. And this? *(Pointing to another parcel)*

KAROLINE. Typewriting-paper, carbon-paper, writing pads, blotting-paper, fountain-pens, and an up-to-date desk lamp! We need that badly!

SPORUM *(Testing the lamp)*. Marvelous!

KAROLINE. Well, we just had to buy a few things. We didn't have anything at all. They've been delivering packages since early this morning.

*(*MAN *enters with multigraph machine)*

KAROLINE. Over there—by the wall!

*(*MAN *follows her directions and exit)*

KAROLINE. That's the new multigraph machine.

SPORUM. Wouldn't it be better to put it over there? *(Points to another place)*

KAROLINE. No. We're going to put the safe there!

SPORUM. A safe!

KAROLINE. Why Mr. Sporum! A safe is indispensable! For important documents and money!

SPORUM. But this is going to cost a fortune!

KAROLINE. We simply had to have these things, Mr. Sporum, and besides the bills won't be in until the first of the month.

SPORUM. Splendid! And then we'll pay everyone, Miss Karoline; we'll pay everyone! We won't throw out anybody! We'll pay! We'll pay! You're a treasure, Miss Karoline. You've done everything so quickly.

KAROLINE. Well, modern client, modern methods. I'm so happy, Mr. Sporum. I've been phoning and ordering and receiving since seven o'clock this morning. Perhaps the Ambassador will send us some more clients, who knows?

SPORUM. What a horrible thought!

KAROLINE. Please, take a look at this, Mr. Sporum—

SPORUM *(Not even glancing at the picture)*. I haven't time now. *(To* CLERK *as he hands him some parcels)* This—goes in the small desk! That—in the new cabinet! This—in the old one! These are power-of-attorney forms! These—are large and small envelopes!

KAROLINE. Please, Mr. Sporum —do take a look at the picture!

SPORUM. In a moment! *(To* CLERK*)* These are heavy linen envelopes for mailing over-seas. These are document files, telegraph forms, cable forms, sealing wax, stamps, pads and rubber bands! Karoline! You're the eighth wonder of the world!

KAROLINE. I've ordered forty-seven different items and forty-three have already been delivered—all on credit!

SPORUM (To CLERK). All right, my boy—you may go now! (CLERK exit) Karoline—give me the Bible! (Takes glasses from it, wipes them and inspects the picture) Splendid! Not too expensive, I hope?

KAROLINE. No.

SPORUM. Credit?

KAROLINE. Of course.

SPORUM. Let's leave it there for the present. I'm terribly nervous. I'll have a good look at it later on and decide then where it belongs.—What are these things?

KAROLINE. This is the new filing cabinet, the latest model, it's fire-proof. This . . . is an adding machine, and this . . . a new typewriter.

(PHONE rings)

SPORUM. Hello? What? The Chrysler Company? Just a minute, please. (To KAROLINE) Somebody wants to demonstrate a car for me! What does it mean? Is that some more of your work?

KAROLINE. Yes. That's Order 24. A little Chrysler . . . on easy payments!

SPORUM. Hello? (Into phone) Well, I'll have a look at it! But without any obligation on my part, of course! Very well . . . Yes! To-morrow morning would be convenient, but I'm a very busy man, you know! Right! (Hangs up receiver) Aren't you over-stepping the mark, Miss Karoline?

KAROLINE. Oh, now really—Mr. Sporum—it's only a little four-seater! Why, every lawyer has one!

SPORUM. A four-passenger! Oh, Karoline . . . what a difference between yesterday and today.

KAROLINE. Oh, please . . . don't remind me! (Takes up a paper)

SPORUM. What is that, Miss Karoline?

KAROLINE. Notes. May I report?

SPORUM. Certainly.

KAROLINE (Pointing to a document). This is a contract, which the President signed.

SPORUM. When did he sign it?

KAROLINE. Last night—at exactly half past nine—in his shirt-sleeves!

SPORUM (Startled). What do you mean—shirt-sleeves?

KAROLINE. He was just about to put on his coat. It was half past nine!

SPORUM. Are you sure?

KAROLINE. Of course, Mr. Sporum. I looked at my watch.

SPORUM. Very well. And what is this other paper?

KAROLINE. This is the company's plan of operation . . . drawn up by the legal department! (Picks up another paper) And this . . . is the result of a little figuring I did last night! I couldn't sleep . . . so I made an estimate of our probable monthly income! We'll be able to meet all current expenses and bank an average of 10,000 per month! In twelve months, that makes . . .

SPORUM. One hundred and twenty thousand . . . and in a hundred years twelve millions! Pretty nice, eh? More than I'd hoped for!

KAROLINE. God bless the Embassy!

SPORUM. Dear God! I can't realize it, Miss Karoline! Is it a vision or a dream? I couldn't sleep all night. *(Changes his tone abruptly)* Thank you, Miss Karoline—you may go now! (KAROLINE *exit.* SPORUM *to himself)* Am I a scoundrel? No —not legally! But I'm no longer the paragon I was yesterday! *(Rises. Glances up at the wall)* It's very beautiful—that picture there! I'm going to buy it! *(Enjoys repeating the words differently)* I'm going to buy *it! I'm* going to buy! I'm going to buy a picture! I *like* it and therefore—*I'm going to buy it!* Why not? ... What am I doing? Talking out loud in an empty room like a radio? What's come over me? Am I crazy? *(The* PHONE *rings.* KAROLINE *enters, carrying a new, bright yellow brief case)* Hello? Yes, of course! Now! Yes, half past four . . . Certainly! Any time! I shall be in all afternoon. I'll be delighted to see him! Goodbye! *(Hangs up phone. To* KAROLINE) Mr. Konrad's secretary! Mr. Konrad is coming here!

KAROLINE *(Excitedly).* When?

SPORUM. He's just leaving. He'll be here in half an hour—and of course—everything is upside down!

KAROLINE. All the better! He'll be impressed . . . *(Almost shouting with joy)* . . . with the activity . . . preparation . . organization . . .

SPORUM. Steady, steady! Calm yourself, Miss Karoline! What have you there?

KAROLINE. A gorgeous, new pig-skin brief case. Order No. 29. *(Puts it on his desk)*

SPORUM. Oh, what a beauty! And we must also prepare for our guest! Have we any cognac, cigarettes, cigars? We must offer him something, you know.

KAROLINE. I'll get them immediately! They'll bring the total number of orders to 51. *(Goes to main entrance.* CLERK *brings in packages)* Give them to me, please! *(Takes packages.* CLERK *exit)*

SPORUM. What are those?

KAROLINE *(Hurriedly placing packages on desk).* Orders 46 and 47! Six boxes of pencils . . . a pencil-sharpener . . . 1,000 paper clips . . . and this thing here . . . is a stapling machine. *(Rushes out)*

SPORUM. Ah! A pencil-sharpener! *(Unpacking the machine)* The dream of my childhood! How I longed for one as a boy! And now— at last—I've got it! *I've got it!*

(Begins trying it out)

KAROLINE *(Returns).* The lady is here.

SPORUM. What lady?

KAROLINE. Yesterday's! The crazy one. *(Enter* LU. KAROLINE *exit)*

LU. Good morning.

SPORUM. Hello. What does this mean? Yesterday you said "goodbye" forever—and now you're here again!

LU. Yes. What have you got there?

SPORUM. A pencil-sharpener! Look at it! The dream of my childhood! The dearest wish of Sporum —the boy! I've waited for it for forty years!

LU. And what are all these packages?

SPORUM *(Gleefully).* Preparation! Organization! Equipment! Do have a seat!

LU. Thank you. *(Sits down and heaves a great sigh)* Ah, my friend . . .

SPORUM. What a deep sigh! *(Sympathetically)* My poor, pretty child—I can guess what it means.

LU. Oh—what a night! *(Wipes away a few tears)*

SPORUM. Poor little thing! It must have been perfectly awful! But at any rate . . . it's all over now! You've done it—so it's done with.

LU. Yes, I've done it . . .

SPORUM. Poor child.

LU. Don't pity me, please! I'm *not unhappy!*

SPORUM *(Sarcastically).* Ah! You're happy!

LU. We don't look at it quite the same way. There's just a little difference. *(Look from* SPORUM*)* I don't think it's of the least importance—legally.

SPORUM. And what is this difference?

LU. I . . . I've met someone. But . . . not him.

SPORUM. Not him?

LU. No. Someone else?

SPORUM. But at ten o'clock last night . . .

LU. I didn't keep the appointment!

SPORUM. Then what did you do?

LU. I didn't go till eleven—and then—not to him, but—to someone else! What did you say these packages were?

SPORUM. Preparation! Organization! Equipment!

LU. Didn't you get too much?

SPORUM. We needed a good many things.

LU. I'm afraid . . . you won't need that many. You won't have so much to do after all! I'm afraid you won't have anything to do!

SPORUM. Why? What's happened?

LU. He caught me! *(Long pause.* KAROLINE *enters)*

KAROLINE *(In a low voice).* Excuse me, but the man is getting impatient about the picture!

SPORUM. Wait . . . my child! The fate of the picture is just being decided! I'll let you know in a few moments! (KAROLINE *exit)* Well . . . so he caught you, eh?

LU. Yes! He caught me . . .

SPORUM. Isn't it funny? Now . . . I don't know what to ask you next?

LU. You should ask me with *whom* he caught me! . . .

SPORUM. Well . . . with whom did he catch you?

LU. With someone else.

SPORUM *(Angrily).* A charming answer, that! I'm so confused! I don't understand at all . . .

LU. Unfortunately, it's very simple! I couldn't meet him for money! I made a last try . . . but I couldn't! So that's that! Now, I'll never try again! I'm happy. It's only you I'm sorry for.

SPORUM *(Rings the bell.* KAROLINE *enters. She leaves the door open behind her).* We don't want the picture, Karoline!

(KAROLINE *beckons through the door.* MAN *enters and removes picture; out with* KAROLINE. LU *and* SPORUM *look blankly to front during this)*

LU. Yesterday . . . I kept hoping I could . . . until the evening. At ten o'clock . . - it still seemed quite likely . . . that we'd both be rich. Then at eleven . . . I decided . . . For a moment I thought of you intensely . . . but I couldn't. I felt sure you wouldn't have expected it of me.

SPORUM. God forbid!

LU. I knew you wouldn't!

SPORUM. And so you decided all by yourself . . .

LU. What difference does that make?

SPORUM. Well . . . did someone help you to decide?

LU. Yes . . . someone did . . . at the last moment!

SPORUM. Who was it?

LU. The other one!

SPORUM (Explosively). And you listened to such a scoundrel?

LU. Scoundrel?

SPORUM (Shouting). Do you mean to say that . . . this unscrupulous blackguard . . . this unspeakable cad . . . exercised more influence over you, than the voice of your own convictions? You . . . you little idiot?

LU. Look here! Why are you calling me names?

SPORUM. I'm not calling you names! I'm talking about this man! To be frank . . . I don't know what I'm talking about! (Sits down very suddenly)

LU (Trying to comfort him). Come . . . be nice to me, darling, won't you? (Points to wall) Look! The map is much prettier than the picture! It's nice and bright! There's imagination in it!

SPORUM. Yes. (To himself, meditatively) What a scoundrel!
        (Pause)

LU. We're sitting here just like yesterday . . . when we were waiting for him!

SPORUM (Bitterly). There's just a little difference.

LU. Which, however . . .

SPORUM (Scathingly). Is not of the least importance . . . legally, I mean. (He bursts out suddenly) It all came so suddenly . . . And now this awful change. Oh, forgive me.

LU. Go ahead! Please shout, if it relieves you!

SPORUM (Shouts). Why, oh why —did all this have to happen?

LU. Because we cheated him!

SPORUM. We?

LU. Well, I did! Or rather . . . I didn't cheat him . . . I merely failed to keep my part of the bargain!

SPORUM. And subsequently, made your offense even more serious by . . .

LU. . . . keeping the bargain with someone else!

SPORUM. And . . . further aggravated the situation . . . by allowing him to . . .

LU. . . . catch me.

SPORUM. Full stop! That will do. I haven't had a case as clearly stated in this office for years! (Forlornly) Goodbye — packages — machines, clips — and envelopes! (Rings bell. KAROLINE enters immediately. She stops in the doorway) Karoline—all the packages must be returned.

KAROLINE. Good heavens!

SPORUM. Karoline! One of your best qualities . . . is that you never ask questions. (KAROLINE tries to speak) In this instance . . . I must particularly request you not to.

KAROLINE. Very well, Mr. Sporum. I'll make the necessary arrangements at once! We've received 51 items. Now, I'll have to count backwards!

SPORUM (As she is about to go). Karoline, there is a tear in your eye.

KAROLINE (Heroically). Two, Mr. Sporum. Two. (Exit)

SPORUM. What a pity! As a matter of fact—well, let's be honest about it—it was beastly of me! But

I'd explained it away so brilliantly to my own conscience! It was one of my best legal efforts!

LU. A legal mind must be a great comfort.

SPORUM. It's a strange thing—it isn't the picture that I mind losing. It's the pencil sharpener. (LU *nods.* SPORUM *hangs his head. Long pause*) I don't suppose he'll forgive you?

LU. That's out of the question.

SPORUM. It must have been a great disappointment to President Konrad.

LU. Yes.

SPORUM. But he didn't have any claims on you . . .

LU. No claims—but hopes—and they hurt more.

KAROLINE (*Entering*). President Konrad is here.

LU (*Running to the door of the apartment*). I'm not here . . . and I haven't been here! (*Runs out*)

SPORUM (*To* KAROLINE). Show him in.

(KAROLINE *goes out and returns with* KONRAD. SPORUM *receives* KONRAD *with great dignity*)

SPORUM. This is an honor, President. Will you have something to drink? Cognac, cigars, cigarettes? Please have a seat here! You're looking very well, indeed.

KONRAD. I'm surprised to hear that, Mr. Sporum. I had a very bad night. What are all these packages?

SPORUM. Preparation! Organization! Equipment!

KONRAD. I see, well, well, . . . may I . . .

SPORUM. Oh! please, Mr. President— (*Indicates* KONRAD *to sit*)

KONRAD. Are we alone?

SPORUM (*Rings bell. Through door*). Karoline? (KAROLINE *appears*) We are not to be disturbed, Miss Karoline. (KAROLINE *nods and exit*) Well sir?

KONRAD (*Sits down*). Can anyone hear me?

SPORUM. Oh, no.

KONRAD. No danger of eavesdropping?

SPORUM. Oh, never! You . . . you alarm me!

KONRAD. I'm afraid I'll have to!

SPORUM. For God's sake . . . has anything happened?

..KONRAD (*Wryly*). It has! Please listen.

SPORUM. Yes, sir! Well . . .

KONRAD. You'll be surprised to hear what I'm about to say, but in the end, you'll realize that I was forced to tell you everything—no matter how unusual it may be.

SPORUM. I am listening, sir.

KONRAD. Last night I got into my car outside of the hotel . . .

SPORUM. At what time?

KONRAD. At eleven! I had a —an—appointment at ten— (*Look between them*)—but it had been previously cancelled!—So, as I've said —at eleven o'clock, I got into my car outside the hotel! Not at the main entrance, but at the side entrance, where the cars are parked. As a matter of fact—it was in front of the service entrance! Please note that: because it's very important—*the service entrance.* Just ahead of my car was a taxi. We both started at exactly the same time, but as the taxi was trying to pull out of the row of cars, it suddenly backed—without warning— collided with us and smashed my brand new headlamps! The lamps had only been fitted to the car the day before. They had been made especially for me at the factory and cost a small fortune! Almost as much as some cars! Well, the taxi smashed them for me and then proceeded to drive off—without paying any attention whatever! I was so furious, that I said to my chauffeur: "Albert, follow that taxi and catch up with it—even if it takes till tomorrow morning!" You see, my car is insured against damage, but the lamps mentioned in the policy, were two cheap lamps, which I had replaced with the more expensive ones, so that I didn't know whether or not the Insurance Company would have to make good my loss! Well, we chased the taxi all over the city—never losing sight of it for a moment! At last, it stopped in front of a house! It stopped—and who do you think got out of it? Hold tight, Mr. Sporum —a waiter at my hotel—and . . . your charming wife, Mrs. Max Sporum! (SPORUM *remains calm and motionless*) The waiter paid the driver, offered his arm to Mrs. Sporum and led her into the house— where, I later learned—he lives! *(Pause)—The waiter!* (SPORUM *still sits motionless*) I was so amazed that I decided to wait! I waited to see when your wife would come out! Well, sir—for your information—they went in at ten minutes past eleven—and it was exactly half past two—when they came out again. (SPORUM *shows no sign of emotion whatever*) Your wife then took a taxi and drove off, but not before she and the waiter had exchanged a long, lingering kiss— which lasted so long . . . that it made me sick to watch it! (KONRAD *pauses, leans back . . . then leans*

forward to SPORUM) Well, what do you say to that?

SPORUM *(With decision).* The case is clear. The Insurance Company *must* pay for the lamps.

KONRAD *(Jumps to his feet).* What? Is that all you have to say?

SPORUM. Yes. The theory of the "navis refecta" . . .

KONRAD. What?

SPORUM. —or—"the renovated ship"—was already known in Roman law. If, in the course of time, every individual part of a ship were replaced by a new part, the vessel, nevertheless, remained one and the same legal entity. The insurance on your care, therefore, includes all the fittings.

KONRAD *(Derisively).* Magnificent! And have you nothing to say to your wife's spending the night with a waiter?

SPORUM. With a waiter?

KONRAD *(Contemptuously).* Well, a waiter of a good hotel, if that makes any difference.

SPORUM. Please don't get excited. You must forgive me if I have only considered the legal aspect. Force of habit, you know . . . but now I'm beginning to understand. So the lady spent quite a time with the waiter?

KONRAD. Quite a time.

SPORUM. And you waited in the street until dawn?

KONRAD. Yes.

SPORUM. In other words . . . you were spying on her?

KONRAD. What does this mean? Are you angry with me?

SPORUM. No. I'm not angry with you, but it seems *rather odd* that you should sit in your car . . . from eleven to half past two, when it had nothing to do with you. What concern was it of yours?

KONRAD. I say! I'm really amazed! I admire you, Mr. Sporum! You've got nerves of steel!

SPORUM. Let's stick to the point. Will you kindly answer a few questions?

KONRAD. Certainly! Fire ahead!

SPORUM (As though cross-examining). You saw the features of the lady under discussion, quite clearly?

KONRAD. Distinctly.

SPORUM. Did she wear a veil?

KONRAD. No.

SPORUM. Wasn't it dark?

KONRAD. She was standing under a street lamp.

SPORUM. Aren't you near-sighted?

KONRAD. No, I'm far-sighted.

SPORUM. I must point out that you had only seen the lady once in your life—that was yesterday—here in this office—and then for a very short time! How is it possible—that you were able to recognize her—in a fraction of a second—on an exceedingly dark night?

KONRAD (Excited). I beg your pardon, but you are examining me, as though I were the defendant! I'm not! I'm the plaintiff!

SPORUM. I beg your pardon, but the plaintiff must prove his case.

KONRAD (Mockingly). I think I understand you, sir. You're the typical husband. You're building me a bridge, over which I may retreat—but retreat is out of the question! I have not told you all! There is something else which makes retreat impossible and—proves my case—as well.

SPORUM. Well?

KONRAD. I spoke to Mrs. Sporum.

SPORUM. When she went in—or when she came out?

KONRAD. When she came out!

SPORUM. And what did you say to her?

KONRAD. I said: "Madame, I've seen what I've seen and I warn you that there will be consequences!"

SPORUM. And what did she say to that?

KONRAD. She said, "You bet." And then she boxed my ears. (They catch each other's eye) She boxed my ears in the presence of the waiter and my chauffeur. It struck me like a blow in the face.

SPORUM (Calmly). She was quite right!

KONRAD (Rises). WHAT?

SPORUM. Why did you spy on her?

KONRAD (Furiously). I was trying to get the taxi's number! I had to have it!

SPORUM. But you didn't have to have it, because the Insurance Company has got to pay you! I've just told you so!

KONRAD. But I hadn't talked to you then . . .

SPORUM. Why didn't you come to me first?

KONRAD. Because you might have said that the Insurance Company didn't have to pay and I might never have found the taxi!

SPORUM. No, but then—you wouldn't have had your ears boxed! That's logic, Mr. President! That's logic!

KONRAD (Glares at SPORUM a minute). Well, we won't discuss the matter any further, Mr. Sporum. The fact is that your wife has boxed my ears in the presence of two witnesses! I'm not going to take her to Court— nor am I going to demand satisfaction from you, but you must realize, that under the circumstances, we cannot continue our relations. Either business or social! I, therefore, trust that you will deem it quite natural, if I avail myself of the cancellation clause in our contract—and terminate it forthwith.

SPORUM *(Gasps)*. Terminate— contract—forthwith . . . *(Faints)*

(KONRAD *rings.* KAROLINE *enters)*

KONRAD *(Ironically)*. Mr. Sporum has fainted—as usual!

(KAROLINE gives him some *water.* SPORUM *recovers. Exit* KAROLINE)

SPORUM. I beg your pardon!

KONRAD. I'm amazed at you! Now—you faint! But a little while ago, when I proved to you that your wife . . . you sat there like a—a—as if it didn't concern you at all!

SPORUM. That was because you gave me the impression of a jilted lover, who wanted to revenge himself on a lady.

KONRAD. Mr. Sporum! Do you know what impression you give me? *(Shaking a finger at him)* Mr. Sporum!—Mr. Sporum!

SPORUM. Well? . . . Well?

KONRAD. You . . . you impress me as a husband who views his wife's infidelity with remarkable tolerance.

SPORUM. What do you mean by that?

KONRAD. "THAT!" . . . you've guessed the very word! *That's* what I mean!

SPORUM *(Shouts)*. Sir!

KONRAD. I'm beginning to see how wise I was in breaking off our business relations!

SPORUM *(Calmly)*. Look here, Mr. President. You're a practical man. You came here yesterday intending to make me your legal representative. Today you've withdrawn your offer. So further discussion is useless. Now then . . . you get out of here and get out as quickly as possible . . . for if you are *not* quick about it . . . I'll land you a kick in the traditional place . . . and with both feet at once! That kick is a specialty of mine!

KONRAD. I shan't give you the chance, Mr. Sporum. *(Starts for the door. Enter* LU)

LU. Ah, Mr. President? You here?

KONRAD *(Close to the door)*. I am just leaving, Madame.

LU. When are we to have the pleasure of seeing you again?

KONRAD. Well . . . I . . . not in the very near future.

LU. Well—you wouldn't find me here in any case! There's no need to make a secret of it to such a good client, is there? *(Turns to* KONRAD) We're going to get a divorce!

KONRAD. Is that so?

LU. Yes! We're going to get a divorce. A perfectly friendly divorce! Baby has been so kind and noble and now he'll be all alone.

KONRAD. Oh, so baby will be all alone, eh? And you?

LU. I'll probably marry again. A distinguished restaurant proprietor. It would be very nice if you would . . .

KONRAD *(Furiously)*. If I became a customer?

LU. Yes! And if you would recommend the restaurant to a few of the better-class Bank Presidents!

It would be so kind of you . . . if you'd give my future husband a lift!

KONRAD. Of course, Madame! I'd be delighted!

LU. My future husband deserves it.

KONRAD. Oh, that's quite irrelevant! *(Pause)*

LU. Will you take a liqueur?

KONRAD. No, thanks. I'll take my leave. Goodbye, Madame! *(To* SPORUM*)* Goodbye—BABY!

(SPORUM *makes as though to kick him.* KONRAD *rushes out)*

LU *(To* SPORUM*))*. Tell me, darling . . . what does "irrelevant" mean?

SPORUM. It means beside the point!

LU *(Relieved)*. Oh, thanks!

SPORUM. Now . . . look at the situation you've placed me in.

LU. Oh, forgive me, Mr. Sporum —but it was a very simple situation! *(Rapidly)* First, he had to act as though I didn't know that you knew! I had to act as though I didn't know that you knew it from him! And you had to act as though—you didn't know that I knew that you knew! That's simple . . .

SPORUM. Awfully simple.

LU. And *irrelevant!*

SPORUM. Ah, I feel so relieved! What joy! The nightmare is over.

LU. Are you happy, darling? As happy as I?

SPORUM. Yes, I *am* happy! I'm really happy!

LU. And you've got me to thank for it again!

SPORUM. Yes . . . again! I do thank you, my child! I'm no longer a scoundrel! I'm pure again. *(To* KAROLINE, *who comes in)* What's happening about the packages?

KAROLINE. They're being returned, just as you said! I've been counting backwards! There were fifty-one and now there are only twenty-six! Twenty-five!

SPORUM. All right, Karoline! It was only a dream!

KAROLINE. A dream?

SPORUM. Yes! And now we're coming back to reality again! Back to a clear conscience. Moral integrity and its natural consequences: beer and salami. (KAROLINE *gets brief case from table)* Are you returning the brief case as well? (KAROLINE *nods. He takes brief case)* Thank heaven! It was too beautiful—Farewell, fickle blonde! Farewell! *(Gives brief case back to* KAROLINE. *She exit with the brief case)*

LU. Well, I'm going too. I'll only stay until the waiter calls for me. I asked him to come here, so I could introduce him to you.

SPORUM. That was very thoughtful of you. Thanks.

LU. What's the matter, darling? Will seeing the waiter hurt you?

SPORUM. Well . . . you know, my child . . . when I come to think of it . . .

LU *(Gently and ecstatically)*. Max! A fairy belongs to the whole world! To people . . . to animals . . . to flowers . . . to waiters . . .

(Pause)

SPORUM. Listen, dear child. I'd like to say something that will surprise you.

LU. Well?

SPORUM. Now . . . I'd like you to kiss me!

LU. Kiss you?

SPORUM *(Embarrassed)* Yes.

LU. Passionately?

SPORUM. Well . . . yes. Please, kiss me passionately.

LU. That's interesting. Yesterday . . . you didn't want to.

SPORUM. That was different. Now, there are no moral obstacles.

LU. Oh yes, there are, Maxie! Brand new ones.

SPORUM. What new ones? *(Enter* KAROLINE) Have you thrown . . .

KAROLINE. No . . . it wasn't a collector . . . it was a gentleman. He is calling for the lady.

LU. Show him in. *(Enter* WAITER) Here he is. The new moral obstacle.

(Exit KAROLINE)

SPORUM. Oh, so you are the waiter in question?

LU. Yes. Let me introduce you. Mr. Sporum—the Scoundrel!

SPORUM. Happy to meet you.

LU. He's my fiancé. I'm going to marry him.

SPORUM. Why?

LU. Because he wants to marry me. The only man a girl should have —is the man who wants to marry her.

SPORUM. That sounds convincing.

WAITER. Mr. Sporum—it was my duty—to interfere—last night! It wasn't that we didn't think of you— we did! Lu cried. She said: "Now Mr. Sporum will have to starve again!"

SPORUM. And what did you say?

WAITER. I said: "What of it?"

SPORUM *(Shaking him by the hand)*. Very considerate.

WAITER. Forgive me, but I didn't feel that we owed you anything.

LU. But *I* do! *(To* WAITER) Now that I've introduced you—wait outside. I have a last request to make of Mr. Sporum. (WAITER *exit*)

SPORUM. Well, my child?

LU *(Comes close to him)*. I want to ask you, darling . . . it's like this! My fiancé is opening a small restaurant . . . I want you to . . .

SPORUM. Eat there?

LU. Oh, no, I needn't ask you that. That goes without saying. We're going to have very distinguished customers—bankers, presidents—Ministers—etc. I want to ask you to do something else for me. You see— there are so many legal difficulties when you buy a restaurant. Contracts — transfers — taxes — fees — commissions — and lawyers are so expensive. Won't you attend to all that for my fiancé?

SPORUM. For nothing?

LU. Yes. For nothing. All right!

SPORUM. All right.

LU. You know . . . I never ask anything for myself . . .

SPORUM. Yes, I know.

LU. But to help others is my specialty. Now, I'm *his* . . . good fairy! You'll do it, won't you?

SPORUM. Certainly. With pleasure.

LU. And . . . for nothing?

SPORUM. Yes . . . for nothing!

LU. Come there to eat—we'll give you a good meal!

SPORUM. For nothing?

LU. Oh, *no!* Not for nothing— but a little cheaper! (LU *leans over his shoulder)* Come and have a look at the place! Make a note of the address: 427 Elizabeth Street. "Restaurant of the Good Fairy!"

SPORUM. Yes. I'll make a note of it. *(Turns on desk lamp. Picks up a pencil and fits it into the pencil-sharpener. He sharpens the pencil very, very slowly)* Just a moment, please—I want to sharpen my pencil —with this—before—they take it away—(To see more clearly, he ad-

justs the lamp. The light illumines his face. He goes on talking in a low voice, while he slowly turns the handle)

LU *(In the meantime, she has tip-toed to the door. The room darkens very gradually. She whispers softly as the door opens slowly and she creeps out).* Four—hundred—and—twenty-seven — Elizabeth Street —

"Restaurant Good Fairy." *(She slips out. The door closes slowly.)*

SPORUM *(Doesn't realize that she has departed. He continues to speak softly, as he turns the handle of the machine).* I am sharpening—my pen-cil—for the first—and last time—with this—lovely—pencil-sharpener . . .

(Stage darkens, as the

CURTAIN FALLS

EPILOGUE

(The MANAGER *steps before the curtain)*

MANAGER. Please don't go, ladies and gentlemen. With your kind permission, I have a little experiment to try for you tonight. *(He recollects himself)* Forgive me. I should have introduced myself. I am the producer of this play. *(He smiles nervously)* I tell you that so that you won't mis-take me for an actor. One has to make these distinctions nowadays, hasn't one? *(He takes the audience more into his confidence)* Now about the experiment. I thought I should take advantage of this moment of silence . . . *(Sounds of scene shifting back stage distract him.)* This mo-ment of SILENCE! . . . *(Silence back stage. Another apologetic smile)* While the scenery is being shifted. . . . Yes. . . . Well, as I was saying, you may think you've seen the end of this play, but you're wrong! That wasn't an ending. Why, when I read the manuscript, I sat down at once and wrote to the author. "My dear friend," I said, "isn't it about time that you authors learned that audi-ences insist on endings that ARE end-

ings? You simply can't leave your characters up in the air the way you've done in this play. The Public wants to know what really becomes of char-acters!" *(His indignation changes to the confidential tone)* Incidentally, I HOPE we managers know what the public wants. I mean to say, where would we managers be if we didn't know? A lot of our plays would fail! *(He draws a letter from his pocket and opens it.)* Well, the author wrote a most gracious reply to my letter. I'll read you what he wrote. *(Read-ing)* "My dear friend," he says, "you are absolutely right." *(He looks more closely at the letter. He con-tinues)* "We authors have fallen into the bad habit of ending our plays with the final curtain, which, of course, is no ending at all, since every story goes on for ages. Of course, you realize that your sugges-tion makes the dramatist's work very much harder. However, I find your argument so convincing that I enclose a little scene I have written especially for your theatre, and which you will be good enough to have performed after the play, so that the audience may gaze for a moment into the future lives of the characters whose acquaintance they have made. I remain most sincerely yours . . . " *(He looks up)* That's all. And that's the experiment we're trying tonight. Now, if you'll be good enough to sit where you are for 10 years more . . . 10 years, yes; we'll show you what really became of the characters in this fairy tale. Of course, most of the 10 years have passed while I've been speaking. That is, the actors have changed their clothes, they have. *(He trns to speak off stage)* Everything ready? *(He is satisfied)* All right. Go ahead. *(To audience)* The 10 years have passed. Now you'll see! LET THE CURTAIN RISE!

(The MANAGER bows and retires behind the curtain. The theatre is slowly darkened. It is pitch black when the curtain rises. The scene is in the same private dining room as in Act I. In the center, is a richly decorated table. Six places have been set. A large basket of flowers is on a chair. At first, nothing is visible. Only LU's voice is heard. She is chatting merrily with KAROLINE.)

LU *(Walking about the table)*. It's sweet of you to help me, darling! You know, darling—I simply adore beautifully appointed tables!

(The lights go up slowly. LU is busy arranging the table decorations. She arranges things and walks to and fro feverishly. Finally, she joins KAROLINE at the table. LU has not changed, but KAROLINE has stoutened. They are both in evening dress. The men who will enter will also be in evening dress. They will look slightly aged and are getting grey. KAROLINE is walking around the table.)

LU. You know, darling, I don't like to rely on others. I'd rather do everything myself. Everything myself. *(Lights go up completely)* Doesn't the table look gay, darling?

KAROLINE. It's really lovely.

LU *(Looking table over)*. Now come and help me scatter the flowers sort of — carelessly! *(KAROLINE helps)* You know, dear, I like cut flowers strewn about far better than the conventional bunches in the middle! *(Takes flowers out of bowl. KAROLINE takes bowl to serving table. They arrange flowers)*

LU. But I can't deny that I'm excited! It's touching, somehow, to think that I've lived to see the tenth anniversary of my marriage!

KAROLINE. And how young you've kept, dear!

LU. That's because I'm happy and I've got my husband to thank for that! He's a perfect husband! Good gracious! *Ten years!* Ten years today . . . we've been married!

KAROLINE. How time flies . . .

LU. Yes. Time flies . . . Put a few more flowers over there. You know, dear . . . I chose this dining room for our anniversary dinner because I've so many memories of the only other evening I spent here . . . ten years ago. It was here that all our fates were decided. Put a few more flowers over there, too, darling. Not so many flowers there. That's too many. *(KAROLINE puts flowers around table during all this)* It'll be strange to dine here with my guests. Please put the place cards on the glasses. It's incredible. I've invited them for eight o'clock and not one of them is here yet. Everyone is late, except you. And what do you think of my husband's being late, too? He ought to be the first to arrive. It's awful for a husband to be late on his tenth anniversary.

KAROLINE. The most important thing is that he was on time for the wedding.

LU. That's true! Oh, dear . . . what time is it?

KAROLINE. It's one minute past eight.

LU. Incredible. Half past eight and my husband isn't here yet! (WAITER *enters*) At last, you've arrived, darling! At nine o'clock! *(Embraces him. They kiss)* What kept you so long, darling?

WAITER. I met a friend and couldn't get rid of him.

LU. Well, sit down, darling! *(He sits in chair placed by* LU) No, get up and have something to drink! *(To* KAROLINE) Give my Charlie something to drink, Karoline! (KAROLINE *gets drink from serving table)*

WAITER. Thanks. Thanks very much.

LU. Now come and help us a little. Let's put the chairs around the table. (KAROLINE *takes chair and puts it at upper end of table.)* No, no, here. *(Indicating other end of table.* WAITER *puts armchair to the end of table)* I like my guests to be seated comfortable . . . not squeezed together like sardines. There's going to be a marvelous dinner. A magnificent capon as big as an eagle. I saw him on the spit. Don't smile. There never was anything like it in your restaurant. The beer was good but the food was simply terrible! That's why you went broke. Have a cigarette. *(Hands box from table)* You weren't born to be a restaurant proprietor. You're lucky they were willing to take you back here. Some people are born leaders, others must serve.

WAITER. If you had married me —things would have gone better.

LU *(Arranging the tables).* Oh, don't say that! We were very wise to part while we were engaged—rather than after we were married!

WAITER. That really doesn't change matters! We parted—that's the point—and you married someone else! It was a good thing for you— but a bad thing for me!

LU. Don't get sentimental. You'd better open the bottle instead! (WAITER *goes to serving table)* We want to be merry tonight! Oh, dear —isn't it awful? Nine o'clock—and my husband isn't here yet! (SPORUM *enters)* At last, darling. Half past nine. *(She embraces him. They kiss)* Why is it that my one and only Max is never on time? Where have you been so long?

SPORUM. One of my students called on me and I couldn't send him away.

LU. When you had no money you were always on time!

SPORUM. Why not? I had nothing to do then. But now—that I'm a university professor . . .

LU *(Interrupts him).* What's the matter with you, Max? Aren't you going to kiss your wife?

SPORUM *(Crossing to* KARO-LINE). Of course I am, but you talk so much that I haven't had a chance to. *(Kisses* KAROLINE)

KAROLINE. Did the children go to bed?

SPORUM. Yes, my angel. Don't worry, they're all asleep.

LU. All six?

SPORUM *(Sighs)*. Yes, all six!

LU *(Busying herself again)*. Don't sigh, Max! You ought to be glad that you have a steady income and six beautiful, healthy children as well! There's nothing nicer than that! Karoline should be very proud of herself!

KAROLINE. And so I am! Still —it's a bit too much!

LU. Well, when your fourth child was born—I told you to call a halt! But, lo and behold—there were two more after that!

SPORUM. It was *my* fault!

LU. Oh, I'm *sure* of *that*, my dear! *(To* WAITER) Let me have those small glasses, please. Thanks. *(Gives glasses to* KAROLINE. *To* SPORUM) As you see, my former fiancé has also been invited! *(*SPORUM *looks around)* Sit down, Max. What are you staring at?

SPORUM. It's funny. This is the first time I've ever been in this room.

LU. Yet it was in this room that I found you . . . in the telephone book! Won't you have a drop of Vermouth? *(To* WAITER) Give him a glass of Vermouth? *(Takes drink to* SPORUM, *puts arm round his neck. To* KAROLINE) Oh, you're looking at my bracelet? It's my husband's anniversary present!

KAROLINE. How many diamonds are there in it?

LU. Forty small ones and five large ones! *(To* WAITER) Did you tell them to give my chauffeur his dinner?

WAITER. Of course.

LU. See that he gets a little champagne. But not too much! Oh, dear . . . Now I'm really upset! It's very rude of my husband to be so late!

It's half past nine! The guests are here—and my husband isn't! *(*KON-RAD *enters)* At last, darling! But it's ten o'clock. *(She embraces him. They kiss)* Why did you keep us waiting? Where have you been?

KONRAD. I had to talk long distance and I couldn't get through for some time. *(Bows to the others)*

LU *(Gets drink from* WAITER). Well, have a drink, dear! We want to be merry tonight! *(He drinks it)* Do you still love me?

KONRAD. Always . . . and forever!

LU. Then have another drink! *(*LU *takes his glass back to* WAITER) Do you love Professor Sporum, too?

KONRAD. Since I have known his life's story . . . I am extremely fond of him! What an attractive table! And wasn't it charming of you to choose *this* room?

LU. Do you still remember?

KONRAD. Oh, don't I, though?

LU *(Pointing to* WAITER). My former fiancé is also here! *(*WAITER *crossing to* KONRAD *offers* KONRAD *a Vermouth with his right hand)*

KONRAD. So—you're a waiter here again ,eh!

WAITER. Yes. But tonight I am one of the guests.

KONRAD. Bravo!

> *(Offers to shake hands with him.* WAITER *quickly transfers glass to left hand. They shake hands.* WAITER *transfers the glass back to right hand and offers it to* KONRAD. WAITER *crosses back to serving table)*

KONRAD *(Drinks)*. Thanks.

LU *(Busying herself again)*. So! Everything is all right now and dinner could be served—if only my husband were here. *(To* KONRAD) You must excuse him for being late—but I'm sure he's doing something in the interests of your firm.

KONRAD. Very likely! We're lucky to have here such a brilliant manager. We owe him to you, little Fairy! It was you who recommended him!

LU. And it was you who made him rich . . . so we're quits! But, dear me! It's half past ten! Isn't it maddening, that my husband isn't here? (METZ enters) At last you're here! At eleven o'clock! (She embraces him. They kiss) How could you be so late? Where have you been? What's been keeping you?

METZ. My secretary delayed me. There were a thousand details to be attended to. (Mutely greets the others. Looks at his watch) Six minutes past eight, exactly!

LU. Don't make excuses! You were all late! Dinner was ordered for eight o'clock sharp and it's really too bad, that my husband and guest of honor—should be the last to arrive!

KONRAD (Jovially). Now look here . . . I can't have the "pride and joy" of my firm run down!

LU (To the others). Ten years haven't been enough for me to teach him to be punctual! Having once been a politician—he can't get out of the habit of being late! He makes me very happy—but he's never on

time! (Kisses METZ) Do you remember this room, where you behaved so badly?

(They join hands and turn back to audience, looking over the room)

METZ. How could I forget it? (Kisses LU's hand)

LU. I've punished you for it with ten years of marriage!

METZ. Punished me? (To the others) Did you hear that? I, who have had ten years of bliss . . . all of which, I owe to my dear little wife!

LU (Interrupts him). Don't be sentimental! It's getting late! Take your seats! You'll find your names on the place cards! (LU sits end of table. They sit down. To WAITER) Tell your comrades outside to start serving dinner! (WAITER goes to the door and gives a signal. He returns to his place and sits down) I hope you're all hungry, because we're going to have such a dinner! (The stage begins to darken) I can say with pride you will have a dinner . . . (It is growing darker rapidly) . . . which I am sure will please you all. (They chatter merrily) I take all the credit for it . . .

(She continues to talk gaily. It becomes almost pitch dark. Nothing can be seen; only the company's merry bantering can be heard, as the curtain falls)

CURTAIN

ANNIVERSARY DINNER

ANNIVERSARY DINNER

COMEDY IN ONE ACT

CHARACTERS

HOST, 50
HOSTESS, 43
DOCTOR, 55
DOCTOR'S WIFE, 45
HIGH GOVERMENT OFFICIAL, 50-55
OFFICIAL'S WIFE, 43-45
A LADY, 30-40
YOUNG MAN, 25-30
DETECTIVE, 48-50
BUTLER
MANSERVANT (silent part)

PLACE : ANY COUNTRY WHERE SUCH A THING CAN HAPPEN

(New acting version of the same author's SOUPER. Produced as curtain-raiser with the one act play PRESIDENT in Vienna, Berlin, Budapest and on the Italian stages. Translated by BARROWS MUSSEY.*)*

ANNIVERSARY DINNER

SCENE: *Dining room of very rich people. A party of about fifteen persons, sitting around a large, oblong, festively decorated dinner-table, in the middle of the room. Dinner is almost over. Left, in the rear corner a small piano with three musicians; one pianist, two violinists. In the rear wall, center, a large double door, open, through which two more rooms of an elegant apartment are visible. A chandelier is lit in each room. In the rear wall of the dining room near the piano, a small door.)*

AT RISE: *As the curtain rises, the* YOUNG MAN *is proposing a toast but no one is paying any particular attention.*

YOUNG MAN. . . . . . . and for that reason and on this account, because we have got to remember that in our social life, in our age of pull and undue influence, it's especially the men who have pull . . . who have pulled . . . and, if I may say so . . . well, the people who have pulled themselves up by their bootstraps deserve simply all the credit in the world. I think everyone here will agree with me when I say, Long life to our beloved and revered host!

(General "Your health!" clinking of glasses; the musicians sound a sustained chord, a flourish)

HOST. Thank you.

(Gay noise; loud conversation)

DOCTOR'S WIFE. "All the credit in the world." That's right. *(To the* YOUNG MAN*)* "All the credit in the world." That's right. *(She drinks)*

THE HIGH OFFICIAL. Now the Doctor's got to speak!

DOCTOR'S WIFE *(A little tipsy).* "All the credit in the world!" That's right. *(To the* HOST*)* Here's to you!

SEVERAL AT ONCE. Here's to our host! Here's to Willy! The Doctor's got to speak! Doctor! Doctor!

DOCTOR *(Declining).* He's all toasted out!

HOST *(Pleading).* Dear, dear Doctor please speak! Don't let us down! Say something! Something with those killing puns of yours . . . Something like that unforgettable speech last year at the "Building and Loan" banquet!—Quiet, please, for the Doctor!—Now, then, dear Doctor, let's have one of those humorous things.

DOCTOR. I really haven't a thing on hand.

HOST *(To his neighbor).* At the "Building and Loan banquet . . . (Laughs) . . .* he gave such a wonderful toast . . . *(Laughs) . . .* that I almost died laughing . . . *(Laughs)*

THE LADY. Then let us hear it! Speech!

HOSTESS. Doctor, do you hear that? We ladies insist! It can't be just agriculture and politics all the time.

DOCTOR *(Rising).* I suppose I dare not disobey orders from the lips of the fair.

ALL *(Applauding).* Bravo! Bravo! Hear! Hear!

HOST. It doesn't matter if you pick on me, too, Doctor! Whatever you say is all right!

DOCTOR *(Amid eager attention).* A word to all those present, even if absent!

YOUNG MAN *(Delighted).* Excellent! Brilliant! *(He laughs)*

273

ALL. Sh! Quiet! Hear! Hear!

DOCTOR. As an old proverb has it, "nothing venture, nothing have." So what do I do? I'll just turn the proverb around, and say, "nothing have, nothing venture!"

(Brief pause. Eager attention)

DOCTOR. Explanation: he that has NOTHING in the bank doesn't VENTURE to give such magnificent suppers.

(Laughter and applause. Then eager attention again)

YOUNG MAN *(With sincere enthusiasm)*. Tremendous! *(Makes a note in a little book)*

DOCTOR. Because that proverb is just like all proverbs. It's silly. But if you reverse it, it makes sense. And I can prove it to you, because certainly any one who VENTURES to give such a supper has NOTHING from it. *(Laughter. The* YOUNG MAN *earnestly takes notes)* Just one thing more. Tonight I'm going to cut it short. *(Protests)* Silence, please. A simple question. Just a question. Why is our host's son like opium? *(Silence)* Eh? *(Silence)* Eh? Give up? All right. They both come from a rich poppy.

(General applause, big success)

YOUNG MAN. It's old, it's old! An old joke! *(Shows his neighbors that the joke is already in his notes)* I had it down in my notebook before!

DOCTOR. Old, did you say? All right, I'll say something new. Listen carefully. *(Raising his glass)* Long life to our esteemed host, my good friend Willy, my faithful old patient!

(General "Here's to him," noise, clinking of glasses, laughter; the musicians sound a flourish. DOCTOR *sits down)*

DOCTOR. Now let's have the bigwig! The Undersecretary!

HIGH OFFICIAL. I beg your pardon . . . Our host first!

ALL *(To the* HIGH OFFICIAL*)*. Our host? No, no, you have the floor!

HIGH OFFICIAL *(Rises and clears his throat)*. Ahem, ahem.

ALL. Hear, hear!

DOCTOR *(In a tone of patronage)*. Now let's just listen to him.

HIGH OFFICIAL *(Modest, excited, with a show of stage-fright)*. Indeed . . . I should not have ventured an utterance in this exalted society . . . particularly after the dazzling remarks just rendered by the Doctor . . . the less so as I dare not risk comparison with his effervescent humor . . . But I feel called upon to make good an omission . . . which I do with the greater satisfaction . . . as I thus have the high privilege of offering a toast to . . . our charming hostess!

(General delight; flourish)

DOCTOR. I'll drink to that, too.

YOUNG MAN *(Gravely)*. Here's to the millionaires! Here's to the ladies of big business!

HOST *(Smiling)*. I thank you in the name of all concerned.

(General conversation, during the course of which the desire makes itself felt for the HOST *to speak. As he protests, every one urges him at once. He thereupon rises, smiling, and starts to talk, unlike the previous speakers, in a deep silence. The* HOST *is about fifty years old, highly elegant, his manner very calm, although a trifle nervous. He smiles softly, as people do who are used to talk condescendingly)*

Ladies and gentlemen, my friends. It is more than flattering to my humble self in this intimate circle of family and friends to hear all these undeserved praises, and I feel moved to make at least some reply. Forgive me if I follow the usual custom in such cases, and begin with a small personal reminiscence. I do it now ... *(Looks at his wrist-watch)* ... right now, a few minutes before midnight, before the end of this day so memorable to me.

ALL. Hear! Hear!

HOST. Ladies and gentlemen! This modest dinner here ... *(General "Oh!" "Oh!")* All right, my friends ... This immodest dinner here ... *(Laughter. Applause)* ... This is an anniversary dinner. *(General "Hear!" "Hear!")* Because ... it was thirty years ago today, this last day of the month of March, exactly thirty years ago today, that a poor boy set out from a very small town and came to our glorious city for the first time. The very small town is not far away from here but ... *(With an appropriate smile)* ... but the boy came on foot. Do you know why? Because he had no money for the train fare. And during the second half of this journey the boy was a barefoot boy. Do you know why? Because his only pair of shoes in which he started this journey fraught with destiny, that pair of shoes went to pieces in the first hour. *(General "Oh!" "Oh!" mixed with laughter)* That boy, ladies and gentlemen, was I. *(Thunderous applause)*

(At this moment the BUTLER *appears in the rearmost room— the drawing-room—and comes somewhat excitedly through the two rooms straight toward the*

HOSTESS, *to whom he whispers respectfully. The* HOSTESS *gets up slowly and goes through the central door into the rearmost drawing-room. The* BUTLER *follows her, both disappearing in the drawing-room.)*

HOST *(Paying no attention)*. Yes, my friends, I was that boy, and I came to this big city with forty-four, I repeat, forty-four little round copper coins in my pocket. With this "capital" ... *(Laughter)* ... with this capital I went to work. Yes, ladies and gentlemen ...

(The HOSTESS *reappears in the rearmost drawing-room, followed by three gentlemen in overcoat, hats in hand, and behind them the* BUTLER. *The first of the three gentlemen is the* DEPUTY DETECTIVE INSPECTOR. *All five walk toward the dining room, which the company, however, does not notice. At the wide open dining room door the three gentlemen pause, and only the* HOSTESS *and the* BUTLER *come into the dining room. The* HOSTESS *stops behind her chair, hiding her excitement under a forced smile; she wants to say something to her husband, but cannot bring herself to do so. She frantically clutches the back of the chair. The* BUTLER *is between her and the* HOST. *Of the three gentlemen in the next room two disappear; the* DETECTIVE INSPECTOR *is only half in view, as if courteously waiting to avoid disturbing the party)*

HOST *(Has meanwhile been speaking as follows)*. ... And with those forty-four coins I founded the fortune that became the basis of one of the greatest enterprises in the country, and which brought me—I do not hesitate to say—such a position not only in business circles but also in political and social affairs . . . *(Notices his wife; solicitously)* What is it, dear?

BUTLER *(Whispers something to the* HOST).

(Brief pause)

HOST *(Agitatedly, but softly and with dignity).* But really . . . What's this . . . *(Catches sight of the* DE-TECTIVE*)* . . . Really . . . I must say . . . I can't think of any reason . . . *(To the* DETECTIVE) Come in please . . . come nearer . . . come in . . .

(The DETECTIVE, *a bearded, mustached, middle-aged man, comes deferentially nearer but stops on the threshold, and bows rather awkwardly to the company)*

HOST. . . . Really, I only want . . . Truly . . . I've not the slightest idea . . .

DETECTIVE *(In a grave undertone).* You'll forgive me, but I don't mean to . . . disturb you . . . That is, when you have company . . .

(Brief pause)

HOST. Really . . . It's quite a surprise . . . I must say . . There's no cause for . . . (HE *breaks off)*

DETECTIVE *(Flashing a badge in his hand).* My name is Joseph Rex, Deputy Detective Inspector Rex, and I am instructed, sir, to ask you . . . to be so kind . . . there's a cab waiting downstairs . . . as to come with me. (HE *pockets the badge. Dead silence. After a brief pause)* While you're getting your hat and coat . . .

I'll . . . (HE *steps modestly slightly backward)*

(Dead silence)

HOSTESS *(Profoundly agitated, but controlling herself, speaks softly, indeed encouragingly, uttering the words with a certain emphasis in order to strengthen her husband's will-power).* Please do take your hat and coat and go with the Inspector.

DETECTIVE *(Modestly).* Only DEPUTY Inspector.

HOSTESS. It must just be some inquiry, some very important information, something urgent . . . or something of that kind . . . that they want from you . . .

HOST *(With a painful smile).* But really, I must say . . . Mister . . . ?

DETECTIVE. Rex.

HOST. Mister Rex . . . this is scarcely the proper way . . . when I'm . . . *(Somewhat louder)* After all, I have guests!

DETECTIVE. I told you . . . take your time . . . There is no rush . . .

HOST *(Loud).* But . . .

DETECTIVE *(Politely but decidedly).* I must beg your pardon, but I have no authority to enter into any discussion with you in the matter. I'm carrying out an order.

HOST *(Nervously smiling).* Are you . . . arresting me?

DETECTIVE. No, sir. Not at all. That is the job of the Chief Inspector at headquarters. My duty is only to take you there, sir, and that—to quote my orders—immediately. Meanwhile my two men will search the house. *(Takes a document out of his pocket)* If you care to read the warrant . . .

(The YOUNG MAN *rises, whispers something to his dinner*

partner, and goes over to the musicians)

HOST. So far as I know, the Penal Code of our State provides that searches of premises . . .

HOSTESS *(Raising her voice).* Willy dear, do be a good boy and get dressed and go with the Inspector. We'll wait for you here.

HOST *(Slowly losing command of himself, yet managing to conceal it, speaks softly, with dignity, but nervously).* Very well, my dear . . . Of course I'll go . . . but nobody can . . . Naturally everyone must take it that . . . I can't in the least understand . . . I'm actually so much shocked . . . It wouldn't be surprising if . . . After all . . I have always done the right thing, always obeyed the dictates of honor and decency. Yes, I may say I have behaved on that principle all my life, and will always continue to do so!

(He speaks the last words in a somewhat louder tone, whereupon the dozing musicians pull themselves together and sound a flourish)

ALL. Sh!

(The music suddenly stops. The YOUNG MAN hustles the musicians out through the small door on the left; he himself remains standing in the room by the door)

DETECTIVE *(After silence has fallen).* I repeat that I have no authority to argue this or any other matter with you, sir; I have to do my duty.

HIGH OFFICIAL *(Modestly, to the DETECTIVE).* Please be assured that we all . . .

HOSTESS *(To the HOST).* Please don't be nervous. Please don't be nervous. Don't—be—nervous. We've —got—to keep cool.

DETECTIVE *(After a pause; politely).* Please, sir, would you mind coming with me?

HOST *(Pushes the chair under the table; to the DETECTIVE).* I point out that I most certainly did not refuse. I . . . You must admit yourself that this unexpected . . . Here among my guests . . . If I were alone, don't think that . . The most innocent person in the world could not help being put out of countenance if . . . I have really every right to be upset . . .

DETECTIVE. If you don't feel well, a few minutes more or less won't make any difference.

(Falls back toward the entrance as though to indicate that he is ready to wait a few minutes if it can't be helped)

HOST *(After a brief pause).* I don't know . . . *(In a suddenly changed tone, humbled)* I hardly believe that that matter of buying the woodland . . . *(Looks toward the DOCTOR)* . . . Because that would . . . You know very well, my dear Doctor, it was in your house on direct urging from one of your friends and "faithful old patients" . . . the powerful Assistant Secretary of . . .

DOCTOR *(Interrupts him, coldly and impersonally).* Asking your pardon. I must request you not to involve me in the matter.

HOST. I didn't . . .

DOCTOR *(Interrupting).* Moreover . . . I'm a physician, so I was interested in your—I don't say "questionable"—but rather exciting business affairs, yes. But only in so far as it was my duty to tell you that exciting transactions raise your already high blood-pressure.

DOCTOR'S WIFE. That's right. He often told me that.

HOST *(To the* HIGH OFFICIAL). At your wife's bridge-party in February . . .

OFFICIAL'S WIFE. After all, I can hardly be held responsible for what my guests may do . . . at a bridge party attended by I don't know how many people . . .

HIGH OFFICIAL *(Interrupting severely)*. Please, my child, do me the favor of not answering.

HOST. The Doctor . . .

DOCTOR. I have already requested you not to involve me.

DOCTOR'S WIFE *(To the* DOCTOR). It's simply beneath your dignity to say anything at all. That kind of thing one just doesn't hear.

OFFICIAL'S WIFE *(Loud)*. That's certainly the most sensible way.

HOST *(To the* OFFICIAL'S WIFE). That evening . . . after your bridge party . . . *(To the* HIGH OFFICIAL) . . . when your fellow government bigwig—you should know that I never mention names—when that man was whispering with your wife . . . after he drank half a bottle cognac . . .

HIGH OFFICIAL *(Interrupting)*. This is not true.

HOST. I saw it with my own eyes.

HIGH OFFICIAL. First, it was not Cognac. It was Scotch. Second, he didn't whisper to my wife.

HOST. All right. He didn't whisper. But your wife whispered to you and to him and you listened and you made notes in a little book, if you don't mind my saying so.

OFFICIAL'S WIFE *(Quite brusquely)*. Really, I must tell you . . .

HOST *(Nervously, to* OFFICIAL'S WIFE). I can't understand how you of all people . . . you and your husband of all people . . .

HIGH OFFICIAL *(Flaring up)*. What are you getting at? *(Great silence)* What, if you please, are you implying with "you, of all people"? *(To his wife)* What does he mean, you of all people?

OFFICIAL'S WIFE *(In great embarrassment)*. Really, you know, in his situation . . . I can understand that he . . .

HOST *(To the* OFFICIAL). I'm surprised that you as my friend . . .

HIGH OFFICIAL *(Interrupting, coldly)*. Excuse me but I considered the present you gave us last Christmas as a token of . . . sorry, I have to tell you the truth . . . as a token of a rather one-sided, let's say non-mutual, attachment. *(Politely)* By no means what is known as friendship. *(Calmly)* I have to make this perhaps harsh but candid statement before witnesses for the record. It's not an improvisation as a consequence of this painful moment. I entered it last Christmas day, just as I'm telling it to you now, in my diary that I've been keeping painstakingly for twenty years. *(To the* DETECTIVE) If you go right now to my house, you can read it, verbatim. It's in the middle drawer of my desk.

OFFICIAL'S WIFE. And if you want further proof—we quickly got rid of your ridiculous present. We gave it away a few days later.

HOST *(Softly, bitterly)*. It was an authentic antique French work of art. A clock made by the famous Boulle for King Louis XIV, two hundred years ago.

OFFICIAL'S WIFE. So what.

HIGH OFFICIAL. We would

have got rid of it even if it were made a thousand years ago.

(At this point three guests who have been sitting with their backs to the audience get up, go slowly around the table and stand in the background. Of those sitting facing the audience two get up a few seconds later but stand by their chairs)

DOCTOR'S WIFE *(To* OFFICIAL'S WIFE*)*. It's no use, Catherine. Never mind. Never mind.

HIGH OFFICIAL. Pardon me but I also feel compelled to state here openly before witnesses, that I as a high government official, sometimes having to deal with matters affecting woodlands, cannot be held responsible for anything that has been said or whispered at my wife's bridge parties . . . and that I consider it really preposterous when somebody . . .

HOST *(Interrupting)*. But I didn't address a word to *you!* I didn't mention *you!*

HIGH OFFICIAL *(Nervously but with dignity)*. President, I take note of that eminently fair statement.

(The YOUNG MAN, *who has meanwhile crept to the door, now finds himself suddenly facing the* HOSTESS *on the threshold, with her looking him in the eyes—Brief pause)*

HOSTESS. Where are you going?

YOUNG MAN *(Very softly, almost whispering)*. Truly, I'm awfully sorry . . . But I told you before that on the dot of eleven forty-five . . . *(Pointing to his watch)* I've got to . . . *(Smiles forcedly)* And now it's past midnight.

HOSTESS. You said *twelve* forty-five.

YOUNG MAN *(Very humbly)*. Sorry . . . It probably doesn't matter . . . but I remember very well . . .

HOSTESS *(Raising her voice)*. You said *twelve* forty-five. Forty-five after midnight.

DETECTIVE *(To the* YOUNG MAN*)*. I am obliged to require you to stay, particularly since no one must leave the apartment during the search. But probably in half an hour you can . . .

YOUNG MAN *(Submissively)*. Certainly, certainly. *(Comes back. Deep, painful silence)* Tremendous!

DOCTOR *(To the* DETECTIVE, *loud)*. Nobody can interfere with my movements if I choose to leave. I am a law-abiding citizen. I have nothing to do with the police.

HIGH OFFICIAL *(Rises, as does his wife)*. What law says we mayn't leave here if we please?

HOSTESS *(To her husband)*. Please, dear . . . go.

(Her energy forsakes her. She suddenly puts her hands over her face, and totters)

HOST *(Tenderly)*. Sweetheart . . . *(Goes to her, and says excitedly to the* BUTLER, *who is waiting with discreet rigidity in the next room)* Water!

(The BUTLER *starts to go, but the* HOSTESS'S *words stop him)*

HOSTESS *(Coming to)*. Never mind. It isn't necessary. There's nothing wrong with me.

OFFICIAL'S WIFE *(To her husband)*. Shall we be going?

DETECTIVE *(Somewhat more severely)*. Kindly remain here. As I just said, those present must not leave the apartment during the search. *(To the* HOST*)* I'm sorry, sir, but I can't wait any longer. *(To the* BUTLER

who is standing in the next room)
Bring the President's things.

(The BUTLER *disappears. Returns immediately with coat and hat, and hands the coat to the* HOST, *who puts it on without help. The* BUTLER *holds the hat)*

DETECTIVE *(While the* HOST *is struggling with the coat; peremptorily).* Help the President with his coat.

(The BUTLER *rushes over to help)*

DETECTIVE. Give him the hat!

(The BUTLER *does so.—Pause)*

HOST *(Brokenly).* We can go now. *(To his wife)* Sweetheart . . . telephone my lawyer. *(He starts to go)*

DETECTIVE. Stop!

(With a slow movement he removes his false beard and mustache and pulls off his wig and his false bushy eyebrows and pockets it all. A smiling, rosy, jovial face, cheerful but stupid and wholly provincial, comes into view. He shouts out loud, explaining, reassuring, joyful)

DETECTIVE. It's me! Rudy! Rudolph! Cousin Rudy Klein! *(To the* HOST, *laughing and jubilant)* The first of April! APRIL FOOL!!!

(Great relief. The YOUNG MAN *hurries like a flash back to his seat)*

HOST. Rudy!

SEVERAL *(Surprised).* Rudolph! Rudy! Rudy Klein!

YOUNG MAN *(Very gravely).* Tremendous. Sensational.

DOCTOR *(Sitting down and heaving a sigh).* Rudolph . . .

(All rejoicing, only the HOSTESS

remains grave. The HOST *takes off his coat and hat. In the neighboring room a* MANSERVANT *appears carrying the after-dinner coffee on a big tray. The* BUTLER *takes it from him.* MANSERVANT *disappears.)*

DETECTIVE *(In a kindly jocose voice, as if nothing had happened, most merrily).* Well, friends, you can just bring on a good supper now to Cousin Rudy, because the joke gave me a terrific appetite. I'm dying of hunger. *(To the* HOSTESS*)* I haven't seen you for a year . . . or more . . . You look fine, Mary dear. *(He kisses the* HOSTESS *on both cheeks. He says jokingly)* I'm not greeting anybody else until I get something to eat! *(He sits down at the table, takes a napkin, prepares to eat, wipes his fork and knife with another napkin. He says laughingly)* Until I've eaten, I don't speak to anybody!

(He takes a plate of appetizers, containing radishes, celery, carrots, olives, etc. He takes a bite of a big stalk of celery. Solemn silence. The BUTLER *enters with the after-dinner coffee tray)*

BUTLER. Coffee, sir?

DETECTIVE *(Eating).* I haven't got anywhere near that far yet!

(The BUTLER *goes out.* MANSERVANT *enters at the same time from the next room and hurries with a plate of meat and potatoes to the* "DETECTIVE," *who helps himself abundantly)*

DETECTIVE *(Helping himself).* It's all very well for you to talk, because you've all eaten; I haven't touched a thing for a long time . . . *(Dips in, chewing)* I came by the afternoon train . . . After all it's more than three hundred miles!

DOCTOR *(Bitterly)*. Well, if that's the only reason you came three hundred miles . . .

DETECTIVE. More, Doctor! More than three hundred! *(To the* BUTLER, *eating)* Look here, old boy. Bring on the beer before I collapse.

(The BUTLER *rushes out. The* "DETECTIVE" *winks shrewdly at the guests.)*

DETECTIVE. Neatly done, hey? First class play-acting from an old dairy-farmer! *(Laughing)* Cousin Rudy, a character-actor! The neatest trick of ye old prankster Rudy Klein! *(Eating)* People at home will be in stitches . . . they'll split their sides laughing when I tell them how frightened you looked . . . all of you!

(The BUTLER *enters with a decanter and pours him a glass of beer. The* "DETECTIVE" *grabs the glass and takes a big gulp. Meanwhile the* HOSTESS *speaks)*

HOSTESS *(Gravely but trying to be natural; to her husband)*. My dear, you started to give a toast before. Do go on with it.

(No more than four or five guest are still sitting around the table near the door with demitasses in their hands; two are already in the next room. The HOSTESS *is standing at the left end of the table, staring at her husband who sits quite brokenly at the other end fixing the* "DETECTIVE" *with a forced, painful smile. The* "DETECTIVE" *goes on eating unperturbed)*

HOST *(Stands up)*. Well . . . *(He raises his glass and says in a very soft voice)* . . . Yes . . . As I was saying . . .

A FEW TIMID VOICES *(Without conviction)*. Hear! Hear!

HOST. Well . . . as I was saying . . . Thirty years ago . . . exactly thirty years ago . . . a boy came barefoot from a small town to the glorious city. That boy . . . ladies and gentlemen . . . was I. *(Here he stops, smiles painfully, and is unable to go on)*

(Dead silence. The HOST *stands a little while more, but does not speak. Finally he slowly sits, and puts down his glass. The guests near the door withdraw slowly to the other room, where the* BUTLER *is passing coffee and cordials. Those who are sitting get up slowly, uncomfortably, and also go out into the next room. No one is left in the dining room except the* HOST, *sitting at the end of the table and smiling sadly, the* HOSTESS *at the opposite end of the table, staring fixedly at her husband, and the* "DETECTIVE," *who keeps on eating)*

DETECTIVE *(Not looking up as he eats)*. Why . . . Was that all?

(Not getting an answer, looks around. Looks at the HOST, *then at the* HOSTESS, *then looks backward in the direction of the guests in the adjoining room)*

DETECTIVE *(Calling to the rear)*. Hey! Folks! Save me a cup of coffee! Very hot!

HOSTESS *(Going behind the* "DETECTIVE," *to her husband, calls out to the* BUTLER)*. Save a hot coffee for Cousin Rudolph!

(She goes to her husband, who gives her his hand, and acts for a moment as if he would lean

against her breast. She gently restrains him, and speaks in a voice choked with tears, forcing herself to put on a jolly tone)

HOSTESS. Go and join your guests, sweetheart!

(The HOST *rises, walks into the other room, where the* BUTLER *hands him after-dinner coffee. The* HOSTESS *watches her husband leave, then, with an icy gravity, sits down at the piano and plays loudly and a little off-tune, a well-known lively number from the latest hit-musical. The "*DETECTIVE*" eats and nods gaily in time with the music. At the sixth or eighth measure of the song the curtain slowly falls. The piano is audible for a little while after the curtain has fallen)*

CURTAIN

GAME OF HEARTS

GAME OF HEARTS

COMEDY IN THREE ACTS

CHARACTERS

Dr. HARRY W. MOORE, 50
LINDA HANSSON, 40
SOPHIE LAURIN, 43
DICK LAURIN, 22
BESS LAURIN, 20
VINCENT REID, 51
CLEM HENNYMAN, 50
HARRIET BELL, 40
MARY PETITO, 23
LIZ PETITO, 21

PLACE : *Act One:* DOCTOR'S OFFICE.—*Act Two:* ROOM AT SOPHIE'S.—
Act Three: DOCTOR'S OFFICE.

(English text by P. G. WODEHOUSE.)

GAME OF HEARTS

ACT ONE

SCENE: *Examining room in* DR. MOORE'S *office, in New York, in the East Seventies. Examining table. Adjustable searchlight floor lamp standing at the head of the examining table. X-ray machine. Scale. A wash basin on the wall. Standing against the wall is a small white medical cabinet, with drawers and a glass top, covered with vials, small medical instruments, boxes, etc. Two doors. One leads to the laboratory. The other to the waiting room which opens on the street. Closets. White doors. Hanging from a hook on the wall is a so-called lead apron and a pair of big lead gloves for fluoroscope examinations. On one side is an electro-cardiograph machine.— October. Afternoon.*

AT RISE: *As the curtain rises, the stage is pitch dark. A single small red bulb glimmers in the blackness. We hear the soft hum of the electro-cardiograph. Only for a short time, though, because the taking of the cardiogram is at an end. The lights go on as* DR. MOORE *switches on the electricity. The red bulb goes out. Three people are on the stage.* VINCENT REID *is lying on the examining table, with the "electrode" wires of the electro-cardiograph machine fastened to his body. He is wearing a white shirt, unbuttoned in front, with the left sleeve rolled up, shorts, socks and shoes. Standing beside him, in a nurse's white uniform is* LINDA HANSSON, *the doctor's nurse, a strong, attractive blonde of forty.* DR. MOORE, *wearing a white office coat, is standing beside the cardiograph machine.*

DR. MOORE. Take off the electrodes, please.

LINDA. Yes, Doctor. *(Starts to remove the wires from* VINCENT)

VINCENT. Unwrapping the parcel.

DOCTOR *(Busying himself with the cardiograph machine).* Don't look so gloomy, Mr. Reid. I didn't take this cardiograph because I was afraid your heart had got worse since I examined you last week . . . but to confirm my impression that you're coming along very well indeed. Today's visit is the last one of the series and the last one for a long, long time, I hope.

VINCENT. Thank you for those kind words, Doctor. Your pep talks are always so convincing.

DOCTOR. You think I'm just stringing you along? Not at all. I don't give pep talks, Mr. Reid, I diagnose. If you ever do have to come back, it will be in the remote future.

VINCENT. And until then?

DOCTOR. Forget that you've ever been in a hospital.

LINDA. Mrs. M. is waiting, Doctor.

DOCTOR. All right, Linda. *(To* VINCENT, *as he takes off his stethoscope and hands it to* LINDA, *who hangs it around her neck and goes on with what she is doing)* Excuse me a minute. Patient in the laboratory waiting for an injection. Don't get dressed. I want to have a look at you under the fluoroscope. *(Starts to go out)*

VINCENT. I am always open for inspection.—Doctor!

DOCTOR *(Pausing at door).* Yes?

VINCENT. Are you unusually

sunny for a heart specialist, or are they all like that?

DOCTOR. Optimistic? I don't know. But I am, and I've never had occasion to regret it.

(He hurries out. Silence. VIN-CENT lies on the examining table. LINDA is removing the wires of the electrodes. With dabs of cotton she wipes off the smears of ointment known as electrode jelly, used in the examination)

VINCENT. What's the time?

LINDA. Four twenty.

VINCENT. Thank you.

LINDA. Yours was the last appointment of the afternoon. It shows how interested Doctor Moore is in you.

VINCENT. Really?

LINDA. He put you last so that he'd have plenty of time to give you.

(Silence. LINDA wipes off the smears of ointment)

VINCENT. Doctor Moore is extraordinarily nice.

LINDA. Yes, he's nice.

VINCENT. Not extraordinarily nice?

LINDA. If you insist. I'm not very fond of superlatives. He's a fine doctor.

VINCENT. And you're a fine nurse.

LINDA. You think so?

VINCENT. I'm positive of it.

LINDA. Thank you.

(Silence. VINCENT sits on examining table)

VINCENT. You must have heard lots of hearts beat. More than most women.

LINDA. Through a stethoscope.

VINCENT. Isn't it the same thing?

LINDA. No.

VINCENT. Which way's better?

LINDA. The way I heard it twenty-four years ago. When I was sixteen and silly. In love, with my head against a boy's chest, listening— without a stethoscope—to his heart jumping and thumping . . .

VINCENT. And bumping?

LINDA. Yes, and bumping . . . *(She writes something in a little notebook)* . . . You've been out of the hospital about six weeks now, haven't you?

VINCENT. Six long weary weeks.

LINDA. Where are you living?

VINCENT. Hotel Monterosa. On Fifty-eighth Street.

LINDA. Is it nice there?

VINCENT. Is it nice anywhere? I have one room. Very dark.

LINDA. That's too bad.

VINCENT. It doesn't matter. It's temporary. In the past I've had many beautiful apartments in Europe.

LINDA. And?

VINCENT. Hitler! Bombs! War! But I'm resigned to it. I'm a guest on this earth. Particularly since . . . *(He points to his heart)*

LINDA. Oh, come on!

VINCENT. What use expensive furniture? A few years . . . or months . . .

LINDA. Patients with heart disease usually survive their doctors.

VINCENT. You think so?

LINDA. They take care of themselves. Dieting . . . rest . . . taking it easy . . .

VINCENT. Still, I sometimes wish I were back at the hospital. At least there was sunshine there. And people around. *(HE takes a white sheet which LINDA hands him and he winds it about himself like a Roman* toga) Ancient Roman Senator. (HE *speaks unpretentiously, smiling a little, without complaining, rather matter of fact*) You know, since I've had this trouble, I don't like to be alone . . . with my memories.

LINDA. Aren't they pleasant?

VINCENT. Too pleasant. That's the trouble. You remember what Tennyson said. "A sorrow's crown of sorrow is remembering happier things." My pleasant memories would torture me to death . . . if I let them. When they discover I'm alone—mostly at night—they come rushing at me, gnashing their teeth.

LINDA. What do you do?

VINCENT. I gnash back. I stand up to them. I tackle them. I slay them.

LINDA. How?

VINCENT. With sleeping pills. Nembutal. Sodium Amytal. Seconal. One pill for each memory . . . though some of them need two.

LINDA. I'm afraid this is upsetting you. Let's not talk about it.

VINCENT. Why not? So long as I'm not alone . . .

LINDA *(Interrupts. In a different tone. Obviously determined to change the subject).* Did they look after you all right there . . . in the hospital?

VINCENT. They were fine. But two months . . . that's a long time.

LINDA *(Matter of fact, with no suggestion of coquetry).* Did you have a pretty nurse?

VINCENT. Exceptionally pretty. But not nearly as attractive as you.

LINDA. Where I come from, they say that remarks like that don't cost you anything. *(Takes his pulse)* And I caught that switch from "pretty" to "attractive."

VINCENT *(While she counts his pulse).* Are you always so observant?

LINDA. Not always.

VINCENT. Why, thank you.

LINDA *(Still counting pulse, brushes a stray lock from his forehead).* Your pulse is good.

VINCENT. If you stroke my head it'll go up.

LINDA. That remark didn't cost you much either.

(She goes to the X-ray machine which is set horizontally, readjusts it to a standing position, getting it ready for the doctor)

VINCENT. You Swedish?

LINDA. American. My parents came from Sweden. Northern Sweden.

VINCENT. Up near the Pole?

LINDA. Not far from it. Why? Do I seem so cold to you?

VINCENT. I didn't say so. But . . .

LINDA. Not that I care.

(Silence)

VINCENT. Swedish girls are the most desirable in the world.

LINDA. Thank you.

VINCENT. And the best.

LINDA. How do you know?

VINCENT. Judging by you.

LINDA. You scatter compliments like bird seed. And that sad little half smile that goes with them. No wonder you've made such a hit with Doctor Moore. Of course, he's an easy mark.

VINCENT. That might have been put more tactfully. Nevertheless . . . thank you.

LINDA *(Begins to apologize).* I didn't mean . . .

(DOCTOR MOORE enters, interrupting her)

DOCTOR. Well?

VINCENT. All ready for you, Doctor. *(Pointing at his Roman toga)* You must excuse my clothes. I've just been murdering Julius Caesar.

> (DOCTOR MOORE *takes the lead apron off its hook and slips it over his head. Puts on the huge lead gloves)*

LINDA. Stand here, please.

> (VINCENT *steps behind the fluoroscopic screen. The* DOC-TOR *switches off the light. The red bulb lights up again, while* LINDA *helps* VINCENT *off with his shirt)*

VINCENT. This always reminds me of a mystery play. You know ... where the lights go out and people rush around screaming, "Here comes the shadow."

DOCTOR. Quiet, please. Take a deep breath.

> *(He presses the fluoroscopic screen closer to* VINCENT's *chest.* VINCENT *sighs heavily.* DOCTOR *moves the screen around, looks into his chest as doctors do)*

DOCTOR. Another deep breath. (VINCENT *sighs again)* Once more please. (VINCENT *sighs again)* Turn around. (VINCENT *turns.* DOCTOR MOORE *scrutinizes him through screen.* VINCENT *sighs deeply)* Thank you I was just going to ask you to do that. All right.

> *(In the darkness* LINDA *quickly helps* VINCENT *put on his shirt again.* DOCTOR *turns on the light.* VINCENT *is again the Roman Senator draped in his toga)*

DOCTOR. Weigh Mr. Reid, please, Linda.

> (LINDA, *with* VINCENT *on the scale, adjusts the balance and records his weight in her little notebook.* VINCENT *starts to put on his clothes. The* DOCTOR *re-adjusts the X-ray machine to its former position, while the following dialogue takes place)*

LINDA. No change.

VINCENT. That's that diet of yours, doctor. I've stuck to it like glue.

DOCTOR. Good. Lose weight, lose weight, lose weight. You've no idea how important it is.

VINCENT. Yes I have. That's why I stick to it. *(He has put on his pants. Now he is busy with his tie. Still without vest and jacket)*

DOCTOR. Linda ...

LINDA *(Smiling)*. Okay. Just off.

DOCTOR. There's a haemoglobin test. And then ... that blood count.

LINDA. I know, doctor. *(Exit* LINDA *into laboratory)*

DOCTOR. Sit down, please. For a few minutes only. *(He takes out several sheets of paper, at which he glances from time to time during the following dialogue:)* This is your case history. *(Leafing through his notes)* Let's just check a few details ... before it's buried in my files. As I've told you, I closed your case to-day. And so now I store your case history with the others. Maybe ... sometime ... one day ... they will make a big book.

VINCENT. I hope so. And an interesting one. Title?

DOCTOR. "One Thousand Heart Cases."

VINCENT *(Impressed)*. Oh!

DOCTOR *(With pencil in his hand)*. Let's just check a few things. *(Looks at his notes)* You're fifty-one.

VINCENT. Yes.

DOCTOR. Born . . .

VINCENT. Yes. (*In answer to* DOCTOR's *reproachful look*) Sorry . . . In Buffalo. My parents came from Vienna.

DOCTOR (*Makes a note on the paper*). The cardiogram will be ready this evening. If you're anxious to know, you can call the office before nine. We'll be here. Meanwhile, I can tell you that the results of today's examination are on the whole good.

VINCENT (*With a somewhat bitter smile*). If you can use that adjective in connection with a man in my position.

DOCTOR. Hundreds . . . thousands . . . millions of people are in your position. And they're still alive. What's more, they often live longer than other people . . . because they take better care of themselves. But never mind that now. We'll come back to it later. You've made a remarkable recovery . . . in the hospital and since. Your heart's responded admirably. Now we've got to keep it that way. You have a grateful, ambitious, obliging, gallant heart.

VINCENT. Thank you for speaking of it so highly.

DOCTOR. I have a pretty clear picture of you, Mr. Reid. So clear that we can get down to the practical side of things. As for instance, where do you go from here?

VINCENT. I'm grateful to you that you're not only interested in my past but in my future as well.

DOCTOR. That's a must with a heart specialist. Besides . . . I've taken a liking to you. You must have noticed it.

VINCENT. Thank you. (*Brief pause*) I'm moved, believe me.

DOCTOR. Well, anyway . . . where do you go from here?

VINCENT. Exactly what I'd like to know.

DOCTOR. You can't go on living as you have. You would lose all the ground you've gained. The cure is a different, a new way of living.

VINCENT (*With that half-smile*). Smoking, alcohol: poison. Forbidden.

DOCTOR. Your list is incomplete. Add . . . the telephone.

VINCENT. How can I escape that?

DOCTOR. Do as I do. If the damned thing rings, let someone else answer it.

VINCENT (*Same half-smile*). Something wrong with yours, too? (*He points to his own heart*)

DOCTOR. Not yet. But there will be. I have a theory that a man can't be a really first-rate heart specialist unless he has a touch of it himself. But let's get on. You mustn't drive a car.

VINCENT. Naturally. Taxi.

DOCTOR. And furthermore . . .

VINCENT (*Half-smile*). No excitement.

DOCTOR. None.

VINCENT. How can you avoid it nowadays?

DOCTOR. You can reduce it.

VINCENT. How?

DOCTOR. By using your head.

VINCENT. I suppose really people ought to spend years in special schools learning how to take care of themselves. They'd live a lot longer, wouldn't they?

DOCTOR. Not necessarily. Who gets a better education in hygiene than a doctor? And doctors don't live longer than other people.

VINCENT. Aren't *you* going to?

DOCTOR. No. Does that comfort you?

VINCENT. I must confess it does rather. It's somehow kind of comforting to think that doctors don't live forever.—And what else mustn't I do?

DOCTOR. One more thing. I've left it for the last because it's the most serious. There's just one thing that's deadly for the heart. Not for a sound heart. For a convalescent one.

VINCENT. You're scaring me.

DOCTOR. I meant to.

VINCENT. And what is so terribly harmful for the convalescent heart?

DOCTOR. Worry. I mean the fashionable, new variety. Worry about the state of the world. Private worries are as old as mankind, but this type is new, and since the last war there's been an epidemic of it. Comes chiefly from reading the papers, listening to the radio . . .

VINCENT . . . and talking to frightened people, cursed with powerful imaginations.

DOCTOR. Exactly. It started back in the fall of '45. Right after the war. It was after they tried out the first atom bombs that my first worry-itis patient turned up. And the contagious disease began to spread. A few years later I thought we had passed the peak, but no. Instead of getting better, it got worse.

VINCENT. And you think the cause is what they call "the troubles of the world."

DOCTOR. To list the causes of the disease I'd have to talk politics, and I don't want to. I'm a doctor. All that interests me is diagnosis and therapy. Still, your phrase covers it well enough. The troubles of this world.

VINCENT. This *doomed* world.

DOCTOR. The world isn't doomed. Mankind may be, but what of it?

VINCENT. I see what you mean. Why bother about trifles?

DOCTOR. If man disappears, the ants will take over, billions, trillions of them—and probably run things extremely well.

VINCENT. Didn't you tell me you were an optimist, Doctor?

DOCTOR. I am. (VINCENT *raises his eyebrows, surprised*) If I were a pessimist, I'd be saying that man will blow up the globe.

VINCENT. They won't dare.

DOCTOR. They'll dare all right, but they won't be able to.—But let's get back to that formula of yours . . . the troubles of the world. That's the cause of this epidemic. And that's the reason you're here now in my consulting room.

    (VINCENT *has meanwhile put on his vest and jacket*)

VINCENT. Really?

DOCTOR. I assure you. (*Glances at his notes*) But we're neglecting our check-up.

VINCENT. For the big book? "Thousand Cases?"

DOCTOR. Yes. Let's get yours completed.

VINCENT. Carry on.

DOCTOR (*Glancing at his notes*). You used to fly.

VINCENT. Yes. First on the West Coast. I was a test pilot in an airplane factory.

DOCTOR. When?

VINCENT. Before the war.

DOCTOR (*Making a note*). And then . . .

VINCENT. My firm sent me to Paris. *(Smiling)* Sounds like a cross-examination.

DOCTOR. It's a medical one. *(Makes a note)* In Paris . . .

VINCENT. I sold planes and engines.

DOCTOR. Successfully?

VINCENT. Very.

DOCTOR. During the war . . .

VINCENT. I did my bit, as the expression is. Air Force.

DOCTOR. I know.

VINCENT. Ground crew. *(Points to his heart)* It was the doctor's fault.

DOCTOR. Fault? You mean his competence, perhaps? *(Makes a note)*

VINCENT That's your opinion.

DOCTOR. Are you ashamed of it?

VINCENT. A flyer's place is in the air.

(Silence)

DOCTOR. And then?

VINCENT. It's difficult . . . painful . . . to tell it like this. Even to a doctor as understanding as you. How much easier it must be to confess in a narcosis.

DOCTOR. I'll make it easy for you.

VINCENT. With an injection?

DOCTOR. No, no injection.

VINCENT. I thought there was an injection for everything nowadays.

DOCTOR. Not for this. My method is to word my embarrassing questions so that you can give the shortest possible answers. Monosyllables. Or, if you prefer it, you can just move your head. *(Shows him)* Yes. No.

VINCENT. Splendid. You make the third degree positively enjoyable. Go ahead.

DOCTOR *(Looking at his notes).* You were married.

VINCENT. Yes.

(The DOCTOR *continues to glance at the sheets and makes notes from time to time)*

DOCTOR. Any children.

VINCENT. Not so far as I know.

DOCTOR. So far as you know?

VINCENT. Twelve years, doctor . . . in *Paris.* You never can tell.

DOCTOR. Twelve years. During which time you were married for . . . ?

VINCENT. Seven years.

DOCTOR. Divorced.

VINCENT. I got my final decree last week.

DOCTOR. Unnecessarily long, that answer. You had only to say yes.

VINCENT. Yes.

DOCTOR. Your wife . . . a Parisian?

VINCENT. Yes.

DOCTOR. You were a prisoner of war . . .

VINCENT. Winter, 1945. Battle of the Bulge.

DOCTOR. Then back to France.

VINCENT. Yes. To my wife.

DOCTOR. She was faithful to you?

VINCENT. I had no doubts.

DOCTOR. Mmmmm . . .

VINCENT. You win. I did have a tiny doubt.

DOCTOR. That's better. You brought her back to America with you.

VINCENT. Yes.

DOCTOR. And then . . .

VINCENT. The night we landed my former boss took us to dinner. Then to a night club.

DOCTOR. Boss danced with your wife.

VINCENT. Till dawn.

DOCTOR *(Looking at his notes).* You said your wife was dressed . . .

VINCENT. In about half as much silk as she should have been.

DOCTOR. Boss liked that.

VINCENT. And how.

DOCTOR. Boss has a million or two.

VINCENT. Eleven.

DOCTOR. Your wife left you.

VINCENT. I told you . . . Eleven.

DOCTOR. You missed her?

VINCENT. Very much.

DOCTOR. Still?

VINCENT. Still.

DOCTOR. Is she beautiful?

VINCENT. No. Attractive, rather. But . . .

DOCTOR. But?

VINCENT. Very exciting . . . to me, at least. Southern French blood, plus Parisian . . . let's say artfulness.

DOCTOR. Come, come, this is all wrong. We seem to have exchanged roles in this conversation. I'm asking short questions and you're giving long answers.

VINCENT. If something hurts me, I like to talk about it. One of my faults.

DOCTOR. A very bad one.

VINCENT. Well, you know, waking up in a double bed with the same woman every morning for seven years . . . it's a bond . . . and it's painful when it ends . . . abruptly.

DOCTOR Others have had the same experience, but in your case it hurts more than usual.

VINCENT. Why in my case?

DOCTOR. Because you didn't just lose an exciting wife, you lost her *to another man*. That's where the agony comes in.

VINCENT. How right you are.

DOCTOR. You look at your watch in the night. One o'clock. You say to yourself "Maybe right now." You close your eyes and you *see* it.

VINCENT. In technicolor. Every word you say is true. Are other people like that?

DOCTOR. A great many.

VINCENT. Are you married?

DOCTOR. I was. From the look on your face I gather that you want to ask if anything of that sort happened to me. It did. I know how you're feeling. But it soon gets better.

VINCENT. Unassisted?

DOCTOR. No. It requires treatment.

VINCENT. What's that?

DOCTOR. Another exciting woman.

VINCENT. Another wife?

DOCTOR. Good God, no. I said woman.

VINCENT. Unattached?

DOCTOR. As unattached as possible.

VINCENT. And it works?

DOCTOR. Like magic. But unfortunately in your case the treatment cannot be applied. You have to be careful.

VINCENT. I see.

DOCTOR. Your slogan must be "Take it easy." I feel sure you understand. If I were a poet, I would say "On the highway of your love life there are signs . . . they don't say STOP, they say SLOW."

VINCENT. I see.

DOCTOR. Which takes us, smoothly and easily, past the first difficult prescription. I must congratulate you on the way you took it. In one leap. No argument. Most unusual.

VINCENT. Well, of course, I'm a man of a certain age.

DOCTOR. It's men of a certain

age who make the most fuss, as a rule. And now my final Doctor's Order.

VINCENT. Not to worry.

DOCTOR. That's right.

VINCENT. Stop tormenting myself about the state of the world.

DOCTOR. Exactly.

VINCENT. That's what I do from morning till night . . . and very often from night till morning. I never realized that that was a sickness.

DOCTOR. I told you; it's an epidemic. The symptoms are . . . anxiety, premonitions of evil, a haunting fear that somehow, somewhere, something is going to happen. Know where your kidneys are?

VINCENT. Here. (Indicates) Right?

DOCTOR. Near enough. Do you know what is above your kidneys?

VINCENT. No. But I'll bet *you* do.

DOCTOR. There are two tiny glands. They secrete a substance called adrenalin. When you worry, you stimulate these glands to overwork and they pour too much adrenalin into your blood. Which affects the heart.

VINCENT. How?

DOCTOR. My dear Mr. Reid, I explain these medical matters to intelligent patients . . . up to a point . . . as long as I feel they serve a purpose. That point has now been reached. No more details.

VINCENT. For fear those glands above my kidneys will secrete too much . . . what was the word?

DOCTOR. Adrenalin.

VINCENT. Thus disturbing my heart action.

DOCTOR. Glad you understand.

VINCENT. It's amazing. Stalin and adrenalin. The United Nations and my kidneys.

DOCTOR. And mine. And everybody else's.

VINCENT. But, if I've been following you correctly, the worry which stirs up all this trouble is curable?

DOCTOR. In my opinion there is one certain cure.

VINCENT. World peace? U.N.?

DOCTOR. No.

VINCENT. Morphine? Cocaine?

DOCTOR. God forbid.

VINCENT. A monastery?

DOCTOR. No.

VINCENT. How about suicide?

DOCTOR. That would do the trick, but my medical oath forbids me to prescribe it. No, what you need is a new way of life.

VINCENT. Well, what must I do?

DOCTOR. You must stop being lonely. Have you any friends?

VINCENT. Not that I know of. Twelve years abroad, you know.

DOCTOR. You lead a completely miserable life.

VINCENT. Indeed I do.

DOCTOR. Well, you can't go on living alone. I won't go so far as to say it's a kind of slow suicide, but there's a distinct resemblance. Here's my prescription. Go and live with a family.

VINCENT. I have no family.

DOCTOR. It wouldn't do you any good if you had. One's own family is no use. Quite the reverse. Relatives make the worst possible material for a family. What you must do is look around and, as soon as possible, pick out a nice, cozy family of strangers and go and live in its warm, calm atmosphere.

VINCENT. An elderly adopted child.

DOCTOR. Exactly. Live with them quietly, placidly, and pay for it ... generously. Pay through the nose. Nothing brings out the tenderness in people so much as being overpaid. How are you fixed for money?

VINCENT. All right.

DOCTOR. You've lost your family the way a man might lose his teeth. When a man loses his teeth, he buys a fine expensive false set. That's what you must do.

VINCENT. Get a false family?

DOCTOR. Yes.

VINCENT. Money can't buy love.

DOCTOR. That was not the experience of your former boss ... or your former wife.

VINCENT. *Touché!*

DOCTOR. There are any number of respectable, not too well off families who would ask for nothing better than a gentle, elderly, *well-to-do* bachelor for a boarder.

VINCENT. Whom they'd murder for his money.

DOCTOR. Oh, only in two or three per cent of cases at the most. But, seriously, it's a common enough arrangement. You see families advertising in the papers all the time. And ... above all ... don't let yourself be bored. Keep busy. Keep moving. Who does nothing, dies. Who doesn't move is lowered into the grave.—Have you a hobby?

VINCENT. I had one.

DOCTOR. What was it?

VINCENT. Flying at break-neck speed.

DOCTOR. That's out of the question now. What else?

VINCENT. Women.

DOCTOR. Also not good now. How about collecting stamps?

VINCENT. Disgusting.

DOCTOR. Painting?

VINCENT. I've tried. No talent, positively.

DOCTOR. What talent have you?

VINCENT. As a relative. I was always a talented relative. I mean I like to help people, to see them through difficulties, to root for them ...

DOCTOR. Now we're getting somewhere. That fits in with what I suggested to you. Go and live with a family.

VINCENT *(Thinking it over).* Interesting ... recently I've given a lot of thought to a family that is very dear to me.

DOCTOR. Nice people?

VINCENT. Yes, and thank you for jogging my memory. There's an elderly lady, a widow, who ... Well, I guess there's no harm in saying so after all these years ... she was my old sweetheart.

DOCTOR. You mean your young sweetheart.

VINCENT. My sweetheart when a boy. My childhood sweetheart. Her son just got married. The three of them live together. I give her a monthly allowance, and she makes some money on the side, renting two small rooms.

DOCTOR. This begins to sound fine. Go on.

VINCENT. The boy is a goldsmith. Works for a jewelry firm. His bride's a secretary or something.

DOCTOR. See much of them?

VINCENT. I'm ashamed to say I've only been there once since I came back to New York. Before the hospital, that was. A tiny place, but pleasant, shiny, clean and cozy *(More and more taken with the idea)* Why, this is wonderful. I'll rent both spare rooms. Thank you for the idea, Doctor. I'll move in.

DOCTOR. You are a man of quick decisions.

VINCENT. Always. Got my divorce that way. One, two, three. Yes, I'll move in.

DOCTOR. And pay them. Generously.

VINCENT. I will. Though they're fond of me aside from that. Sophie . . . the widow . . . still calls me "the hero of the air" and "The Eagle."

DOCTOR. Really?

VINCENT. Oh, yes, I'm a romantic figure there.

DOCTOR. Here, too.

VINCENT. Here? Where?

DOCTOR. In this office.

VINCENT *(Pleased)*. Honestly?

DOCTOR. Haven't you noticed the way I've probed into your case? Like a psychoanalyst. You interest me. I like the atmosphere that surrounds you. I get a sense of your romantic Viennese background.

VINCENT. Thank you.

DOCTOR. In the way you smile, in your attitude towards life, in your very inconsistency I find . . . something of the vague, melancholy unrest of the world today.

VINCENT. You put these things so well. Ever write poetry?

DOCTOR. No.

VINCENT. Play an instrument? Piano?

DOCTOR. Violin.

VINCENT. I like the violin. My wife preferred the piano.

DOCTOR. Forget about your wife. Tell me about this family.

VINCENT. The last time I said goodbye . . . the way she looked at me . . .

DOCTOR. Sophie?

VINCENT. Yes. I'm still a hero to her.

DOCTOR. You don't think she's fallen in love with you again?

VINCENT. No. And yet, now you mention it, it might be. Or on the other hand, I might be just a conceited ass. *(Silence.* VINCENT *smiles)* Being put on a pedestal makes me feel wonderful. You, too?

DOCTOR. Oh, definitely.

VINCENT *(Dreamily)*. Dear Sophie. She's not very bright.

DOCTOR. Lucky woman. Only the people who are not very bright can get through these modern times safely. Does she know you're rich?

VINCENT. Of course.

DOCTOR. Then I see nothing surprising in her falling in love with you.

VINCENT *(That certain half-smile)*. You're a realist.

DOCTOR. An incorrigible realist. What's she like . . . apart from not being one of our great thinkers?

VINCENT. Sophie is the sweetest, most dignified old lady in the world.

DOCTOR. Age?

VINCENT. Forty-three.

DOCTOR *(Surprised)*. You regard that as old?

VINCENT. I knew her when she was nineteen.

DOCTOR. Then she is old. What does she look like . . . if anything?

VINCENT. We-ell . . . you might describe her as still in the running. But not dangerous to me . . . from a medical viewpoint. Not the way my wife was . . . or would be . . .

DOCTOR. Will you kindly leave your wife out of this.

VINCENT. She is gentle . . . and sweet . . . and restful.

DOCTOR. Why didn't you marry her twenty-four years ago?

VINCENT. I wanted to. But . . . *(He breaks off)*

DOCTOR. But?

VINCENT. It just struck me that the same thing has happened to me twice. Sophie and I were engaged. I was poor then. She left me for a rich man. Then . . . the rich man went broke and died.

DOCTOR. They do.

VINCENT. But she manages.

DOCTOR. And now she'll manage even better. Rent both rooms at once. And keep gorging them with money. Have they a car?

VINCENT. No.

DOCTOR. Buy them one. Then . . . new furniture. Later . . . a house.

VINCENT. The thought of money seems to obsess you.

DOCTOR. So it will them. You'll see. Love which doesn't need lubrication doesn't exist. What you will be doing is spending your money to prolong your life. A very good investment. I told you I was a realist. And you have already mentioned that your sweetheart-when-a-boy was fonder of money than she was of you.

VINCENT. And that still hurts, after twenty-four years.

DOCTOR. You're much too easily hurt. But I think your future is going to work out nicely.

VINCENT. So you feel that I have a future?

DOCTOR. A very bright one. I'll take a look at this new family of yours some day next week, if I have time.

VINCENT. You're very kind, Doctor. More so than I deserve.

DOCTOR. They'll take good care of you, I hope. You'll be calm and happy. What's the boy like?

VINCENT. Wonderful. He's mine. My son.

DOCTOR. What do you mean, your son?

VINCENT. I'm his father.

DOCTOR. Are you sure?

VINCENT. Well, I think so . . . and Sophie thinks so.

DOCTOR. You mean . . . you had an affair with her?

VINCENT. Why, Doctor, didn't they teach you in medical school that it's rather difficult to create a child without . . . that sort of . . .

DOCTOR. Hmm . . . But you told me you had no children.

VINCENT. That was before we became friends.

DOCTOR. And does the boy know?

VINCENT. He doesn't even suspect. Sophie got married before he was born. *(Brightening)* But Sophie knows. And I know.

DOCTOR. I envy you. You'll have a lovely romantic life with them in their little home.

VINCENT *(Sentimentally)*. He's just been married.

DOCTOR. What's his wife like?

VINCENT. Marvellous. Always merry and bright.

DOCTOR. Well, upon my word, it begins to look like the perfect sanatorium for you.

VINCENT. That's what I think.

DOCTOR. Move in. Move in at once. And above all—

VINCENT. Gorge them with money. I will.

DOCTOR. Little presents at first.

Birthdays. Christmas. Mother's Day. Then big ones. A car. A house.

VINCENT. Of course. I'll give them everything.

DOCTOR. Only don't make a will in their favor.

VINCENT. You're afraid they might not take such good care of my health then?

DOCTOR. I won't say that. But as a doctor I never advise a will in favor of the people you live with. Safety first . . . if you know what I mean.

VINCENT. Your opinion of families seems a little low.

DOCTOR. Families, unfortunately, are made up of people.— Where do they live?

VINCENT. Forty minutes out of New York. They've rented a little house. You can't imagine the charm of those little cottages, a stone's throw from the city.

DOCTOR. I can. I have one myself. (Sighing) But I've been living alone in it a long long time.

VINCENT. A little house . . . simple but lovely.

DOCTOR. Garden?

VINCENT. Yes.

DOCTOR. Just the thing for you. You'll be living there in 1955, '56, '57, '58, '59, '60 . . . and beyond that. You'll live to be a hundred.

VINCENT. Only a hundred?

DOCTOR. Maybe more.

VINCENT. Thank you. (Gets up, sighs, starts to go) Well, here I go. Away from the world, to put my head in the sand. (With self-mockery) the "fearless flyer"! Once he soared through the sky. Now when there's trouble, he goes and hides his head in the sand like a damn fool ostrich in the African desert.

DOCTOR. Maybe the ostrich wasn't such a damn fool, after all. What do you suppose the great generals, the great military geniuses of World War II did when enemy bombers came over the African desert? They couldn't improve on the ostrich's technique. They not only hid their heads in the sand; they hid their entire armies as well. Learn from the ostrich. A strategic genius.

(LINDA comes in, glances at her wrist watch and winks at the DOCTOR)

DOCTOR (Glancing at his watch). Thank you, Linda. (To VINCENT) I'm seeing a patient at five. Sorry. I'll have to be moving. (As LINDA helps him off with his long white coat and hangs it in the closet) When will you see these people?

VINCENT. What time is it now?

DOCTOR. Ten to five. (In his shirt sleeves, starts to scrub his hands at the washstand)

VINCENT. I'll go this very evening. I can't wait. You've given me a new lease on life. I'm so happy. To think it never occurred to me when I was there. When I left, I sighed, I remember. At the time I didn't know why I was sighing, but I do now. I was subconsciously envying them for their quiet happy life. Now I envy them consciously.

(Meanwhile LINDA has handed the DOCTOR a towel)

DOCTOR (Drying his hands). Be sure to give Linda their address.

VINCENT. I will.

(LINDA helps the DOCTOR on with his coat)

DOCTOR. Which way do you go?

VINCENT. Uptown. To have early dinner.

DOCTOR *(Glancing at his watch hurriedly)*. I'm going downtown and in a hurry. *(Hurrying out)* So long, Linda. *(His hand on doorknob)* Goodbye, Mr. Reid.

VINCENT. I wish you'd call me Vincent.

DOCTOR. No.

VINCENT. Why not?

DOCTOR. It spoils the relationship between doctor and patient.

VINCENT. Sure?

DOCTOR. Absolutely. *(He goes out)*

VINCENT *(To* LINDA, *who is straightening up the office)*. He's not so nice as I thought. *(Writing address on a slip of paper)* Here's the address he was asking for.

LINDA *(Takes the slip)*. Thank you. I will give it to him.

VINCENT *(Smiles at her)*. He's a lucky man, that doc.

LINDA. Why?

VINCENT. For having such an efficient assistant. Do you always remind him so promptly when he's due some place?

LINDA. It's what I'm paid for.

VINCENT. You know, I have a great respect for order and method. I suppose you have a big book outside . . . address, date, hour, minute, everything neatly entered?

LINDA. Oh, no. It's simpler than that. When the doctor wants to leave and can't get rid of a patient, he presses a hidden button there . . . *(She points)* . . . and I come in and give him the high sign. You didn't notice him pressing it?

VINCENT. No.

LINDA. Nobody does. The quickness of the hand deceives the eye.

VINCENT. Like a sort of Indian ropetrick. You give your boss's secrets away pretty freely.

LINDA. Not to everyone. *(She opens the door to the waiting room, reaches for his overcoat and hat on a nearby clothes tree and brings them in)* So you're leaving your hotel and moving in with a family?

VINCENT. Yes. How did you know?

LINDA. I have ears.

VINCENT. Shell-like ears . . . and an alabaster brow. It's nice of you to take such an interest in the patients.

LINDA. I always do.

VINCENT. How do you feel about this plan of mine of moving in with a family?

LINDA. I always say, follow the doctor's advice.

VINCENT. This was his advice.

LINDA. Then follow it.

VINCENT. You have no views of your own?

LINDA. Plenty. But you're the doctor's patient, not mine.

VINCENT. Too bad. I'm sorry.

LINDA. *(Trying to change subject)*. Is the old lady nice?

VINCENT. What old lady?

LINDA. The one you're going to live with.

VINCENT. Oh . . . Yes, very nice. And not so old, either. What does that quizzical look mean?

LINDA. You seem in great spirits.

VINCENT. I am. Whenever I make a good quick decision, I fizz like a bottle of pop. Though, as a matter of fact, this one wasn't mine; it was Doctor Moore's, bless him.

LINDA *(Hands* VINCENT *his overcoat)*. You appear more enthusiastic about him than you were a moment ago.

VINCENT. You're interested in my opinions?

LINDA. I'm interested in all the patients.

VINCENT. All?

LINDA. I was exaggerating a little. Not all.

VINCENT. Only one or two?

LINDA. Maybe.

VINCENT. Perhaps only one?

LINDA. *(Embarrassed)*. You ask too many questions.

VINCENT. *(Putting on his overcoat, while* LINDA *helps him)*. You're right. I'm crazy. No wonder. Thanks.

LINDA *(Hands him his hat, smiling)*. Goodbye . . . and good luck.

VINCENT. Thank you. *(He takes out his wallet and starts to give her a bill)*.

LINDA. What's that for?

VINCENT. You're blushing. Why don't you take it?

LINDA. Put it away.

VINCENT *(The wallet still in his hand)*. But why not?

LINDA *(Annoyed)*. Put it away. *(*VINCENT *shrugs, puts wallet back in his pocket)*

LINDA. I've been too nice to you. That's why.

VINCENT. I still don't get it.

LINDA. I wouldn't want you to think I did it . . . hoping for a tip.

VINCENT. Hoping for what, then?

LINDA. Hoping . . . for nothing, I guess. That's what's nice about it.

VINCENT. You really are a peach. I've said it before and I'll say it again . . . Scandinavian women are the finest in the world. But you're making this very difficult for me. Can't you understand that I want to do something to show my appreciation of your kindness the fourteen times I've been here?

LINDA. Only thirteen.

VINCENT. Do you always keep the score so carefully?

LINDA. No.

VINCENT. Thank you . . . Well, here's a thought. Let me take you to dinner . . . at the Colony . . . whenever you say. Afterwards, an hour or so at one of the quieter night clubs.

LINDA. It would be wasted on me. I don't drink, smoke or dance, and seeing what the ladies of Café Society are wearing is not one of my passions.

VINCENT. Have you any passions?

LINDA. I have.

VINCENT. Such as . . . ?

LINDA. One you wouldn't expect in a nurse.

VINCENT. What's that?

LINDA. Nursing.

VINCENT. Ye gods! Injections? Temperature? Feeling pulses? Listening to hearts going pit-a-pat?

LINDA *(Defiantly)*. Yes.

VINCENT. Well, you must get all you want of that here.

LINDA. Not enough. For once . . . it's just a dream, but . . . just for once I'd like to nurse somebody . . . for a long long time . . . somebody I loved. But so far I've been out of luck. The ones I nursed I didn't love. The ones I loved weren't sick.

VINCENT. Very remiss of them.

LINDA. I guess I'm like a small part actress, who ought to be happy playing her little bit night after night . . . but deep in her heart she's waiting . . . waiting for the role of her life.

(Silence)

VINCENT *(Simply)*. May I kiss you?

LINDA. Why?

VINCENT. Why not?

LINDA. Instead of a tip?

VINCENT. No.

LINDA *(Ironically)*. Do I have an exciting effect on you?

VINCENT. No.

LINDA. What effect do I have?

VINCENT. Shall we say . . . one of goodness? *(Suddenly becomes suspicious)* Wait a minute! Did you hear what I was telling the doctor?

LINDA *(Pointing with her head)*. Sometimes when I'm out there in the laboratory I can hear what's being said in here. Accidentally. The wall is thin. But sometimes I listen on purpose.

VINCENT. Which was it this time? Accident?

LINDA. No. Purpose. (VINCENT *moves his face nearer to* LINDA's *lips as if to kiss her.* LINDA *draws away her head slightly. She speaks very simply, without a smile)* Mr. Reid, I was forty last birthday.

VINCENT. A mere child.

LINDA. I have gray hairs.

VINCENT *(Looking at her hair)*. I don't see any.

LINDA *(Raising her cap a little)*. Here.

VINCENT *(Looking)*. Pooh! Two or three.

LINDA *(Putting her cap back again)*. Or four. Or five.

VINCENT. They suit you. *(Again bends close to her face)* May I?

LINDA *(Earnestly, without coquetry)*. Why? I ask you again.

VINCENT. Let's say . . . for goodbye. Or . . . *(Uncertainly)* . . . should I say . . . *(Quickly making up his mind)* No, it's for goodbye.

LINDA *(Ironically)*. That's your final decision?

VINCENT. Yes. *(Bends close to her again)* May I?

LINDA *(Simply)*. If you're careful.

VINCENT. Careful? What do you mean?

LINDA. A professional warning. Make it short and . . . let's say dispassionate. Remember what the doctor said.

VINCENT. I will. *(Kisses her)* Was that "dispassionate" enough?

LINDA. Well, I wouldn't call it a criminal assault. But it lasted longer than was strictly necessary.

VINCENT. You speak as a woman?

LINDA. No. As a nurse.

VINCENT. I'll make it shorter next time.—Are you married?

LINDA *(Indignantly)*. What an insulting question to ask . . . after . . .

VINCENT. How right you are. Excuse it, please. I'm a fool. So long.

(He goes out)

CURTAIN

ACT TWO

SCENE: *Evening of the same day, about seven o'clock. Very simply, cozily furnished living-dining room in the little house occupied by* SOPHIE *and her family, forty minutes from New York. Door in the rear wall. Right: window. Left: fireplace.*

AT RISE: *On stage are* DR. MOORE, SOPHIE, BESS, DICK. BESS *is pressing shirts on an ironing board.* DICK *mixes cocktails and pours them into four glasses.* DR. MOORE *is saying goodbye to* SOPHIE.

DOCTOR. No, I really must go, Mrs. Laurin. Mr. Reid went to a restaurant but *(Taking a look at his watch)* . . . he may walk in at any minute, and I'd rather he didn't find me here. To be frank, I came in such haste because—as you certainly know—he comes to his decisions in a flash. It's possible that he immediately took a taxi and will be here in a moment.

SOPHIE. He called up to say he would be arriving around seven.

DOCTOR. But it's also possible that on the way here he'll think it over, stop the driver, and order him to head for the North Pole.

SOPHIE *(Laughing)*. How well you know him! *(Ingratiatingly)* Just one more, Doctor?

(DICK *offers* DOCTOR *drink*)

DOCTOR. Thank you, no, really. I must be off. I told him I hadn't intended to come here till next week, but . . .

SOPHIE. Yes?

DOCTOR. I suppose I'm fussy by nature, and . . . well, it's odd, but I've become very fond of Mr. Reid.

SOPHIE. Not odd at all. Everybody likes him.

DOCTOR. Yes. Why, even my nurse, who's always so cool and distant, seems to take a special pleasure in treating him.

SOPHIE. I'm not surprised.

DOCTOR. Well, it's a very good thing, because what he needs now is care and kindness. That's why I advised him to move here. And . . . I said to myself . . . I'll run right out and take a look at that little house of yours.

SOPHIE *(Sweetly)*. He's lucky to have a doctor like you.

DOCTOR. And a guardian angel like you.

SOPHIE. Oh, Doctor.—All your instructions will be carried out. *(Reeling off)* Early to bed, morning walks, afternoon rest, no smoking, nothing to drink . . . loss of weight . . .

DOCTOR. And above all . . .

SOPHIE *(With a knowing smile)*. Yes, yes, I know. No worry.

DOCTOR *(Very gravely)*. And most crucial . . .

SOPHIE. No excitement.

DOCTOR. None whatsoever. Not the least.—I think that's about all.

SOPHIE. Except the slippers.

DOCTOR *(Laughing)*. You remember that?

SOPHIE. Of course. *(As if reciting a lesson)* Tight shoes keep the blood from circulating through the feet, but in comfortable slippers . . .

DOCTOR. Right.

SOPHIE. He shall have his comfortable slippers. I've learned something new.

DICK. Mamma knows everything, but she still goes on learning all the time.

SOPHIE. And we're not to tell him you were here.

DOCTOR. Better not, I think. He would start letting his imagination run away with him. Of course there wasn't really the slightest necessity for me to come, but I'm very glad I did. I can see that this is exactly what he needs. May I have a drop of that nice drink, after all.

(DICK *offers a glass.* SOPHIE *also gets him one.* BESS, *too)*

DOCTOR *(Laughing).* Quick service! Thank you, thank you. *(He takes* SOPHIE'S *glass)* It's the same as we had before?

SOPHIE. Yes.

DOCTOR. What do you call it?

BESS. Hot martini.

DOCTOR. *Hot* martini?

BESS. Because it's made of three things . . . gin, vermouth and a kiss. *(Showing her glass)* Gin and vermouth . . . (DICK *and* BESS *sip a little from their glasses)* . . . and . . . (THEY *kiss each other)* That's it.

DOCTOR. Charming. *(Lifts his glass, looking at* SOPHIE. SOPHIE *takes a glass)* Here's to you.

(DOCTOR *and* SOPHIE *drink)*

SOPHIE. Well, really, though I've only known you for fifteen minutes, Doctor . . . (SHE *kisses him on both cheeks)* . . . let's make ours a hot martini, too. Because you're so kind to my dear Vincent.

DOCTOR *(Delighted).* My dear lady, I'm quite overcome. How glad I am that I yielded to that impulse and came to this little house out of a fairy story.

SOPHIE *(Flattered).* Oh, Doctor.

DOCTOR. Presided over by the Good Fairy in person.

DICK. You said it, Doctor. *(Puts his arm around* SOPHIE'S *shoulder)* A Good Fairy is just what she is . . . my dear mother!

BESS *(Ironing).* The very word for my mother-in-law, doctor.

SOPHIE. Dear Vincent, how happy he'll be in that clean, quiet room upstairs, looking out on the garden. And then in the evening a cozy corner by the fire. Reading . . .

DOCTOR. But not listening to the radio.

SOPHIE. No, the singing commercials are so upsetting. And what's worse, the news. The victrola . . . *(Points to it)* . . . plays what he wants to hear, not the things this wicked world frightens us with all day long.

DOCTOR. That's right. Exactly what I was saying. *(Enthusiastically)* This is exactly the peaceful atmosphere I pictured.

SOPHIE *(Coyly).* But you came anyway, to make sure.

DOCTOR. Oh, well, I felt responsible. (SOPHIE *dabs at her eyes)* You mustn't cry.

SOPHIE. But it's so wonderful to think of my dear Vincent being here . . . my childhood playmate. We'll do everything to make him happy.

BESS. Everything. Won't we, Dick?

DICK. I'd like to see the man who wouldn't be happy with Mamma and Bess around.

DOCTOR. I quite agree. Well, I really must tear myself away, or you'll be having me for a boarder, too. *(Starts to go, then stops, recalling something)* You'll find Mr. Reid very grateful. And he's a very generous man. He was telling me all the wonderful things he wants to give you.

SOPHIE. But, Doctor, we don't want anything.

DOCTOR. I'm afraid you'll get it. He's just longing to give you presents. You needn't worry. He can afford it.

SOPHIE. What matters is the spirit. And good health.

DOCTOR. Especially good health.

SOPHIE. Not the spirit?

DOCTOR. I wouldn't know. That's out of my line. (A car is heard stopping outside) Hello. A car.

SOPHIE (Pushing the curtain aside and looking out). It's not he. It's only those girls next door.

DOCTOR (Concerned). Are there girls next door?

SOPHIE. A couple of small time dancers. The two Petito sisters.

DOCTOR. Are they pretty?

SOPHIE. Very.

DOCTOR. Too bad.—Well, now I must run along. (Starts to go. Stops) What sort of girls are they?

SOPHIE (Meaningfully). Well . . .

DOCTOR. Questionable girls?

SOPHIE. No question.

DOCTOR. Then for heaven's sake keep them away from Mr. Reid.

SOPHIE (Grimly). I will.

DOCTOR. Do. It's important. Goodbye.

SOPHIE, DICK, BESS. Goodbye. —So long.—Goodbye.

(DOCTOR goes out hurriedly.— The OTHERS begin to push the furniture around, to form a cozy corner in front of the fireplace)

SOPHIE (Moved). There aren't many doctors like that.

BESS. I'll say there aren't.

SOPHIE (Dabbing her eyes). And there aren't many men like Vincent.

BESS. Were you very much in love with him, Mom?

SOPHIE. I don't suppose any silly girl of nineteen was ever more in love.

BESS. But you married Willy Laurin.

DICK. And quite right, too. My father, Willy Laurin, was a fine man.

SOPHIE. He certainly was. He had a true Viennese heart of gold.

BESS. Which of them are you crying for, Mom . . . Vincent, the doctor or your late husband?

SOPHIE. All three.

(During the preceding dialogue and that which follows they set up a cozy corner at the fireside. They place the evening paper beside the arm chair and near it a bottle of beer and a plate of pretzels. They cushion the back of the chair with soft pillows. There is only one armchair at the fireplace)

SOPHIE. Well, if he wants to sit and rest by the fire, he'll be comfortable there.

(THEY put a reading lamp beside the chair. DICK sits for a moment in the chair, while BESS adjusts the light to the proper level for a man reading the paper. Outside a storm has broken, with gusts of wind and rain. Thunder. Meanwhile THEY speak)

SOPHIE. Poor Vincent. He'll be caught in the storm.

BESS. Hasn't he a car?

SOPHIE. He's not allowed to drive.

DICK. Well, he can take a cab.

SOPHIE. But think of the time it takes to get into a cab . . . and out of it. (Suddenly remembering) The slippers! We've forgotten the slippers! (Takes a pair of slippers from *a drawer and puts them by the chair)* They help the blood to circulate. (SHE *looks at the cozy corner with an inspecting glance)* Well, I think we've done everything now *(Meditatively)* I wish we had a cat to sit on his lap.

BESS. Maybe he doesn't like cats.

SOPHIE. No, there's that, of course.

(SHE leaves the "corner" and takes up some sewing. BESS goes back to the ironing board. DICK opens a book. The next moment a car stops outside and then DOORBELL rings. ALL jump up and go out to open the front door. Noisy, warm greetings in the foyer. Then THEY enter with VINCENT, who comes in with a broad smile. HE is laden with boxes)

VINCENT *(Gay, too loud)*. What weather! It's raining cats, dogs, pitchforks, axes and hammer handles.

SOPHIE *(Beginning to take care of him. Quietingly)*. Now, now, you mustn't get excited. Nice and quiet now. It's just raining rain.

VINCENT. Dear Sophie. Always so matter-of-fact and literal. Well my arrival is symbolic, Sophie. Here I am, out of the raging storm into the calm haven. What a heavenly, restful atmosphere.

SOPHIE. It's always like that here, Vincent. (VINCENT *takes roses out of a box and hands them to her)* Vincent! Two dozen American Beauties! How wonderful! Thank you! *(Pricks her finger on a thorn)* Ouch! A thorn! And such a big one.

(SHE dumps the roses on to the table, sticks her finger in her mouth and sucks it. DICK examines the thorn. BESS dashes

over to a drawer. EVERYBODY *acts with the haste and despair befitting a serious accident)*

VINCENT. Oh! Bleeding!

DICK *(Looking at the thorn)*. It's enormous. Like a dagger. Does it hurt, Mamma?

SOPHIE *(Sucking her finger)*. It does rather. Bess, iodine, please. There in the first aid kit.

VINCENT. This is a tragedy.

BESS. Here you are, Mom. (SHE *paints* SOPHIE's *finger with the iodine)* You poor thing.

DICK *(Putting cotton wool on* SOPHIE's *finger)*. Hold it there a minute.

VINCENT. I'm really most awfully sorry. Nothing could have been further from my intention than to make you welter in your gore.—I ought not to have brought roses.

BESS. Mom only likes one kind of flower—pink carnations.

VINCENT *(Slapping his forehead)*. I'm a fool. I knew that once, but I forgot.

SOPHIE *(With a sigh and a coquettish smile)*. Oh, well, Vincent, it was very long ago. (SHE *puts the roses in a vase)*

VINCENT *(Giving DICK a box)*. This is for you, Dick.

DICK. Why, say, that's swell of you, Mr. Reid. *(Opens box)* Look, Mamma! Bess!

SOPHIE *(Takes out a handful of neckties)*. Beautiful silk neckties. Pure silk. And so many of them.

BESS. Too bad Dick only wears bow ties.

VINCENT. Just my luck.

DICK. Now, Bess . . . I'll be glad to wear these, too. If only for Mr. Reid's sake.

BESS. Like fun you will. I know you. Tomorrow they'll go in the ash can.

VINCENT. Really? Well, I hope this won't. (*Opens a small box, looking at* DICK) It's for your wife. Something for a secretary.

(SOPHIE *takes the box*)

SOPHIE. A gold pen! Solid gold! Even the barrel! And a gold pencil! Look at them, Dick. You're the goldsmith of the family.

DICK (*Examines the pen expertly*). Twenty-four carat. They don't use any better gold than that. (HE *gives the box to* BESS)

BESS. Thanks so much. (SHE *smiles at* DICK)

DICK. I see in your eyes the words "I'd rather have had . . ."

BESS. There's always an "I'd rather have had" in a girl's eyes.

DICK. You'd rather have had . . . what? Come on, spill it.

BESS. Well, if I must say . . . a wrist watch.

VINCENT. First thing tomorrow I'll . . .

BESS. No, no, please. Don't bother, I'll exchange it myself. (*Mumbling*) It means spending a whole lot extra. (SHE *goes back to the ironing board*)

SOPHIE (*Reproachfully*). Bess!

VINCENT. I didn't quite catch that.

SOPHIE. It was nothing, Vincent, nothing. (SHE *pushes him into an armchair. It's not the same chair, though, that they set up at the fireside earlier*) Do sit down . . . in this nice soft chair.

BESS. Cushions, Dick.

DICK. Coming over! (HE *puts a cushion at back of chair*)

BESS. The footstool.

(DICK *quickly brings it from a corner*)

SOPHIE (*Bringing another cushion*). And another cushion. (SHE *puts it alongside the first, and* VINCENT *sits down*)

DICK (*Placing footstool at his feet*). Upsy-daisy!

(SOPHIE *pats the cushions into place.* DICK *sets a little table with a bottle, glasses and a box of cigars beside the chair*)

VINCENT (*Putting his feet on footstool*). This is solid comfort! But you oughtn't to coddle me this way.

SOPHIE. It isn't too cold for you?

VINCENT. No.

SOPHIE. Nor too warm?

VINCENT. No. Just right. Thank you one and all. I'm much obliged. You're angels. (ALL *sit down*) And now let me tell you something. Listen carefully, my darlings. Sophie, you'll never guess why I've come here.

SOPHIE (*Pretending ignorance*). You've come to supper, haven't you?

VINCENT. Rather . . . to breakfast.

SOPHIE. What?

VINCENT. Without going into an elaborate introduction—I want to stay here.

SOPHIE. Stay here?

VINCENT. Live here. For ever . . . or as long as I do live. I ought to begin by explaining that the doctor has ordered me a quiet, peaceful life.

SOPHIE (*Pretending to be painfully surprised*). Oh, Vincent! You haven't . . . ?

VINCENT. No, I haven't anything serious the matter with me. Just a heart that's misbehaving a little.

SOPHIE. Heavens!

VINCENT. And the doctor insists that I escape from what city people call living and take up my abode with some nice quiet family. I thought of you right away.

SOPHIE. How sweet of you, Vincent. You couldn't have come to a better place. But your heart . . .

VINCENT. Oh, let's forget my heart.

SOPHIE. Dick, put those cigars away this minute. And the drinks, too. (VINCENT *smiles, while* DICK *puts the cigars and drinks away)* You mustn't even look at them.

VINCENT. You ought to have been a nurse, Sophie.

SOPHIE. I did think of it once.

VINCENT. You wanted to be a nurse?

SOPHIE. You don't like nurses? Nor do I.

VINCENT. Of course, there are nurses *and* nurses.

SOPHIE. But, Vincent, you've taken my breath away. Just to think of you living here with us! *(Sweetly)* I'll fix your room up myself. It's so quiet. The windows open on the garden.

VINCENT. Can you see next door from the windows?

SOPHIE. Yes. Why?

VINCENT. I saw two darned pretty girls on the porch there when I came in. Friends of yours?

SOPHIE *(Icily)*. No . . . and we don't want them to be. *(Throwing a serious glance at* VINCENT, *as she remembers the doctor's warning).* God forbid.

VINCENT *(Laughing)*. I understand. Thank you, Sophie. (HE *turns to* DICK) Well, Dick, old man. Let's have a look at you. (HE *takes both*

of DICK's *hands, looks at him softening, speaks happily)* You're a fine, healthy specimen.

SOPHIE. With a sweet face.

DICK. I got it from mother.

VINCENT *(Pointing at* DICK's *book)*. What are you reading?

DICK. The life of Benvenuto Cellini. The greatest goldsmith in history.

VINCENT *(Sentimental)*. I used to read all the time once. Only I read the life stories of flyers.

DICK. I know. I envy you. You used to be an aviator, Mr. Reid?

SOPHIE. Call him "Uncle Vincent."

DICK *(Embarrassed)*. Aw, gee, Mamma, not right away. Let's get acquainted first.

SOPHIE. But, Dick . . .

VINCENT *(With that half-smile)*. Don't rush him, Sophie. I was just that way at his age. Took me quite a while to warm up to people. *(Smiling at* DICK) Don't be afraid, Dick. I won't kiss you.

BESS. *I* will (SHE'*kisses* DICK. HE *returns the kiss passionately)*

SOPHIE. Aren't they cute? Like love-birds. I love to see them together. So do other people. Dick's boss often takes them out to dinner and a night club.

VINCENT *(Cut to the quick)*. The boss?

DICK. Yes. Bess is a wonderful dancer. My boss loves to dance with her.

VINCENT *(After a pause)*. Well, that's fine. (HE *is silent for a moment)* But we ought to be fixing up the business arrangements. You have two rooms upstairs for rent, yes?

SOPHIE. Yes. Two.

VINCENT. I'll take 'em both.

SOPHIE. Oh, but only one of them will be free. The school teacher, Miss Bell, who has it, is moving out on Monday. The other's taken.

VINCENT. Who by?

SOPHIE. An elderly gentleman.

VINCENT. Shoot him out.

SOPHIE. I don't think he'd go.

VINCENT. Not even for money?

SOPHIE (Uneasily). I don't think so.

VINCENT. Lots of money?

SOPHIE. I don't think so.

VINCENT. We'll see. My experience is that elderly gentlemen have their price. In the meantime I'll do with one room. (Looks around) I'll be down here with you all the time, anyway. I like this room, Sophie. But what it needs is a couple of soft, thick rugs. And you must have a maid. I'll attend to all that. And later on . . . if there is any "later on" for me . . . I'll buy a house . . . for you and the family and me.

(DICK wrinkles his nose)

SOPHIE. Children! Our dreams are coming true! Why, Vincent, it's just like a fairy story.

VINCENT. You wait. I mean to do you proud.—How many steps are there up to this room of yours?

SOPHIE. Only eighteen.

VINCENT. It's wonderful. This place might have been constructed to my own specifications.—Hey, Dick, don't bury your nose in that book. You'll ruin your eyes.

(DICK takes no notice)

SOPHIE. Dick, thank Uncle Vincent for thinking of your eyes.

BESS (Ironing). I thank you for my grouchy husband.

DICK (Looks up from his book). It isn't that I have a grouch, Mr. . . . Vincent. But there are two things that always get my goat . . . having to talk when I'm reading and . . .

VINCENT. . . . being ordered around.

BESS. That's right.

VINCENT. Just the way I was at his age.

DICK (To Vincent, warmly). You aren't sore?

VINCENT. Not in the least. I think you're fine, Dick. I like your character, what I've seen of it . . . and I liked the way you sneered at me when I was bragging about my money.

DICK (Sincerely). My heart belongs to the poor. (Goes on reading)

VINCENT. I think Dick's swell.

BESS. Take a bow, Dick.

DICK (Without looking up from his book). Yes, darling.

SOPHIE (Ingratiatingly). Evening paper, Vincent? (SHE hands it to him)

VINCENT (Refusing it after a cursory glance). My doctor would snatch it out of my hand and dance on it. Wrong kind of reading for me. "Airplane crash . . . Burning wreck . . . Charred bodies."

SOPHIE (With the paper in her hand). Don't look at the headline, Vincent. Read the subhead. "Five uninjured." Just imagine the happiness in those five families. Daddy home. Mother home. Brother-in-law a little shaken but otherwise all right. It's a delightful story, if you know how to read it.

VINCENT. Sophie, do you remember a book called "Pollyanna"?

Sophie. Yes.

VINCENT. You didn't write it, did you?

SOPHIE. No.

VINCENT. I was wondering.—
You're such a ray of sunshine.

SOPHIE (*Cocking her ear toward the foyer*). How funny! That's what Mr. Hennyman always says.

VINCENT. Mr. Hennyman being who?

SOPHIE. The man who lives upstairs. Your future neighbor. An artist. He's so sweet.

VINCENT. I'm not so sure that I want a sweet neighbor.

SOPHIE. He's as gentle as a lamb.

VINCENT. Fine, if you're fond of lambs. . . .

SOPHIE (*Pointing toward the foyer*). The reason I mentioned him was, I just heard his key in the lock. He's been on a trip, and he's just come back.

(*Outside, the door slams shut. BESS stops ironing. DICK closes his book and gets up. BOTH are smiling happily*)

SOPHIE. You and he will be the greatest friends. You see. I've told him lots of nice things about you.

VINCENT. Sophie, you're marvelous.

(HE *kisses* SOPHIE *on forehead as* CLEM HENNYMAN *comes in He is in his fifties. He wears a cheap suit and is laden with boxes, as Vincent was.* HE *is taken aback at seeing* VINCENT *kissing* SOPHIE. BESS *and* DICK, *like a pair of affectionate puppies who have not seen their master for a long time, throw themselves at* CLEM, *embrace him, laughing and shouting*)

BESS, DICK (*Together*). Clem! Henny! Thank goodness, you're back, Clem, dear! Gee, it's good to have you back.

CLEM (*Beaming*). Dick! Bess! Dick! Bess! Hello, Mrs. Laurin, how are you?

SOPHIE. How are *you?* About time you came home! (CLEM *hands* SOPHIE *a hat box*) More presents! How many times have I told you not to be so naughty?

(VINCENT *stands aside, very much out of it in this wild burst of welcome.* CLEM *gives boxes to* DICK *and* BESS)

BESS (*Eagerly opening her box*). Trust Clem not to come home empty-handed.

CLEM. Say, look, I've been on the road for three weeks. Why wouldn't I bring you something?

(CLEM *is speaking to Sophie and the two young people, but glances from time to time at* VINCENT, *who stands aside silently, sourly observing how much more successful* CLEM'S *presents are than his*)

SOPHIE (*Squeals delightedly as* SHE *takes a strikingly stylish green and pink hat from her box*). Look! Oh, do look at this, everybody! But, Clem, didn't it cost a fortune?

CLEM. No, *ma'am.* Dirt cheap. I only wish I could have afforded something better.

DICK (*Taking a flashlight out of his box*). A double-powered flashlight! Gee! (HE *flashes it on and off and whoops with joy*) Fantastic! You know I was planning to buy one of these tomorrow?

BESS (*Squealing as* SHE *takes a sweater out of her box*). Oh, Clem, it's out of this world! You can't say *this* was cheap?

CLEM. Practically given away. There's kind of a defect in the weave.

BESS. My great big blue-eyed dream man!!

(SHE *starts to throw herself on* CLEM'S *neck.* SOPHIE *tries the hat on and squeals as she sees herself in the mirror*)

SOPHIE. Look! Look!!!

BESS. Wonderful!

CLEM. Just a simple little number. Got it at a sale.

SOPHIE. Sea-green velvet with pink carnations! *(Coquettishly).* Pink carnations! You remembered! It's so gorgeous, I'll wear it even in the house. I'll wear it while I'm washing the dishes. *(With the hat on her head, holds out her hand to* CLEM) It's the compliment that touches me . . . you thinking me young and attractive enough for anything as gay and youthful as this.

CLEM *(Taking her hand).* Shucks! You're the youngest and loveliest woman in the world, Mrs. Laurin . . . to me. *(Seeing her finger)* Hurt your finger?

SOPHIE. A thorn . . . the roses . . . *(Realizes that she has forgotten to introduce* VINCENT) Gracious! Whatever will you think of me? And you, Vincent, just standing there and not a peep out of you! This is Clem Hennyman, Vincent. Clem, meet Vincent Reid. *(She takes her hat off)*

CLEM *(Very coldly).* How do you do?

VINCENT *(Friendly).* How do you do?

(CLEM *looks at* VINCENT *with unmistakeable hostility, making a wry face*)

SOPHIE *(Seeing this, becomes loquacious and in her great embarrassment chats too brightly, with forced gaiety).* He brought me the roses. Red roses. Aren't they wonderful?

My childhood friend. Vincent. Remember? I told you about him. Vincent Reid. He was working for an airplane firm. In Paris. Yes. For ten years. It was ten, Vincent? Or was it twelve? He married a French girl, then he was a prisoner of war, then he came back here, then he got a divorce . . . and here he is.

CLEM *(Visibly displeased).* Ah . . . that's him?

SOPHIE *(After two overwhelmingly sweet smiles, to both of them).* Yes. (SHE *puts the hat in the box*)

CLEM *(Dryly).* The rich Vincent Reid.

SOPHIE *(Sweetly).* The *nice* Vincent Reid.

(CLEM *stares at* VINCENT, *sizing him up*)

VINCENT *(Amiably, pointing at himself).* Height, five eight. Weight, one forty-nine.

SOPHIE *(Pointing to* CLEM). He's been living upstairs . . . oh, for a long, long time.

VINCENT. Yes.

(Silence)

CLEM *(Looking at* VINCENT *thoughtfully).* Strange.

VINCENT *(Who likes neither the word nor* CLEM). What do you mean, strange?

CLEM. You're kind of different from what I pictured you.

VINCENT. Really? In what way?

CLEM. Well, considering that there was a time when Mrs. Laurin. . . .

VINCENT. Yes?

CLEM. Well, let's put it this way. She tells me she was once sort of sweet on you.

VINCENT. And you expected me to be more glamorous?

CLEM *(Irritated).* Yes, I did.

VINCENT. The years take their toll, Mr. . . . Mr. . . .

CLEM *(Barely concealing his antipathy)*. Hennyman.

VINCENT. Sorry I'm not the Romeo a sentimental elderly gentleman imagined me.

CLEM. I'll say you're not. Not by a damn sight.

SOPHIE *(Placatingly)*. Clem, dear.

VINCENT *(Surprised)*. "Clem"?—"Dear"? *(As SOPHIE looks at him frightened)* I thought he was a roomer.

SOPHIE. He is. And . . . his name is Clement. Clem.

VINCENT *(Staring before him resignedly. Begins to understand)*. I thought it was Hennyman.

CLEM *(Irritated)*. Clem *and* Hennyman.

SOPHIE. Clem . . . please . . .

CLEM *(Interrupting)*. As you very well know, Sophie . . .

VINCENT. Oh. "Sophie!"

CLEM *(Furious)*. Yes . . . SOPHIE! *(To SOPHIE, loudly)* As you very well know, Sophie, I'm a man who speaks his mind. He asked me if I expected him to be more glamorous, and I said yes. And I say it again. *(Painful silence)*

SOPHIE. Do sit down, both of you.

(The TWO MEN are motionless. BESS, worried, has been glancing alternately at CLEM and VINCENT. SHE goes on ironing. DICK looks, then tactfully resumes his reading. SOPHIE, between the two men, looks from one to the other, frightened. Long, painful pause)

VINCENT. Extraordinary.

CLEM. What's "extraordinary"?

VINCENT. The sudden tension in the air.

CLEM *(Aggressively)*. What tension?

SOPHIE. Clem, do stop working yourself up!

VINCENT. Is that bad for him, *too?*

SOPHIE. It's bad for anybody. Now, Clem, listen to me. I have to tell you. Mr. Reid . . . Vincent . . . is coming to live here.

CLEM *(Scowling)*. Coming to live here?

SOPHIE. Yes.

CLEM. Here in this house?

SOPHIE. Yes.

VINCENT. I'm renting a room.

SOPHIE *(Again too-too cheerfully, to stop the tension)*. Isn't it wonderful, Clem? I'm so happy. Vincent's just wonderful. You'll like him. You'll love him.

CLEM *(Darkly)*. Oh, yeah?

VINCENT. So that's the elderly lamb in the next room.

SOPHIE. Yes.

CLEM. Say, where do you get that "elderly" stuff? That's the second time you pulled it. Maybe you object to my age?

VINCENT. Not at all.

CLEM. Maybe you object to me living in the next room?

SOPHIE. Of course he doesn't. What makes you think so?

CLEM. The tone of his question. *(To VINCENT)* And what's all this about lambs?

VINCENT. She said you were as gentle as a lamb.

CLEM *(Furious)*. Say, listen . . . I . . . I . . .

SOPHIE Now, Clem! This isn't like you!

(BESS and DICK step up affec-

tionately to CLEM, *who has been standing near them, and try to calm him, whispering:* . . . *"Clem"* . . . *"Dear!"* . . . *"Clem!" etc.)*

CLEM *(To* VINCENT). I . . . I don't like you.

VINCENT *(Beginning to lose patience).* It's mutual.

BESS, DICK. Clem . . . dear . . . Clem. . . .

CLEM *(Moved).* At least you two are fond of me.

SOPHIE *(Pouting).* And I.

CLEM *(Melting).* You too, Sophie.

SOPHIE. Kiss me. (CLEM *kisses* SOPHIE *on forehead.* VINCENT *makes a wry face)* Clem is a very remarkable man, Vincent.

VINCENT. I noticed it.

SOPHIE. And Vincent is a great man, Clem.

CLEM. Who said so? Did *he?*

SOPHIE. He's a flyer.

VINCENT. I was.

SOPHIE. Clem's an artist. A creative man. A painter.

CLEM *(Irritably).* I was. But I never got anywhere. Matter of fact, right now I'm a travelling salesman. I work for a firm that outfits bathrooms?

VINCENT *(Scornfully).* Bathrooms?

CLEM *(Boiling).* Yes, bathrooms . . . and everything that goes into them. Grin all you like. I'm not ashamed of it. I install all the fixings . . . mostly the ones you're grinning about so hard.

VINCENT. Aren't you going to a lot of trouble to camouflage a useful, if inelegant, detail of interior decoration?

CLEM *(Angrily).* It's worth trouble to avoid calling a spade a spade.

SOPHIE. You're making such a fuss, Clem, over a trifle.

CLEM. Well, look how he keeps grinning at me. The man who owns the sky! All right . . . *(Exploding)* . . . if you want my story, here it is. I used to be an artist, but nobody would buy my pictures. So now I'm trying to make a living installing rest rooms in gas stations. Like it or not.

VINCENT. I always like a good rest room. Much better than a bad painting.

CLEM *(Wounded).* My job's not a romantic one, but the bird of my heart soars high above the clouds.

VINCENT. That's neat. Your own?

CLEM. No. Tennyson.

SOPHIE. He reads all the great poetry. He's an artist through and through. *(Looks at* CLEM *with awe)* A dreamer.

CLEM *(To* VINCENT). You could never penetrate the depths of my soul.

VINCENT. If you don't mind my saying so, that's one of my lesser worries.

(SOPHIE *takes a small picture from the mantelpiece)*

SOPHIE *(To* CLEM). May I show him this?

CLEM *(Sullenly).* If you like.

VINCENT. *(Taking picture).* Wonderful.—A battleship.

CLEM. No. Hold it further away.

VINCENT *(Doing so).* Oh, I see. St. Patrick's Cathedral.

CLEM *(Wounded).* No.

VINCENT. What then?

CLEM. A self-portrait. (HE *snatches the picture from* VINCENT *and flings it hysterically into a far corner of the room)*

SOPHIE. Clem? How can you?

CLEM (*Furiously*). He's making fun of me.

VINCENT. I wasn't. Don't be so damn touchy. Take that idiotic chip off your shoulder. This is a hell of a welcome for me to get, when I'm this family's best friend.

CLEM. This family's *rich* friend.

VINCENT. You make me sick.

CLEM. I do, do I? Say listen. (*Bitterly frank*) Why do you suppose they're all so nice to you? Because of your money, that's why.

SOPHIE. Clem, that was a dreadful thing to say.

VINCENT. Jealous fool!

SOPHIE. My goodness . . . both of you getting so excited . . . for no reason. Why should he be jealous? Who of?

CLEM (*Hysterical*). How did I get mixed up in this fight with a fellow I've only known for five minutes?

SOPHIE (*Would like to side with both of them*). You've known him for ever so long, Clem. I've told you so much about him.

CLEM. And I didn't like what you told me. (*To* VINCENT). Put that in your pipe and smoke it.

VINCENT. The doctor won't let me smoke.

(SOPHIE, *between them, throws frightened glances at them*)

BESS. May I say a word?

VINCENT. Do.

BESS. We're wandering from the subject a little, aren't we? We *were* talking about the room.

VINCENT. Smart girl. You're quite right. Let's get back to it.

CLEM (*In a tone of cross-examination*). For how long do you intend to rent this room?

VINCENT (*To* SOPHIE). Is he the landlord?

CLEM. No, I'm not the landlord, but I'd very much like to know how long you plan to stay here.

VINCENT. Forever. And when you get out of the other room I'm going to take that, too.

CLEM. The hell you are! You'll get it over my dead body.

VINCENT. How nice if that could be arranged. (CLEM *sputters*). All right, keep calm. For the time being, I'm only interested in the room the school teacher is vacating.

CLEM. You're not going to have that, either.

SOPHIE. Really, Clem! That room belongs to me.

CLEM. I don't care. He's not going to get it. I don't want to be next door to someone dropping his shoes all over the place.

VINCENT. I'll put them under my pillow.

CLEM. Do you think I'm going to share the bathroom with you?

VINCENT. We won't use it together.

CLEM. I won't stand for it, I tell you. (*To* SOPHIE, *with childish spite*) I'll take the other room, too.

VINCENT. I'll double the gentleman's offer, blind.

CLEM. There you go! Money! But your damned money doesn't mean a thing in this house. They don't care about it here.

VINCENT. A minute ago you were saying that it was only my money that made them nice to me.

CLEM. Yes, a minute ago. And now I'm saying the opposite. I'm not pigheaded. (*More and more vehemently*). Their love is not for sale. If you want to get love for money, there's only one way . . . buy a dog.

SOPHIE *(Almost crying)*. Clem!

CLEM *(Upset)*. Yes, but did you hear him? "I'll double the gentleman's offer." Capitalistic louse!

VINCENT. The decision would seem to be up to you, Sophie.

SOPHIE *(Girlishly lowering her eyes)*. Clem Hennyman's been here a long time.

DICK *(Looks up from his book)*. He came here the night when he ran away from home because his wife beat him up.

SOPHIE. And he's been here two years.

DICK. Poor old Clem. He's an unhappy man. He's a martyr.

BESS. Clem's a saint.

CLEM. You hear? Do you think I'm going to leave people like them? I only wish I could spend the next hundred years living with them.

SOPHIE. Clem's so grateful.

VINCENT *(Simply)*. What does he pay?

SOPHIE *(Embarrassed)*. Who?

VINCENT. Clem Hennyman.

SOPHIE *(More and more embarrassed)*. For what?

VINCENT. For his room. *(Silence. DICK turns away. BESS irons feverishly. VINCENT asks again, simply:)* What does he pay?

SOPHIE *(Dropping her eyes)*. Nothing.

CLEM *(His voice breaking)*. No, they don't make a profit out of loving me. They lose money. *(His voice more and more choked)* Yes, sir, they're supporting me . . . till something turns up. *(In a very choked voice)*. Those are my shirts Bess is ironing.

BESS. Quite all right, Clem. A pleasure. *(Irons with gusto)*

CLEM. When I say *my* shirts, Dick bought them.

SOPHIE. And I washed them.— Poor dear, he ran away from home that night in a pair of pink pajamas.

VINCENT. And they got up a trousseau for you, like a bride?

CLEM. Yes, they did.

VINCENT. Did you bring your hope chest?

CLEM. They took pity on me because life had kicked me around.

(The family become sentimental as CLEM dabs at his eyes. SOPHIE, DICK and BESS caress and soothe him with short words of comfort . . . "There, there," "Cheer up, Clem," "Now, now, now" . . . CLEM feels sorrier and sorrier for himself)

CLEM. They love me because I'm impractical and helpless . . . a dreamer . . .

VINCENT. Maybe that's why *I* love you.

CLEM. I'm not meant for this world.

VINCENT. No, I can see how it might get on without you.

(SOPHIE has poured out a drink with her back to VINCENT and CLEM. DICK picks up the footstool and goes with BESS to the fireplace where BOTH are busy with the "cozy corner.")

SOPHIE *(Without turning, sweetly)*. Sit down, dear. We've fixed up a little nest for you by the fire.

VINCENT. Thank you. *(Starts for the only armchair by the fireplace)*

CLEM. Thank you. *(Plants himself in this armchair)*

BESS *(To VINCENT, explaining)*. This is his place. We call it "Clem's

Corner." *(To* CLEM, *sweetly, offering each thing in turn).* Beer, pipe, matches, paper . . .

DICK *(Lovingly, with the footstool in his hand).* Lamp, glasses . . . *(Placing footstool at* CLEM'S *feet)* Upsy-daisy!

CLEM. Thank you, children, thank you. *(Putting his feet on footstool pretends to read the paper)*

BESS. Dear old Clem. Nice to have you here again. After three long weeks! We missed you, dear! (SHE *kisses him on the top of his head.* SOPHIE *turns)*

VINCENT. Exactly as I pictured the scene . . . except that I thought I'd be the man in the armchair.

SOPHIE. But, Vincent, you will be . . . in *this* armchair. *(Shows him the chair where he sat before)*

VINCENT *(Smiling bitterly).* My sweetheart when a boy!

CLEM *(Pretending to read the paper. Dryly).* That's all over.

VINCENT. You think so?

CLEM. Well, isn't it?

VINCENT *(Challengingly).* Not for me. And maybe not for her.

CLEM *(Excitedly, aggressively).* Well, I say it is, and I'll tell you why. (HE *rises, threateningly)*

SOPHIE *(Frightened).* Bess, go get supper started.

BESS *(Seeing that* SOPHIE *is sending her out for fear of an unpleasant scene).* Okay, Mom. *(Pats* SOPHIE'S *arm)* Relax.

SOPHIE *(Tremulously).* I'll try.

BESS. Come on, Dick. (SHE *goes out.* DICK *starts after her)*

CLEM *(In a trembling voice).* We're going to have a showdown.

(DICK *stops a moment)*

SOPHIE *(Nervously, peremptorily).* Go on, Dick, help Bess.

DICK. Yes, Mamma, sure. (HE *goes out, reluctantly)*

SOPHIE. Clem, *please.* Don't be so . . .

CLEM. Well, he makes me sick. Calling you his sweetheart.

VINCENT. "When a boy."

CLEM *(Irritated).* "Boy" nothing. You were twenty-seven. I know. She was nineteen. I know. And she was in love with you. I know. I know everything. *(Suddenly getting very excited again, slams down paper)* You! . . . Quit meddling with our happy lives. You've nothing in common with anybody here. Not with her or her son or her daughter-in-law. Get the hell out with your money.

VINCENT *(To* SOPHIE). What does he mean, he "knows everything"?

SOPHIE *(Tremulously).* Not everything, Vincent.

CLEM *(Suspiciously).* Hey? What's all this?

SOPHIE *(Beginning to lose control).* But I'll tell him everything now. *(To* VINCENT, *excitedly)* I won't have him thinking . . .

VINCENT *(Interrupting).* He can think any damn thing he likes, for all I care.

CLEM. You've been keeping something from me.

SOPHIE. Yes, and I can't stand it any longer. *(To* VINCENT). Now that you're going to be here with us, I want my whole life to be an open book to Clem.

VINCENT *(Agitated).* Sophie, pipe down.

SOPHIE *(Savagely).* I won't!!!

VINCENT. He won't like it.

SOPHIE *(Excitedly)*. I don't care. I won't have him thinking that your only claim to live here is your money. *(To* CLEM, *solemnly but in a trembling voice)* Clem, I have a confession to make ...

VINCENT *(Interrupting, upset)*. Sophie, for God's sake! Don't ...

(HE *grabs her arm.* SHE *breaks away)*

SOPHIE *(To* CLEM). Dick ... My son ...

CLEM. Yes? Yes?

SOPHIE. This man is his father. (SHE *covers her face)*

CLEM. Well, I'll be ... hornswoggled!

(VINCENT *puts his arms around* SOPHIE's *shoulder)*

VINCENT *(To* CLEM). So now you know.

CLEM. Well, I'll be ...

VINCENT. Yes, you said that before.

(Brief pause. SOPHIE *weeps softly)*

CLEM *(Abruptly)*. Unhand that woman!

VINCENT. Oh, was I handing her? I'm sorry. (HE *lets go of* SOPHIE)

CLEM *(Brokenly)*. This is kind of a shock.

VINCENT. I thought it might be.

CLEM. I see it all now.

VINCENT. What do you see?

CLEM. You've come to live here because you want to marry Sophie.

VINCENT *(Only to tease* CLEM). It's a thought. Clemmy, I believe you've got something there.

SOPHIE *(Wrought up. Sincerely)*. I won't marry you, Vincent. No. Never. Don't worry, Clem. Never. Do you hear?

VINCENT. Don't get worked up, Sophie. I haven't asked you. *(To* CLEM) If you're so madly in love with my Sophie ... er ... *our* Sophie, why don't you marry her yourself?

SOPHIE *(In tears)*. He can't, poor lamb. His wife won't give him a divorce.

CLEM. That's what's killing me.

VINCENT. But I thought she beat you up?

CLEM. Not before witnesses. She'd deny it, and the judge would believe her. You'd believe her, too, if you saw what a sawed-off little half portion she is.

VINCENT. These small women often pack a whale of a punch.

CLEM. Don't I know it!

VINCENT. What made her exercise it on you?

CLEM. That I'll never tell a soul. And it's no good looking at me like that, Sophie. I won't ever tell you, either. But I'll say this. I came out of the affair with great credit.

VINCENT. You speak in riddles, Clemmy.

SOPHIE. He's a man of mystery. That's what makes him so fascinating. *(Timidly, on the verge of tears)* He keeps dropping vague hints ... and sometimes he behaves rather oddly ...

VINCENT. Just sometimes?

SOPHIE. Do you know what I think? I believe he had all that trouble with his wife because he's ... a virgin.

VINCENT. A ... *what?*

CLEM. That'll do now! Of all the absurd ideas! Please!!! Isn't it enough that you should come popping up out of the past! *(More and more distraught)* Dick's father!

That's what I call competition! Good God! Sophie, what have you done to me?

SOPHIE. Whatever it was, I did it twenty-four years ago.

CLEM *(Wildly jealous)*. How did it happen?

VINCENT *(Reprovingly)*. Why, Mr. Hennyman! You don't want the details?

CLEM. I do want the details! All of them! Sophie . . . My Sophie . . . an adultress!

VINCENT. Adultress, my foot.

CLEM. How did it happen, Sophie? Relieve me.

VINCENT. "Relieve me" is good.

SOPHIE. *(Bashfully, with tears in her voice)*. Well . . . we were in love . . .

CLEM. Go on.

SOPHIE. And one night . . . one summer night . . . we were in the woods . . . two pure, innocent children . . . holding hands . . . and a storm came up . . . a terrible storm. Drenched and shivering, we took refuge in a rickety, abandoned shack. That's all?

CLEM. That's *all?*

SOPHIE. As a matter of fact, it was more like a hurricane than a storm. Hail, wind, rain, thunder, lightning. A ninety year record. If you don't believe me, you can go to the Public Library and look it up in the back papers.

CLEM. I won't go to the Public Library. What happened in the shack?

SOPHIE. It was the twelfth of August.

CLEM. What happened in the shack?

SOPHIE *(Trembling)*. Afterward,

when I knew I was to become a mother, I told Vincent.

CLEM. Very civil.

SOPHIE. Vincent, like a gentleman, wanted to marry me at once. But about the same time the rich Willie Laurin proposed too. I told Laurin the truth. Without hesitating an instant, he said it made no difference to him. So . . . the next week I married Laurin.

VINCENT. Which didn't prevent Dick being my son.

SOPHIE. But calling me an adultress . . . that's outrageous! *(In a choked voice)* Vincent hadn't any money. Willie Laurin had.

VINCENT *(With suppressed bitterness, burlesquing his words)*. And as a mother it was your sacred duty to consider what was best for your child.

SOPHIE. Exactly. I sacrificed myself for the good of my child.

CLEM. The question is, which of those two men was really the gentleman?

VINCENT. Who's bringing up that idiotic question?

CLEM. I am, and I'll tell you why. So that Sophie won't think so highly of you. You proposed to her under moral pressure.

VINCENT. Clem, you extend the bounds of possibility.

CLEM. Laurin married her without pressure. He was the gentleman.

VINCENT. So that's settled. How do you feel now, buddy? Better?

CLEM *(Exploding)*. No. And I never will.

VINCENT *(Losing patience)*. I can't see where your kick comes in. You knew Dick wasn't *your* son.

CLEM. I knew.

VINCENT (*Shouting*). He had to be somebody's son, hadn't he?

CLEM. I guess so.

VINCENT. There's no guessing about it—he *had*. Well, then, as long as he's not your son, isn't it all the same to you whose son he is?

CLEM. No!

VINCENT (*At the end of his rope*). Are you trying to dictate retroactively by whom Sophie is to have a son?

CLEM. She can have a son by anyone who doesn't come here to rent a room.

VINCENT. I don't follow your train of thought.

CLEM. Yes, you do. Being the father of her son, you'll use it as an excuse to marry my fiancée.

VINCENT (*Tongue in cheek*). She used to be *my* fiancée . . . a state of affairs temporarily interrupted by her brief marriage. Naturally the moment she lost her husband she automatically reverted to her old status. So if she's anybody's fiancée, she's mine. Not that I wish to pursue the matter. Just keeping the record straight.

CLEM (*To* SOPHIE). You see! That's one of those sophisticated quibbles of his that give me stomach ulcers.

SOPHIE (*Angrily*). Didn't you hear me say I wouldn't marry him?

CLEM (*Stubbornly*). You will too.

SOPHIE (*Almost furiously*). Clem! What is this?

CLEM (*To* VINCENT). No sense fooling ourselves. Many years ago she turned you down because of money. She'll give me the brush off for the same reason.

SOPHIE (*Stamping her foot*). Clem!

CLEM (*Hysterically*). You will! You will! You'll leave me flat! To sink into the gutter! To rot! To die! (*To* VINCENT, *shouting*) And wipe off that silly smile, you homewrecker! (HE *approaches him threateningly*)

SOPHIE. Clem, for heaven's sake!

CLEM. There was always a suspicious light in her eyes when she talked about you. I used to wonder why. (*With a very bitter, dramatic laugh*) Now I know! Ha, ha!

VINCENT. Clem, you're a ham.

SOPHIE (*Pleadingly, in tears*). But Clem darling . . . all that belongs to the past.

CLEM (*Very excited*). Not for me it doesn't! (*To* VINCENT, *in exasperation*) For two years . . . every time I've looked up and seen a flyer in the sky . . . it's been like a dagger in my heart. "There he is," I said to myself. "Her hero." Her "eagle..! I read the reports of every crash . . .

VINCENT. Hoping for the best?

CLEM. And when you were in the hospital and she used to phone asking how you were . . .

VINCENT. You were eagerly expecting the final bulletin?

CLEM (*Trembling with excitement*). Yes, I was. And then you got better. But that won't help you. I'm not a bad sort . . . I can love deeply but . . . in self-defense I'm downright dangerous! (*His eyes flaming with implacable hatred. Hoarsely*) I'm going to kill you.

VINCENT. My dear Clem! Think of that little old electric chair.

CLEM. You don't suppose I'm such a sap that I'd stick a knife into you and get myself arrested? I'll kill you with excitement. You won't have a minute's peace here. I'll see to it. A couple of heart attacks, and you'll be finished.

SOPHIE. Clem! You've gone mad!

CLEM (*Frighteningly. Irresponsible*). I think I have! My life's been turned upside down today! Our life! Your past and my future! Nothing matters any more! One of us will have to die! (HE *whips out a pistol*)

SOPHIE. Clem!!!

(CLEM *points the gun in the air and fires twice unmistakably at the ceiling. Keeps shouting hysterically*)

CLEM. Quiet home!!! Peaceful home!!!

(BESS *and* DICK *rush in from the kitchen*)

BESS (*Screaming*). What's happened?

(DICK *runs to* CLEM *and wrenches the gun from him*)

DICK. What's all this, Clem?

(VINCENT *sits down and puts his hand over his heart*)

SOPHIE (*Screaming, appeals to both, in turn*). Clem! Vincent! Clem! Vincent!

CLEM. (*Gasping*). That'll give you a rough idea. That was just a sample. (*Shrieking*) A sample!

(*Forgetting about* VINCENT, BESS, DICK *and* SOPHIE *flutter solicitously around* CLEM, *who pants for breath, reeling*)

SOPHIE. You want a tablet. Quick! Water, Bess!

(BESS *runs up with a drink of water.* CLEM *takes a tablet from his pocket and swallows it*)

VINCENT. What's that?

SOPHIE (*In tears*). Nitroglycerin. A precaution. Doctor's orders. Clem

has to be careful about getting excited.

VINCENT. You don't say? He, too?

CLEM. Did you think you had a monopoly?

(*The* FAMILY *take care of* CLEM. *There is nothing wrong with him.* CLEM *sits back in his place.* HE *picks up paper*)

BESS. What a fright you gave us! What was it all about?

DICK (*Looking at pistol*). Clem . . . a gun!

BESS. For heaven's sake, Mom!

SOPHIE (*In a trembling voice*). No harm's done, thank God. Clem got a little upset, but he's all right now. (*Very nervously*) You must promise me, all of you, never never to speak of this again. Never! (*Turns to* VINCENT) Are you all right, Vincent?

VINCENT. Quite, thank you. I was in the war. He couldn't scare me with a thousand pistols. Next time bring a cannon or two. Bring a howitzer, Henny.

CLEM. Mr. Hennyman.

VINCENT. Mr. Hennyman.

CLEM. I'll bring a cannon. Dick, give me back my gun.

DICK. I will not. (HE *puts it in his pocket*)

(*There is exciting* KNOCKING *on the door.* HARRIET BELL, *the school teacher from upstairs rushes in*)

HARRIET (*Hysterically*). What's the matter? What's happened? (SHE *rushes to* CLEM)

SOPHIE. Nothing, Miss Bell, nothing. Vincent, this is Miss Harriet Bell, the teacher, who lives upstairs. Clem's neighbor . . . (*With a pained smile*) . . . who's leaving on Monday.

HARRIET (*Looks around, still frightened, meanwhile tenderly stroking* CLEM'S *head*). Tell me you're not hurt, Mr. Hennyman.

CLEM. No, no, I'm quite all right, Miss Bell, thank you.

VINCENT (*Shouts, to* HARRIET). You, too???

HARRIET (*Furiously*). What do you mean, "you, too"?

SOPHIE. Vincent, please!

(*The* DOORBELL *rings.* ALL *look up.* DICK *hurries out, leaving sitting-room door open.* SOPHIE *speaks despairingly*)

SOPHIE. Company! They had to pick a moment like this!

(DICK *can be heard and seen through the open door with* MARY *and* LIZ, *the two pretty dancers from next door. They have rushed over frightened by the shots*)

DICK (*To the* GIRLS). It's nothing, I tell you, nothing.

SOPHIE. Who is that?

DICK (*Appears in doorway with* MARY *and* LIZ). The dancers from next door. The Petito sisters.

SOPHIE. I like their nerve!

(MARY *comes in, still breathless*)

MARY. Oh, Mrs. Laurin, do excuse this intrusion ... but we thought something had happened ... and we thought if there was anything we could do ... we thought ...

(*Meanwhile* LIZ *and* DICK *have come nearer, too.* HARRIET BELL *stands beside* CLEM, *stroking his head lovingly*)

SOPHIE (*Sharply*). Well, you thought wrong. We don't need anything, thank you.

DICK (*To the* GIRLS). I told you

it was all right. It must have been a car backfiring.

LIZ (*To* VINCENT, *smiling sweetly*). I was sure it was pistol shots.

HARRIET. Clem, promise me you're not in trouble.

CLEM. No, no, ... really ... dear Miss Bell. Thank you so much. You're mighty kind.

VINCENT (*Ingratiatingly to the* GIRLS). I hope you weren't terribly frightened.

SOPHIE (*Icily, to the* GIRLS). So kind of you to drop in. But you needn't worry about us. We don't have murders here.

CLEM (*With the paper in his hand, to himself*). We will!

BESS (*Frigidly dismissing the* GIRLS). Good night. Thank you *so* much.

(SHE *pushes* MARY *gently to the door.* MARY *pauses on threshold*)

MARY. All right, all right, don't twist my arm! The nerve of some people! Instead of being grateful ... Come on, Liz.

SOPHIE (*Hurrying them with a gesture*). Goodbye.

MARY (*With a coquettish smile, to* VINCENT). So long.

(VINCENT *bows gallantly.* MARY *goes out*)

LIZ (*Following her to the threshold*). All the same ... (SHE *sniffs*) ... there's a smell of gunpowder in here.

SOPHIE. And worse than that, a cheap, stinking perfume. Open the window, Bess.

LIZ (*To* VINCENT, *with a coquettish smile*). So long.

(VINCENT *bows.* LIZ *goes out, laughing*)

VINCENT *(To* SOPHIE*)*. They're cute.

SOPHIE. Common little tramps. The nerve of them, barging in here!

VINCENT. It was Clem's fault. I didn't fire the shots.

(HARRIET *unexpectedly explodes and begins to speak to* VINCENT *with the fury and rapidity of a machine gun)*

HARRIET. I don't know who did the shooting and I don't care, and I don't even know what happened and I don't care what happened . . . I don't even know who you are . . . but I do know that something happened to dear Clem, and I believe you're responsible, and if you want to know what you can do, you can go straight to hell . . . and quick.

VINCENT. Fine language from a school teacher.

HARRIET *(Excitedly)*. I don't care if I am a school teacher. I'd rather give up my profession than be polite to anyone who hurts dear Clem.

SOPHIE *(Angrily, very loud)*. Well, really! You don't have to get so worked up about it, Miss Bell! Clem doesn't need your protection!

HARRIET *(Much louder than* SOPHIE*)*. All right, all right, I've known for a long time that you're jealous of me, you lovesick old hussy! *(Screaming)* You needn't be afraid, I'm leaving on Monday . . . and if you want to know, that's *why* I'm leaving! (SHE *rushes out, slamming the door furiously)*

CLEM *(With the paper still in his trembling hands)*. Quiet home! Peaceful home! (HE *slams the paper down, speaks to* VINCENT *in a choked voice)* And now to finish this once and for all, let me give you a piece of advice. It's the same the old maid gave you but I'll put it more politely. Leave this family in peace.

VINCENT *(That little smile)*. But I'm very fond of them.

BESS *(Almost in tears)*. But . . . but what was all this about?

SOPHIE *(Peremptorily)*. Didn't I tell you never to speak about it again?

CLEM *(To* VINCENT*)*. All right, you're fond of them. Let's talk about it, man to man. Make a will leaving your money to them, instead of fooling around with roses.

VINCENT. That's an idea. Make a will . . . and die.

CLEM. Everybody dies.

VINCENT. My doctor says no. *(Suddenly)* No, I'll be damned if I do! I don't want to die. I want to live. The longer the better. Years and years and years, trying to be happy in this unhappy age. Escaping from this dreadful world into . . .

CLEM *(Interrupting)*. Not into *this* family. No, sir! I'm the escapist here. And you're not going to marry Sophie. *(To* DICK *and* BESS, *who are staring at him)* That's what he's after.

SOPHIE. Clem! How can you think that of me? (SHE *cries)*

BESS. Clem, you're crazy.

DICK *(Throws his arm about* SOPHIE's *shoulder)*. Mamma, for heaven's sake.

VINCENT. I don't want to seem critical, but I do think you might have told me that this house was infested by Clem Hennyman. It might have been simpler if you had kicked me out the moment I arrived.

BESS. But Mom loves having you here.

CLEM *(Cruelly)*. Mom loves money.

(SOPHIE, *sobbing in* DICK's *arms, utters a piercing scream*)

DICK. Clem! How can you?

BESS *(To* VINCENT*)*. She wanted you here, but she wanted Clem, too.

CLEM *(Bitterly)*. Clem costs money.

SOPHIE *(Sobbing)*. I never said that, Clem! Never! Never!

VINCENT. You wanted us both, Sophie?

SOPHIE. Why shouldn't I?

CLEM *(Getting calmer)*. Now ... listen, Mr. Reid. Now . . . that the storm's over, I believe I can discuss this thing quietly. I don't say you must give up hope.

VINCENT. This is wonderful news.

CLEM. I'm not a heartless man. I'm beginning to think that we might find a little corner for you somewhere in our family circle. But first, let's see the will.

VINCENT. Awfully kind of you.

CLEM. I can't rob them of the chance to be your heirs. That's all I'm interested in . . . the future of those two young people . . . and the baby they're expecting.

VINCENT *(Looks at* DICK, *moved)*. A baby?

BESS *(Buries her head on* CLEM's *shoulder, happily)*. Clem!

DICK *(Deeply moved)*. Clem, that was wonderful of you.

SOPHIE *(Moved, delighted)*. Clem's a prince.

DICK *(Still moved)*. Really, there are times . . . like this one . . . when I feel as if Clem were my father.

VINCENT. I thought that was coming. I could have betted on it.

CLEM. Yes, sir, their future must be provided for. The trouble with us selfish old swine . . .

VINCENT. I beg your pardon?

CLEM. You and me. The trouble is we keep thinking about our future, and we don't have any future. No! No! Grin all you like. We sick, worn-out old men . . .

VINCENT. You allude to . . . ?

CLEM. You and me. We've got to think about other people's futures, if we've got a spark of decency in us.

VINCENT *(To* SOPHIE, *with a bitter smile)*. Is he right? Do you want me to make that will?

SOPHIE *(Plaintively)*. He's right. But you're right, too, if you don't. You're both right. *(Sobbing)* Everybody's right except me.

VINCENT *(With a sardonic smile)*. Very well. I'll go and see my lawyer . . . right away. If he's gone to bed, I'll rout him out. (HE *shakes hands all around.* HE *is deeply disappointed, but smiles and pretends to be very affectionate)* Goodbye, my dears. Goodbye, Dick, old man. Goodbye, Bess, angelface.

(The FAMILY *is startled at the excessive warmth of his farewell)*

DICK. But we'll be seeing you again soon?

SOPHIE. What's your hurry, Vincent?

CLEM *(Icily)*. How about getting on with supper, Bess?

BESS. All right, Clem dear. (SHE *goes out)*

SOPHIE *(To* VINCENT, *frightened)*. You say goodbye as if you were leaving us forever.

DICK. I hope that's not so.

SOPHIE. Where are you going?

VINCENT. I told you. To my lawyer. You needn't stare at me that way. Goodbyes should always be said with a lot of warmth, because you never know what might not happen. Think how easy it is to get run over, crossing the street. You ought to make a point of saying goodbye every time as if it was goodbye forever. That's one of the things you learn when you're a flyer. Who can be sure of tomorrow? Nobody. Not just flyers . . . even creative artists who install toilets.

CLEM *(Roused)*. An invention a damn sight more useful to the human race than your airplanes.

VINCENT. And not nearly so dangerous. *(Raises his hand gayly, waving goodbye with a flourish)* Goodbye! (HE *goes out)*

(During what follows, DICK sets the table very simply for four, taking a tablecloth out of a drawer, also knives and forks, four plates, etc. SOPHIE takes the slippers from beneath the arm chair and hands them to CLEM)

SOPHIE. Take off your shoes.

CLEM. Why?

SOPHIE. Do as you're told.

(CLEM starts to take off his shoes. SOPHIE kneels on the floor and helps him)

CLEM. My ministering angel! But why? So early? Before dinner?

SOPHIE *(Reciting)*. In circulatory disorders the limbs, particularly the feet, are not sufficiently supplied with blood. Shoes squeeze the blood out of the feet. Slippers let it in.

CLEM *(Stands up, takes a step in slippers)*. Sure feels good.

SOPHIE. I knew it would.

CLEM. Where did you learn that?

SOPHIE. I read about it.

(THEY sit down at the table, as BESS brings in the soup tureen. CLEM says grace under his breath. SOPHIE serves the soup. THEY eat)

CLEM. Darned good soup. Fine, rich soup. *(Joyfully)* There's garlic in it.

SOPHIE. Just a speck. Garlic's good for the blood vessels.

(THEY eat)

BESS. Think he'll make a will?

CLEM. If there's a shred of decency in him.

BESS. I'm not thinking of us. I'm thinking of the baby.

DICK *(Puts his arm around her)*. My darling!

CLEM. What a sweet motherly girl our Bess is.

SOPHIE. A jewel.

BESS. You're a jewel, Mom. And you, Dick. And you, Clem.

CLEM *(Delighted)*. And here . . . here . . . he tried to sneak in here! That . . . that . . . *(Breaks off. Then, with a weird smile)* Funny. I can't get it out of my head. Care to hear a dreamer's secret dream? The fantasy of an ex-artist?

SOPHIE. Of course, Clem.

CLEM. Remember when I told him to make a will with you as beneficiaries . . . and then we might make a place for him here?

BESS. Yes.

CLEM. Amazing the way an artist's mind works. Like a flash. The moment I said it, the plot of a wonderful mystery story darted into my mind. A complete novel. Listen. *(THEY listen attentively. HE speaks like a writer telling the plot of his drama)* He makes a will. We take him in here with us. Everything goes fine. He's sitting pretty and he's happy. But I'm not happy.

SOPHIE. Why not?

CLEM. Because I hate his insides. You know why, Sophie. So there you are . . . he's feeling fine, I'm feeling lousy. I glue on a false beard and go out and buy rat poison. One evening I put a good big dose of it in his soup.

BESS. Goodness!

CLEM. He dies. You inherit his money. The baby's in the chips.

DICK. But what did you get out of it?

CLEM. Not a thing. I wander away in my false beard. Disappear. Vanish. You never see me again. Never. I perish somewhere far away. *(In a choked voice)* But I've paid for all your kindness.

(Brief pause)

SOPHIE *(Gently)*. I call that dreadful, Clem.

CLEM. Just an idea. Crossed my mind. If I were a writer, I'd write it up. Just a sentimental mystery story, with a message at the end.

(Brief strained silence. DICK *and* BESS *eat)*

SOPHIE. To me . . . even this dreadful idea only proves how deeply you love us. You're a great heart, Clem. A great hunk of red, warm heart.

CLEM *(Moved)*. Thank you, sweet.

SOPHIE. Drink your soup. It's getting cold.

(ALL drink soup. Silence)

CLEM. I hate him.

SOPHIE. Calm down, dear.

CLEM *(Very softly)*. I hate him.

SOPHIE. Clem, be quiet.

(CLEM, soundlessly with flashing eyes, distinctly forms the words with his lips)

CLEM *(Silently)*. I hate him.

CURTAIN

ACT THREE

SCENE: *The examining room of* DR. MOORE'S *office, same scene as Act One.*

AT RISE: *It is next morning. On stage are* DR. MOORE *and* VINCENT.

VINCENT. So there you have it, doctor. That's the story of my plunge into quiet family life.

DOCTOR *(With a look of distaste on his face)*. I see.

VINCENT. To put it in a nutshell, the sand was fine but there was an ostrich in it already.

DOCTOR. I see. And what happened after you left there?

VINCENT. I went home. I use the word "home" in a loose sense. I mean to my hotel.

DOCTOR. You were feeling a little bitter, no doubt?

VINCENT. A little, I must confess. I felt . . .

DOCTOR. Yes? Go on.

VINCENT. It's rather an embarrassing thing to say out loud. It sounds so . . . corny.

DOCTOR. Then whisper it.

VINCENT. Well, then . . . I felt . . . *(As though quoting, with self-mockery)* I felt "alone in the world."

DOCTOR. You should have phoned me. I told you I'd be at the office till late in the evening.

VINCENT. To tell you the truth, I wanted to be by myself after this . . . shock. Because, I confess . . . no use trying to hide it . . . it was a shock. I went on thinking all night long.

DOCTOR. You didn't sleep?

VINCENT. No. I took a walk of a few miles.

DOCTOR. Where?

VINCENT. In my room. Up and down. I was trying to figure out what the hell I was going to do.

DOCTOR. What did you tell them when you left?

VINCENT. I told them I was going to my lawyer's to make a will, as Mr. Hennyman suggested. *(Sad little smile)* I could see the family thoroughly approved of the idea. They're completely under the spell of this . . . er . . . somewhat rare phenomenon; a hysterical old man.

DOCTOR. From what you've told me, he doesn't deserve such a scientific label. Let's be unscientific. He's a swine.

VINCENT. No. Just a human being fighting tooth and nail for what he considers his happiness and stopping at nothing to get it. Quite understandable.

DOCTOR. You're a philosopher.

VINCENT. And the philosopher is always the one who is kicked out. He shakes the dust from his feet, shrugs and goes on.

DOCTOR. Well, perhaps some sort of a case could be made out for Mr. Hennyman. What astonishes me is that your Sophie . . . that she could fall for a fellow like that.

VINCENT. Want some words of wisdom from the classics? Quote: "Of all the paths that lead to a woman's love, pity's. the straightest." Unquote. Seventeenth century.

DOCTOR. You read the old English authors?

VINCENT. No. I read Barlett's Book of Familiar Quotations. *(Pause)*

DOCTOR *(Meditatively)*. Well, well, well.

VINCENT. What's on your mind, Doctor? Not another family, I hope?

DOCTOR. No. I was just thinking that it was a sad story and wondering which of us two was the fool.

(HE *takes* VINCENT'S *pulse and counts, with an eye on his watch*)

VINCENT. If you'll allow me to say so, I think we both were. We let our imaginations run away with us. Life isn't quite so simple as men of good will think it is. *(After a moment's pause)* Anyway . . . all that makes no difference. Your advice . . . or rather prescription . . . was fine. You're an excellent doctor.

DOCTOR. I don't like a patient criticizing his doctor. Even though he's flattering. Makes me envy horse-doctors. *(Letting go of pulse)* Seventy-two.

VINCENT. Is that good?

DOCTOR. Excellent . After what you've been through, plus a sleepless night, your pulse hasn't gone up a beat. You're in fine shape. *(Thinking. At a loss)* Well, and now what?

VINCENT. God loves me, after all, it seems.

DOCTOR. Yes?

VINCENT. Just after I walked out on them, I thought of another solution. An idea occurred to me. That's what kept me racking my brains till morning. Then I made up my mind in a flash.

DOCTOR. Another of your famous quick decisions?

VINCENT. That's right.

DOCTOR *(Paternally, smiling)*. I wonder when you're going to get some sense.

VINCENT. Not for a long time, I hope. Getting sense is the first sign of senility.

DOCTOR. Well, my impulsive young fellow, what was the decision you came to?

VINCENT. You can see from my face that I think it's a good one. As a matter of fact, it wasn't really one of my "famous quick decisions," because I was mulling the thing over all through the night. At that I was lucky . . . only to take one night over it . . . because . . . however much you try to kid me along . . . life has become scandalously short for me. I have to step lively. You told me to try to be happy right away.

DOCTOR. Well?

VINCENT. No good. Nothing doing. But now . . .

DOCTOR. Yes?

VINCENT. Can you put yourself in the place of a man of fifty-one who knows he's living on borrowed time . . .

DOCTOR. Well?

VINCENT. . . . and so no longer shrinks from anything in the world?

DOCTOR *(Trying to guess)*. You . . . just a minute, now . . . you met those two sexy wenches next door.

VINCENT. Yes. They're something.

DOCTOR. Oh, my Lord!

VINCENT. How did you know . . .

DOCTOR. You didn't speak to them?

VINCENT. Not more than a couple of words. *(Laughing)* Why? Did you think that was the new solution? No, Doctor, I may be a fool, but I'm not a damned fool. (HE *presses the hidden button*) By the way, how did you know there were a couple of girls next door?

DOCTOR. What are you doing?

VINCENT. I pressed the secret buzzer.

(LINDA *comes in and, as in Act One, glances at her watch, then nods and winks at the* DOCTOR *just as before*)

DOCTOR. Yes, Linda?

LINDA. Appointment.

(SHE *nods again and signals with her eyes*)

VINCENT. You're a mendacious female, Linda. I pressed the button.

DOCTOR. Why?

VINCENT. I told you I'd found a new solution in place of the one that didn't work out. *(To* LINDA, *emphatically)* Because it didn't work out at all. It was a wash-out and a total bust!

LINDA. You needn't shout. I knew it would be.

VINCENT. How did you know?

LINDA. Maybe because I was wishing so hard for it to fail.

DOCTOR. Why were you wishing that?

LINDA. Medical considerations. And plain common sense. The idea of banking on a childhood sweetheart . . . at your age.

VINCENT. What do you mean, my age? Are you implying that I am old?

LINDA. I'm not implying anything.

DOCTOR. And what's the new solution? Come on, let's have it.

VINCENT. You'll be flabbergasted. Or . . . maybe . . . you won't even be surprised.

DOCTOR. Well, what is it?

VINCENT. It's ever so much better than our first idea. But I'm afraid it's going to cost you your nurse. (HE *looks at* LINDA *meaningfully*)

LINDA. Why are you staring at me?

VINCENT. I'm observing your reactions.

LINDA *(To the* DOCTOR, *matter-of-factly)*. He's a very inexperienced man if he can't see through such a transparent person as me.

VINCENT. I never claimed to be an accomplished Lothario.

LINDA *(Arranging the things on the medical cabinet)*. Look! He can still blush. I like that. It makes him twenty years younger.

VINCENT. Should I be?

LINDA. No, not you. *I* should.

VINCENT. If there's one girl in the world who doesn't need to be younger it's you.

LINDA. He delivers commonplaces with such deep conviction. I like that, too. *(Turns her back while rummaging among the things on the medical cabinet)*

VINCENT *(At a loss, staring at her back)*. You . . . you . . . (HE *turns abruptly to the* DOCTOR) Shall I tell you my idea about Linda's future?

DOCTOR. I know it.

VINCENT. What?

DOCTOR. Your idea. About her future.

VINCENT. Since when?

DOCTOR. Since the moment you came into the office an hour ago.

You're not the only one who can make quick judgments.

VINCENT. No?

LINDA *(Answers instead of* DOCTOR). No, sir.

VINCENT *(Still embarrassed, to the* DOCTOR). But . . . it's a kind of confession. My plans about her future . . .

LINDA. Don't upset yourself with confessions. It's bad for you. And it isn't such startling news to us as you think.

VINCENT. No?

LINDA. No, sir.

VINCENT *(To* LINDA). Still, I'd like to have your views on the subject. Just a few words . . . or, if you'd rather, just one word . . . as it might be "Yes."

LINDA. I never can understand why men attach such tremendous importance to words.

VINCENT. Failing words, what do you suggest that I should do? Kiss you again?

DOCTOR. "Again?"

LINDA *(To* DOCTOR). You're surprised?

DOCTOR *(Embarrassed)*. Not at all.

VINCENT. Shall I explain?

LINDA. No. Nobody asked you to explain.

VINCENT. No, doctor?

DOCTOR *(Snappishly)*. No.

(DR. MOORE *goes over to the glass-topped medical cabinet by the wall, still crowded with vials, small medical instruments, boxes, test tubes, etc.)*

VINCENT *(To* DOCTOR). Why not? Has Linda mentioned this . . . incident to you?

DOCTOR *(Rummaging among the*

instruments). There are women who don't always feel the need of speech.

VINCENT. And she . . .

DOCTOR. . . . is one of them *(Morosely)* And there are men who don't always feel the need of being spoken to.

VINCENT. And you . . .

DOCTOR. And I am one of them. —I have eyes. When you watch two people together, both dressed, you can be mistaken. But when you watch a woman in conversation with an undressed man, you can't. No possibility of error. And as for the kissing . . . you would do well to control yourself.

VINCENT. What are *your* views on that point, Linda?

LINDA. Do what the doctor tells you. My guess is that he'll tell you there's a golden mean in everything.

VINCENT *(To* DOCTOR*).* By the way, how was the cardiogram yesterday?

DOCTOR. All right. (VINCENT *shrugs)* You seem skeptical.

VINCENT. I don't take a heart specialist's good news at its face value. There's a school of thought that considers lies an important part of therapy.

DOCTOR. God preserve all doctors from intelligent patients.

LINDA *(Practically putting* VINCENT *in his place).* Your condition is quite satisfactory.

VINCENT. Ah, I believe *you.*

LINDA. Why?

VINCENT. Because if my condition weren't good, you wouldn't dream of . . .

LINDA. Dream of what?

VINCENT *(Hand on lips).* I didn't say a word.

LINDA *(Menacingly).* You'd better not.

VINCENT *(At a loss, while* LINDA *is rummaging around among the small objects).* Now I really don't know what to do.

LINDA. Always do what the doctor says.

VINCENT. But what does the doctor say?

DOCTOR. Take off your coat.

VINCENT. What for?

LINDA. You heard what the doctor said. Take it off.

(SHE *starts to wash her hands in the basin.* VINCENT *looks at* DOCTOR *in a puzzled way and takes off his coat)*

DOCTOR. Hang it on the hook. (VINCENT *does so.* DOCTOR *picks out and examines hypodermic needles from among the instruments on the medical cabinet)*

DOCTOR. The law requires people applying for a marriage license to present a certificate showing that they have taken a blood test.

VINCENT *(Brightening, to* LINDA*).* That means you agree.

LINDA. I wash my hands.

VINCENT. Like . . .

LINDA. Like Pontius Pilate. Saying—and I quote—"I am innocent of the blood of this just person."

VINCENT. Unquote. (LINDA *scrubs her hands vigorously.* VINCENT *turns to the* DOCTOR) So . . . You're pleased with the result of the dialogue between the dressed girl and the undressed man.

DOCTOR. "Pleased" is perhaps a little too strong.

VINCENT *(Pointing at needles which* DOCTOR *is selecting).* Still, you're helping things along.

DOCTOR. I won't stand in the way of any natural, healthy develop· ment . . . not even if . . .

VINCENT. Not even if?

DOCTOR *(Annoyed)*. Stop cross-examining me.

VINCENT. I believe you're mad, Doctor.

DOCTOR. Of course I'm mad. Why shouldn't I be, losing the best nurse God ever made?

VINCENT *(To* LINDA*)*. Is he correct in saying he's losing his nurse?

LINDA. He knows best what he's losing.

VINCENT. But a few words on the subject from *you* . . .

L I N D A *(Drying her hands)*. Words, words, words . . . Don't men ever think of anything except words?

(SHE *flings towel into hamper on floor, pretending to be angry)*

DOCTOR. Come on, Linda. Move the chair into the light.

LINDA. Yes, doctor.

(SHE *pushes a chair under the beam of the search light)*

VINCENT. Doctor, I have a feeling that you're suppressing something you'd like to shout from the house tops.

DOCTOR *(Ignoring this)*. Sit down.

VINCENT. Shall I, Linda?

LINDA. Do what the doctor says.

(VINCENT *sits down.* LINDA *pushes up another chair for the* Doctor. DOCTOR *sits down at* VINCENT'S *left)*

DOCTOR. Roll up your sleeve.

VINCENT. Which arm?

LINDA. This one nearest the doctor, silly.

(VINCENT *rolls up his left sleeve. Standing behind them* LINDA *helps him and turns light directly on his bare arm)*

DOCTOR *(With the hypodermic needle in his hand)*. Tourniquet. *(Taking a rubber tube,* LINDA—*still behind them—prepares tourniquet)* Alcohol.

LINDA. Yes, doctor. *(Rubs a spot on* VINCENT'S *arm with cotton wool dipped in alcohol)*

VINCENT. Oh, Doctor . . . I asked you before . . . How did you know about those girls next door . . . the ones you called "sexy wenches"?

(LINDA *frowns. She quickly takes off the rubber tube from* VINCENT'S *arm and moves be-hind him to his right)*

LINDA. What girls? Next door to where?

VINCENT *(Looking up at her)*. Jealous?

LINDA *(Nervously)*. Don't be so silly.

(DOCTOR *brings the needle closer to* VINCENT'S *arm)*

DOCTOR. No talking now.

VINCENT *(To* LINDA, *pointing to his left arm)*. Do you still deny that you gave your consent to this pre-marital operation?

LINDA. Who says I gave my consent?

VINCENT. You're aiding and abetting him.

LINDA. That's what I'm paid for.

DOCTOR *(Annoyed, seizes* VIN-CENT'S *arm with his left hand)*. Keep your arm still.

VINCENT *(Pushing back* DOC-TOR'S *hand)*. Pardon me. Just a mo-ment. *(Exasperated)* Damn it, I'm entitled to a little information when

I'm about to shed my blood. Doctor, in puncturing me with that damned needle, have you Linda in mind?

DOCTOR. I have the law in mind. Sit still now. Keep your arm quiet. Make a fist.

LINDA (*Peremptorily*). Don't ask so many questions. Make a fist.

(VINCENT *makes a fist of his left hand*)

DOCTOR. Tourniquet.

(*As* LINDA *starts to put the tourniquet on again, the* DOCTOR *again brings the needle close to* VINCENT'S *arm*)

VINCENT. One moment, Doctor. (*To* LINDA, *who loosens the tourniquet while the doctor withdraws the needle and makes an exasperated gesture*) Will you take good care of me?

LINDA. Yes.

VINCENT. How good?

LINDA. Better than you'd get from the best nurse in the world.

VINCENT. Until my dying day?

LINDA. Or until mine.

VINCENT. And . . . you still won't say . . .

DOCTOR (*Losing patience*). Tell him, tell him, tell him! For the love of Pete tell him!

LINDA. What?

DOCTOR (*In furious outburst*). The one thing, you fool girl, that he's been dying to hear you say ever since he's known you, why in hell, I don't know. For God's sake spit it out, you dope, spit it out once and for all before I lose my patience.

VINCENT (*Surprised, to* DOC-TOR). Why are you suddenly so eager to push this thing along?

DOCTOR (*Angrily*). What did you expect? Didn't I tell you I wouldn't stand in the way of two such natural forces rushing head on at each other?

VINCENT (*Still surprised*). You told me yesterday . . .

DOCTOR. Yes, and now it's to-day and I tell you different. First because after all you went through last night it's the finest thing that could happen to you. This girl and your heart will be the best of friends and will keep each other young for a hundred years. That's one reason. There's another.

VINCENT. What's that?

DOCTOR. Well, to be quite frank, I'm glad she's going to get married . . . and not to me.

LINDA (*Startled*). Doctor!

DOCTOR (*To* VINCENT). Since that incident in my life . . . you know . . . I told you . . . I've been clinging like a coward to my free bachelor life . . . but in the past year or two . . . growing older and older . . . I've been haunted by one fear . . . that in spite of myself there would come along some time a woman I'd lose my head over and marry. Now I can breathe a sigh of relief. The danger is over.

VINCENT. Why? (*After a brief pause*) Linda's not the only woman in the world.

(*Brief pause*)

DOCTOR. She was for me. Don't gape at me like that, Linda. Go ahead, spill it. Go on, tell him, don't be so coy, get it over with.

LINDA (*Dropping her eyes*). I love you, Doctor Moore.

VINCENT (*Flabbergasted*). What!

DOCTOR (*Withdrawing the needle. Very embarrassed*). What was that you said?

LINDA (*Trying without too much success to be matter-of-fact*). I said that I love you. You, Dr. Harry W. Moore. You. I like Mr. Reid very much. In fact, I've never been so fond of one of your patients in all these years. He's decent, he's good looking, he's slightly pathetic and entirely lovable. Any woman he married could consider herself lucky. To be honest, I didn't have a moment's hesitation about marrying him. And I'd have done it . . . if you hadn't exploded just now. But you did, and just in the nick of time you blurted out something that made me find my tongue. Then you shouted at me to "spill it." All right, Doctor, that's what I'm doing now. Please listen. I've been in love with you for years. Don't keep on trying to look indifferent. I realize it's no news to you. You've known it well enough all along. But you weren't interested. I don't blame you. You burned your fingers once, and you didn't want it to happen again. Since then you've only listened to the heart beats of people who paid you to.

DOCTOR. That's not true. I remember once . . .

LINDA (Interrupting). I know. Once you wanted to listen to mine . . . through a stethoscope . . . and free, at that. I wouldn't let you. It was just about the time I fell so much in love with you . . . and realized that there was no response . . . and I'd have died rather than open my blouse for you.

DOCTOR. Oh come, Linda. I was a doctor.

LINDA. And have you the slightest idea how hard I've been fighting to see you only as a doctor? I can't do it, not even after all these years of watching you work in this room. But what could I do? Until today you kept silent. So I kept silent, too. Today at last you opened your mouth. So I opened mine.

DOCTOR (Embarrassed). So women also cling to words, words, words.

LINDA. So it seems. You've noticed that?

DOCTOR. Yes, and here's another thing I noticed. In spite of all this, you frowned when Mr. Reid mentioned those two girls. You were jealous.

LINDA. Yes, I was . . . but only because he said *you* told him they were sexy.

(VINCENT *stands up smiling, and very slowly puts his coat on*)

DOCTOR. Hello. What's this?

VINCENT. Another of my quick decisions. The best to date. (HE *goes to wash basin*) Here . . . *you* take your coat off. (HE *washes his hands*) Linda, take that needle away from him. *(To* DOCTOR) Sit down.

(DOCTOR, *at a loss, stands by the chair*)

VINCENT *(To* DOCTOR). Didn't you hear me? Sit down. (DOCTOR *sits in the chair.* VINCENT *speaks to the* DOCTOR *while washing his hands*) I'll tell you something. Ever since I got here today I've had a curious feeling that not I but *you* should have been sitting there. Now I'm amazed . . . a little late, perhaps . . . that I ever had the nerve to take that chair.

DOCTOR (Embarrassed). Well . . . then?

LINDA (Coldly). Please roll up your sleeve.

(*The* DOCTOR *looks at her sternly and after a moment's hesitation stands up, takes off his coat, flings it on the floor, and determinedly sits down again in the chair where* VINCENT *sat before and starts to roll up his left sleeve.* LINDA *calmly picks up the coat, dusts it and hangs it on the hook. Goes back to the* DOCTOR *and says to* VINCENT *who has just dried his hands)*

LINDA. Tourniquet.

(With the needle in her hand, SHE *sits down in the chair where the* DOCTOR *was sitting before, while* VINCENT *grabs the rubber tube and quickly ties it around the* DOCTOR'S *arm)*

DOCTOR. And what about him? *(Points to* VINCENT *with his right hand)*

LINDA *(Holding the needle ready for use near the* DOCTOR's *left arm)*. In our house there'll be two nice rooms for rent, too . . . for a quiet, elderly gentleman . . . two quiet rooms complete with doctor and nurse . . . assuming he's interested in renting them.

VINCENT *(That certain sad little smile)*. Interested? Me? The world champion of quick decisions?

DOCTOR. That answer was too long again. All you had to say was: yes.

VINCENT. Yes.

(As the moment threatens to become emotional)

LINDA *(To* VINCENT*)*. Alcohol.

*(*VINCENT, *eager to help, rushes to grab bottle and cotton from the medical cabinet and quickly rubs the* DOCTOR's *arm. Then* HE *steps aside, holding bottle and cotton in his hands)*

LINDA *(To the* DOCTOR*)*. Make a fist.

DOCTOR *(Smiling, makes a fist. Tries to conceal his emotion by teasing her)*. Won't your hand tremble?

LINDA. It never trembles. Why should it now?

DOCTOR. I just thought it might.

LINDA *(Touching the* DOCTOR's *arm gingerly with the point of the needle)*. You thought wrong. Keep your arm quiet.

*(*DOCTOR *and* VINCENT *are motionless.* LINDA *jabs the needle in the* DOCTOR's *arm and slowly draws blood out of it. Silence)*

CURTAIN